T.S. ELIOT

A Study in Character and Style

T.S. ELIOT
A Study in Character and Style

Ronald Bush

New York   Oxford
OXFORD UNIVERSITY PRESS
1983

Copyright © 1984 by Oxford University Press, Inc.

Library of Congress Cataloging in Publication Data
Bush, Ronald.
T.S. Eliot, a study in character and style.

Bibliography: p.
Includes index.
1. Eliot, T.S. (Thomas Stearns), 1888–1965.
2. Poets, American—20th century—Biography. I. Title.
PS3509.L43Z6466 1983   821'.912   83-4259
ISBN 0-19-503376-0

Since this page cannot legibly accommodate all the copyright notices,
the following page constitutes an extension of the copyright page.

This printing (last digit):   9 8 7 6 5 4 3 2 1

Printed in the United States of America

*In Memory of Lillian Schneyer
and Esther Schneyer Bush*

Preface

This book started as a question: how did the author of *The Waste Land*, one of the most highly charged, dramatic poems of the twentieth century, come twenty years later to write a masterpiece of deferred immediacy like *Four Quartets*? Eliot's development, it hardly needs saying, points beyond itself and calls up other questions—questions of what modernism was, why it flourished and why it eventually became a lifeless fossil rising over the landscape of contemporary literature. Had new literary currents changed Eliot's course, affecting his verse at the same time that they altered the literary assumptions of his generation? That would be the simplest explanation of the growth and decline of the modernist movement, but it fails to satisfy. In Eliot's case, although it is possible to locate figures who influenced him after his thirty-fifth year (Marianne Moore, St.-John Perse and Stéphane Mallarmé come to mind), the causes of his evolution were there from the beginning.

Recalling the great French poet who said his complete works "datent de quinze ans," the elements of Eliot's later verse can be found in his first mature poems. This is not to say he did not change. He did— radically—but his development worked out potential he had always possessed. Like the modernist movement as a whole, his early work nurtured two conflicting literary forces he had inherited from the romantics. At mid-career these forces were each so strong only the power of a master could join them. Then in Eliot as in his contemporaries the bond between the forces snapped, and the international style of 1922 became a thing of the past.

The inclinations I am referring to are complex, but for the purposes of a preface, simplification may serve: first, a tendency, inherited from French symbolism, toward a literature stripped both of outside reference and of the voice of the poet who presided at its birth—a poetry, so to speak, of pure music. And opposing that, a disposition, already pronounced by the time of Wordsworth, toward fidelity to the subtlest expressions of the innermost self—a disposition which would lead to the extraordinary internal monologues of the twentieth century. For a brief moment in the late teens and early twenties, these forces reinforced one another, so that in the masterpieces of high modernism we find, as Eliot found in the *Cantos* of Ezra Pound, a "nearly continuous identification . . . of form and feeling."[1] In *The Waste Land* or *Ulysses*, an ornate pattern of myth and music coexists with the most radical kind of emotional sincerity. But by the time of the *Four Quartets* or *Finnegans Wake*, the modernists' understanding of sincerity (and of the self) had been transfigured. No longer driven to seek their buried selves, Eliot and Joyce were free to pursue their symbolist inclinations to an extent unprecedented in English writing.

Much of the work of this study involved tracing the way these two streams of modernism grew, interacted and diverged in Eliot's poetry and criticism. I soon realized, however, that to treat a poet's career this way is to assume that what is most important in it is a literary intelligence, alive to inherited possibilities and free to work those possibilities out without personal constraint. With few writers is this assumption more than provisionally true. It is especially misleading in the case of Eliot, whom Randall Jarrell has called "one of the most subjective and daemonic poets who ever lived, the victim and helpless beneficiary of his own inexorable compulsions [and] obsessions." (Jarrell added: "From a psychoanalytical point of view he was far and away the most interesting poet of [the] century.")[2]

As his admirers have always known, the power of Eliot's early verse comes from an almost unbearable tension between romantic yearning and intellectual detachment. Significant areas of Eliot's psyche are invested in both, and, forced to choose, we would have to say that the yearning, not the intellect, dominates. Eliot was not the kind of second-order artist who, as Henry James says about George Eliot, "proceeds from the abstract to the concrete" and whose "figures and situations are evolved, as the phrsse is, from [the] moral consciousness."[3] Eliot made that clear when he criticized Edgar Lee Masters for writing a poem of ironic autobiography which lacked foundation in the sensuous reality of individual consciousness. Masters, Eliot said, "sometimes fails in a situation . . . because he does not fix before you the contact and cross-contact of souls, the breath and scent of the room. His mind is reflective, not evocative. . . . In descriptive passages . . . we have a vision from the moral emotions, not an immediate application of all the senses."[4]

This is not to say that the moral frames of Eliot's finished poems are to be taken simply as reflex defenses against the discomfort of unexpectedly full experience. Eliot remembered that "I never knew my grandfather: he died a year before my birth. But I was brought up to be very much aware of him: so much so, that as a child I thought of him as still the head of the family—a ruler for whom *in absentia* my grandmother stood as viceregent. The standard of conduct was that which my grandfather had set; our moral judgments, our decisions between duty and self-indulgence, were taken as if, like Moses, he had brought down the tables of the Law, any deviation from which would be sinful. Not least of these laws, which included injunctions still more than prohibitions, was the Law of Public Service" (TCC, 44). As Eliot hints in what follows these remarks, this need always to choose "between duty and self-indulgence" was an extremely uncomfortable one. But he adds that after much contemplation he had come to the conclusion that "it is a very good beginning for any child, to be brought up to reverence such institutions, and to be taught that personal and selfish aims should be subordinated to the general good which they represent." And we may apply the latter remark to his own life and poetry.

Whatever its psychological roots, Eliot's rage for order, his need to impose clear moral outlines on the world, was the source of real clarity, stability and good, not only in his writing but in his personal relations. If his first marriage was torn apart by an instinctive New England revulsion from the vivacious creature his romantic impulses had tempted him to marry, it is also true that Eliot cared for his wife at the cost of great personal suffering and that he refused to give up a suffocating job at Lloyd's bank because it would have meant leaving Vivien without a pension in the event of his death. As regards his poetry, if he sometimes disfigured an emotional sequence with a rigid and unsuitable frame,[5] his frames (witness "Prufrock") often redeem verse that might have degenerated into mawkish self-pity. In the infrequent instance when the emotional source and the intellectual armature of a poem coincide, it is Eliot's intellectual clarity that raises his work a step above the achievements of his greatest contemporaries. Eliot once said that what flawed the most serious poetry of Ezra Pound was that Pound rarely "has an image of the maximum concentration, an image which combines the precise and concrete with a kind of almost infinite suggestion."[6] It is just this combination, I think, that makes a minor poem like "A Song for Simeon" instantly memorable and the emotional force of many of Pound's Cantos opaque until the third reading.

Still, "A Song for Simeon" *is* a minor poem. In the major poems, obvious in *The Waste Land,* less obvious in *Four Quartets,* Eliot's power is a result not of feeling and intellect working hand-in-glove but of powerful emotion held in powerful check. So constructed, the poems mime the central configuration of their author's psyche. Consider this epistolary remark, which for the casual reader of Eliot might seem exaggerated, but which represents one of the most telling confessions Eliot ever made. Writing at Easter 1928 to his religious confidant William Force Stead, Eliot told Stead that he needed the most severe kind of discipline. It was, according to Eliot, a question of compensation. Nothing, he said, could be too ascetic, too violent, for his needs.[7]

The discipline that Eliot sought in his life, and felt he achieved only sporadically, permeates his work, where his success was more frequent, though never complete. If we forget this tension between what may be variously seen as impulse and discipline or sympathy and judgment, if we forget what may be generalized as the conflict between the "inside" and "outside" perspectives of Eliot's work, then we lose touch with what makes it most valuable and most characteristic. And if we choose to read Eliot's work primarily in terms of its anti-romantic attitudes, we are guilty of a shallow Puritanism of the kind that Eliot, thinking of his own experience, differentiated in 1920 from the vital Puritanism of the American tradition. Describing the decadence of the Jacobean dramatist Philip Massinger, Eliot wrote that

> What may be considered corrupt or decadent in the morals of Massinger is not an alteration or diminution in morals; it is simply the disappearance of all the personal and real emotions which this morality supported and into which it introduced a kind of order. As soon as the emotions disappear the morality which ordered it appears hideous. Puritanism itself became repulsive only when it appeared as the survival of a restraint after the feelings which it restrained had gone (SW, 133–34).

If Eliot pursued the modernist dialectic between music and monologue throughout his career, then, it was not simply because he possessed the finest critical intelligence of the age; it was also because the dialectic was grounded in his character. A need to encounter his personal demons and a need to control them, a rebellious self-assertiveness and a compulsive self-censorship, began their quarrel in his psyche before he began to think of them as poles of stylistic choice and long before he was aware of them as issues in contemporary literature. Which is probably why his "rhythmic grumbling" has had such resonance in our time. The circumstances of Eliot's life made his acceptance of acquired conventions of speech repellent. He came instinctively to distrust received forms, and his aversion harmonized with his generation's dislike of rhetoric and later with the deconstructionists' awareness of the rhetoricity of language itself. Other writers incorporated the stylistic fashions of the time into their work or attempted to ignore them. Eliot seems to have had little choice. His genius fulfilled what his character demanded. It thus was no accident that when he walked into Ezra Pound's London flat, Pound did not need to tell him to "remember the date (1914) on the calendar" and could remark that Eliot had "actually trained himself *and* modernized himself *on his own*." [8] To quote Conrad Aiken, who envied Eliot's combination of personal authority and absolute contemporaneity, "how sharp and complete and *sui generis* the whole thing was, from the outset. The *wholeness* is there, from the very beginning—and that can be said of perhaps no other living poet." [9]

Recognizing the truth of Aiken's assertion, the present study assumed its final form. At that moment my interest in Eliot as typical modernist gave way to a fascination with the sources of Eliot's lifelong stylistic ambivalence. But to account for those sources, I had to make certain assumptions about the connections between character and style. And so, though this is a book about Eliot's poetry, it is also something more. Like the "critics of consciousness," I am less interested in the man who wrote the poems than in "the implied being who gradually assumes form as the work is created."[10] Yet I must agree with the Renaissance English critic George Puttenham that a man's work cannot be completely separated from his life. In Puttenham's words, as a man is "tempered and qualified, so are his speeches and language at large."[11] Or to put it in the terms of a recent psychoanalytic critic, what we call poetic voice, like any other kind of speech, is bound up with the matter of character. Style, like character, is a habitual mode of bringing our preconscious impulses into harmony. And just as it is impossible to recognize a man's character unless we understand the internal pressures he lives with, so it is impossible to understand his style unless we first recognize the impulses it serves to repress, channel and adapt.[12]

What follows, then, examines the motives not only of Eliot's writing but of his life. It considers how some of Eliot's experiments amplified his suppressed impulses and did or did not exacerbate the tensions that accompanied them, and how others seem to have been founded not in the amplification but in the evasion of impulse.[13]

In one way the focus of my study never changed. It remains an inquiry into why and how Eliot's poetry evolved from *The Waste Land* to the *Four Quartets*. Part I examines the poems that best exemplify the tensions in Eliot's work from "Prufrock" to *The Waste Land*. Parts II and III consider Eliot's emotional and stylistic adjustments after 1922.

Arlington, Massachusetts R.B.

Acknowledgments

I wish first to acknowledge the kindness of strangers. A grant from the National Endowment for the Humanities paid for research travel and gave me a chance to begin. Grants from Harvard and Caltech helped fund the rest. For library assistance, I am indebted to the staffs of the Houghton Library, Harvard University (especially Susan Halpert); the Beinecke Library, Yale; the New York Public Library; the Humanities Research Center at the University of Texas, Austin; the Huntington Library; the libraries of King's and Magdalene Colleges, Cambridge; to Patricia Willis, Curator of the Marianne Moore Collection, Rosenbach Museum, Philadelphia; and to Bart Feather, Archivist, Milton Academy, Milton, Massachusetts.

Which leaves the friends who helped make the book. Elise Paschen untangled the footnotes, and Elizabeth Catenaccio meticulously read the proofs. Stephanie Golden, editor and classmate, saved me from a hundred errors and cajoled, argued and persisted until I had written a better book than I thought I could. Jerry McGann and Mac Pigman volunteered last-minute advice and reassurance. Andy Delbanco came up with necessary information on short notice.

And finally there are four people whom I cannot thank enough: David Perkins, whose readings sustained my faith in the project, Judy Baumel, whose suggestion set the material free and whose encouragement kept me going, Walton Litz, whose extraordinary good nature gave of time and support beyond the limits of teacher or friend, and Marilyn Bush, who will know how much she meant.

Contents

Part I: Character and Style: 1888–1922

Chapter 1   Ghostly Selves, 3
Chapter 2   "The pathology of rhetoric," 17
Chapter 3   "I would meet you upon this honestly": "Gerontion," 32
Chapter 4   "The poet's inner world of nightmare," 41
Chapter 5   "Unknown terror and mystery": *The Waste Land,* 53

Part II: "A New Form and Style": 1923–34

Chapter 6   New Life: *The Hollow Men,* 81
Chapter 7   "Desire and control," 103
Chapter 8   "Explaining to himself": *Ash Wednesday,* 131
Chapter 9   "Beyond music," 157

Part III: "Costing Not Less Than Everything"

Chapter 10   "Our first world": *Burnt Norton,* 183
Chapter 11   "A new and shocking valuation": *Four Quartets,* 208

Notes, 239
Index, 277

Abbreviations

ASG   *After Strange Gods: A Primer of Modern Heresy.* The Page-Barbour Lectures at the University of Virginia, 1933. New York: Harcourt Brace, 1934. (Also published London: Faber and Faber, 1934.)

CP   *The Complete Plays of T. S. Eliot.* New York: Harcourt Brace, 1967. (Also published as *T. S. Eliot: Collected Plays.* London: Faber and Faber, 1962.)

CPP   *The Complete Poems and Plays of T. S. Eliot 1909–1950.* 1952; rpt. New York: Harcourt Brace, 1962.

ED   *Elizabethan Dramatists: Essays by T. S. Eliot.* London: Faber and Faber, 1963. (Also published New York: Harcourt Brace, 1962.)

Facs.   *The Waste Land: A Facsimile and Transcript of the Original Drafts Including the Annotations of Ezra Pound.* Edited and with an Introduction by Valerie Eliot. New York: Harcourt Brace, 1971. (Also published London: Faber and Faber, 1971.)

FLA   *For Lancelot Andrewes: Essays on Style and Order.* Garden City, N.Y.: Doubleday Doran, 1929. (Also published London: Faber and Gwyer, 1928.)

KE   *Knowledge and Experience in the Philosophy of F. H. Bradley.* London: Faber and Faber, 1964. (Also published New York: Farrar, Straus, 1964.)

OPP   *On Poetry and Poets.* 1957; rpt. New York: Noonday-Farrar, 1969. (Also published London: Faber and Faber, 1957.)

SE   *Selected Essays.* 1932; rpt. New York: Harcourt Brace, 1960. (Also published London: Faber and Faber, 1951.)

SW   *The Sacred Wood: Essays on Poetry and Criticism.* 1920; rpt. New York: University Paperbacks, Barnes and Noble, 1966. (Also published London: Methuen, 1928.)

TCC   *To Criticize the Critic and Other Writings.* 1965; rpt. New York: Noonday-Farrar, 1968. (Also published London: Faber and Faber, 1965.)

UPUC   *The Use of Poetry and the Use of Criticism: Studies in the Relation of Criticism to Poetry in England.* Charles Eliot Norton Lectures for 1932–33 at Harvard University. 1933; rpt. London: Faber and Faber, 1967.

PART ONE

Character and Style
1888–1922

CHAPTER ONE

Ghostly Selves

There is no theory that is not a fragment, carefully prepared, of some autobiography.

Paul Valéry

The whole history of Lawrence's life and of Lawrence's writings . . . is the history of his craving for greater intimacy than is possible between human beings, a craving irritated to the point of frenzy by his unusual incapacity for being intimate at all. His struggle against over-intellectualized life is the history of his own over-intellectualized nature.

T.S. Eliot, from a review of *Son of Woman: The Story of D.H. Lawrence*

In June 1933, at the end of his first year in America since 1914, T.S. Eliot traveled from his rooms in Harvard College to Milton Academy to address the graduating class of his old preparatory school. He was forty-four, he suspected his poetic career was over and he had just decided to leave his wife. Reacting with childhood memories called up by New England, these reminders of his advancing years reinforced one of Eliot's deeply ingrained habits—brooding about the pattern of his life. Now, about to return to England and to undeniable middle age, he more than ever felt the urge to sort out how his life had changed. Speaking to American adolescents of his own social class, unexpectedly he dropped his usual reserve. In his speech, which was more than characteristically charming, he spoke of his personal life with uncharacteristic candor. He became so charming and so candid, in fact, that his audience never recognized the seriousness of what he said. Even forty years later one of his biographers would call the address beguiling and nothing more.[1]

Eliot's Milton Academy remarks, like the poems and plays he wrote soon afterward, inevitably revert to "The Jolly Corner," Henry James's story about a ghostly confrontation with the self he might have been had he never gone abroad.[2] Instead of addressing the boys in front of him, who, Eliot said, had their minds on more important things anyway, Eliot called up "the ghost of myself at the age of seventeen or thereabouts . . . [who is] skulking somewhere about this hall." And as he invoked this reluctantly attendant figure, the ambivalence he felt about the changes in his life grew apparent. On one hand he was disturbed about the problems his youthful character had caused him, and he told his audience, "I should like to face him and say. . . . 'See what a mess you have made of things.'" But having just renounced marriage and married life, he was not entirely sure he had not left the most vital part of himself behind. His anxiety slipped out in the form of a comically exaggerated wish to "cow" his antagonist, who, he said, "does not like me any better than I like him." In the midst of this he offered three pieces of advice that he had "learned . . . in life. . . . by hard experience"—advice which, coming out of a year of soul-searching, was more revealing than anyone in Milton that day was likely to understand.[3]

Two of Eliot's remarks speak directly to his later poetry and to the experience that made him different from the schoolboy and aspiring poet he had been. Filled with the ironies of being a world-renowned writer whose celebrity masked a ruined marriage and a barren pen, and yet of having rescued a spiritual vocation out of the ruin, Eliot counseled: "Don't admire or desire success"; it cannot be distinguished from failure; the important thing is to be steadfast in your determination to "find out the right thing to do and then do it," and not to flinch from the choices that inevitably arise. According to another piece of his advice, some choices are "irrevocable and, whether you make the right one or the wrong one, there is no going back on it. 'Whatever you do,' I wish someone had said to me [when I left Milton], 'don't whimper, but take the consequences.'"[4]

The first of these observations would lead eight years later to Krishna's injunction in "The Dry Salvages": "do not think of the fruit of action. / Fare forward." The second throws a terrible personal gloss on the conclusion to *The Hollow Men:*

> *This is the way the world ends*
> *Not with a bang but a whimper.*

Together they hint at the suffering that lay behind the crises of Eliot's life and at the drastic measures he sometimes took to resolve them. For Eliot, who was exquisitely aware of his effect on other people, decisions that involved his intimates were full of responsibility, guilt and anguish.[5] After long vacillation, he made them by force of will and executed them quickly. After almost a decade of thinking about separating from his wife, for example, he left her without warning, and with only a note from his solicitor for explanation. His remarks at Milton show how he had come to see important personal decisions as tests of strength, and had grown contemptuous, with the stridency of a man fending off his own weakness, of people whose "whimperings" get in the way of their judgment. His poetry, though, tells what life according to such principles cost him. In the poems written after *The Waste Land,* even rapture is inevitably shadowed by discomfort, as in the famous lines from *Ash Wednesday,* where an "enchanted" maytime is felt as something ominous, something that needs to be overcome with the aid of "strength beyond hope and despair."

Eliot's contempt for "whimpering" had also affected his poetics. In 1924, sounding the keynote of a *revised* literary program, he wrote that "not our feelings, but the pattern which we may make of our feelings, is the centre of value."[6] This statement differs considerably from the most fundamental of his earlier assumptions about poetry, which can be gauged from the first piece of advice he offered the students at Milton in 1933. With a flash of the conviction which made him the poet he was by the end of his adolescence, he admonished: "Whatever you think, be sure that it is what you think; whatever you want, be sure that it is what you want; whatever you feel, be sure that it is what you feel. It is bad enough to think and want the things that your elders want you to think and want, but it is still worse to think and want just like all your contemporaries."[7]

"Whatever you feel, be sure that it is what you feel," besides illuminating Eliot's surprising respect for Hemingway,[8] catches the spirit of his young manhood, when he plotted rebellion against the conventions of Unitarian Boston. It also helps make sense of Eliot's expatriation, and before that of his student year abroad. For the young Eliot, Boston was a place where feelings were subjected to the requirements of duty— a duty formulated by social rather than religious prescription. But for his brooding conscience and his poetic vocation, he might have been Chad Newsome sailing for the uncorseted experience of France. And like Chad Newsome, he sailed against the strenuous objections of his mother. ("I cannot bear," Charlotte Eliot wrote him, "to think of your being alone in Paris, the very words give me a chill. English-speaking countries seem so different from foreign [ones].")[9]

More than a comment on Eliot's European exile, his Milton Academy remark about feeling points to the much-misunderstood rationale of his early verse. Everyone who reads *The Sacred Wood* remembers the sentence, "The progress of an artist is a continual self-sacrifice, a continual extinction of personality" (SW, 53). But few recall that in the same volume Eliot condemned Tennyson for "the acquisition of impersonal ideas which obscure what we really are and feel, what we really want, and what really excites our interest" (SW, 154). In ways that are infrequently acknowledged, Eliot played fast and loose with the words "personal" and "impersonal" in his early essays, and did not emphasize certain assumptions about poetry which, baldly stated, made him extremely uncomfortable. The most significant of these turn up in his discussion of Blake, where he wrote that "honesty" is the "peculiarity of all great poetry," and that a poet should write "from the centre of his own crystal" (SW, 151, 54–55). He made the point with greater force and subtlety when he said a few months earlier in an uncollected piece that "great simplicity is only won by an intense moment or by years of intelligent effort, or by both. It represents one of the most arduous conquests of the human spirit: the triumph of feeling and thought over the natural sin of language."[10]

These formulations share a common premise. Avoiding conventionalized ways of feeling and writing requires literary sophistication, but the poet *must* bypass convention to convey his real experience, his real feelings and thought. There is no suggestion that feelings must be dutifully controlled here—nothing about the moral patterns we build out of our experience or our destiny to outgrow "the majority of human passions" (SE, 212). Only a call for the exact presentation of all experience and a hint that the honest presentation of experience may be the most moral (and the most arduous) of human endeavors.

To desire the "triumph of feeling and thought over the natural sin of language" was for Eliot as much a personal necessity as a critical slogan. As for Emerson before him, Eliot's only means of protecting the authenticity of his inner life against repression was through the rigorous honesty of literary craft.[11] It was this function of poetry he confessed in his 1953 essay "The Three Voices of Poetry," where he wrote that the lyric poet "is oppressed by a burden which he must bring to birth in order to obtain relief. Or, to change the figure of speech, he is haunted by a demon, a demon against which he feels powerless, because in its first manifestation it has no face, no name, nothing; and the words, the poem he makes, are a kind of form of exorcism of this demon" (OPP, 107).

But when Eliot exhorted the students of Milton Academy to be sure their wishes, thoughts and feelings were genuinely their own, he also suggested that for him the task was never easy. A man does not emphasize the need to "be sure" of feelings unless he is himself habitually questioning them. Eliot's remark bespeaks a mind used to distrusting spontaneity and relying on conscience not only for moral guidance but also for emotional censorship. In his youth he was determined—even compelled—to acknowledge his inner life, but the most deep-seated of his inhibitions told him that feelings and wishes were not to be trusted. Out of this tension grows the ambivalence of his early poetry and criticism. Devoted to the ideal of emotional honesty, Eliot's early work scorns the easy expression of sentiment with what can only be called an excessive animus. In *The Sacred Wood*, for example, only a page after Eliot praises Blake's "sincerity," he assails him for failing to develop the kind of "impersonal point of view" that would have avoided "the crankiness, the eccentricity, which frequently affects writers outside of the Latin traditions" (SW, 156, 157).

That Eliot as a child was capable of emotional impressions of extraordinary power and delicacy, no one will doubt who has read "The Dry Salvages," where some of these childhood impressions are preserved in the Missouri and Massachusetts landscapes. The young Eliot adored his warm-hearted but uneducated Catholic nursemaid, Annie Dunne, but soon learned that warmth and sensitivity were not important traits of the man he was expected to be.[12] The model his earnest, devoutly Unitarian and self-improving mother held up to him was his Moses-like paternal grandfather, William Greenleaf Eliot, whose sermons Emerson praised and whose standards of conduct were based on the ability to distinguish "between duty and self-indulgence."[13] The Eliots were descended from seventeenth-century New England Puritans. Only because William Greenleaf Eliot believed it his duty to give up the settled life of the Northeast and minister to the needs of the frontier had the poet been born in St. Louis. (Even so, his mother and father made sure he spent his summers in Massachusetts.) And Eliot's St. Louis had a strong Boston flavor. As young Tom was not allowed to forget, his grandfather had helped found "the symbols of Religion, the Community and Education"—the local church and school and college—to teach children "that personal and selfish aims should be subordinated to the general good which they represent" (TCC, 44).

Thus Eliot internalized his family's ideals of self-denial and rational prudence long before Irving Babbitt's Harvard lessons in the evils of romanticism. It became second nature for him to question the value of emotion in general and of the claims of his own authentic emotional life in particular. And if this constant self-questioning lacked some of the ancestral Puritan fear of eternal damnation, it also lacked the Puritan compensation of periodic emotional release. What it retained, and retained with a vengeance, was a perpetual feeling of unworthiness—a sense of inadequacy attendant on a life of self-examination. Conditioned to distrust emotional expression, Eliot came to devalue his strongest experiences and secretly doubt his own worth. As Brigit Patmore (who was close enough to Eliot and his wife Vivien to go dancing with them in London on Sunday afternoons) put it, "He was pleased with nobody—all [fell] short of his desired perfection—but. . . . [he was also full of] worried and self-accusatory apologies."[14] If the life he lived in his poetry made him feel better about himself, it was never for long. One remembers words that Colby, a young pianist, speaks in *The Confidential Clerk:*

> [the garden of my music is] no less unreal to me
> Than the world outside it. If you have two lives
> Which have nothing whatever to do with each other—
> Well, they're both unreal.

> (CP, 245–46)

Or, to quote Lord Claverton, Eliot's alter ego in *The Elder Statesman:*

> Some dissatisfaction
> With myself, I suspect, very deep within myself
> Has impelled me all my life to find justification
> Not so much to the world—first of all to myself.
> What is this self inside us, this silent observer,
> Severe and speechless critic, who can terrorise us
> And urge us on to futile activity,
> And in the end, judge us still more severely
> For the errors into which his own reproaches drove us?
>
> (CP, 317)

Like so many children, Eliot could not fail to strive for the intellectual rigor and accomplishments of his elders. The finest English poet of his generation, he would in time become as forceful a religious figure as his grandfather and as good at banking and publishing as his father was at brick-making. But these accomplishments, being unrelated to a need for emotional self-fulfillment, provided no real satisfaction. After every success, Eliot felt empty. There were times, in fact, when he could only regard the congratulations of his friends as a rude joke. When Conrad Aiken, for example, praised his 1925 *Poems,* Eliot replied "not with a letter, but with a printed page torn out of *The Midwives' Gazette,* on which he had underlined in ink" four grotesquely amusing phrases: *"Blood—mucous—shreds of mucous—purulent offensive discharge."* [15]

For the full extent of Eliot's potential for despondence, though, one turns to his account of Henry Adams. In 1919 Eliot described Adams's life as a way of admonishing himself. "His very American curiosity," Eliot wrote, "was directed and misdirected by two New England characteristics: conscientiousness and scepticism. . . . This is conspicuously a Puritan inheritance . . . conscience lays upon them the heavy burden of self-improvement. They are usually sensitive people, and they want to do something great; [but] dogged by the shadow of self-conscious incompetence they are predestined failures." Adams, according to Eliot, was "aware, as most Bostonians are, of the narrowness of the Boston horizon. But working with and against conscience was the Boston doubt: a scepticism which is difficult to explain to those who are not born to it." [16]

When he wrote that, Eliot felt he had escaped. He had conquered the Boston doubt by allying himself with the artistic sensibility of Henry James, whose novels he praises in the Adams essay for being at once "sensuous and intellectual." And yet there is a real poignancy in the fact that Eliot remains troubled, even in his superior position. For all his words about the life of art, we can still hear the uneasiness in his voice when he says that Adams was predestined to fail at doing something great. Failure, for Eliot, was unthinkable. Not to achieve the civic prominence of his grandfather or the business success of his father meant making himself vulnerable to his family and to their internalized representative in his own conscience. And it also called up fears of exposing himself as a creature of self-indulgent emotionalism. This fear of failure, combined with a horror of a bloodless New England success, kept Eliot on a psychological treadmill that accelerated until he broke down in 1921. The strain is obvious in a letter he wrote about the time of the Adams essay, in which he confessed how much the American publication of his work meant to him. "You see," he explained, "I settled [in England] in the face of strong family opposition, on the claim that I found the environment more favourable to the production of literature. This book is all I have to show for my claim—it would go toward making my parents contented with conditions and toward satisfying them that I have not made a mess of my life, as they are inclined to believe."[17] Three weeks later, he added tellingly, "My father has died, but this does not weaken the need for a book at all—it really reinforces it—my mother is still alive."[18]

But to rehearse these pressures toward family conformity is to tell only half of Eliot's story. In his early defenses of poetry, and in the philosophy to which he was drawn as a young man, Eliot set what he called the "intellectual and puritanical rationalism"[19] of his upbringing against itself. He used, in other words, the tools of skepticism to construct a case for the life of the heart. And if his account of the life of the heart appears more limited than, say, Emerson's, we should not rely too much on appearances. For Eliot no less than Emerson, the salvation of the spirit is at stake, though the issues first seem to concern prosody rather than preaching.

Eliot's drift toward philosophy, striking even before the subject became the serious study of his postgraduate years, was precisely an attempt to justify the value of the affections. Looking back in 1952 he distinguished his early desire to study philosophy in its "older meaning" of "insight and wisdom" from the prevailing motivation of the Harvard philosophers who were "beginning to suffer from a feeling of inferiority to the exact scientist[s]" and who were likely to become "imitation mathematicians."[20] Eliot took the work of philosophers not as the statement of absolute laws but as "insight" and personal "vision."[21] He once wrote that "those who have read philosophy with complete detachment from any schools have trained themselves to look for just those aspects of any author which are most personal; have followed with keenest interest his doubts, his prejudices, his hesitations, his confessions, here and there, of failure; have sought always for the peculiar flavour of the man's thought in the man's own words."[22] His tendency to put philosophy in the service of something warmer and more "personal" than reason even went so far as to make him once forget his innate skepticism and, for a few brief months, became a convert of the philosopher Henri Bergson,[23] at which time Bergson's *An Introduction to Metaphysics* came to support the method of poems like "Rhapsody on a Windy Night."[24]

Whether writing about Bergson, however, or the more sophisticated F. H. Bradley, Eliot's discourses on philosophy do not represent the origin of his poetic vision. His philosophy and his poetry involve parallel attempts to resolve the personal problem that stung him into all his writing—the painful and fundamental split in his psyche between thought and feeling. Eliot was describing himself, I believe, when in unpublished character sketches of the twenties and thirties he portrayed the primary influence on his early work, the French symbolist poet Jules Laforgue, as a young man of ardent feelings and a gift for abstract thinking who desired his every feeling to have a philosophical justification so that thought and feeling should cooperate toward a fullness of life.[25] For Eliot, though, more than fullness of life was at stake, at least if we take the phrase to mean simply making life more intense. His very self-esteem seemed to depend on finding a philosophical justification for feeling. It is this quest which he takes up on the first page of his doctoral dissertation on Bradley, where Eliot takes pains to describe feeling as one of the respectable components of consciousness.[26]

Before his ventures into philosophy, only the poetry he began writing as an adolescent justified his inner life. In its mock-romantic cadences, he subsumed both parts of his double bind, integrating what might be called his buried and "acquired" selves (remember his words about Tennyson's *"acquisition* of impersonal ideas").[27] Eliot confessed as much when he recalled the experience of reading Laforgue and finding his poetic voice. It was not, he said, as if he had deliberately chosen a "poet to mimic," but as if he had begun to write "under a kind of daemonic possession."[28] "There is a close analogy," he added on another occasion, "between the sort of experience which develops a man and the sort of experience which develops a writer. . . . it is certainly a crisis; and when a young writer is seized with his first passion of this sort he may be changed, metamorphosed almost . . . from a bundle of second-hand sentiments into a person."[29]

The subject of Eliot's early poetry is precisely the dilemma his philosophical studies would try, unsuccessfully, to resolve. Caught between the conflicting paths to self-esteem represented by the life of feeling and the life of thought, he turns from trying to reconcile the two to dramatizing their struggle.[30] In his first volume of poetry, *Prufrock and Other Observations,* Eliot gave life to sensibilities suffering his own conflicted energies, only to exorcise them through the violence of satire. "The Love Song of J. Alfred Prufrock," to name only the most famous example, begins with ardent feelings calling out for fulfillment, but soon echoes with the mocking irony of an intellect that is anything but cooperative. Dogged like his creator by the Boston doubt, Prufrock is oppressed by "eyes that fix you in a formulated phrase"—eyes that continually question the value of his emotional life.[31] Nor can he escape this scrutiny, since it is only by acceding to it—identifying with it—that he frees himself from the fearsome authority which it represents. The cost of this freedom, though, is permanent alienation from his inner life. Against the grain, and at considerable psychic cost, he is ruled by an acquired self that suffocates him and leaves him feeling like a servant in his own world. In the words of the poem,

> an easy tool,
> Deferential, glad to be of use,
> Politic, cautious, and meticulous. . . .

To forswear his ironic stance and assert his emotional needs is just not in Prufrock's power. Simply to consider it is to conjure up the likelihood of disapproval, retribution and paralysis. It's no accident, then, that his monologue begins and ends with reveries of escape followed by intimations of ether and drowning. To Prufrock, emotional release necessarily entails the prospect of psychic disintegration.

Prufrock's love song moves toward an erotic vision of a group of women at a tea party. Their arms, "braceleted and white and bare," provoke the insurgence of his buried life, and their pillowed heads push the conflict of his divided selves to the point of crisis. The same moment occurs much amplified in one of Eliot's other early love songs. In "La Figlia Che Piange," the poem Eliot chose to conclude the *Prufrock* volume, the women at the top of the stairs are telescoped into one woman, who dominates the poem and who focuses the ambivalence of Eliot's speaker toward his emotional life.

The title, "La Figlia Che Piange," means "the young girl weeping." It is in Italian because the inspiration for the poem came from a scene on an antique Italian stele that Eliot was told to look for on a trip to Italy, but never found. Out of that beginning, he wrote a dramatic lyric that invokes the romance of Italy and at the same time suggests that the romance is irrecoverable, untranslatable. The poem's Virgilian epigraph catches both the glamor and the disturbing quality of this experience. Eliot took it from the first book of the *Aeneid,* where Aeneas encounters his mother, Venus, disguised as a beautiful young girl. Aeneas suspects, though, that the girl is a goddess, and half-afraid of offending her, he asks: "Maiden, how shall I name thee?" On that note of polite caution mixed with awe, Eliot's speaker begins addressing the girl of his reveries:

> Stand on the highest pavement of the stair—
> Lean on a garden urn—
> Weave, weave the sunlight in your hair—
> Clasp your flowers to you with a pained surprise—
> Fling them to the ground and turn

> With a fugitive resentment in your eyes:
> But weave, weave the sunlight in your hair.

Standing on "the highest pavement of the stair," the young girl plays a part like Dante's Beatrice. To imagine oneself in relation with her is to acknowledge the moral efficacy of love and the value of one's affections. But these acknowledgments are almost impossible for Eliot's characters, since they energize impulses that are associated with terrible retribution. Faced with the image of the girl in his revery, the dandified speaker of this poem responds with a Prufrock-like doubleness. Threatened by his desires, he retreats into the weary irony of a self-consciously arch phrase:

> Fling them to the ground and turn
> With a *fugitive resentment* in your eyes. . . .

But the needs of his emotional life refuse to be denied. In the midst of his ironic detachment, we sense the power of an obsession. The poetic organization of the first stanza stresses what would in any case be four emphatic monosyllables:

> *Stand* on the highest pavement . . .
> *Lean* on a garden urn . . .
> *Clasp* your flowers to you . . .
> *Fling* them to the ground . . .

The force behind these imperatives, all of which attempt to freeze an action into one definable gesture, suggests just how much psychic energy Eliot's speaker must exert to keep the girl's image from becoming vivid and uncomfortable. These stage directions are more than the reflections of an achieved aesthetic detachment. They are part of the poem's inner psychic struggle, in which the dandy anxiously battles to immobilize the girl's image in a tableau fixed and colored by the conventions of his acquired self. Try as he may, though, his attempts prove ineffective. The dandy cannot keep his desire from endowing the girl with a charm as powerful as her ability to unsettle him. And so, in the last line of the first stanza, which is also the end of the poem's first movement, an insurgent burst of lyricism disencumbers the girl's image, and all but effaces the dandy's emotional detachment:

> But weave, weave the sunlight in your hair.

Then, as so often in Eliot's poetry, the beginning of a new stanza signals a new stage of emotional conflict. In stanza two, the impulses behind the poem's ironic voice regroup and the voice employs stronger measures to avoid involvement. For one thing, the imagined encounter is recast from the imperative to the less immediate conditional perfect form that Eliot also uses near the end of *Prufrock:*

> So I *would have had* him leave,
> So I *would have had* her stand and grieve. . . .

More obviously, the speaker protects his ironic stance by splitting himself up into a participant lover ("he") and "I," the detached observer who is now entirely outside the encounter. But even these stratagems cannot ward off the suppressed emotion that is the poem's most distinctive signature. This time, two similes follow the re-enacted scene, and they betray an increased intensity that clarifies the emotional significance of the young girl:

> So he would have left
> As the soul leaves the body torn and bruised,
> As the mind deserts the body it has used.

The dandy, by comparing the lover's desertion of his beloved to the mind's desertion of an exploited body, suggests that at some level, man and girl, lover and beloved, are projections of his own psyche, and that *la figlia*, the young girl, is an image of his own emotional life. It is not surprising, then, that the similes are sympathetically weighted toward the body. Though the word order connects the speaker with mind and soul—the agents of a New England sensibility—the dandy's strongest identification is with the buried emotional life suggested by the heart, the body and the girl. The twice-deserted corpse in his similes thus presents the suppressed desolation characteristic of his own history. He has been cut off from his vital center by an acquired self, and the split seems like the separation of death. Like Prufrock, he is suspended between two identities, unable to enjoy either. It is this tension, this torment, that is mirrored in the syntax of the first simile, where either the body or the soul can be modified by "torn and bruised."

Eliot's drama has by now reached a kind of climax. In the second sentence of the stanza, and at the midpoint of the poem, the dandy's sentimental revery sours, and a multi-syllabic diction announces his increased detachment:

> I should find
> Some way incomparably light and deft,
> Some way we both should understand. . . .

The stanza ends in a line borrowed from Laforgue ("Simple and faithless as a smile and shake of the hand"),[32] and the strong word "faithless" is charged with a hatred that comes from being faithless to oneself. Only the end of the stanza checks an intensity that has become too painful, and allows for the creation of a new emotional equilibrium. As the third stanza begins, the dandy has placed his revery in the past tense, and, once more detached, can afford a last lingering reflection:

> She turned away, but with the autumn weather
> Compelled my imagination many days,
> Many days and many hours:
> Her hair over her arms and her arms full of flowers.

With the change in tenses comes a change from spring flowers to autumn weather (always less threatening to Eliot's speakers than the stirrings of April), along with the dandy's resumption of a comfortable, self-deprecating turn of phrase: "I should have lost a gesture and a pose." Although the girl reappears in a brief lyrical moment, the present danger is over.

It is clear, though, that the dandy has not resolved his ambivalence. The next to last line suggests his obsession will be perpetuated, and the same psychological sequence will be repeated:

> Sometimes these cogitations still amaze. . . .

As with the ancient mariner, the dandy's unconscious needs require him to retell his story until he understands the bond between himself and his suffering victim. Wondering how "they should have been to-gether," he is troubled by midnight thoughts which, though pathetic, remind us of Eliot's own reflections on the possibility of reconciling intellect and feeling. But as the dandy cannot resist telling his story in the language of the "Boston doubt," we may assume he will never re-alize his desire. In Virgil's words, used as the poem's epigraph, he will continue to ask *"O quam te memorem virgo."* But, as he is no Aeneas, his goddess will remain unnamed and unknown. She will continue to weep, and, weeping, provide an image of his imprisoned existence—a for-saken figure of unfulfilled life.

Eliot, of course, unlike the dandy he created, could name his demons by writing poetry. But at this stage of his career he was no more able to dispel a constant feeling of emotional alienation than was his surro-gate. Poetry integrated his life only for a moment. And philosophy, at least when employed by his skeptical intelligence, could not by itself confirm the value of his emotional life. The only way to do that was to ground his yearnings in an object capable of satisfying them, and so achieve a sense of completion, justification and peace. But since there was a part of Eliot that could never quite believe in the reality of other human beings, all paths were blocked but two. Unless he first submitted to despair, he would, sooner or later, give himself up to God. After the fact of his conversion, the pattern of his life cannot help but remind us (as it reminded him) of Dante. In 1930, a man who had given up his aspiration for earthly things, Eliot looked back and summed up the wisdom of his youth. The trigger of his reflection was Baudelaire, but Eliot could not speak of Baudelaire without invoking his spiritual ancestor:

> The romantic idea of Love is never quite exorcised, but never quite sur-rendered to. In *Le Balcon* . . . there is all the romantic idea, but something more: the reaching out towards something which cannot be had *in,* but which may be had partly *through,* personal relations. Indeed, in much ro-

mantic poetry the sadness is due to the exploitation of the fact that no human relations are adequate to human desires, but also to the disbelief in any further object for human desires than that which, being human, fails to satisfy them. One of the unhappy necessities of human existence is that we have to "find things out for ourselves." If it were not so, the statement of Dante would have, at least for poets, have done once for all (SE, 379).

The remark reminds us unmistakably of one of the most famous passages in the *Convivio,* and of Dante's own roots in Saint Augustine:

The loftiest desire of each thing, and the earliest implanted by Nature, is the desire of returning to its first cause. And since God is the first cause of our souls, and has created them like unto Himself . . . the soul desires most of all to return to Him. And just as a pilgrim who travels by a road on which he never went before thinks that every house which he sees from afar is an inn, and on finding that it is not fixes his trust on some other, and so from house to house until he comes to the inn; so our soul as soon as ever she enters on this new and hitherto untrodden path of life bends her gaze on the highest good as goal, and therefore believes that everything she sees which appears to have some good in itself is that highest good. . . . small goods appear great to her, and therefore her desires are directed to these. So we see little children fixing their chief desire on an apple; then as they go farther they desire a small bird; then going farther still, fine clothes; after this a horse, then a mistress; after this moderate riches, then great, and afterwards the greatest wealth. And this comes to pass because in none of these things does a man find that of which he is in quest. . . . a wise traveler arrives at the goal and rests; the man who misses the way never arrives at his goal, but in much weariness of mind ever with greedy eyes keeps gazing before him (*Convivio* IV.12).

There was for me neither rest nor reason. I carried about my pierced and bloodied soul, rebellious at being carried by me, but I could find no place where I might put it down. Not in pleasant groves, not in games and singing, not in sweet-scented spots, not in rich banquets, not in the pleasures of the bedchamber, not even in books and poetry did it find rest. All things grew loathsome, even the very light itself; and whatsoever was not he was base and wearisome to me (*Confessions* IV.7).

This, then, was the pattern that, once Eliot "found it out" for himself, made sense of the confusion of his past. But it came very late. Before the mid-twenties Eliot could find neither meaning nor order in his life. During that period, all he knew was the torment of conflicting desire, amplified by a fear that if he ever honestly asked himself whether his desire could be satisfied, he would be forced in all honesty to answer no. We can reconstruct his fear from the questions that are implied, only to be evaded, in *The Waste Land.* And we can reconstruct what it felt like to think about it from words Eliot later put in the mouth of Harry, in *The Family Reunion:*

What I see
May be one dream or another; if there is nothing else
The most real is what I fear. The bright colour fades
Together with the unrecapturable emotion,
The glow upon the world, that never found its object;
And the eye adjusts itself to a twilight
Where the dead stone is seen to be batrachian,
The aphyllous branch ophidian.

(CPP, 249)

In his teens and twenties this combination of craving and disappointment seemed unending. It was what first attracted Eliot to the great nineteenth-century analysts of the human heart. And it was what prompted him in 1919 to explain how Stendhal and Flaubert, men of more than the common intensity of feeling, were able to understand the "awful separation between potential passion and any actualization possible in life":

It is this intensity, precisely, and consequent discontent with the inevitable inadequacy of actual living to the passionate capacity, which drove them to art and analysis. The surface of existence coagulates into lumps which look like important simple feelings . . . which the patient analyst disintegrates into more complex and trifling, but ultimately, if he goes far enough, into various canalizations of something again simple, terrible and unknown. The Russians point to this thing, and Turgenev seems almost at times to have had some glimpse of it. Beyle [Stendhal] and Flaubert do not point, but they suggest unmistakably the awful separation between potential passion and any actualization possible in life. They indicate also the indestructible barriers between one human being and another.[33]

CHAPTER TWO

"The pathology of rhetoric"

Every man must know that an attempt is rarely made to communicate im-
passioned feelings without something of an accompanying consciousness
of the inadequateness of our own powers, or the deficiencies of language.

William Wordsworth

Parler n'a trait à la réalité des choses que commercialement.

Stéphane Mallarmé

> I gotta use words when I talk to you
> But if you understand or if you dont
> That's nothing to me and nothing to you
> We all gotta do what we gotta do. . . .
>
> T.S. Eliot, from *Sweeney Agonistes*

Eliot wrote "La Figlia Che Piange" just after the end of his "romantic
year" in Paris, 1910–11.[1] More or less consciously, he had gone to France
to bolster the Laforguian pose of his verse with a full continental persona. Through Laforgue's mixture of propriety and dilettantism, he
wanted to gain a Parisian nonchalance about matters of the head and
heart. And from the pains he took to transform himself, from the length
of time the year in France colored his poetry and from the tenacious
way he clung to Paris during the remainder of his youth, we may guess
at the internal disturbance that prompted his pilgrimage. During 1910–
11, Eliot attempted to change himself from the inside out—he actually
altered his handwriting, for instance.[2] And along with the poems written in his new hand, he brought back a hundred treasured memories,
from reading *Crime and Punishment* in French translation to playing a
part in the demonstrations of the *camelots du roi*. (The first would be
revived in the murdered young women of *Sweeney Agonistes* and *The
Family Reunion;* the second is recalled in the *Coriolan* fragments.)[3] Three
years after his return from France he would write Conrad Aiken that
he thought the only way of sustaining his poetry was to live in Paris, a
dream he conceded was impossible.[4] Then three years after that, to get
out of the worst dry spell he had ever known, he "started writing a few
things in French and found I *could*" (his concluding ellipsis is as telling

as it is poignant). Even as late as 1936, he would confess in a melancholy mood that his early work was simply the product of "cross-fertilisation from Symbolist Poetry" which one or other of the generation of the nineties would inevitably have made superfluous had any of them lived into the new century.[5]

But however desperately Eliot reached out to France, the eyes of New England remained with him. Having gone to Paris because it represented "surtout, à mes yeux, la *poésie*," [6] he underwent "my only conversion, by the deliberate influence of any individual" at the feet not of some Parisian poet but in Bergson's lecture hall.[7] He recovered from that conversion not through the auspices of the muse, French or otherwise, but through a bout of skepticism abut the way Bergson philosophically justified the inner life. The crisis caused Eliot to reject Bergson's "optimism" [8] and turn to the course of rigorous philosophy which he pursued back at Harvard in 1911. Around 1913 he started a dissertation on one of Bergson's severest critics, F. H. Bradley,[9] and by 1914 he was on the verge of becoming a professor of philosophy at Harvard and a minor priest of the Boston doubt.

What prevented him from remaining at Harvard was not simply his discomfort in that role. His fear of emotional suffocation was real enough, but it proved no match for the anxiety he felt at the thought of disappointing his family. To settle him for poetry required the outside support of friends who took the side of his romantic aspirations and in effect shamed him into following the life of art. On a traveling fellowship in Germany when the war broke out, Eliot came to Merton College, Oxford, in August 1914 and a month later met Ezra Pound. By 1915, thanks to the efforts of Pound, Bertrand Russell (who had been Eliot's teacher at Harvard) and others, he had acquired English publications, an English job and an English wife. Though he would work on his Bradley dissertation for another year and review for the philosophy journals for a few years more, Eliot had made an English niche, and it was organized around "the production of literature." The problem was that he had already outgrown his first poetic voice, and he felt stymied whenever he tried to shape the increasing emotional alienation he had felt since 1911 into convincing poetic form.

It is now clear that although Eliot complained about the barrenness of the years between his return from France and his establishment in England, the problem was neither a lack of something to say nor writer's block. According to what Eliot told Virginia Woolf, soon after writing "La Figlia Che Piange" he underwent an emotional upheaval.[10] The result of that upheaval was a series of a dozen or so poems, never published, centering on a flight from the world of the city into a desert-like visionary landscape. These were the poems he later pillaged for *The Waste Land* and which were finally deposited with the *Waste Land* manuscript in the New York Public Library.[11] Eliot projected at least two of them—"The Love Song of St. Sebastian" and "A Debate Between Body and Soul"—as long poems, and was still thinking of going on with the "Debate" as late as March 1918.[12] What prevented him from publishing them was a dissatisfaction with his way of writing that corresponded to his dissatisfaction with the world of polite society. A manner like Laforgue's, which depended on the cadences of *vers de société*, was a half-way measure. Retaining the voices of the parlor, it cautiously mocked them as well. But it could not sound the depths of the buried life, and it would not do to render the desert journeys of a saint or a romantic visionary. And though Eliot listened for other voices, he heard nothing he liked. So, temporarily dispossessed of a voice, he hunted for English jobs and contacts, and his hunt turned into something more. At twenty-nine, he wrote that "any poet, if he is to survive as a writer beyond his twenty-fifth year, must alter; he must seek new literary influences; he will have different emotions to express" (TCC, 177). From 1915 Eliot undertook this search for new influences in earnest, and involved himself in the contemporary literary scene. Seeking a new voice, he entered a public dialogue through the medium of journalism and altered not only himself but the way England thought about poetry. The central term in that dialogue was "rhetoric."

Eliot, of course, had cut his teeth on Symons' *The Symbolist Movement in Literature,* a book that introduced French symbolism as "this revolt against exteriority, against rhetoric." Early in his study, Symons recounted Verlaine's advice "Take eloquence, and wring its neck!" and told his readers Verlaine's example showed that French verse could be written without rhetoric.[13] In London, Eliot found still others who had heeded Verlaine's call. Yeats, invoking Verlaine's famous dictum, later wrote:

> The revolt against Victorianism meant to the young poet a revolt against irrelevant descriptions of nature, the scientific and moral discursiveness of *In Memoriam*—"When he should have been broken-hearted," said Verlaine, "he had many reminiscences"—the political eloquence of Swinburne, the psychological curiosity of Browning, and the poetical diction of everybody. Poets said to one another over their black coffee . . . "We must purify poetry of all that is not poetry," and by poetry they meant poetry as it had been written by Catullus . . . by the Jacobean writers, by Verlaine, by Baudelaire.[14]

And when Eliot arrived in London, he found that Ezra Pound—his immediate predecessor—had written:

> As for there being a "movement" or my being of it, the conception of poetry as a "pure art" in the sense in which I use the term, revived with Swinburne. . . . [In our generation] Mr. Yeats has once and for all stripped English poetry of its perdamnable rhetoric.[15]

Little wonder that Eliot would remember his English initiation the way he did—"The question was still: where do we go from Swinburne? and the answer appeared to be, nowhere."[16] Or that he would, in the most programmatic of his essays, denounce the rhetoric of the Victorians in the intonations of Verlaine, Yeats and Pound: according to "The Metaphysical Poets," "Keats and Shelley died," while "Tennyson and Browning ruminated" (SE, 248).

But if Eliot came to see the task of modern poetry as keeping literature free from rhetoric he did not accept the criteria of his contemporaries in a mechanical way.[17] As we have seen, possessed of an enormous sensitivity to the inadequacy of his own acquired habits of thinking and feeling, Eliot wrestled with the problem of conventional expression long before he realized it was a preoccupation of his generation. He was exquisitely aware of the insincere, conventional component of his most characteristic gestures and once wrote Richard Aldington that his ability to write English prose derived in part from a disposition to rhetoric he had inherited from generations of preachers and orators, a disposition that gave his prose a rather rheumatic pomposity.[18] Eliot even came to understand his own, and by implication, all philosophy as an inadequate expression of something deeper than either thought or speech. Along with making the pronouncements cited in chapter one, he liked to quote Bradley's *mot* "Metaphysics [is] the finding of bad reasons for what we believe upon instinct."[19] And his consciousness of acquired thought, gesture and speech as rhetorical was one of the things that had drawn him to Laforgue's anatomy of conventional poses and had led him, in "Prufrock" and "Portrait of a Lady," to satirize Boston speech. In fact, the "Portrait," using images of Flaubert's, gives us Eliot's most succinct statement of the matter:

> And I must borrow every changing shape
> To find expression . . . dance, dance
> Like a dancing bear,
> Cry like a parrot, chatter like an ape.[20]

In 1917, then, when Eliot was given the opportunity to record a series of "Reflections on Contemporary Poetry" for *The Egoist*, explaining modern poetry in relation to the problem of rhetoric seemed an appropriate way to address both his own preoccupations and those of his audience. The first of the "Reflections" begins, "One of the ways by which contemporary verse has tried to escape the rhetorical, the abstract, the moralizing, to recover (for that is its purpose) the accents of direct speech, is to concentrate its attention upon trivial or accidental or commonplace objects."[21] The importance of those accidental objects in Eliot's own verse will be addressed in chapter four. In the meantime, it is worth noting the characteristic quickness with which Eliot slides from asking how best to escape rhetoric into wondering whether it can be done at all. In the third of his "Reflections," Eliot reviewed Harriet Monroe's anthology *The New Poetry,* and wryly considered the spectacle of "a whole generation, and not merely an isolated individual here and there, [arising] as one man to wring the neck of rhetoric." He added, "as for the escape from rhetoric—there is a great push at the door and some cases of suffocation. But what is rhetoric? . . . There is rhetoric even among the new poets."[22]

The question is well worth asking: what is rhetoric? Even more interesting: what did it mean to Eliot? At the minimum, rhetoric involved more than poetic decorum and more than the duplicity of language. It engaged the matter of insincerity, of the way acquired gesture betrayed human impulse and facilitated what Eliot would call "the human will to see things as they are not" (SE, 111). And as such it required from the poet not an application of new precepts but a caustic introspective scrutiny that was at least as much a matter of self-examination as of aesthetic discipline. And so Eliot ends the third of his "Reflections" not with a definition of rhetoric and a general prescription for its cure, but with a call for literary "intelligence, of which an important function is the discernment of exactly what, and how much, we feel in any given situation." As so often in his prose, he puts his primary emphasis on honest feeling, and his awareness of the abuse of language is really a sensitivity to ways expression can betray the inner self. But note that even as he attends to levels of emotional honesty, Eliot puts at least equal stress on a writer's need for intelligence, and makes intelligence sound more like a gatekeeper than a gardener. The implication, here, I think, is that some of Eliot's horror of dishonest feeling is in fact a horror of feeling in general. We need not wonder that he suspected it was impossible to escape rhetoric, or that he began to believe his proper subject was the dramatization of the soul's eternal imprisonment in the rhetorical conventions of its own gestures.

To speak of Eliot's preoccupation with rhetoric after 1917 is inevitably to invoke his renewed interest in Elizabethan drama. Eliot once wrote that his poetry had begun with a "study of Laforgue together with the later Elizabethan drama."[23] But it would be more accurate to say that his serious—even calculating—study of the Elizabethans came after his first reading of Laforgue and grew out of a fascination with what he saw as the quintessential Elizabethan "vice." Around 1919 Eliot wrote a series of essays in which he diagnosed the Elizabethan mind as it appeared in Marlowe's "simple huffle-snuffle bombast" and Shakespeare's "perverse ingenuity of images."[24] In general, Eliot asserted,

> Rhetoric, a particular form of rhetoric, was endemic, it pervaded the whole organism; the healthy as well as the morbid tissues were built up on it. We cannot grapple with even the simplest and most conversational lines in Tudor and early Stuart drama without having diagnosed the rhetoric in the sixteenth- and seventeenth-century mind.[25]

As in his "Reflections on Contemporary Poetry," in these articles Eliot never precisely defines what he means by rhetoric. The tone of contempt in the remarks just quoted, however, speaks volumes. The occasion for it was Eliot's May 1919 review of a volume of essays on romantic literature written by George Wyndham, a review which stands at the center of Eliot's conquest of London. Not only does the review knit together the most important threads of the London poetry Eliot had already written, it serves as a gunsight for the more important work he was about to undertake. In analyzing Wyndham, Eliot focused what were to be the over-riding concerns of the essays of the next four years.

The particular importance of Eliot's review of Wyndham is latent in its title: "A Romantic Patrician." It points to Wyndham's status as an upper-class man of letters but it also suggests that Eliot is approaching a type similar to his own. (He would call Henry Adams a "Sceptical Patrician.") For Eliot, Wyndham stood for a kind of perversely well-educated Victorian reader who began with the age's disposition toward sentiment and went on to acquire a second weakness. Examining such a reader, Eliot instinctively seized on the particular combination of linguistic failings he knew best and moved toward a general criticism of style. It is a remarkable performance, and most remarkable for the ease with which he accommodates failings he maintains are the hallmarks of two different centuries:

> Wyndham was a Romantic; the only cure for Romanticism is to analyse it. . . . Romanticism is a short cut to the strangeness without the reality, and it leads its disciples only back upon themselves. George Wyndham had curiosity, but he employed it romantically, not to penetrate the real world, but to complete the varied features of the world he made for himself. . . .
> . . . An understanding of Elizabethan rhetoric is as essential to the appreciation of Elizabethan literature as an understanding of Victorian sentiment is essential to the appreciation of Victorian literature and of George Wyndham (SW, 31–32)

We begin here to see where Eliot's nineties-like aversion might be leading. In "A Romantic Patrician," he presumes a connection between the unreal linguistic world of bombast and the equally unreal landscape of romanticism. Though he holds that the Elizabethans were rhetorical realists (that is, their rhetoric did not affect their feeling or their thought), Eliot discovers how easy it is for a Victorian mind of a certain inclination to ignore that discrimination and romanticize Elizabethan eloquence as it romanticizes the rest of experience. Once such a mind had internalized Elizabethan practices, it would be more divorced from its experience than ever. It would, in Eliot's words, be confirmed in (the phrase cannot be over-emphasized) *"the pathology of rhetoric"* (SW, 30).

The importance to Eliot's development of this discovery is patent.

Eliot habitually associated rhetoric with the Puritan as well as the Elizabethan mind, and especially with his own family background. Accusing Wyndam of both sentiment and rhetoric, he is clearly rediscovering and reformulating the central antinomy of his own temperament.

By 1923 the contrast between Elizabethan (which had by now become late Renaissance) and Victorian sensibilities would cause him to posit a historical dissociation of English sensibility. But that was four years in the future. During his early London period, Eliot's musings about what seemed to him an inescapable connection between Elizabethan rhetoric and Victorian romanticism were much more tentative. In May 1919, thanks to George Wyndham, his thinking crystallized, and he took up a slogan: "the pathology of rhetoric." Even before that, his attraction to Elizabethan drama and Victorian poetry had provided texture for a striking and distinctive series of satires.

Two of these poems—"Cousin Nancy" and "Burbank with a Baedeker: Bleistein with a Cigar"—were still on Eliot's mind when he diagnosed Wyndham's diseased sensibility. Tellingly, both concern New England. When he writes, for example, that Wyndham was a "Romantic, riding to hounds across his prose, looking with wonder upon the world as upon a fairyland," he was remembering the cadences of "Cousin Nancy," a 1915 poem about a certain kind of New England girl, which begins:

> Miss Nancy Ellicott
> Strode across the hills and broke them,
> Rode across the hills and broke them—
> The barren New England hills—
> Riding to hounds
> Over the cow-pasture.

> Miss Nancy Ellicott smoked
> And danced all the modern dances;
> And her aunts were not quite sure how they felt about it,
> But they knew that it was modern.

The way Cousin Nancy Ellicott uses her "modern" attitudes to enact a fairy-tale transformation of "the barren New England hills" corresponds to Eliot's account of the way George Wyndham transformed the "real world" into features of a "world he made for himself." Nancy's romanticism serves to make her feel privileged. She is a figure out of the Boston 1890's, rendered by a technique Eliot learned from Pound. In "Les Millwin," written shortly before "Cousin Nancy," Pound comically suggests the limitations of his subjects by presenting them through their characteristic cliches:

> The *turbulent* and *undisciplined* host of art students—
> The *rigorous deputation* from "Slade"—
> Was before them.

With arms *exalted,* with fore-arms
Crossed in great futuristic X's, the art students
Exulted, they *beheld* the *splendours* of *Cleopatra.*

This is also the strategy of Eliot's poem, in which we sense Nancy behind "strode" and "broke." The boastfulness of "danced all the modern
dances" is hers, as is the gleeful judgment that "her aunts were not
quite sure how they felt about it, / But they knew that it was modern."
Her New England might as well be a Hollywood set.

The poem's last line, however, goes beyond social satire. Here Eliot
borrows from Meredith's "Lucifer in Starlight" and presents the intellectual guardians of Victorian culture, Ralph Waldo Emerson and Matthew Arnold, as a mock-angelic "army of unalterable law." After twelve
lines of aggressively prosy straightforwardness, though, the old-fash-
ioned eloquence of that phrase, which Eliot must have enjoyed before
his judgment censored his pleasure, releases complex emotional rever-
berations. As it becomes clear that the phrase "army of unalterable law"
is more important for its sound than for its meaning, the poem uses
the eloquence of the phrase to energize a turn against its own rhetoric.
(The respected position of Matthew Arnold, Eliot later wrote, derives
not from his guardianship of the faith but from "the power of his rhetoric," which he used to "usurp the place of Religion" and "divorce Religion from thought" [SE, 383, 385].)

The emotional center of the poem, then, is a revulsion against not
only Nancy but Matthew and Waldo, in other words against both sides
of Eliot's divided temperament. Together betokening an unbridgeable
gap between sentiment and rhetoric in the New England mind, first
Nancy and then Waldo is offered as an ideal, only to be exposed as cut
off from both experience and reality. If anything Eliot is more disgusted with the respectable Waldo, whose magniloquence he felt as his
own.

"Cousin Nancy," though, is only a practice piece. The concerns it
represents receive a much more sophisticated treatment in a poem Eliot
wrote three years later. It is traditional to approach "Burbank with a
Baedeker: Bleistein with a Cigar" by recalling Pound's account of the
origins of its composition: "At a particular date in a particular room,
two authors . . . decided that the dilutation of *vers libre* . . . had gone
too far. . . . Remedy prescribed "Emaux et Camées" (or the Bay State
Hymn Book). Rhyme and regular strophes." (Eliot later added, "We
studied Gautier's poems and then we thought, 'Have I anything to say
in which this form will be useful?' And we experimented. The form
gave the impetus to the content.")[26] And it is true that in "Burbank,"
Eliot's play of irregular diction against "rhyme and regular strophes"
does produce much of the poem's bite:

Princess Volupine extends
A meagre, blue-nailed, phthisic hand

> To climb the waterstair. Lights, lights,
> She entertains Sir Ferdinand
> Klein.

But more than the tour de force of dark comedy that Robert Graves and Laura Riding found,[27] "Burbank" is a serious exercise in presenting the New England "disposition to rhetoric" Eliot had come to recognize in himself. In his review of Henry Adams's *Education,* written about a year after "Burbank," Eliot remarks on the way Adams, unlike Henry James, is divorced from the emotional aspect of his experience and asks his readers to compare two passages: "Henry Adams in 1858 and Henry James in 1870 (both at still receptive ages), land at Liverpool and descend at the same hotel."[28]

In "Burbank," with Europe figured as Venice, an Adams-like compatriot succumbs to the New Englander's inability to understand either the beauty or the evil of the Old World:

> Burbank crossed a little bridge
> Descending at a small hotel;
> Princess Volupine arrived,
> They were together, and he fell.

Burbank is immature, all intellect and no sensation. In the words of the Adams review, he is a New England Paul Dombey, asking questions when mere questioning is no longer appropriate. Consequently he arrives at the fate that Eliot would ascribe to George Wyndham:

the world was an adventure of himself. It is characteristic that on embarking as a subaltern for Egypt he wrote enthusiastically: "I do not suppose that any expedition since the days of Roman governors of provinces has started with such magnificence; *we might have been Antony going to Egypt in a purple-sailed galley.*" This is precisely the spirit which animates his appreciation of the Elizabethans. . . . Wyndham was enthusiastic, he was a Romantic, he was an Imperialist (SW, 27; emphasis mine).

"Burbank" presents the sentiment "we might have been Antony." But as Burbank is an extension of Eliot and not Wyndham, his mind ends up by reminding us of New England. As with the last line of "Cousin Nancy," the poem's rhetoric is poignant and effective because Eliot seems to have responded to it himself.[29] In the second and third quatrains, Burbank hears the siren song of literary romanticism and exploits the attractiveness of some of the most resonant lines of English poetry. In the process, he reminds us of Prufrock, who also drifted under the waves to the accompaniment of an exquisite lyricism. But Burbank's romanticism is more educated than Prufrock's. His sea-girl is a Venetian princess become Cleopatra, and his lyric enticement is remembered Elizabethan eloquence. The consequences of his delusion, therefore, are more overwhelming. His fate? Immersion in sentiment, followed by death by water:

> Defunctive music under sea
>   Passed seaward with the passing bell
> Slowly: the God Hercules
>   Had left him, that had loved him well.
>
> The horses, under the axletree
>   Beat up the dawn from Istria
> With even feet. Her shuttered Barge
>   Burned on the water all the day.

Innumerable commentators have pointed to the literary echoes here.[30] But to take Eliot's references to George Chapman, Shakespeare and John Marston as invocations of a more heroic age is to miss the emotional point of the writing. These stanzas do not present a narrator's mock-epic comment on Burbank; they render Burbank's own sensibility. Blind to the moral world of his citations, Burbank is possessed by their sound. And swept up by such a "romantic" response, he not surprisingly apprehends sensuality as subhuman. Thus the comedy becomes even darker when Bleistein appears, whom we see not through the lens of an objective narrator but through Burbank's refined yet debilitating sensibility. In the fourth quatrain Eliot leaves Burbank's operatic musing to show us how repulsive the real world is when it is examined through the haze of fairyland.

> But this or such was Bleistein's way:
>   A saggy bending of the knees
> And elbows, with the palms turned out,
>   Chicago Semite Viennese.
>
> A lustreless protrusive eye
>   Stares from the protozoic slime
> At a perspective of Canaletto.

"Burbank" turns on the irony of the last line. Are we watching as Bleistein puzzles over a Canaletto canvas that Burbank prizes? Or are we watching Bleistein gaze at Venice itself, a city that Burbank idealizes by thinking of it as "a perspective of Canaletto"? In other words, is the poem directing us to share in Burbank's disdain for Bleistein's philistinism, or are we being made aware that to Burbank, life is nothing but an aesthetic object? The question is answered in the concluding lines which ridicule Burbank as he "avoids" the city's squalor to "think" and "meditate" on Byron's "ruins" and Ruskin's "seven laws."

But "Burbank" does not only underscore the dangers of aestheticism. It also raises a second, related danger: historicism. The poem asks us to ponder history and condemn Burbank's idolatry of a past that never was. It is common to put this aspect of "Burbank" in different terms, and to invoke one of the most famous sentences in Eliot's most famous essay, "Tradition and the Individual Talent":

> The historical sense involves a perception, not only of the pastness of the past, but of its presence (SW, 49).

What is interesting, though, is that "Burbank" fails to live up to that imperative, just as it fails to live up to Eliot's intentions as he explained them in a 1933 lecture on modern literature. His aim, he said, was the same as James's in "The Aspern Papers": "To get Venice"—the real "centre" of interest—indirectly by making a multitude of references call up something about the city. The idea was to achieve a "complete fitness of place and action."[31]

These remarks say a great deal about the poem Eliot wrote and the one he didn't. James's story concerns an American scoundrel who makes love to the niece of a great poet's abandoned mistress to get at the poet's papers. The point is to move us with the suffering of the niece, who repeats her aunt's blighted love affair in the key of tragicomedy. James, it is clear, modeled the dead poet after Byron, and fashioned the Venice of the story after the Venice of the fourth book of *Childe Harold's Pilgrimage* (the source of Eliot's phrase "Time's ruins").[32] The Venice of "The Aspern Papers" is a city of immemorial suffering, a testimony to the darkness of the human heart. In the story, we occasionally hear the city's chattering society, but in the major scenes Venice functions (as does Rome in "Daisy Miller" or in *The Portrait of a Lady*) to objectify the inevitability of failed desire and failed hope in human affairs. In "The Aspern Papers," however, as in "Burbank," the protagonist fails to see this Venice, and does not understand his own actions. James's scoundrel is an "antiquarian" who rhapsodizes on "the general romance and the general glory" of history and art and is blind to the real value of the present moment. In the sequence which seems to have inspired "Burbank," he recalls a time when he ate ices under the winged lion of Mark, sometimes speaking to tourists temporarily disencumbered of their Baedekers. In the midst of his memories, the great basilica looks out on the tempered gloom, calling up somber truths which the lounging editor chooses to ignore. In the next paragraph, he encounters the niece, and fantasizes that he is Romeo, little realizing that he is involved in an affair as dark and sorrowful as Shakespeare's. The passage needs to be quoted at length:

> I was seldom at home in the evening, for when I attempted to occupy myself in my apartments the lamplight brought in a swarm of noxious insects, and it was too hot for closed windows. Accordingly I spent the late hours either on the water—the moonlights of Venice are famous—or in the splendid square which serves as a vast forecourt to the strange old church of Saint Mark. I sat in front of Florian's café eating ices, listening to music, talking with acquaintances: the traveller will remember how the

immense cluster of tables and little chairs stretches like a promontory into the smooth lake of the Piazza. The whole place, of a summer's evening, under the stars and with all the lamps, all the voices and light footsteps on marble—the only sounds of the immense arcade that encloses it—is an open-air saloon dedicated to cooling drinks and to a still finer degustation, that of the splendid impressions received during the day. When I didn't prefer to keep mine to myself there was always a stray tourist, disencumbered of his Bädeker, to discuss them with, or some domesticated painter rejoicing in the return of the season of strong effects. The great basilica, with its low domes and bristling embroideries, the mystery of its mosaic and sculpture, looked ghostly in the tempered gloom, and the sea-breeze passed between the twin columns of the Piazzetta, the lintels of a door no longer guarded, as gently as if a rich curtain swayed there. I used sometimes on these occasions to think of the Misses Bordereau and of the pity of their being shut up in apartments which in the Venetian July even Venetian vastness couldn't relieve of some stuffiness. Their life seemed miles away from the life of the Piazza, and no doubt it was really too late to make the austere Juliana change her habits. But poor Miss Tina would have enjoyed one of Florian's ices, I was sure; sometimes I even had thoughts of carrying one home to her. Fortunately my patience bore fruit and I was not obliged to do anything so ridiculous.

One evening about the middle of July I came in earlier than usual—I forgot what chance had led to this—and instead of going up to my quarters made my way into the garden. The temperature was very high; it was such a night as one would gladly have spent in the open air, and I was in no hurry to go to bed. I had floated home in my gondola, listening to the slow splash of the oar in the dark narrow canals, and now the only thought that occupied me was that it would be good to recline at one's length in the fragrant darkness on a garden bench. The odour of the canal was doubtless at the bottom of that aspiration, and the breath of the garden, as I entered it, gave consistency to my purpose. It was delicious—just such an air as must have trembled with Romeo's vows when he stood among the thick flowers and raised his arms to his mistress's balcony. I looked at the windows of the palace to see if by chance the example of Verona— Verona being not far off—had been followed; but everything was dim, as usual, and everything was still. Juliana might on the summer nights of her youth have murmured down from open windows at Jeffrey Aspern, but Miss Tina was not a poet's mistress any more than I was a poet. This however didn't prevent my gratification from being great as I became aware on reaching the end of the garden that my younger padrona was seated in one of the bowers. At first I made out but an indistinct figure, not in the least counting on such an overture from one of my hostesses; it even occurred to me that some enamoured maidservant had stolen in to keep a tryst with her sweetheart. I was going to turn away, not to frighten her, when the figure rose to its height and I recognised Miss Bordereau's niece.[33]

As James's scoundrel dreams of a romanticized Romeo, Burbank dreams of Antony, each distorting both Shakespeare and his own life. But in place of James's vivid presentation of Tina's suffering, in the suggestive fragments of the Epigraph to "Burbank," assembled from several sources, we are given only a tissue of allusions to the eternal Venice:

> *Tra-la-la-la-la-la-laire—nil nisi divinum stabile est; caetera fumus—the gondola stopped, the old palace was there, how charming its grey and pink—goats and monkeys, with such hair too!—so the countess passed on until she came through the little park, where Niobe presented her with a cabinet, and so departed.*

We may speculate that Eliot intended to make the poem a Jamesian weighing of American idealism against European realism. But the preoccupation that took possession of his intentions is revealed in the emphases of what he actually wrote. Deprived of an emotional counterweight, the poem speaks of the unreality of the world to a sensibility in the thrall of what Eliot would formulate a year later as "the pathology of rhetoric."

After "Cousin Nancy" and "Burbank," and just after his 1919 Wyndham review, Eliot pursued the problem of rhetoric in a series of other essays.[34] In "Whether Rostand Had Something About Him," for example, revised as "Rhetoric and Poetic Drama" for *The Sacred Wood*, he brought his interests in Elizabethan literature and in the contemporary scene together. "Rostand" returns to the skepticism Eliot had expressed about his generation's attempt to "wring the neck of rhetoric" and concludes:

> At the present time there is a visible preference for the "conversational," the style of "direct speech," opposed to the "oratorical"; but this conversational style may and does become itself a rhetoric, in becoming a fixed convention applied to any matter, not invariably issuing out of the matter treated but imposed upon it. Certain writers have indeed succeeded in obtaining, at times, the effect of direct or simple speech desired; but the avoidance of the rhetorical expression of older writers has become a form, or has separated into a variety of forms or rhetorics which impede, as often as they assist, the expression of feeling. What is overlooked is the fact that there is no "conversational" or other form which can be applied indiscriminately.[35]

In response, Eliot looks to the example of Elizabethan drama to instruct his own age, and notes that while it is said to have "grown out of its early successes of rhetorical expression," even in its maturity it did not forswear the use of certain kinds of rhetoric for particular effects. The examples he gives are personal touchstones, tokens of a literature capable of self-consciously exposing the thing Eliot distrusted most in his own life: an ineradicable need to self-dramatize.

> Shakespeare when he chooses, when the situation requires it, is as "rhetorical" as either Kyd or Marlowe. The moments occur when a character in the play *sees himself* in a dramatic light:

> *Othello:* And likewise say that at Aleppo once. . . . .
>
> *Coriolanus:* If you have writ your annals true, 'tis there,
> That like an eagle in a dovecote, I
> Fluttered your Volscians in Corioli. . . . .
>
> *Timon:* Come not to me again; but say to Athens,
> Timon has built his everlasting mansion
> Beyond the beachèd verge of the salt flood. . . . .

and in "Antony and Cleopatra," when the old captain is inspired to see Cleopatra in this dramatic light:

> The barge she sat in. . . . .

Eliot explains the point of these examples with reference to "modern" literature and the authority of "actual life":

> What is very rare in modern drama, either verse or prose, is the dramatic sense on the part of the characters in the play themselves. We are given plays of realism in which the parts are never allowed to be consciously dramatic, for fear, perhaps, of their appearing less real. But in actual life, or in those situations in our actual life which we enjoy consciously and keenly, we are, at times, aware of ourselves in this way, and these moments are of very great usefulness to dramatic verse. . . .
>
>   . . . as a writer of poetic drama [Rostand] is superior to Maeterlinck, whose drama, in failing to be dramatic, fails also to be poetic. . . . [Maeterlinck's] characters take no conscious delight in their dramatic-poetic rôle—they are sentimental; while Rostand's characters, enjoying awareness, are thereby preserved from sentimentality.[36]

The "situations in our actual life" that Eliot refers to are, however, not just "ours" but his—the ones he had satirized since "Prufrock." In his own experience speech and behavior were expressions of an acquired self—conventional, role-playing, mask-like. Normally, he finds this lack of connection to inner life appalling. But part of him, during special moments, is able to enjoy the spectacle "consciously and keenly." *These* moments "are of very great usefulness to dramatic verse." They allow the poet to swell out his language by incorporating styles which the Georgians and Imagists were forced to reject. More importantly, they allow the poet to render a certain kind of non-sentimental "awareness"—an awareness of the human need to create and sustain an artificial self.

Note, however, that Eliot is careful to limit the claims he makes for such moments. To say that characters then cease to be sentimental is not the same as saying they acquire dignity or nobility. He will later remind us that in speaking about the Turk of Aleppo, Othello was only *"cheering himself up.* . . . *endeavouring to escape reality"* (SE, 111). Still later he will add that "our lives are mostly a constant evasion of ourselves, and an evasion of the visible and sensible world" (UPUC, 155). All these observations, though, are anticipated in a 1919 essay where he praises the great French "anatomist of the heart," Marivaux, for his "exposition of the gradual appearance and selfconsciousness of love" and for making us aware of the self-deceiving "motives and interests which bring it about." Marivaux was concerned, Eliot says, with " 'petits mouvements du coeur,' half conscious."[37] In these moments, when the heart becomes aware of its own rhetoric, its own self-dramatization and self-deception, we see clearly the interaction of love, cupidity and self-deception that for Eliot constitutes the tragedy of the human condition.

CHAPTER THREE

"I would meet you upon this honestly": "Gerontion"

Men are deeply immersed in illusions and dream images; their eye glides only over the surface of things and sees "forms"; their feeling nowhere leads into truth, but contents itself with the reception of stimuli, playing, as it were, a game of blindman's buff on the backs of things.

Nietzsche

Although I have saved it for consideration here, the poem that best represents the concerns of the last chapter is neither "Cousin Nancy" nor "Burbank" but "Gerontion." Still fixated on the relation between rhetoric and romantic self-deception, in "Gerontion" Eliot again draws on moments in Elizabethan and Jacobean drama to represent the consequences of a paralyzing disposition toward rhetoric. Eliot composed it in the same season (perhaps in the same month)[1] that he reviewed Henry Adams's *Education,* and like the *Education,* the poem provides "a remarkable confession of" the New England mind. Its speaker has a sensibility like the Adams Eliot describes, who, caught between conscience and the Boston doubt, is a man who "could believe in nothing." Also like Adams, Gerontion is "unaware that education—the education of an individual—is a by-product of being interested, passionately absorbed" with something or someone outside himself. And, imagining himself as a "gull against the wind," Gerontion flies as Eliot pictured Adams—"with the wings of a beautiful but ineffectual conscience beating vainly in a vacuum jar." His "sense has cooled" and, like the hero of the *Education,* wherever he steps, "the ground [does] not simply give way, it [flies] into particles." Consequently, he lives in the same prison that confined Adams—an "egotism" in which, in the words of the poem's epigraph, life has "nor youth nor age/ But as it were an after dinner sleep/ Dreaming of both."

A canceled epigraph makes the poem's subject even clearer. Like so many of Eliot's early poems, "Gerontion" is a mixture of exorcism and self-indulgence. It gives us the pain of Eliot's inner life and also his drive to distance it. The epigraph from *Measure for Measure* which Eliot retained evokes both sympathy and judgment, but emphasizes the second: in *Measure for Measure,* the Prince advises his charge to regard anything but heavenly life as a dream, and to think of ordinary life as unreal. But this epigraph originally shared space with a second, which announced the poem's reverberating distress. On an early typescript, following "Dreaming of both," Eliot added: *"Come 'l mio corpo stea / nel mondo su, nulla scienza porto."* [2] The line comes from *Inferno* XXXIII, where Dante hears Fra Alberigo say that because Alberigo betrayed his guests, his soul was taken while he lived. ("How my body stands in the world above, I have no knowledge.") [3]

Standing at the beginning of "Gerontion," Dante's words foreshadow the alienation of Gerontion's mind from his body, and dramatize the isolation of his consciousness from the world of sense. In the circle of hell inhabited by Alberigo, it is impossible even to see, because the wind generated by Satan's wings freezes the sinners' tears into an opaque screen of ice. The pilgrim tells us, "And although, as from a callus, through the cold all feeling had departed from my face, it now seemed to me as if I felt some wind."

Befitting that canceled epigraph, "Gerontion" chronicles the development of Prufrockian anesthesia into sensory dessication. "Prufrock" had rendered a split between two selves and a displacement of sexual energy into fantasy; in "Gerontion," man is dissociated from his own sensory world. ("I have lost my sight, smell, hearing, taste and touch: / How should I use them for your closer contact?") The poem's dominant element, therefore, is not water, which has the power to dissolve rigidities of the self. It is a Dantesque cold wind that blows in the vacuum between self-consciousness and the inner life. This wind embodies a ceaseless randomness which cannot find an end and yet cannot die. As such it defines a type of emotional frontier that remains constant in Eliot's mature verse:

> The goat coughs at night in the field overhead;
> Rocks, moss, stonecrop, iron, merds.
> The woman keeps the kitchen, makes tea,
> Sneezes at evening, poking the peevish gutter.
>   I an old man,
> A dull head among windy spaces.
>
>   ("Gerontion")

> The river's tent is broken: the last fingers of leaf
> Clutch and sink into the wet bank. The wind
> Crosses the brown land, unheard. The nymphs are departed.
>   (*The Waste Land*)

>   Alas!
> Our dried voices, when
> We whisper together
> Are quiet and meaningless
> As wind in dry grass. . . .
>
>   (*The Hollow Men*)

              And God said
Prophesy to the wind, to the wind only for only
The wind will listen.

                                        (*Ash Wednesday*)

Tumid apathy with no concentration
Men and bits of paper, whirled by the cold wind
That blows before and after time. . . .

                                        ("Burnt Norton")

In common, these excerpts recognize that unless the affections find their appropriate object, there can be no firm self, no substance. Life unrelated to the affections is weightless, subject to the winds of random impulse, motion without final end.

But there is another major component to the winds in "Gerontion," and that is the movement of empty talk—a speech that has become unmoored from its emotional springs and has degenerated into rhetoric. Gerontion's talk does not correspond to his inner reality, nor does it let him grasp the reality outside him. It serves only to postpone silence, and keeps him from acknowledging the truth of his condition. His speech, if we wish to dignify his mutterings with that word, is a series of shifting postures shoring up a self that he himself constantly questions. Appropriately, Hugh Kenner once connected his windiness with Eliot's essay "Seneca in Elizabethan Translation." Gerontion, Kenner noted, falls into the pattern Eliot defined when he wrote that "the 'beliefs' of Stoicism are a consequence of scepticism; and the ethic of Seneca's plays is that of an age which supplied the lack of moral habits by a system of moral attitudes and poses. . . . The ethic of Seneca is a matter of postures. The posture which gives the greatest opportunity for effect . . . is the posture of dying: death gives his characters the opportunity for their most sententious aphorisms—a hint which Elizabethan dramatists were only too ready to follow."[4] But Kenner, I think, should not have taken Eliot's moralizing at face value. Gerontion's monologue is filled with self-dramatization and self-deception, but not just because of his lack of "moral habits." Gerontion also lacks contact with, on the one hand, "what we really are and feel, what we really want, and what really excites our interests," and, on the other, "the real world."

In all likelihood, "Gerontion" started as a recasting of Tennyson's "Ulysses," which, though its egocentric point of view deprived it of the narrative clarity of Dante's "seaman's yarn," Eliot called a "perfect poem." ("Tennyson's Ulysses," he said, was "a very self-conscious poet" [SE, 210, 211].) Like Ulysses, Gerontion presents himself in a landscape transformed by his own desolation, a psychological terrain where things he once loved have cooled, diminished and turned into inconveniences. Compare the way the two poems open:

Here I am, an old man in a dry month,
Being read to by a boy, waiting for rain.
I was neither at the hot gates
Nor fought in the warm rain
Nor knee deep in the salt marsh, heaving a cutlass,
Bitten by flies, fought.
My house is a decayed house,
And the jew squats on the window sill, the owner,
Spawned in some estaminet of Antwerp,
Blistered in Brussels, patched and peeled in London.
The goat coughs at night in the field overhead;
Rocks, moss, stonecrop, iron, merds.
The woman keeps the kitchen, makes tea,
Sneezes at evening, poking the peevish gutter.
                              I an old man,
A dull head among windy spaces. . . .

　It little profits that an idle king,
By this still hearth, among these barren crags,
Matched with an aged wife, I mete and dole
Unequal laws unto a savage race,
That hoard, and sleep, and feed, and know not me.

Eliot's innovations are at first merely technical. Tennyson had suggested Ulysses's alienation by the distant way—"aged wife"—he names Penelope. Forswearing Tennyson's descriptive phrase, Eliot renders the same condition with a mental sequence. Gerontion thinks of his "woman" as one who pokes "the peevish gutter": a gutter is a sputtering fire, and by identifying the woman with the action of poking it, he suggests the nature of their marriage. In the same way, Eliot transforms Tennyson's "barren crags" into a miniature mental drama, which is sometimes confused with a catalogue: "Rocks, moss, stonecrop, iron, merds"—Gerontion's prospect turns bleaker with every added word.

Finally, though, Gerontion's rose-colored glasses provide the emotional center of the poem's first verse paragraph. Here Eliot remembers how Tennyson's Ulysses cheered himself up with his own rhetoric ("drunk delight of battle with my peers, / Far on the ringing plains of windy Troy"). But, updating Tennyson, he utilizes effects like the ones he had created in "Burbank." Like Burbank, Gerontion turns his world into a fairyland of his own desires. It is, for example, a place where cool sense can be warmed by "hot gates" and "warm rain." But in "Gerontion," this fairyland is only the first circle of hell, just a step in the direction of what Eliot elsewhere calls

　　　　　　　the final desolation
　　Of solitude in the phantasmal world
　　Of imagination, shuffling memories and desires.

　　　　　　　　　　　　　　　　　(CPP, 365)

This deeper part of the inferno, as we encounter it in the third verse paragraph of "Gerontion," holds the George Wyndhams of the earth: people caught in the trap of their own rhetoric. Here, what Gerontion "knows" is that he has turned his back on the possibility of salvation ("neither fear nor courage *saves* us"), and that he has "no ghosts." Using the word "ghosts" as Colby Simpkins will use it in *The Confidential Clerk,* Gerontion means he has no filial ties, and he recalls Eliot's account of Aeneas, whose filial piety is rooted in the recognition of a more than human "bond."[5] To have knowledge of spiritual "failure / Towards someone, or something, outside of myself," as Eliot suggests in one of his plays, generates unexplained feelings of guilt.[6] Aware of that guilt ("what forgiveness?"), Gerontion yet chooses to turn his back on it. Like Burbank, he has a taste for the grand phrase, and he rationalizes:

> After such knowledge, what forgiveness? Think now
> History has many cunning passages, contrived corridors
> And issues, deceives with whispering ambitions,
> Guides us by vanities. Think now
> She gives when our attention is distracted. . . .

In this logic, there is no need to feel guilty about isolation: others are, after all, only history, and history is an abstraction. Gerontion urges himself insistently to "think now," but he has no desire to think, and his refrain is only a substitute for thought.

This section of the poem is extraordinarily difficult for two reasons. First, its references are deliberately vague, suggesting the way Gerontion's self-justifications have refined themselves into a kind of neurotic subtlety. "Whispering ambitions," for example, recalls Prufrock's "muttering retreats" and suggests a mental disturbance of a preconscious kind. From the evidence of the manuscript, even Pound did not understand the purpose of this vagueness. Failing to find syntactic clarity, he recommended revision. Eliot ignored the recommendation.

The greatest difficulty of the passage, however, lies not in its shadowy syntax but in the subtle precision of its dramatic technique, its ability to delineate psychic movement by quiet implication. Here, Pound was not antagonist but model, and Eliot's procedures recall a poem like "The River Merchant's Wife," where a deserted bride remembers her younger self as "without dislike or suspicion" and poignantly suggests their subsequent arrival. In dramatizing the emotional curve of Gerontion's rationalizations, Eliot depends a great deal on such precisions. When Gerontion counsels himself, for example,

> Think now
> History has *many* cunning passages. . . .

he is not yet bemoaning the existence of History's bewildering complexities. In that case just the plural ("passages") would suffice, and the word "many" would be superfluous. But Gerontion is not complaining. Instead he comforts himself with the thought that history has *many* "issues" (exits) *other than this one*, and he begins to hope that his vanity may lead him to one of them. Warming to the subject, he reiterates, "Think now / She gives when our attention is distracted" (as it is now). But this optimism is difficult even for Gerontion to sustain, and he soon falters. The "and" which begins his next phrase has the force of "but," and it introduces an afterthought, a recollection of the sour "gifts" of the past and one overpowering "fear":

> *And* what she gives, gives with such supple confusions
> That the giving famishes the craving. Gives too late
> What's not believed in, or if still believed,
> In memory only, reconsidered passion. Gives too soon
> Into weak hands, what's thought can be dispensed with
> Till the refusal propagates a fear.

Continuing, Gerontion's self-exhortation ("think") is almost hysterical, but once again he manages to find an excuse not to think. Instead, he consoles himself with more precautionary advice: "Neither fear *nor courage* saves us." His point: we needn't exert ourselves—a tranquil thought which leads to the conclusion that *"These* tears" (the particular tears that prompted the guilt behind the question "What forgiveness?") "are shaken *from the wrath-bearing tree."* They are therefore not tears of contrition, and they may be comfortably ignored. For another moment he is safe.

When Gerontion takes up his attempt to reason away guilt and fear in the next verse paragraph, however, the "you" that he had earlier implied by speaking of "we" becomes a presence. The identity of that presence hardly matters, though many readers have puzzled over it. What does matter is that, addressing a single person, Gerontion hardens his argumentative stance and shows us the distilled essence of the thousand real or imagined times he has defended himself against "someone, or something, outside of myself." (Since he knows he is divided from his buried self, this "you" may not even be an outsider.) Not his interlocutor, but his posture of self-defense counts. Like one of the characters in the *Inferno,* he cannot escape it.

As he faces his mysterious adversary, the emotional content of Gerontion's posturing is again implied but never stated.

> The tiger springs in the new year. Us he devours. Think at last
> We have not reached conclusion, when I
> Stiffen in a rented house. Think at last
> I have not made this show purposelessly
> And it is not by any concitation
> Of the backward devils.
> I would meet you upon this honestly.

After entertaining the prospect that he and his partner might be delivered from their poisoned circle in the new year (one thinks of John Marcher's desire for deliverance in James's "The Beast in the Jungle"), Gerontion casts himself in a drama on the verge of conclusion and tries to conjure up a satisfactory denouement. His former "think now" becomes with eager anticipation "Think at last," and he implies he will tell all: "I have not," he says, "made this show purposelessly." His "I would meet you upon this *honestly*" suggests a moment of recognition, and his "I that was near your heart" makes us anticipate the kind of retrospective vision that ends a certain kind of play. Here, in part improvising and in part borrowing, Eliot makes consummate use of his study of Elizabethan rhetoric. "This show" is adapted from the climactic scene (Act III, scene iv) of Tourneur's *The Revenger's Tragedy,* where Vendice achieves his revenge. And "I that was near your heart" comes from the finale of Middleton's *The Changeling,* where Beatrice-Joanna reveals her conspiracy.

But we should not pay too much attention to Eliot's sources. Eliot wants us to attend not to his models but to his mood. Using rhetorical cadences he sometimes aped thoughtlessly himself, he shows how Gerontion tries "to escape reality" by turning the harshness of self-recognition into the occasion for acting out an "aesthetic" attitude for his own delectation (SE, 111). Thus, as A. D. Moody points out, he feels free to alter his borrowings.[7]

Caught in Eliot's censure, though, Gerontion cannot "escape reality." Even as mouthing the grand words of Middleton and Tourneur cheers him up, his anxiety will not go away. Apparently longing for resolution, Gerontion begins "Think at last" and sounds as if he is pressing for conclusion in the very next scene: "We have," he says, *"not* [i.e. not yet] reached conclusion, when I stiffen in a rented house." And he continues, "I have *not* made this show purposelessly / And it is *not* by any concitation / Of the backward devils." But notice that each emphatic reiteration of "not" tells us that he mistrusts his own claims; though he protests the contrary, he fears he *has* reached conclusion, and that his show (his speech) was purposeless after all. Thus although the grandiloquent notions of his speech advance his belief that his dessicated condition is only the necessary ascetic prelude to an imminent redemption, he voices that belief in a series of questions, and we begin to doubt his sincerity. In truth, with each question he cries out to be told that his dessication is *not* part of the denouement and that his passion will one day be restored:

> I have lost my passion: why should I need to keep it
> Since what is kept must be adulterated?
> I have lost my sight, smell, hearing, taste and touch:
> How should I use them for your closer contact?

Gerontion, then, seems at some level always aware of his own windiness. And in the last verse paragraph, where he experiences a genuine horror of who he is, he emerges into almost full consciousness of his own role-playing. Realizing his "small deliberations" serve to "excite the membrane" of his own ego, his honesty clears the air. After it we are prepared for the poem's conclusion. In the silence of the space that precedes the poem's final lines throbs Gerontion's version of Prufrock's "overwhelming question" along with the terrifying answer the question would require were Gerontion ever brave enough to ask it: What end would my conversion serve? None.

As the last verse paragraph begins, that question and that answer balloon into an apocalyptic vision of decay. But even in his despair, Gerontion couches his appalling vision in the form of a question, and this question too is an implicit plea for survival as he was: "What will the spider do [if I surrender myself?] / Suspend its operations, will the weevil / Delay?" He neither wishes to surrender his old self nor believes that if he did it would serve any purpose, and the ambivalence of his question anticipates a similar sequence in "Burnt Norton":

> Will the sunflower turn to us, will the clematis
> Stray down, bend to us; tendril and spray
> Clutch and cling?

In Eliot's manuscript version of the poem, Gerontion returned to paralysis aided by the cynicism of a hollow phrase:

> De Bailhache, Fresca, Mrs. Cammel, whirled
> Beyond the circuit of the shuddering Bear
> In fractured atoms. *We have saved a shilling against*
> *oblivion*
> *Even oblivious.*
>
> Tenants of the house,
> Thoughts of a dry brain in a dry season.

In revision, however, Eliot improved the ending considerably. The lines "Gull against the wind, in the windy straits / Of Belle Isle, or running on the Horn" voice Gerontion's wrenching desire for liberation and the open sea. They are comparable to Prufrock's "I have seen them riding seaward on the waves" or *Ash Wednesday*'s apostrophe to the "spirit of the river, spirit of the sea." In "Gerontion," it is only when the old man releases these last, most repressed yearnings, that his full hopelessness comes over him. As he projects his fate on the doom of a bird in a storm, his resigned withdrawal rises to the full height of sadness:

> White feathers in the snow, the Gulf claims,
> And an old man driven by the Trades
> To a sleepy corner.

"Gerontion," then, is a dazzling exposition of rhetorical insincerity. But that alone does not account for its power. Some of its depths—its attention to the European political situation, for example, or its awareness of scriptural texts—fall outside the notice of my argument. One other innovation, however, is directly related to the issues I have been discussing. What I have in mind is a quality that led one of Eliot's readers to remark that his poetry contains "the tension and terror of a world nearly but not wholly revealed."[8] It is this quality that gives an extended section of "Gerontion" its novelty:

> In depraved May, dogwood and chestnut, flowering judas,
> To be eaten, to be divided, to be drunk
> Among whispers; by Mr. Silvero
> With caressing hands, at Limoges
> Who walked all night in the next room;
>
> By Hakagawa, bowing among the Titians;
> By Madame de Tornquist, in the dark room
> Shifting the candles; Fräulein von Kulp
> Who turned in the hall, one hand on the door.

Here the tension between Eliot's sympathy and his disapproval is at the point of snapping. Bearing symbolic names, Mr. Silvero and company are satiric types of Western decadence, but they are also something more. What at first seems an allegorical tableau on second glance seethes with the suppressed energy of Gerontion's inner life. Representations of unconscious anxiety, Mr. Silvero, Hakagawa, Madame de Tornquist, and Fräulein von Kulp in stunted gestures mime Gerontion's own desire and guilt. He is, remember, a sensibility who, like Prufrock, feels diminished and suffocated. But his consciousness is less insulated than Prufrock's was from eruptions from below. The figures in the lines I have quoted evoke an unspoken menace, which Eliot elaborates with effects drawn from his favorite conspiracy melodramas, *The Duchess of Malfi* and *The Revenger's Tragedy*. The dark room, the claustrophobic corridors, the whispers that arise out of fear and provoke it, give us a "dominant tone"—which, as Eliot once wrote, is the only kind of dramatic unity that matters (SW, 135). But a dominant tone may unify more than drama, and the details of this passage suggest a kind of action which the theatre before Beckett and Pinter rarely attempts.

Gerontion first comes to us accompanied by associations of dreams. And though he has no desire to prolong his dreaming, he clearly has no choice. To render Gerontion's experience, Eliot of course uses Dante's visionary technique, in which truths arise out of the world of night. But he also dabbles in that other kind of dreaming which is discussed on the psychiatric couch. In this kind of dream objects appear as representatives of pre-conscious impulse and provide us with reliable indications of a life we would not otherwise know.

CHAPTER FOUR

"The poet's inner world of nightmare"

When you're alone in the middle of the night and you wake
   in a sweat and a hell of a fright
When you're alone in the middle of the bed and you wake
   like someone hit you on the head
You've had a cream of a nightmare dream and you've got the
   hoo-ha's coming to you.
Hoo hoo hoo

from Sweeney Agonistes

"Gerontion"'s dream-like sequence corresponds to a persistent preoccupation in Eliot's prose. In "Reflections on Contemporary Poetry" (1917), in the same paragraph where he announced the intention of contemporary verse "to escape the rhetorical," Eliot also recognized its tendency "to concentrate . . . attention upon trivial or accidental or commonplace objects."[1] According to Eliot, it is possible to avoid rhetoric in this way because of the "universally human" ability to "attach the strongest emotions to definite tokens." Eliot here acknowledges the relevance of this truth to the Imagist movement, which he diplomatically refers to as one of the significant "recent American currents" in poetry. But though Eliot verges on Pound's pronouncement that "the natural object is always the *adequate* symbol,"[2] his meaning has a coloring very much his own. His nuancing, moreover, is only hinted at in the sentence that would eventually fix the notion in the minds of his readers—"The only way of expressing emotion in the form of art is by finding an 'objective correlative'; in other words, a set of objects, a situation, a chain of events which shall be the formula of that *particular* emotion" (SW, 100).

For Eliot, escaping rhetoric involved evading the rigidity of the acquired self, something he was able to do only through the agency of poetry and only, it appears, in two modes of awareness. One, being possessed by another poet or another culture, has been treated by Hugh Kenner in *T.S. Eliot: The Invisible Poet*. The other, giving his everyday self up to unexplained but powerful images, was a happening that occurred frequently enough for Eliot to make of such "digressions" a constant of his earlier poetry:

> Is it perfume from a dress
> That makes me so digress?
>
> ("Prufrock")

> I remain self-possessed
> Except when a street piano, mechanical and tired
> Reiterates some worn-out common song
> With the smell of hyacinths across the garden
> Recalling things that other people have desired.
>
> ("Portrait of a Lady")

> I am moved by fancies that are curled
> Around these images, and cling:
> The notion of some infinitely gentle
> Infinitely suffering thing.
>
> ("Preludes")

Only "accidental" images, it seems, were spared by Eliot's inner censor from being diluted by his acquired self. Only accidental images could make him aware of something below that self, some "infinitely gentle / Infinitely suffering thing" that frequently felt like the source of "other people's desires" or the secrets of a "world" that was not his own. As he wrote in reference to Marianne Moore:

For a [reticent] sensibility . . . the minor subject . . . may be the best release for the major emotions. Only the pedantic literalist could consider the subject-matter to be trivial. . . . We all have to choose whatever subject-matter allows us the most powerful and most secret release. . . .[3]

And so prized were what we may call these *images trouvailles*, these oases of emotional intensity in an otherwise unemotional existence, that Eliot was eager to cultivate them even when they assumed nightmarish coloring. To be emotionally alive, though it meant living in terror, was better than being dead. Fortunately, though, only some of the images were nightmarish. The more soothing of them assumed the shape of a childhood memory, as Eliot would recount from the distance of middle age:

I suggest that what gives [an author's imagery] such intensity . . . is its saturation—I will not say with "associations," for I do not want to revert to Hartley—but with feelings too obscure for the authors even to know quite what they were. And of course only a part of an author's imagery comes from his reading. It comes from the whole of his sensitive life since early childhood. Why, for all of us, out of all that we have heard, seen, felt, in a lifetime, do certain images recur, charged with emotion, rather than others? The song of one bird, the leap of one fish, at a particular place and time, the scent of one flower, an old woman on a German mountain path, six ruffians seen through an open window playing cards at night at a small French railway junction where there was a water-mill: such memories may have symbolic value, but of what we cannot tell, for they come to represent the depths of feeling into which we cannot peer (UPUC, 147–48).

These images are saturated with feelings "too obscure" for the poet to know and represent depths into which he "cannot peer." Eliot is not eager to know or to peer because knowing and seeing would destroy the feelings by making them a part of speech. They must be preserved as fragments, free from logical argument or conscious symbolism. Intact and isolated they are proof and reassurance that "depths of feeling"—the genuine "sensitive life"—exist and occasionally emerge triumphant. In the words of Edward in *The Cocktail Party,*

> The self that can say "I want this—or want that"—
> The self that wills—he is a feeble creature;
> He has to come to terms in the end
> With the obstinate, the tougher self; who does not speak,
> Who never talks, who cannot argue. . . .
>
> (CPP, 326)

In the period of "Gerontion" and *The Waste Land,* Eliot's poetry is obsessed with disclosing the self "who does not speak" and exposing "the self that wills." Consequently, his prose of the same period is devoted to establishing a theoretical basis for discriminating between the two selves. Eliot addresses the problem most rigorously in his Ph.D. thesis on Bradley. Many of his readers have found it convenient to think about his poetry in terms of that thesis, where Eliot characterizes not only what I have been calling the "acquired self" but *any* self as an abstraction from experience.[4] For Bradley, the only valid way of speaking about what we ordinarily call "selves" or "souls" is through a term like "locus of experience" or "point of view" or "finite center."[5] And using Bradley does give us a way to conceptualize the poetry's presentation of experience and allows us to discount the naive view that the poet's work is continuous with his breakfast conversation. A problem arises, however, when critics superimpose the terms of Eliot's dissertation on a few of his famous essays (especially "Tradition and the Individual Talent") and speak of his rigorously "impersonal" poetry. In an early and admirably lucid formulation of the Bradley element in Eliot, for example, Hugh Kenner claims that the study of Bradley freed Eliot from anxiety about the reality of social poses "by affirming the artificiality of *all* personality including the one we intimately suppose to be our true one; not only the faces we prepare but the 'we' that prepares."[6] But this manifestly does not account for the emphasis we have seen Eliot put as late as 1920 on the way Blake, in his "honesty" and "sincerity," "was naked, and saw man naked, and from the centre of his own crystal" (SW 154–55).

During this period, Eliot was willing to use any amount of acid skepticism to destroy the claims of "the self that wills" on the life of feeling and could, in the context of a philosophical disquisition, dare to assert that any self is an artificial construct. But at the same time he very much wanted to believe in the existence of a "centre" to "his own crystal"—what he once called "the substratum of our being" (UPUC, 155). In his criticism, where he was less constrained by logical necessity, his need to assert a life deeper than the poses of rhetoric frequently makes itself felt. So, in one of his essays, he wrote that poetry, far from being "impersonal" in any abstract sense, gives "the undertone, of the personal emotion, the personal drama and struggle, which no biography, however full and intimate, could give us" (SE, 180). In this perhaps logically indefensible assertion of an individuality "below the intellect" (SW, 118), he was sustained before 1923 by the writings of Rémy de Gourmont, whose influence pervades *The Sacred Wood*.[7] It was under Gourmont's aegis that the theory of Eliot's early poetry crystalized and it was largely due to Gourmont that Eliot adopted his confusing and extremely deceptive use of the terms "personal" and "impersonal." When Eliot called in the same volume for an "impersonal theory of poetry" (SW, 53) and for the necessity of a "personal point of view" (SW, 117), he was doing no more than drawing out the apparent paradoxes of Gourmont's *Promenades philosophiques,* quoted a year or so before by Ezra Pound: "Etre impersonnel c'est être personnel selon un mode particulier: Voyez Flaubert. On dirait en jargon: l'objectif est une des formes du subjectif."[8]

Simply put, for Gourmont, personality as we ordinarily conceive it is nothing more than a potentially suffocating shell, a cortex of received responses, attitudes and ideas that has nothing to do with life. Our real life takes place on the surface of the unconscious, where our emotions respond to new sensation. *This* life has its own, authentic personality, which consists in the flavor of its emotional response; it constitutes a unique sensibility, apprehensible through the manifestations of its private world of perception. In words Ezra Pound loved to quote, "A very few only . . . can transform directly the acts of others into their own personal thoughts; the multitude of men thinks only thoughts already emitted, feels but feelings used up, and has but sensations as faded as old gloves."[9]

Once Gourmont had dissociated "personality" into two senses, however, it became perfectly possible for Eliot to characterize it as something to be both wished for and disdained. In the vulgar sense of the word, to write out of one's personality is to express one's conditioned self and write cliches; in this sense, to achieve an "impersonal point of view" is to avoid second-hand sentiment. But adopting Gourmont's revised sense of "personality," great literature is always "the transformation of a personality into a personal world of art" (SW, 139), and it is *im*personal ideas that "obscure what we really are and feel, what we really want, and what really excites our interests" (SW, 154). E. M. Forster, altering Eliot's usages slightly, explains the matter with characteristic elegance:

> Modern critics go too far in their insistence on personality.
>
> They go too far because they do not reflect what personality is. Just as words have two functions—information and creation—so each human mind has two personalities, one on the surface, one deeper down. The upper personality has a name. It is called S.T. Coleridge, or William Shakespeare, or Mrs. Humphry Ward. It is conscious and alert, does things like dining out, answering letters, etc., and it differs vividly and amusingly from other personalities. The lower personality is a very queer affair. In many ways it is a perfect fool, but without it there is no literature, because unless a man dips a bucket down into it occasionally he cannot produce first-class work. There is something general about it. Although it is inside S.T. Coleridge, it cannot be labelled with his name. It has something in common with all other deeper personalities, and the mystic will assert that the common quality is God, and that here, in the obscure recesses of our being, we near the gates of the Divine. It is in any case the force that makes for anonymity. . . . The poet wrote the poem, no doubt, but he forgot himself while he wrote it, and we forget him while we read. What is so wonderful about great literature is that it transforms the man who reads it towards the condition of the man who wrote, and brings to birth in us also the creative impulse.[10]

Gourmont's dissociation of personalities corresponds, of course, to Eliot's fundamental intuition that one's public self and its habitual expressions are a sham and that one's true self—"what we really are and feel"—is connected with a private world. Delighted with Gourmont's formulations, which approximated Bradley's but grew out of the study of literature, Eliot ventilated his critical essays with Gourmont's phrases and Gourmont's technical vocabulary.[11] In "Tradition and the Individual Talent," full of Gourmont's subtleties,[12] in his best New England manner Eliot calls the poet's work "impersonal" and points out how little poetry has to do with what is ordinarily called personal emotion. But he also remains true to the romantic attitude that "the business of the poet" is to express his feelings. And in the following two citations, which span the period from 1917 to 1922, he uses Gourmont's discriminations to help express his horror of men who have allowed themselves to be cut off from their "core of vital emotions":

> Both were endeavoring to escape . . . the too well pigeonholed, too taken-for-granted, too highly systematized areas, and,—in the language of those whom they sought to avoid—they wished "to apprehend the human soul in its concrete individuality."
>
> "Why," said Eeldrop, "was that fat Spaniard, who sat at the table with us this evening, and listened to our conversation with occasional curiosity,

why was he himself for a moment an object of interest to us? . . . we were able to detach him from his classification and regard him for a moment as an unique being, a soul, however insignificant, with a history of its own, once and for all. It is these moments which we prize, and which alone are revealing. For any vital truth is incapable of being applied to another case: the essential is unique. . . ."

"What you say," replied Appleplex, "commands my measured adherence. . . . when a man is classified something is lost. The majority of mankind live on paper currency: they use terms which are merely good for so much reality, they never see actual coinage."

"I should go even further than that," said Eeldrop. "The majority not only have no language to express anything save generalized man; they are for the most part unaware of themselves as anything but generalized men. They are first of all government officials, or pillars of the church, or trade unionists, or poets, or unemployed; this cataloguing is not only satisfactory to other people for practical purposes, it is sufficient to themselves for their 'life of the spirit.' Many are not quite real at any moment. When Wolstrip married, I am sure he said to himself: 'Now I am consummating the union of two of the best families in Philadelphia.' "[13]

The lack of any moral integrity, which I think is behind all the superficial imbecilities of contemporary English verse . . . is disguised in various ways; the disguise often takes the form of noble thoughts, and (in serious prose writers also) in an endless pomposity. It is the mark of the man who has no core, no individual moral existence, to be possessed with moral notions, be goaded by the necessity of continual moral formulations.[14]

The full subtlety and importance of Eliot's discrimination, however, can be found in another essay, "Philip Massinger," the crux of which is a citation from the pages Gourmont devoted to Flaubert in his *Problème du style:*

La vie est un dépouillement. Le but de l'activité propre de l'homme est de nettoyer sa personnalité, de la laver de toutes les souillures qu'y déposa l'éducation, de la dégager de toutes les empreintes qu'y laissèrent nos admirations adolescentes;

and again:

Flaubert incorporait toute sa sensibilité à ses oeuvres. . . . Hors de ses livres, où il se transvasait goutte à goutte, jusqu'à la lie, Flaubert est fort peu intéressant. . . .

Of Shakespeare notably, of Jonson less, of Marlowe (and of Keats to the term of life allowed him), one can say that they *se transvasaient goutte à goutte* . . . (SW, 139–40).

Here is the center of Gourmont's theory of true and false personality. "La vie est un dépouillement," or as Eliot elsewhere translates it: "to be free we must be stripped, like the sea-god Glaucus,[15] of any number of incrustations of education and frequentation; we must divest ourselves even of our ancestors. But to undertake this stripping of acquired ideas, we must make one assumption: that of the individuality of each human being."[16] More importantly, here is the center of Gourmont's theory of literature, and of the paradox of personality and impersonality: The true artist transfuses himself (*se transvasait*) into his work. Or, as Eliot says elsewhere, "the creation of a work of art . . . consists in the process of transfusion of the personality, or, in a deeper sense, the life, of the author into the character" (SW, 118).

Gourmont's paradox lies in the fact that the more a work has to do with the personality of the artist—that is, the superficial acquired personality—the less personal the work is, the less connected with his buried life. The truly personal work must be composed of material free of the artist's superficial attitudes. To act as the "definite token" of uncontaminated feeling or as a magnet that will attract the deepest impulses of the self, it must be composed of elements that are objective, foreign, other. Hence only the apparently "impersonal" work can convey an artist's core of subjectivity, his authentically personal emotion. According to a passage of Gourmont which follows the one quoted by Eliot, such is the process by which Flaubert's *Bouvard et Pécuchet,* a book that "seems like a catalog of little experiments which any industrious man could easily achieve," can also be "so personal, so woven as it were from nervous fibres that no one has ever been able to add to it a page which did not produce the effect of a piece of cloth on a tulle dress."[17]

It is significant, moreover, that Gourmont in his example chooses not a poet but a novelist and not just a novelist but the great collector of things, Flaubert. Because fiction deals with stories and not feelings, facts and not coloring, it can be a possible new point of departure for poets. This is especially true for Eliot, who again and again praises the "unique worlds" of James and Conrad, Joyce and Wyndham Lewis.[18] Eliot took Flaubert as an early master,[19] and he pushes his poetry toward the pole of narrative whenever he is not caught up in the grip of song. But something Eliot adds to Gourmont's remarks about Flaubert alerts us that another kind of writing competed with fiction in his admiring gaze.

Eliot excerpts Gourmont's remarks on Flaubert in an essay on the Elizabethan dramatist Philip Massinger, and that essay is surrounded by other essays on playwrights and the theory of plays ("The Possibility of a Poetic Drama," "Euripides and Professor Murray," "Rhetoric and Poetic Drama," "Notes on the Blank Verse of Christopher Marlowe," "Hamlet and His Problem," "Ben Jonson"). Throughout these essays Eliot reiterates a central preoccupation: in the necessary "slight distortion of *all* the elements in the world of a play or a story," an artist's world can become the expression of "personality," and reach down to a "complex tissue of feelings and desires" (SW, 142, 119). In Gourmont's formulation, "The work of a writer must be . . . the enlarged reflection of his personality. The only excuse a man has for writing is to write himself—to reveal to others the kind of world reflected in his individual mirror."[20]

And so in reference to Aeschylus and Shakespeare, Aristotle and Flaubert, Eliot writes that "permanent literature is always a presentation: either a presentation of thought, or a presentation of feeling by a statement of events in human action or objects in the external world" (SW, 64–65). About Euripides he says, "The essential is to get upon the stage this precise statement of life which is at the same time a point of view, a world—a world which the author's mind has subjected to a complete process of simplification" (SW, 68). And about Jonson, he tells us that "Jonson's characters conform to the logic of the emotions of their world. . . . the worlds created by artists like Jonson are like systems of non-Euclidean geometry. They are not fancy, because they have a logic of their own. . . ." (SW, 116–17).

Apparently addressed to the subject of drama, these observations and the essays they punctuate have nothing to say about the nuts and bolts of theatre. Announcing his admiration for drama, Eliot is in fact concerned with the way it objectifies a point of view, an internal world, a sensibility. Hence he says almost nothing about dramatic structure or plot and singles out plays like Jonson's which contain characters who do not so much *"act upon* one another" as *"fit in* with each other," and which have a "single and simple" emotional effect (SW, 112–13). In this view, dramatic unity has less to do with action than with "an emotional unity, let the emotion be whatever you like. It must have a dominant tone; and if this be strong enough, the most heterogeneous emotions may be made to reinforce it" (SW, 135). If this emotional unity, this "dominant tone," exists, it is because of a deeper unity than plot—a unity derived from the subconscious expression of the dramatist: Jonson's simplification, according to Eliot, "consists largely in reduction of detail, in the seizing of aspects relevant to the relief of an emotional impulse which remains the same" (SW, 120).

Eliot's ideal, then, is a series of scenes or dramatic monologues, held together by a "dominant tone" and existing to express the "emotional impulse" of their creator. Under the guise of making Jonson new for the twentieth century, he simplifies Jonson's meticulously plotted work and describes something that looks forward to *The Waste Land* more than it looks back to *Volpone*. Any doubt about that disappears when we note that Eliot, at the conclusion of his remarks on Jonson, prophesies the future of twentieth-century literature. Knowing what Jonson was about, Eliot announces, we can "apply him, be aware of him as a part of our literary inheritance *craving further expression*. Of all the dramatists of his time, Jonson is probably the one whom the present age would find the most sympathetic, if it knew him" (SW, 121; emphasis mine).

But before going on to consider the work Eliot was planning, it is useful to explore one more model his preoccupations were drawing him toward. Behind his flirtation with fiction and drama stands a fascination with another mode of representation, also hard and thick with objective facts, and also suffused with feeling. The similarity between poetry and dreams, the subject which began this digression on Eliot's criticism, was by the beginning of the twentieth century a less than fashionable topic—it had too many associations with Victorian poetry. Yet dreams, nightmares, hallucinations and visions had been Eliot's interests at least since his undergraduate days, when he combined those interests with an interest in mysticism. A substantial portion of his doctoral dissertation concerns "imaginary objects," in which category Eliot groups the content of dreams and hallucinations with the content of literature.[21] Then, too, Eliot's poetry is crammed with dreams, starting with the "Preludes" and culminating in *The Family Reunion:*

> You have gone through life in sleep,
> Never woken to the nightmare.

> (CPP, 234)

The subject of dreams in Eliot, I suspect, has received so little emphasis because he so often dissociated himself from the dreamy vagueness that in his view characterized much of romantic poetry. In his essay "Swinburne as Poet," Eliot berates Swinburne because his "meaning is merely the *hallucination of meaning,* because language, uprooted, has adapted itself to an independent life of atmospheric nourishment" (SW, 149; emphasis mine). But even in that essay, Eliot *praises* Swinburne for the brave independence of his dream world. ("The world of Swinburne does not depend upon some other world which it simulates; it has the necessary completeness and self-sufficiency for justification and permanence. It is impersonal, and no one else could have made it"—SW, 149.) Elsewhere, Eliot's invocations of dreams suggest the poetry he was about to write more than any other topic of his prose. An early and important case in point occurs in remarks he made about the Noh drama in 1917. Here Eliot brings the subjects of dreams and drama together, and suggests the point of his developing interest in the stage.[22] Noting the way a Noh-play called *Awoi No Uye* revolves around the image of a folded red kimono, Eliot praises the way Japanese drama stimulates the imagination through fully visualized but mysterious detail. He then comments:

Dreams, to be real, must be seen.
　　When we speak of the Noh as dreamlike, we do not imply any attenuation of emotion, nor imply that the emotions of dreams are essentially different from the emotions of waking. . . . but the ways of approaching these emotions are diverse. The Japanese method is inverse to that with which we are familiar. The phantom-psychology of Orestes and Macbeth is as good as that of Awoi; but the method of making the ghost real is

different. In the former cases the ghost is given in the mind of the possessed; in the latter case the mind of the sufferer is inferred from the reality of the ghost. The ghost is enacted, the dreaming or feverish Awoi is represented by the "red kimono." In fact, it is only ghosts that are actual; the world of active passions is observed through the veil of another world.

A dream then, is for Eliot an intensified form of drama—a drama of the soul; and the best play is only the approximation of a dream. In their very essence dreams "enact," dramatize, "represent" the inner world of the dreamer. In fact, as Eliot suggests, dreams are the only way of getting at that inner world, since the private "world of active passions" must be only an abstraction "inferred from" the reality of its manifestations, which alone are "actual." Since they provide unexplained particulars charged with emotion from below, and are thus more authentically involved with our buried lives, dreams give the prototype for lyric poetry. True vision, as Eliot says elsewhere, "is significant detail, particularly of movement, sensation, thought."[23] In commenting on the Noh, Eliot suggests that the Japanese had found a way to convey such vision, and that the best way to describe it was via "images" and—images in motion—dreams. Such a method, Eliot adds, "prevents rhetoric" and achieves "ghost lovers, with as fine a strangeness in their way as any lovers of Webster or Ford."

What Eliot says about dreams in the passage quoted above, of course, might be taken as a more or less conventional statement about visionary literature. Other remarks, however, suggest that when Eliot spoke of dreams, he *meant* dreams. These remarks suggest that he was much taken with the way dreams came unbeckoned and how they overpowered the waking self, with the way their emotional charge was unexpected and discontinuous, and with the way they dramatized disturbing conflicts which the dreamer could not otherwise approach. For Eliot, who constantly longed for access to "the depths of feeling into which we cannot peer,"[24] dreams were one of a very few open avenues to self-discovery, and one of the triggers of poetic creation. He illustrates his fascination with them in an unpublished lecture when he notes that "an 'image,' in itself, is like dream symbolism, is only vigorous in relation to the feelings out of which it issues, in the relation of word to flesh."[25] Elsewhere, musing on the way dreams remain mysterious while at the same time exercising the dreamer to great curiosity about their meaning, he notes of a poem of William Morris that it intends "to produce the effect of a dream. It is not necessary, in order to enjoy the poem, to know what the dream means; but human beings have an unshakeable belief that dreams mean something" (OPP, 22).[26] Later in his career, writing in *The Listener,* he remarks on the way the actions of dreams are overcharged with unexplained emotion, and explains how they exemplify an ideal fusion of lyricism and dramatic action:

There is a flight above, at which poetry and drama become one thing: of which one is often reminded in passages of Homer or Dante. We often feel with Shakespeare, and now and then with his lesser contemporaries, that the dramatic action on the stage is the symbol and shadow of some more serious action in a world of feeling more real than ours, *just as our perceptions in dreams are often more ominously weighted than they are in practical waking life.*[27]

Three months after the publication of his Jonson essay he also remarks how even a nonsense statement can be effective in certain contexts when "it appears to be a tremendous statement, like statements made in our dreams" (SW, 148).

One feature that many of the citations just noted share is especially significant as we approach *The Waste Land*. In his observations about the "possessed" and "feverish" dreamer of *Awoi No Uye,* in his statement about the anxiety involved in wanting to know what dreams mean, in the way he suggests that dreams in general are "ominously weighted," Eliot suggests the kind of dreams that were most important to him, and anticipates the kind of dreams he will recount in his work. When we speak of the dream-like quality of *The Waste Land,* what we really mean is that it feels like a nightmare, and for good reason. "Nightmares" presided over Eliot's London life, his taste in literature and his perception of poetry. At the very beginning of the first of his "Reflections on Contemporary Poetry," he seizes on two examples to illustrate the doctrine of the emotion-laden "token": first a ghoulish image of Donne's that reappears in "Whispers of Immortality":

> When my grave is broke up again . . .
>   And he that digs it, spies
> A bracelet of bright hair about the bone. . . .

And secondly the example of "the Russian novel, with its curious trick of fastening upon accidental properties of a critical situation, and letting these in turn fasten upon the attention to such an extent as to replace the emotion which gave them their importance."

It is accidental details that "fasten upon the attention" that Eliot uses to chilling effect in the passage from "Gerontion" that chapter three considered. And it is exactly such accidental detail that he finds at the center of a nightmare. In the remarks just quoted, Eliot means Dostoevsky when he speaks of the "Russian novel." In another article he identifies what parts of Dostoevsky he has in mind, and why they are important:

> If you examine some of Dostoevsky's most successful, most imaginative "flights," you find them to be projections, continuations, of the actual, the observed: the final scene of the "Idiot," the hallucinations at the beginning of the same book and in "Crime and Punishment," even (what is more questionable) the interview of Ivan Karamazov with the Devil—Dostoev-

sky's point of departure is always a human brain in a human environment, and the "aura" is simply the continuation of the quotidian *experience of the brain into seldom explored extremities of torture.*[28]

Eliot was attracted, clearly, by the way Dostoevsky charged accidental images in painful scenes, like the fly buzzing around Nastasya's corpse in the "final scene of the 'Idiot,'" with the full immediacy and dark meaningfulness of nightmare.[29] But this power, if anything, is also what distinguishes the special flavor of Eliot's own brand of imagism as it enters *The Waste Land.* As an elucidation of the link between "Geron-tion" and *The Waste Land* Eliot's remarks about Dostoevsky could only be bettered by another passage he wrote eleven years later. Speaking about Tourneur's *Revenger's Tragedy,* he glanced back at a phase of life he had passed through and—blissfully—left behind:

> [This, chiefly, is what gives *The Revenger's Tragedy*] its amazing unity—an intense and unique and horrible vision of life; but [it] is such a vision as might come, as the result of few or slender experiences, to a highly sensi-tive adolescent with a gift for words. We are apt to expect of youth only a fragmentary view of life; we incline to see youth as exaggerating the im-portance of its narrow experience and imagining the world as did Chicken Licken. But occasionally the intensity of the vision of its own ecstasies or horrors, combined with a mastery of word and rhythm, may give to a ju-venile work [we may read here *The Waste Land* as well as *The Revenger's Tragedy*] a universality which is beyond the author's knowledge of life to give, and to which mature men and women can respond. . . . The cyni-cism, the loathing and disgust of humanity, expressed consummately in *The Revenger's Tragedy,* are immature in the respect that they exceed the object. Their objective equivalents are characters practising the grossest vices; *characters* which *seem merely to be spectres projected from the poet's inner world of nightmare, some horror beyond words* (SE, 165–66; emphasis mine).

CHAPTER FIVE

"Unknown terror and mystery": *The Waste Land*

. . . He kept her, as they circulated, from being waylaid, even remarking to her afresh as he had often done before, on the help rendered in such situations by the intrinsic oddity of the London "squash," a thing of vague, slow, senseless eddies, revolving as in fear of some menace of conversation suspended over it, the drop of which, with some consequent refreshing splash or spatter, yet never took place.

> Henry James, *The Golden Bowl*

The idea is to take something familiar, something to which people have emotional associations, and change it enough to make it alien. The most difficult thing of all is to get the ambiences, the cold crispness of Hoth, the swampiness of Dagobah. For Dagobah, I slowed down and used many gull, tern and shorebird sounds, along with sea lions, dolphins and the pump at a water-treatment plant, sounds that kept things low-pitched, croaking, slithering.

> Benn Burtt, sound effects expert for *Star Wars, New York Times,* June 9, 1980.

Because the material [of the psychoanalytic novel] is so clearly defined . . . there is no possibility [in it] of tapping the atmosphere of unknown terror and mystery in which our life is passed and which psychoanalysis has not yet analysed.

> T.S. Eliot, "London Letter," *The Dial,* September 1922

From the summer of 1915, when Eliot married Vivien Haigh-Wood and decided for England and a life of poetry, his "inner world of nightmare" had all too many correspondences with the world of outer events. In a gesture of surrender, hoping to overcome his chronic detachment from life, Eliot had in two months courted and wed the sometime governess, sometime painter, sometime ballerina he first met at an Oxford punting party. Yet there was hardly a time when his high-strung and sickly wife was not a problem. And when his parents, who disapproved of the emotional and financial demands Vivien made upon Eliot, summoned him home and threatened to cut off his support (they later half relented), the problems were compounded. The Eliots lived for a while with Bertrand Russell, without whose financial help they could not have gone on. Eliot taught grammar school, but hated it because preparation for teaching invaded even his sleep. He secured a job with Lloyd's bank, but spent almost as much time preparing extension school lectures and working on occasional essays. And he drove himself unmercifully trying to produce the literature that would justify his rebellious behavior and satisfy all "that I have not made a mess of my life."[1] But the more he drove himself, the less he produced. He wrote nothing good enough to publish between mid-1915 and mid-1917, and then after the period of the quatrain poems and "Gerontion" again nothing between summer 1919 and summer 1921.

Almost as soon as they married, Vivien Eliot, who Bertrand Russell said showed "impulses of. . . . a Dostojevsky type of cruelty"—she "lives on a knife-edge, and will end as a criminal or a saint"[2]—exacerbated all the internal dissonance Eliot had addressed in his early poetry. At first charmed by Vivien's combination of acute sensitivity and unashamed brashness, Eliot quickly saw it turned against himself. Vivien held him to standards of emotional forthrightness he wished to but could not sustain. According to Lyndall Gordon, there was a "disastrous 'pseudo-honeymoon' at Eastbourne," with Vivien "not far from suicide." Then came the parties at which Vivien, feeling Eliot's disapproval of her lack of restraint, either exaggerated her behavior or publicly accused him of hypocrisy. Just a month after their marriage, Russell watched their *danse macabre* and wrote,

> She is light, a little vulgar, adventurous, full of life—an artist I think he said, but I should have thought her an actress. He is exquisite and listless; she says she married him to stimulate him, but finds she can't do it. Obviously he married in order to be stimulated. I think she will soon be tired of him. She refuses to go to America to see his people, for fear of submarines. He is ashamed of his marriage, and very grateful if one is kind to her. He is the Miss Sands type of American.[3]

Vivien complicated everything. She forced Eliot to quarrel with his parents just when he was feeling anxious over his foreign escape. And she reinforced many of the intricacies of his troubled identity. Like his mother she seemed to adore him in one moment and question his strongest impulses in the next. But Vivien's sarcasm was directed against Eliot's New England self and not its emotional antagonist. The tangled result was that her disapproval was soon compounded with his mother's, threatening both parts of Eliot's delicate equilibrium. Eventually she must have appeared both his just punishment and the very image of the authority he had transgressed. In one vein of his poetry her eyes are telescoped with his mother's, leading to the transformation of Prufrock's "eyes that fix you in a formulated phrase" into *The Hollow Men*'s "eyes I dare not meet in dreams." Little wonder that in *The Waste Land,* "the awful daring of a moment's [sexual] surrender" generates feelings of "a broken Coriolanus."

In January 1919, before Eliot and his father had a chance to reconcile, his father died. According to Vivien's diary his reaction was "most terrible."[4] Soon after, he wrote, "This does not weaken the need for a book at all—it really reinforces it—my mother is still alive. . . . a great deal hangs on it for me."[5] In December Eliot mentioned wanting to get started on "a long poem I have had on my mind," and in February he wrote his brother Henry, "I am thinking all the time of my desire to see [mother]. I cannot get away from it. Unless I can really *see* her again I shall never be happy."[6] Just before his mother came with his sister and brother to visit him Eliot began work on his long poem, but her visit stopped him cold. She did not get along with Vivien, whom Eliot whisked away to the country whenever he could. She also had lost none of the force of her New England ideals (she proved "terrifyingly energetic"), and when she left England Eliot, who had passionately desired not confrontation but reassurance and approval, felt once again a failure. By September he was weak and ill, and wrote that he felt extremely "shaky, and seem to have gone down rapidly since my family left."[7] That was when Lloyd's bank gave him leave. In October, attacked by depression, indecisiveness and fear of psychosis, he went alone to Margate for a rest-cure. There, building on fragments he had been collecting since he came to London, he wrote part of *The Waste Land.* According to Valerie Eliot he returned from Margate on November 12, and set out with Vivien on the eighteenth for Paris, where he left Vivien in Pound's care. He then went to Lausanne, where he would place himself in the hands of a Dr. Vittoz and complete the first draft of his poem.[8]

Many times during this period Eliot sensed he was trapped in a bad dream. In 1916 he distinguished his London from his Harvard life by telling Conrad Aiken the latter now seemed "a *dull* nightmare."[9] London with Vivien was anything but dull, and Eliot's confessions to John Quinn in 1922 make it clear that it was difficult for him to dissociate the nightmare within and the nightmare without: he told Quinn that whenever he got tired or worried, he recognized the old symptoms ready to appear, and that he found himself under the strain of trying to suppress a vague but intensely acute horror and apprehension. Perhaps the greatest curse of his life, he said, was the associations imagination suggested with various noises. He could not abide living in a town flat, therefore, because he could never forget the lives and disagreeable personalities of his neighbors.[10]

Eliot's horror and apprehension, his obsession with neighbors' noises and his inflamed perception of noise in general all manifest themselves in the poem he wrote. *The Waste Land* would rehearse some of Eliot's most painful experiences and finger psychological knots that he could not consciously consider. But anxiety blocked him in the fall of 1921, and Conrad Aiken tells us that "although every evening he went home to his flat hoping that he could start writing again, and with every confidence that the material was *there* and waiting, night after night the hope proved illusory: the sharpened pencil lay unused by the untouched sheet of paper."[11] Eliot, however, had to write. He would later gloss Housman's comment "I have seldom written poetry unless I was rather out of health" with the statement that it revealed "authentic processes of a real poet. . . . I understand that sentence."[12] Poetry was the way he explored and exorcised his discomfort, and in 1921 the burdens of his demon ("[the lyric poet] is haunted by a demon . . . and the words, the poem he makes, are a kind of form of exorcism of this demon")[13] were the worst he had ever known. A memory of the therapeutic effects of composition sent him to his sharpened pencils night after night, and his preoccupation with emotional sincerity, recently honed on the maxims of Rémy de Gourmont, insisted that he confront his demon honestly. Though the poem he was about to write, like his earlier poems, would distance his suffering by raising a moral framework around the demon (that was part of the therapeutic magic), this time the demon would be stronger than the scaffold. Dante's "ordered scale of human emotions" (SW, 168) was very much on Eliot's mind in 1921, as was the indirect mythic presentation of moral states; but even more pressing was a desire to dredge up what he really was and felt.

On the evidence of the manuscripts collected by Valerie Eliot, "The Fire Sermon" was the first full movement of *The Waste Land* Eliot attempted.[14] Out of the fragments he had been collecting since 1914, at Margate Eliot chose a passage already several years old as a starting point:

> London, the swarming life you kill and breed,
> Huddled between the concrete and the sky,
> Responsive to the momentary need,
> Vibrates unconscious to its formal destiny,
>
> Knowing neither how to think, nor how to feel,
> But lives in the awareness of the observing eye.
> Phantasmal gnomes, burrowing in brick and stone and steel!
> Some minds, aberrant from the normal equipoise
> (London, your people is bound upon the wheel!)
> Record the motions of these pavement toys
> And trace the cryptograms that may be curled
> Within these faint perceptions of the noise
> Of the movement, and the lights![15]

This is a programmatic statement, an announcement that ⟨
Fire Sermon" would consist of a hypersensitive record of tw
London's teeming crowds and the "cryptogram" of significat
around them.[16] Eliot's portraits would be the stuff of journa
method spiritual analysis, his manner nightmare-gothic, and I ...no-
tional subject the emptiness of lives bound upon the wheel of passion
and misdirected by the values of the modern city.

That was the program, but the way Eliot phrased it would not do.
(Pound later dismissed it with a slash of red ink and a disgusted
"B——S.")[17] To conform to the standards Eliot and Pound had been
enunciating for several years, Eliot's theme would have to be embodied
in comment-free dramatic vignettes. And when Eliot finally conjured
these vignettes out of the air, his program fell away and his writing was
in the power of his demon. Heeding advice he had recently given others ("the bad poet is usually unconscious where he ought to be conscious, and conscious where he ought to be unconscious. Both errors
tend to make him 'personal' "),[18] Eliot seized on images and impressions that had struck his imagination and did not belabor their moral
significance.[19] Beginning with "The Fire Sermon," he drew on memories of London formed during the preceding summer, when his attention was sharpened to visionary intensity by the presence of his
mother;[20] on scenes from his own life, particularly from his life with
Vivien;[21] and on the horrible noises and the disagreeable neighbors he
complained of to John Quinn.[22] Through all of these, like wine through
water, ran the nightmarish emotional charge of Eliot's vague but intensely accute horror and apprehension of the "unknown terror and
mystery in which our life is passed." As Eliot said about Jonson's plays,
that was enough to give the fragments a "dominant tone," a "unity of
inspiration that radiates into plot and personages alike."[23] What he had
sensed at the very bottom of Jonson's constructions became the primary—almost the only—unity of his own poem. To appropriate Richard Poirier on a famous collection of popular songs, the fragments
"emanated from some inwardly felt coherence that awaited a merely
explicit design, and they would ask to be heard together even without
the design."[24]

Some of Eliot's *images trouvailles* were drawn from actual nightmares.
When Bertrand Russell, for example, told him about a hallucination
Russell had that London Bridge would collapse and sink and the whole
great city would "vanish like a morning mist,"[25] Eliot suffused it with
the energy of a nursery rhyme gone mad and made it the keynote of
his finale. Other images drew on literary nightmares, or combinations
of literature and fact, but were no less imaginatively transformed. Out
of his recollections of the murdered young women in Dostoyevsky's
Crime and Punishment and *The Idiot* (and of an actual incident of a man

murdering his mistress),[26] Eliot created yet another poetic sequence about the mangling of "La Figlia Che Piange." Participating in the sense of emotional strangulation that suffuses that early poem, the betrayed women in *The Waste Land* also absorb the complex ambivalence associated in Eliot's mind with Vivien. These women anticipate Harry's murdered wife in *The Family Reunion* and Sweeney's murdered neighbor in *Sweeney Agonistes.* They are also the immediate successors of the girl in Eliot's abandoned long poem of the mid-teens, "The Love Song of St. Sebastian," who was strangled by her neophyte-lover between his bleeding knees.[27] Unlike "St. Sebastian," which was to have one strangling episode as centerpiece, *The Waste Land* has many, all brief (some, like "Philomela," nearly invisible). Together they provide an undercurrent to the poem, dominating it the way a buried incident that is too terrifying to confront dominates a nightmare and occasionally breaks its surface. As Hugh Kenner observed many years ago, this buried sequence ties together a number of guilty protagonists and a long list of potential or real corpses: the hyacinth girl, Ophelia, "that corpse you planted last year in your garden," "bones cast in a little low dry garret," and so on.[28]

The subject of *The Waste Land*'s literary borrowings, now that it has been raised, commands a moment's reflection. It should be clear by now that contrary to the assumptions of generations of readers, for Eliot literary borrowings were more appropriations of other people's feelings than tools for ironic comment. He once put it this way: "Immature poets imitate; mature poets steal; bad poets deface what they take, and good poets make it into something better, or at least something different. The good poet welds his theft into a whole of feeling which is unique, utterly different from that from which it was torn" (SW, 125). In *The Waste Land* as elsewhere in his writings, images borrowed from other writers serve the same purpose as images found in everyday life—they provide nuggets of the objective world charged with feelings and untarnished by the deadening, conventional rhetoric of Eliot's personal will. They are thus uncontaminated by the acquired self, rooted in what lies below it and good fodder for a new "whole of feeling." Hence the presence in *The Waste Land* of Ovid's sweet-singing nightingale or Shakespeare's intensely mourned Ophelia.

But there is another way that the literature of the past makes itself felt in *The Waste Land,* a way that also has nothing to do with allusion as we normally think of it. We have seen that in poems like "Burbank with a Baedeker," the resonant poetry of the past is likely to become simply the rhetoric of the present. In *The Waste Land* Eliot's pervasive speaker—if one may use the word "speaker" to describe a vehicle for the "dominant tone" of subconscious feeling—is intensely aware of the literaryness, the rhetorical quality, of his utterance. Much of the poem's poetic sophistication comes from this self-consciousness, which is the enormously subtle dramatization of Eliot reacting against his own inherited disposition to rhetoric.[29] As in not only Eliot's own experience but the fictional lives of Prufrock and Gerontion, one of the terrors of the speaker of *The Waste Land* is that he has forfeited life to books, and is trapped in ways of thinking and feeling acquired through convention. To use Eliot's bitter phrases, his emotional life is a terminal victim of "the pathology of rhetoric" and the "pastness of the past." And so in a sequence like the opening of "The Fire Sermon"—one of the finest and most terrifying passages of the poem—the other horrors of Eliot's nightmare are compounded by a self-consciousness that shadows every attempted escape from an isolated emptiness into the imaginative richness of poetry. In a passage like the following, every allusion has implied quotation marks around it and so renders a self-consciousness on the part of the speaker as much as it alludes to something outside the poem. (Where else in our poetry can a poem like Verlaine's "Parsifal" be sounded—a wondrously passionate poem considered by itself—and yet be charged with the coldness of irony simply by the context of its new surroundings? In *"Et O ces voix d'enfants"* Verlaine expressed indescribable aspiration; here the short line expresses that and also an ironic awareness that poetry is only literature, and to quote poetry is less to relieve genuine feeling than to succumb to monkish temptation.)

> The river's tent is broken: the last fingers of leaf
> Clutch and sink into the wet bank. The wind
> Crosses the brown land, unheard. The nymphs are departed.
> Sweet Thames, run softly, till I end my song.
> The river bears no empty bottles, sandwich papers,
> Silk handkerchiefs, cardboard boxes, cigarette ends
> Or other testimony of summer nights. The nymphs are departed.
> And their friends, the loitering heirs of city directors;
> Departed, have left no addresses.
> By the waters of Leman I sat down and wept . . .
> Sweet Thames, run softly till I end my song,
> Sweet Thames, run softly, for I speak not loud or long.
> But at my back in a cold blast I hear
> The rattle of the bones, and chuckle spread from ear to ear.
> A rat crept softly through the vegetation
> Dragging its slimy belly on the bank
> While I was fishing in the dull canal
> On a winter evening round behind the gashouse
> Musing upon the king my brother's wreck
> And on the king my father's death before him.
> White bodies naked on the low damp ground
> And bones cast in a little low dry garret,
> Rattled by the rat's foot only, year to year.
> But at my back from time to time I hear
> The sound of horns and motors, which shall bring

Sweeney to Mrs. Porter in the spring.
O the moon shone bright on Mrs. Porter
And on her daughter
They wash their feet in soda water
Et O ces voix d'enfants, chantant dans la coupole!

Below the level of allusion, the passage presents the characteristic emotions of *The Waste Land*. Melancholy, loss, isolation and fear of a meaningless death adhere to "impersonal" objects in a "world" of awareness. The elements of this world arise from observation and memory (sometimes literary), and they strike us as complex sensations that have not been homogenized into a univalent pattern—a nameable feeling. But behind the pieces we sense an emotional logic that is "constantly amalgamating" (SE, 247) fragments into a single vision, and we are drawn into the poem's "point of view." Once we have given ourselves over to the emotional pressure of the poem we accept its coherence as we would accept the sequence of events in a dream, where objects quite often have an order, an emotional charge and a significance very different from the ones they have in waking consciousness. (Think of how often, for example, familiar people or objects terrify us in a nightmare when the same images in our sight or in our daydreams would not make us think twice.)

The opening movement of "The Fire Sermon" is "Hell" as Edward describes it in *The Cocktail Party:*

What is hell? Hell is oneself,
Hell is alone, the other figures in it
Merely projections.[30]

It takes its dominant tone from a series of surrealistic images in which subconscious anxiety, as in a bad dream or a psychotic delusion, is projected onto human and non-human objects. Harry, in *The Family Reunion*, describes it this way:

I could not fit myself together:
When I was inside the old dream, I felt all the same emotion
Or lack of emotion, as before: the same loathing
Diffused, I not a person, in a world not of persons
But only of contaminating presences.

(CPP, 272)

But what Harry describes, the opening of "The Fire Sermon" presents. In it, emotional fantasies, sometimes of self-loathing, extend through a series of unconnected images in a medium where ego-integration seems to be non-existent. In synechdochic progression, a river, falling leaves, the brown land, bones, a rat, Ferdinand, his brother and his father, Mrs. Porter and her daughter all become extensions of a whole (but not continuous) state of anxiety. Eliot's speaker (if—again—

one can use that noun in a case where utterance seems to come from below the level of ordinary speech), projects his feelings of isolation, vanished protection and loss first onto the river, whose tent of leaves is "broken" (the inappropriately violent adjective emphasizes the feeling of grief behind the loss), and then onto the falling leaves, which animistically have fingers that "clutch" for support as they sink into decomposition and oblivion. Then defenselessness becomes a shrinking from attack as the leaves fade into the brown land, "crossed" by the wind. (Ten lines later the crossing wind will become a "cold blast" rattling sensitive bones and, metamorphosed, the insubstantial malevolence of a "chuckle spread from ear to ear.") Still later, after an interlude of deep-seated loss, isolation turns into self-disgust as the "speaker" projects himself into a rat with a human belly creeping softly and loathsomely through the vegetation. (Both rat and vegetation are extensions of the decomposing leaves.) And as this horrified fascination with the process of decomposition increases, the rat's living body merges with a corpse's and the "speaker" apprehends himself first as rotting and sodden flesh, feeling "naked on the low damp ground," and then as dry bones, rattled by the rat's foot as he was rattled before by the cold wind. (In a nightmare one can be both rat and bones.)

In the conclusion of the passage, the threatening vital force which had been apprehended as the wind's blast reasserts itself as raucous sound and the impinging moon, and the poem reacts once again with revulsion, now animating the behavior of Mrs. Porter and her daughter, who insulate themselves in a vivid but ineffective gesture. (According to the bawdier versions of a popular ballad, their "feet" are a euphemism and the soda water is a prophylactic douche; one does not need to know that to feel the compulsive defensiveness in their unexplained washing.)

There is more. The opening of "The Fire Sermon" is not simply an English version of the kind of French poetry that uses symbols to express the ambivalence of the subconscious mind. Eliot's poetry is self-dramatizing. In the way it echoes literature of the past and in its self-conscious use of elevated or colloquial language, it dramatizes a Prufrockian sensibility with a subtlety unavailable to the Eliot of 1911. In the passage we are considering, this sensibility is caught between two double binds: a yearning for the vitality of common life combined with a revulsion from its vulgarity; and an inclination toward poetry combined with a horror of literature. This vacillation, superimposed over the poetry's *progression d'effets,* brings the world of unconscious impulse into contact with the humanized world of language. In "The Fire Sermon" *this* drama begins as the literary word "nymphs" emerges from a series of more or less pure images. As it unfolds, the phrase "the nymphs are departed" suggests Eliot's desire to recuperate his lost sense of fullness in a world of pastoral poetry, and for a moment Eliot appropriates

Spenser's voice. "Sweet Thames, run softly, till I end my song." The immediate result is a disgust with modern life worthy of Burbank. Hence the following three lines, where that disgust can be heard in a series of jolting colloquialisms. But both Eliot's poetic nostalgia and his disgust with the quotidian soften in the ninth line: there is a real sorrow in the speaker's statement that the "nymphs" and their vulgar friends have deserted him, a sorrow sounded in the repetition of "departed" twice in two lines. When the speaker reassumes the linguistic personae of the past in the *glissando* of the next three lines, therefore, it strikes us as a gesture taken *faute de mieux*. That is, we sense by this point that Eliot's speaker already has some awareness that the great phrases of the past are as unreal as they are beautiful. As his reminiscence (shall we call it memory?) of Spenser's "Prothalamion" sounds, we detect a note of self-consciousness in the nostalgia, as if the voice inhabiting the lines were feeling its own inauthenticity. When yet a third quotation is added to the Psalms and to Spenser, this discomfort, which stems from an awareness of the inadequacy of rhetoric to sustain true feeling or ward off grief, explodes in mid-flight. "But at my back," the speaker begins, and we expect to hear the rest of Marvell's immortal lines: "But at my back I always hear / Time's winged chariot hurrying near." Instead, the feeling of desolation which had called up the line swells out into bitterness: even the cherished texts of the past cannot charm away the bleak realities of life. To pretend that they can is a fraud. In Keats's "Ode to a Nightingale," this chilling realization generates yet two more sublime verses: "Adieu! the fancy cannot cheat so well/As she is famed to do, deceiving elf." In *The Waste Land,* the same realization shatters Eliot's poetic continuity, and causes him to interrupt Marvell's lines with a sardonic assertion of the primacy of the here and now:

> But at my back in a cold blast I hear
> The rattle of the bones, and chuckle spread from ear to ear.

Unlike Burbank then, this speaker is aware of the pathology of his rhetoric; all his literary utterances remind him of it. No sooner does he begin to transfigure the death of his father with it in the language of *The Tempest,* than he rebukes himself with an unidealized image of death. The image is close to pure terror; it is his own death as well as his father's that obsesses him:

> While I was fishing in the dull canal
> On a winter evening round behind the gashouse
> Musing upon the king my brother's wreck
> And on the king my father's death before him.
> White bodies on the low damp ground. . . .

The same pattern repeats itself three lines later, only this time the sequence has become more agitated:

But at my back from time to time I hear
The sound of horns and motors, which shall bring
Sweeney to Mrs. Porter in the spring.

This tune is not Spenserian, and its leering swell mocks the legendary powers of music itself. Finally, the last line combines the highest reaches of expressive eloquence with an icy rejection of eloquence itself: "*Et O ces voix d'enfants, chantant dans la coupole!*" Oh those voices. Oh those children's voices.

In passages like this one, then, the anxiety we feel has two sources: a sequence of anxiety-charged images and the increasingly agitated self-laceration of a speaker conscious of his own rhetorical bent. Fueling both is a terrified awareness of death and a near-desperate sense that there is no escape from it. The pattern, moreover, resembles a certain kind of nightmare: a situation both desired and feared arises. Then, fueled by underlying desire, the situation develops. Meanwhile a dream censor is trying to suppress the clarity of the situation and terminates the sequence before the significance of a briefly glimpsed climax can be elaborated.

This configuration describes a great many of the separate vignettes that make up the first three movements of *The Waste Land*. What connects them is precisely what connects the disparate segments of our most distressing dreams. When we do not wake up after our first approach to a piece of heavily charged psychic material, we quite often play out the same pattern in situations that have different manifest elements but draw on the same body of latent content. That is, when the dream censor is able to agitate and then shatter a fantasy that gets too close to some forbidden truth, the forces that initiated the fantasy start the whole struggle again. In each segment, the same impulses reappear veiled in different objects or personae, unifying them from below. A dramatic situation emerges, intensifies mysteriously, reverberates with frightening tension and then, just before the situation is clarified, disperses; then a new situation arises that seems comfortingly different but is in fact the same anew.[31]

I use the analogy of nightmare here with premeditation, but also with some diffidence. There are, of course, other, more subtle, ways of making sense of the tensions, the dramatic unity and the emotional progression of the first three movements of *The Waste Land,* and the best of them use a vocabulary generated to describe related examples of post-romantic poetry.[32] Yet, dealing with a poem whose emotional immediacy has been slighted for so many years, I think it is of real use to apply an analogy drawn from common experience. And I would point out that the analogy is sanctioned by Eliot's own prose.

"The Burial of the Dead" begins as a voice remarks on the cruelty of "Memory and desire." Then, transformed, these feelings are absorbed

in a dramatization. But the woman in the dramatization seems unconscious of the desire that conjured her up. We know of it by inference,
from the particulars of her vision. She is oblivious to it, and she is just
as oblivious to her own anxieties. We read them from the defensive
stance of her protestations: why, we must guess, is she so eager not to
be identified as Russian? Her interjection, apparently meaningless, is,
in Eliot's words, a "tremendous statement, like statements made in our
dreams" (SW, 148).

Her appearance in the dream, however, comes to an abrupt end.
There is something, apparently, she is afraid to face: "In the mountains, *there* you feel free." Apparently, *here* you do not. Why? Her non
sequitur in the next line does not tell us, although it speaks of her
uneasiness. But before her uneasiness is allowed to grow the scene is
over. It is Marie's evasion that leads to the next verse paragraph, which
vibrates with a terror of what cannot be evaded even as we ask ourselves what it has to do with the story we have just heard. The paragraph ends, moreover, with a line (Eliot stole it from "Meditation IV"
in Donne's *Devotions*) that represents a threshold over which the poem's
voice cannot step: "I will show you fear in a handful of dust."

The next three scenes repeat a sequence the first verse paragraph
began: the desolation latent in *Oed' und leer das Meer* is profound enough
to foreclose further examination, and the latent content of the thing
"One must be so careful [of] these days" is too threatening to name.
Finally, in a conclusion that resembles the end of a nightmare sequence, the narrative becomes so agitated it cannot continue, and is
shattered by an unexpected incident and a feverish inquisition. Without warning an unexplained encounter verges on some kind of recognition ("There I saw one I knew, and stopped him, crying, 'Stetson!' "),
then explodes. There follow three hysterical questions, two lines of reverberating prophesy and then, from out of nowhere, Baudelaire's
"You! hypocrite lecteur!"—a fragment which, in context, confronts us
like the menacing ravings of a lunatic. Whatever charges Eliot's memory and desire from below has come so close to the surface that the
sequence can no longer contain it, and so disintegrates.

At the center of "The Burial of the Dead," and at the center of the
nightmare of *The Waste Land*, lies the episode of the Hyacinth garden.
Like Marie's summer memory, the episode begins on the note of romantic desire, this time with full-throated song, slightly melancholy,
but rising to an unqualified yearning to have the romance of the past
restored. Wagner's lyric acts as an epigraph to the drama that follows.
As the German suggests a love lost and remembered, the girl who now
appears before the speaker recalls a luminous moment when love *re-
named* her, and made her part of the spring: "They called me the hyacinth girl." As in "La Figlia," the girl's condition mirrors the speaker's
own emotional life, caught for a second in one of its infrequent blos-

somings. But his moment of self-transcendence—transcending himself through love and transcending his always hollow-sounding voice through images—fades. His qualification "Yet" suggests he is again conscious of himself, and places us at the center of one of Eliot's recurrent obsessions. If his speaker can sustain his love into eternity, if this moment can be made the foundation of a set of permanent values, then his emotional self will have been validated and the warnings of his acquired self will be proved worthless. If, however, the moment cannot be sustained, if the promise of love turns out to be illusory and "the awful separation between potential passion and any actualization possible in life"[33] is as real as he suspected, then the worst of his fears will have been realized, and he will be trapped forever in an emotional waste land where "eyes fix you in a formulated phrase."

What then transpires can only be suggested by a reading alive to the way Eliot's poetry renders small movements of the heart. Eliot's speaker tries to prolong his memory and the feelings attached to it, and we hear his feeling swell in two pronounced spondees: "Your arms full, and your hair wet." But a second caesura introduces the plaintive words "I could not":

> I could not
> Speak and my eyes failed, I was neither
> Living nor dead, and I knew nothing,
> Looking into the heart of light, the silence.
> *Oed' und leer das Meer.*

Could he not speak because speech had been transcended or because the limitation of speech prevented him from fulfilling the moment? Did his eyes fail because he experienced what was beyond vision or because sight prevented him from the vision that he sought? Did he know nothing because worldly knowledge had fallen away or because he understood the nothing that is the ultimate truth? We would need to answer all of these questions if the speaker's statements were not given in the past tense. Since they are, it is clear that the questions they imply are his as much as ours. Looking back at his moment in the garden, the speaker ponders the issues on which his life turns. He has reached a moment like the one Celia describes in *The Cocktail Party:*

> I have thought at moments that the ecstacy is real
> Although those who experience it may have no reality.
> For what happened is remembered like a dream
> In which one is exalted by intensity of loving
> In the spirit, a vibration of delight
> Without desire, for desire is fulfilled
> In the delight of loving. A state one does not know
> When awake. But what, or whom I loved,
> Or what in me was loving, I do not know.

And if that is all meaningless, I want to be cured
Of a craving for something I cannot find
And of the shame of never finding it.

(CPP, 363)

In the Hyacinth garden episode, Eliot dramatizes both Celia's "dream" and her wondering afterwards "if that is all meaningless." Reliving his failure to speak, to see, to know, the voice of *The Waste Land* gives us the agonized speculation of a man asking ultimate questions and being unable—or afraid—to answer. And since the sequence itself not only contains a dream but enacts one, this speculation swells out into another "tremendous statement," cast in a timeless present participle and balanced between the possibilities of nihilism and a mystic vision. Is he "looking into the heart of light" or the "silence"? As Celia puts it,

Can we only love
Something created by our own imagination?
Are we all in fact unloving and unlovable?
Then one *is* alone, and if one is alone
Then lover and belovèd are equally unreal
And the dreamer is no more real than his dreams.

(CPP, 362)

These questions, wrung out of Eliot by the most rigorous discipline of honesty, hang over the first three sections of *The Waste Land* as the "menace of conversation" hangs over James's party in the epigraph to this chapter. They appear to represent Eliot's deepest fears: that we are alone, that what seems our most authentic emotional life is an illusion, that we are consequently worthless, and that reality itself is meaningless.

The Waste Land itself returns continually to that moment and those questions, as if to some feared truth which its speakers would do anything to avoid and yet are doomed to confront. As with a criminal returning to the scene of his crime (a murdered girl, a buried life), all things lead to that. And along the way of this compulsive, nightmarish vacillation, every instrument of answering the doubts, of testing the truth, is itself questioned. Nothing, not the authority of history or of literature or of language itself is allowed to go unsuspected in this horrified interrogation of the moment in the garden. History may be lies, literature may be rhetoric, memory may be illusion, the rambling self may be but an artificial construct, sensation may be hallucination, even language may be a "natural sin." [34] And—uncannily—at the center of this nightmarish questioning stands the figure of Tiresias. How many of Eliot's readers have noticed that the figure he affixed to his disembodied narrator, the figure who unites all the dream's men and all the dream's women, is also at the center of Freud's archetypal myth of the tormented human psyche turned back against itself—the Oedipus myth?[35]

2

One has only to compare the dramatic concentration of the Hyacinth garden episode with Eliot's exploration of the same anxieties in "La Figlia Che Piange" to realize the power of *The Waste Land*. The psychic material once distanced with the aid of Laforguian irony and later with the comic disproportions of the quatrain poems is now isolated and exposed. What had made the earlier poems compelling was the uneasiness that pervaded their formal polish. Deft as they were, and as much as they claimed to be the accounts of an outsider, a double anxiety persistently filled the distance between observed and observer: a Jamesian anxiety that the very fastidiousness which defends the observer from vulgarity also serves to prevent him from participating in what Shakespeare and then Joyce called "life's feast"; and a deeper anxiety that if the observer ever broke through his fastidiousness he would discover the feast was a sham. In Eliot's poems before "Gerontion" the first anxiety makes the observer's distance intolerable. The second renders the thought of giving it up unthinkable. Together they activate the circle of approach and withdrawal that gives Eliot's early poetry its considerable fascination.

In *The Waste Land,* the deeper of these anxieties is brought closer to consciousness than one would have believed possible. It is just below the surface, and the threat of its rising terrifies not only Eliot's "different voices" but also the narrative voice that stands behind them. Even the most unthinking and resistant of the poem's characters find themselves being pushed toward a moment of discovery that will tell them whether the "silence" at the "heart of life" is meaningless or not. Eliot's drama moves from a revulsion from the mode of cultured life to a revulsion from the mode of common life, facing in endless succession the fear that both are shells around a core of emptiness. Even adolescent yearnings—the moment in the Hyacinth garden—constantly threaten to reveal themselves as the ghoulish manifestation of something other than love. At the heart of the poem is a sense of worthlessness, not only the worthlessness of the present but the probable worthlessness of the past and the future. This sense of pervasive worthlessness, called into resurgence by the biographical events recounted at the beginning of this chapter, was undoubtedly at the root of the vague but intensely acute horror and apprehension Eliot told John Quinn in 1922 he had been straining to suppress.[36]

Given the correspondence, moreover, between the never-to-be-repeated intensity of *The Waste Land* and the psychological conditions,

amounting to a full-scale breakdown, under which the poem was written, one is compelled to ask whether one was the result of the other.
Was *The Waste Land* made possible by a disruption in Eliot's conscious
life and a breakdown of his psychological defenses? That, it seems to
me, is one of the most interesting of the many problems that surround
the poem.

In his case study of Eliot, the psychiatrist Harry Trosman cites two
of Eliot's remarks that relate the composition of *The Waste Land* to his
emotional breakdown. (Valerie Eliot, who reproduces the first in the
Waste Land Facsimile volume, reports that Eliot told her specifically that
he was here "describing his own experience of writing ["What the
Thunder Said"]"):

> . . . It is a commonplace that some forms of illness are extremely fa-
> vourable, not only to religious illumination, but to artistic and literary com-
> position. A piece of writing meditated, apparently without progress, for
> months or years, may suddenly take shape and word; and in this state long
> passages may be produced which require little or no retouch.

> I know, for instance, that some form of ill-health, debility or anaemia,
> may . . . produce an efflux of poetry in a way approaching the condition
> of automatic writing—though, in contrast to the claims sometimes made
> for the latter, the material has obviously been incubating within the poet,
> and cannot be suspected of being a present from a friendly or impertinent
> demon. What one writes in this way may succeed in standing the exami-
> nation of a more normal state of mind; it gives me the impression, as I
> have just said, of having undergone a long incubation, though we do not
> know until the shell breaks what kind of egg we have been sitting on. To
> me it seems that at these moments, which are characterised by the sudden
> lifting of the burden of anxiety and fear which presses upon our daily life
> so steadily that we are unaware of it, what happens is something *negative:*
> that is to say, not "inspiration" as we commonly think of it, but the break-
> ing down of strong habitual barriers—which tend to re-form very quickly.
> Some obstruction is momentarily whisked away. The accompanying feeling
> is less like what we know as positive pleasure, than a sudden relief from
> an intolerable burden.[37]

Based on these remarks and Eliot's psychiatric history, Trosman links
the fragmentation and animistic energy of *The Waste Land* to Eliot's
disturbance, breakdown and recovery:

> From a psychological point of view, Eliot's achievement lay in utilizing the
> content of his narcissistic regression for creative purposes. Having experi-
> enced a failure in response from need-satisfying and narcissistically ca-
> thected self-objects, he found himself empty, fragmented, and lacking in a
> sense of self-cohesion. As he began to reintegrate, he turned his previous
> adversity to poetic advantage. In a highly original manner, and perhaps
> for the first time in literature, he made narcissistic fragmentation a basis

for poetic form and alienation of self legitimate poetic content. The ideational and effective content of his psychic restitution, the expression of his attempt to reconstitute the fragmented elements of the split in his self became the new voice of *The Waste Land.*

Vittoz [the therapist who treated Eliot in Lausanne] was helpful by providing a framework for reintegration, satisfaction in completing simple tasks, and a religious philosophy reminiscent of Eliot's early youth. Vittoz could not, however, provide Eliot with insight into the basis of his disorder, and it is possible that the working out of the poem with the reactivation of experiences from the past, the mixing of memory and desire, and the unification of isolated and fragmented parts of the self may have been a form of partial self-analytic work. When Eliot wrote toward the end of the poem, "These fragments I have shored against my ruins" (line 430), he described a process of partial integration that brought about a relief from his personal grouse against life.[38]

Beneath the jargon of contemporary psychiatry there is a great deal of sense here. It is certainly likely, for example, that the mythic organization of *The Waste Land,* which Eliot imposed on the poem in the last stages of composition,[39] did represent an attempt to "reconstitute" a personal world—to give it a meaning, a shape and an order which were not in the original fragments. Nevertheless, it seems to me that *The Waste Land* is both more and less than the product of reintegration Trosman suggests. For one thing, the subterranean voice of the poem has as much to do with Eliot's theory of poetry as with his breakdown. For another, the final shape of the poem seems to have had more to do with Eliot's collapse than with his recovery.

The Waste Land, we saw, congealed around the intellectual program announced by "London, the swarming life you kill and breed." When Eliot started to assemble the first of his complete sections, he intended to hold modern life up to spiritual analysis and he consciously chose to present his material as fragments. In no simple sense, then, can we say that the initial fragmentation of the poem was the expression of a disabling emotional disturbance. Eliot, however, did not simply supply examples to illustrate preconceived types of moral decay. *The Waste Land* would be wooden had he done so. Instead, following the procedures described above, he allowed poetic scenes to arise out of *images trouvailles:* observed situations, disconnected mental pictures, overheard sounds, all of which imposed themselves on his imagination. It was at this point in composition that the lock on his unconscious must have broken. Guided by the principle of rigorous emotional honesty that he had been following since his Harvard days, Eliot's habits of composition led him to open a door he could not close. Later he would describe precisely this kind of unexpected marriage of impulse and technique in remarks occasioned by the publication of Ezra Pound's selected poems:

Those who expect that any good poet should proceed by turning out a series of masterpieces, each similar to the last, only more developed in *every way*, are simply ignorant of the conditions under which the poet must work, especially in our time. The poet's progress is dual. There is the gradual accumulation of experience, like a tantalus jar: it may be only once in five or ten years that experience accumulates to form a new whole and finds its appropriate expression. But if a poet were content to attempt nothing less than always his best, if he insisted on waiting for these unpredictable crystallizations, he would not be ready for them when they came. The development of experience is largely unconscious, subterranean, so that we cannot gauge its progress except once in every five or ten years; but in the meantime the poet must be working; he must be experimenting and trying his technique so that it will be ready, like a well-oiled fire-engine, when the moment comes to strain it to its utmost.[40]

By 1921, Eliot's cultivation of visionary drama, of a "continous identification of form and feeling,"[41] of the mysteriously charged details of dreams and nightmares, had together managed to weaken the clamp on the impulses of his inner life. Then, combined with the enormous emotional pressure of his family situation, they managed to break it altogether. Supplying portraits for his nightmare, Eliot charged them with his own inner hell and produced the first three sections of *The Waste Land*. Between the time his "strong habitual barriers" had momentarily broken down and the time they re-formed, the technical procedures he had made second nature did their job.

Most of what I have described as the poem's nightmare—"The Burial of the Dead," "A Game of Chess" and "The Fire Sermon"—was written or assembled at Margate and just after, in October and November of 1921. In the last two sections, written in the sanitarium at Lausanne, the poem turned from fire to water. That is, in Eliot's words, turned from "anxiety and fear" to "relief from an intolerable burden." The Thames maidens at the end of "The Fire Sermon" anticipate the drowned sailor in "Death by Water" and the releasing of an old self with its interminable tensions. And the last section of the poem—"What the Thunder Said"—strikes us, to quote D. W. Harding, as "corresponding to the precarious situation of a man who has partially recovered from a psychological collapse but remains aware of the formidable obstacles still ahead of him."[42]

When Eliot recovered, however, and the strong barriers were once again in place, he looked at his poem and shuddered. Remembering his return from Lausanne, Eliot would recall that "it was in 1922 that I placed before [Pound] in Paris the manuscript of a sprawling, chaotic poem,"[43] and his words give us a strong sense of how the emotional honesty of his new mirror struck him. The exaggeration of the remark—the draft Pound saw was certainly sprawling, but most of the "chaos" was in Eliot's mind—says a great deal about why Eliot was so

willing to give up his work to Pound for alteration.[44] (As it turned
out, Pound altered it relatively little.) Having composed one of the most
terrifying poems of a terrifying century, Eliot—in Paris and even before—struggled mightily to civilize a "grouse against life" that now
seemed objectionable. In August he would write that "Dostoevsky had
the gift, a sign of genius in itself, for utilizing his weaknesses; so that
epilepsy and hysteria cease to be the defects of an individual and become—as a fundamental weakness can, given the ability to face and
study it—the entrance to a genuine and personal universe."[45] And in
the last stages of polishing Eliot tried to "utilize" the record of what
must have seemed his own "fundamental weakness" by making it part
of a moral structure. According to a decade-old pattern, after venting
his emotional life, he felt compelled to gather it up and order it in a
way his ancestors would approve of.

The Eliot of 1922 was not only a disciple of Rémy de Gourmont but,
by turns, also a proponent of Irving Babbitt, T. E. Hulme, Charles
Maurras, Georges Sorel and Julien Benda. Even had he been convinced of his poem's emotional coherence, that is to say, allowing *The
Waste Land* to suggest moral chaos would have meant repudiating an
important part of his character. As Benda put it in a book Eliot called
essential, the ideal writer is one who "allows intelligence and judgment
to predominate over sentiment in the composition of his work."[46] The
problem was how to contain *The Waste Land* within a frame of judgment without vitiating its emotional authority.

Eliot solved his problem by recourse to a technique he had observed
in Joyce. In a 1923 review of *Ulysses* that is now as famous as *The Waste
Land*, Eliot spoke of "the mythical method":

> In using the myth, in manipulating a continuous parallel between contem-
> poraneity and antiquity, Mr. Joyce is pursuing a method which others must
> pursue after him. They will not be imitators, any more than the scientist
> who uses the discoveries of an Einstein in pursuing his own, independent,
> further investigations. It is simply a way of *controlling*, of *ordering*, of *giving
> a shape and a significance* to the immense panorama of futility and anarchy
> which is contemporary history. It is a method already adumbrated by Mr.
> Yeats, and of the need for which I believe Mr. Yeats to have been the first
> contemporary to be conscious. It is a method for which the horoscope is
> auspicious. Psychology (such as it is, and whether our reaction to it be
> comic or serious), ethnology, and *The Golden Bough* have concurred to make
> possible what was impossible even a few years ago. Instead of narrative
> method, we may now use the mythical method. It is, I seriously believe, a
> step toward making the modern world possible for art. . . .[47]

Often as this passage has been invoked to identify the central concerns of *The Waste Land*, the truth is that it belongs to the period when
Eliot was reshaping, not composing, his poem. As the words I have
emphasized suggest, it points to the way Eliot "controlled" and "or-

dered" something that was given to him more than it describes how he proceeded from the beginning. As an account of *The Waste Land* as a whole it is a dismal failure, for, as Hugh Kenner has pointed out, "it is difficult to believe that anyone who saw only the first four parts [of *The Waste Land*] in their original form would believe that 'the plan and a good deal of the incidental symbolism' were suggested by Jessie Weston's book on the Grail Legend, or that *The Golden Bough . . .* had much pertinence."[48] It is difficult, as Kenner explains, because the manuscript clearly shows that most of the Frazer and Weston imagery got into the poem only at the very end and that Eliot superimposed this material piecemeal onto sections that had been written earlier. Furthermore, the "myth" exists more in the suggestions of the belated title and in the notes than in the poem itself.

What is remarkable is that Eliot did not ruin his poem in that last reshaping, something for which we have Ezra Pound to thank. In his revision Pound concentrated on local infelicities more than on the integrity of the whole and kept Eliot from brooding about his lack of outline for several crucial days or weeks. What A. Walton Litz has called the "spurious"[49] grail legend plot in *The Waste Land* belongs more to our misreading than to the poem itself. The poem still vibrates much as it did before Eliot framed it, although its mythical overlay emphasizes certain overtones at the expense of others. The chapel perilous, for example, which cryptically appears at line 388, provides one more site where a fearsome ultimate question must be asked, and thus rhymes with the implied and explicit questioning in "The Burial of the Dead."

The final questions we can never answer. It may be, for example, that Eliot had some kind of short-lived religious illumination during the process of re-envisioning the fragments of his poem, and that his reshaping points to the recognition of a pattern in his life that he had not seen before.[50] Whatever the motivation of these last changes, *The Waste Land* survived them. Like *Crime and Punishment* or *The Brothers Karamazov*, though the poem is stamped with the mind of a middle-aged conservative, it claims its authority from the suffering and doubts of a rebellious youth.

3

It becomes increasingly more difficult, though, to say the same about the poetry that followed *The Waste Land*. Whereas Eliot's poetic and critical allegiances had been consistently divided before 1922 between romantic honesty and classical order, internal monologue and controlling myth, in 1922 that balance began to shift. The causes of the shift were many and had to do with new friendships and with Eliot's changing position in London society. But the most important of them seems to have involved Eliot's reaction to having finally achieved the kind of poetry he had for so long been trying to write. Eliot looked back on *The Waste Land* and the state of mind that produced it and saw himself "naked" as even Blake had not dared to be. And, consciously or unconsciously, he decided that he could not, would not continue to write that kind of poetry. He could not strive to write a poetry that continually sensitized his own internal fragmentation and brought him unbearable anxiety. As the next chapter will show, starting in 1922, and before his conversion, Eliot's poetry and criticism ceased to applaud "the transformation of a personality into a personal work of art" (SW, 139) and began envisioning creation as a process in which the poet, through the rigors of akesis, effaces his sensibility in traditional personae, traditional images and traditional patterns of feeling and thought. A token of this turning appeared when Eliot brought out a preface to the second edition of *The Sacred Wood*. In that preface, written in 1928, Eliot explained that he had "passed on to another problem not touched upon in this book: that of the relation of poetry to the spiritual and social life of its time and of other times" (SW, viii). As we shall see, at least for a while the procedure that Eliot chose as best suited to relating poetry to the "spiritual and social life" of its time was the method of *Sweeney Agonistes,* in which myth and the popular imagination were combined to create figures that were unconnected to personal sensibility.

There were other kinds of writing, however, that appealed to Eliot in these years as alternatives to the intense dramatic representation of inner reality. And one of these begins to appear in the last movement of *The Waste Land.* Its emergence was to have profound effects on the remainder of Eliot's career.

As the *Facsimile* volume notes, Eliot wrote Bertrand Russell in October 1922 that "it gives me very great pleasure to know that you like *The Waste Land,* and especially Part V which in my opinion is not only the best part, but the only part that justifies the whole, at all" (129). There is no question that "What the Thunder Said," much of which was written in a sudden fit of emotional release, is enormously moving. Eliot's speaker is here removed from the "swarming life" of London and among the mountains. And even though "There is not even silence in the mountains," the change suggests a condition of momentary release from his recurring nightmare. Where perfumes once "drowned the sense in odours" and the bones once crawled with slime, now "Sweat is dry" (l. 337) and "Dry bones can harm no one" (l. 391). From the first line we have the sense of someone amid a break in an emotional storm straining his faculties for some sign of what will happen next. He is yearning for "a damp gust / Bringing rain" and yet also intensely aware of the possible return of the terrors he has lived with—relivings of "the frosty silence" in the Hyacinth garden and reappearances of the woman who draws "her long black hair out tight." Line 389 suggests a mo-

ment's peace, when the grail quester has finally been given a moment's
respite before he asks the doom-laden question that has grown to haunt
him. But lines 344 and 345 ("red sullen faces sneer and snarl / From
doors of mudcracked houses") tell us we are as much in the world of
Browning's "Childe Roland"—a poem Eliot greatly admired[51]—as in
the world of Jessie Weston.

As Eliot wrote John Quinn, the greatest curse of his life came from
noises and associations noises called up.[52] It is therefore natural that
the aura of anticipation in "What the Thunder Said" should be presented through the sense of hearing, and that the great relief of the
section be announced by sounds (the hermit-thrush song of lines 357–
58, and the tripartite voice of the thunder in the conclusion). The poetry of "What the Thunder Said," in fact, vacillates between highly
charged sensations of sound and sight. Moreover, in the twenty-nine
lines of the "water-dripping song" (331–59), which Eliot told Ford Madox Ford were the only *"good* lines in *The Waste Land,"*[53] the poetry
also hovers between the precise representation of sound and the stylized rhythms of incantation:

> Here is no water but only rock
> Rock and no water and the sandy road
> The road winding above among the mountains
> Which are mountains of rock without water
> If there were water we should stop and drink
> Amongst the rock one cannot stop or think
> Sweat is dry and feet are in the sand
> If there were only water amongst the rock
> Dead mountain mouth of carious teeth that cannot spit
> Here one can neither stand nor lie nor sit
> There is not even silence in the mountains
> But dry sterile thunder without rain
> There is not even solitude in the mountains
> But red sullen faces sneer and snarl
> From doors of mudcracked houses
>   If there were water
>   And no rock
>   If there were rock
>   And also water
>   And water
>   A spring
>   A pool among the rock
>   If there were the sound of water only
>   Not the cicada
>   And dry grass singing
>   But sound of water over a rock
>   Where the hermit-thrush sings in the pine trees
>   Drip drop drip drop drop drop drop
>   But there is no water. . . .

This is a repetitive charm. It bespeaks an enormous amount of psychic energy working to displace images into an aural pattern. Both the speaker's anguish in the awful recognition that there is "no water" (once again, a negative pointing to a strong positive desire) and his pained apprehension of the "rock" around him are distanced by hypnotizing incantation. The rhythmic sequence "water . . . rock . . . Rock . . . water . . . road . . . road" lulls us so that we must force ourselves to notice certain clear but unpleasant images:

> Sweat is dry and feet are in the sand
> . . . .
> Dead mountain mouth of carious teeth that cannot spit . . .   ·
> . . . .
>   red sullen faces sneer and snarl
> From doors of mudcracked houses. . . .

Eliot's music here is a counterpoint between the themes of "rock" and "water," and it resolves itself into the second theme. By the fifth line the phrase "Here is no water" has been transformed into "If there were water," a conjurer's formula that swells in line 338 to "If there were only water." By line 347 the force of desire in the lines is so strong that the charm acquires the rhythm of a litany, a litany which calls into existence a spring, and a pool, but whose strongest magic lies in what follows. For a second, the poem breaks through to the only area of Eliot's visionary geography whose attraction is strong enough to counter the pressure exerted by his anxiety. The place "Where the hermit-thrush sings in the pine trees / Drip drop drip drop drop drop drop" is the emotional terrain of Eliot's childhood, the place where "the wind blows the water white and black" ("Prufrock"), the place where one can hear "The cry of quail and the whirling plover" (*Ash Wednesday*) and the place where one knows the "scent of pine and the woodthrush singing through the fog" ("Marina"). In no other poem, however, is the force of the vision as great as in these lines from *The Waste Land,* where the thrush's song stands as the culmination of an incantatory pattern twenty-eight lines long. Not even in the Hyacinth garden episode do we find an epiphany like this, where every hint of self-consciousness has been effaced by a complex of chiseled image and precisely heard song. The line "drip drop drip drop drop drop drop" is not only an accurate reproduction of the voice of the *Turdus aonalaschkae pallasii,* which Eliot heard as a boy;[54] it is also a piece of pure music which represents complete gratification. It is the only gift of water in the poem. Little wonder that these lines came to Eliot in a great surge of release, or that Eliot should have subsequently felt closer to them than to anything else in his poem.

The "water-dripping song" is a major poetic success. But the cost of that success turned out to be considerable. By introducing so strong a dose of incantation into his poetry, Eliot unleashed a chemical capable of dissolving the delicate balance between music and psychic drama that characterizes the work of his early maturity, a balance which he maintained for a while in common with his fellow modernists. Like Joyce, Pound, Lawrence, Stevens and Woolf, Eliot emerged from his juvenilia into a period where music and internal monologue were held in a powerful but precarious balance. But starting with the "water-dripping song," music—the tendency in post-symbolist verse toward a "musical pattern of sound and a musical pattern of the secondary meanings of the words which compose it"[55]—began to tip the scale. No better description of this changing equilibrium can be offered than Eliot's own: in his first essay on Milton, oblivious to the application of what he said to his own verse, he berated Joyce and Milton for "an auditory imagination abnormally sharpened at the expense of the visual." Eliot went on to say that, in Joyce after the middle of *Ulysses* and in *Paradise Lost,* "the inner meaning is separated from the surface, and tends to become something occult, or at least without effect upon the reader until fully understood" (OPP, 162). In the same essay, he contrasted Milton's involutions to those of Henry James, and concluded:

> The style of James certainly depends for its effect a good deal on the sound of a voice, James's own, painfully explaining. But the complication, with James, is due to a determination not to simplify, and in that simplification lose any of the real intricacies and by-paths of mental movement; whereas the complication of a Miltonic sentence is an active complication . . . deliberately introduced into what was a previously simplified and abstract thought. The dark angel here is not *thinking* or conversing, but making a speech carefully prepared for him; and the arrangement is for the sake of musical value, not for significance. . . . reality is no part of the intention. . . . syntax is determined by the musical significance, by the auditory imagination, rather than by the attempt to follow actual speech or thought. . . . The result with Milton is, in one sense of the word, *rhetoric* (OPP, 160–61).

In Eliot's case the allure of music was slightly different, but the effect was much the same. Starting with a genius for assonance, internal rhyme, and melodious cadence ("There will be time, there will be time / To prepare a face to meet the faces that you meet"), at the beginning of his career Eliot disciplined his propensities toward incantation. As a result of his association with Pound and Imagism, and his admiration for James, Flaubert and Joyce, his verse explored "intricacies and by-paths of mental movement." *The Waste Land* takes Eliot as far along that path as he was to go. The poem, that is, gives us Eliot's maximum push toward what Pound was to call the prose tradition in verse. As such it resembles a number of other modernist masterpieces, typically written in the middle and not at the end of their authors' careers: *The Tower, Women in Love,* the first half of *Ulysses,* "Sunday Morning," *To the Lighthouse.*

After *The Waste Land,* Eliot's writing, though it did not abandon the effort to map small movements of feeling and thought, did lose its keenness to dredge up the mind's subterranean reaches. As in the 1936 essay on Milton, Eliot retained a vestige of a distrust for the rhetorical deceptiveness of the auditory imagination, but at the same time allowed it to alter his creative work. As early as 1933 he would write that Matthew Arnold's account of poetry "does not perhaps go deep enough" because Arnold was not

> highly sensitive to the musical qualities of verse. His own occasional bad lapses arouse the suspicion; and so far as I can recollect he never emphasises this virtue of poetic style, this fundamental, in his criticism. What I call the "auditory imagination" is the feeling for syllable and rhythm, penetrating far below the conscious levels of thought and feeling, invigorating every word . . . (UPUC, 118–19).

By 1942 Eliot had so far acceded to the pull of one pole of his literary heritage that he recorded the lessons he had learned *entre deux guerres* under the title of "The Music of Poetry." And of course the major poem of his later years—the work that competes for our admiration with *The Waste Land* even as it calls attention to *The Waste Land*'s rejected virtues—is entitled *Four Quartets.* The path to the *Quartets* was one in which Eliot followed his symbolist inclinations to their conclusion. It is littered, however, with what can only be called embarrassments—what Conrad Aiken called "beautiful gibberish":[56]

> Where shall the word be found, where will the word
> Resound? Not here, there is not enough silence
> Not on the sea or on the islands, not
> On the mainland, in the desert or the rain land. . . .
>
>   *(Ash Wednesday)*

In his last major critical essay, "From Poe to Valéry" (1948), Eliot by implication locates himself at the end of the symbolist tradition. And nowhere is that essay clearer about how far he had come from *The Waste Land* than in the way it dismisses Poe and Poe's dreaming:

> What is lacking is not brain power, but that maturity of intellect which comes only with the maturing of the man as whole, the development and coordination of his various emotions. I am not concerned with any possible psychological or pathological explanation: it is enough for my purpose to record that the work of Poe is such as I should expect of a man of very exceptional mind and sensibility, whose emotional development has been in some respect arrested at an early age. *His most vivid imaginative realizations are the realization of a dream:* significantly, the ladies in his poems and tales are always ladies lost, or ladies vanishing before they can be em-

braced. Even in *The Haunted Palace,* where the subject appears to be his own weakness of alcoholism, the disaster has no moral significance; it is treated impersonally as an isolated phenomenon; it has not behind it the terrific force of such lines as those of François Villon when he speaks of his own fallen state (TCC, 35; emphasis mine).

In this passage Eliot characteristically reflects on himself while he analyzes a literary predecessor. In doing so he gives us an emblem of the metamorphosis that divides the two halves of his literary career. Here, to the best of his capabilities, T.S. Eliot, the literary arbiter of the English-speaking world in the year of his Nobel Prize, has left the nightmare-haunted figure of thirty-three-year-old Tom Eliot behind.

PART TWO

"A New Form and Style"
1923–34

CHAPTER SIX

New Life: *The Hollow Men*

May there not be superior beings amused with any graceful, though instinctive attitude my mind may fall into, as I am entertained with the alertness of a Stoat or the anxiety of a Deer? Though a quarrel in the streets is a thing to be hated, the energies displayed in it are fine; the commonest Man shows a grace in his quarrel— By a superior being our reasonings may take the same tone—though erroneous they may be fine— This is the very thing in which consists poetry; and if so it is not so fine a thing as philosophy— For the same reason that an eagle is not so fine a thing as a truth.

John Keats

It is often said that Eliot's movement from *The Waste Land* to *The Hollow Men* was a natural one, but nothing could be further from the truth.[1] In 1922, far from wishing to add a sequel to *The Waste Land*, Eliot wanted to put it and the pain associated with it out of his mind. In November of that year he wrote his friend, the poet and novelist Richard Aldington, *"The Waste Land* . . . is a thing of the past . . . I am now feeling toward a new form and style" (*Facs.*, xxv). And from Arnold Bennett's journal, we know something about what "new form" and new "style" he meant. According to what Eliot told Bennett, he had "definitely given up that [*Waste Land*] form of writing, and was now centred on dramatic writing. He wanted to write a drama of modern life (furnished flat sort of people) in a rhythmic prose 'perhaps with certain things in it accentuated by drum-beats.' "[2] As Eliot revised *The Waste Land* he was reading Aristophanes, and during the next several years he wrote a number of essays advocating the value of ritual-like stylization in drama, the cinema, ballet and poetry.[3] His conscious intentions were drawing him inexorably toward the sketches which he later entitled *Sweeney Agonistes: Fragments of an Aristophanic Melodrama.*[4] But, as Eliot admitted on more than one occasion, his conscious intentions were very poor guides to the important work he produced.[5] Between his statement to Aldington and the writing of the *Sweeney* sketches, Eliot's life altered and caused his interest in rhythmically stylized art to be grafted onto work that was more closely linked to *The Waste Land* than he had foreseen.

In 1923 Eliot lived through the worst year of his marriage. In April, Vivien, bedridden with "nerves" and colitis, nearly died from her doctor's treatment, and Eliot, constantly ill himself, became exhausted from his wife's demands, his job at the bank, and his journalism. It was then that he wrote John Quinn, "I am worn out, I cannot go on" (*Facs.*, xxvii). And it was then that Eliot, never one to permit his life to remain uncontrolled for too long, began reaching for new sources of support. In the mid-twenties he radically remade his life, from the way he spent his days to the way he ordered his ideas. The psychological, intellectual and spiritual ramifications of his remaking will provide the subject of chapter seven. But since it is impossible to approach *The Hollow Men* without some understanding of that change, I would like briefly to consider it here. In the introduction Eliot wrote in 1924 to a slim volume of Valéry and in the Clark Lectures he delivered in 1926, we can see the lines of force that were to control his new poetry and his new poetics.

In late 1920, when Eliot was collecting essays to be published in *The Sacred Wood*, he had compared Paul Valéry unfavorably to Dante and had criticized Valéry for "exorcising" philosophy from modern poetry (SW, 159–60). But by 1924, when Eliot published an introduction to Mark Wardle's translation of Valéry's "Le Serpent," he demonstrated an intimacy with Valéry's verse that indicated deep personal interest.[6] In it, Eliot wrote that Valéry "extended" and "completed" his personal emotions in *impersonal* verse. And in the way that he spoke, Eliot called up their common ancestry. Connecting what he called Valéry's "classicism" to the "tradition" of French verse, Eliot wrote that Valéry reintegrated "the symbolist movement into the great tradition." Further, Valéry represented the "completion" and the "explanation" of the "experimental work of the last generation," and he raised "the music, the fluidity" of Jules Laforgue to new heights through a poetic organization of a much higher intellectual order than Laforgue's.[7]

It is hardly necessary to point out how closely related these comments were to Eliot's thinking about his own poetry. For Eliot, who had begun his career as an imitator of Laforgue, to write that Valéry was the "completion" and "explanation" of Laforgue, he must have already questioned some of his most cherished assumptions. After many years of vacillating between a drive to represent his inner life and a drive to order it, he now was willing to let the balance tip toward the "intellect" and toward "classicism." In the central statement of his introduction, already alluded to in chapter one, he made this unmistakable. Valéry, in Eliot's words, recognized "the truth that not our feelings, but the pattern which we may make of our feelings, is the centre of value."

And though this precept went against the grain of Eliot's creative impulse, for the rest of his career Eliot strove to impose it on his poetry. Looking at the Clark Lectures, which Eliot began to prepare in the spring of 1924, we can see at least some of what this meant. In what follows, I would like to examine the unpublished manuscript of those lectures at some length.[8] Delivered at Cambridge University in early 1926 and then forgotten, the Clark Lectures supply information heretofore unavailable about Eliot's new critical attitudes and the way they affected *The Hollow Men.*

These eight "Lectures on the Metaphysical Poetry of the Seventeenth Century" applied new standards to old preoccupations—the problems of poetic excellence and poetic tradition. Less than four years after he championed the "massive music of Donne" (SE, 250), Eliot now argued that Donne's sensibility represented a *dissolution* of the fusion of thought and feeling to be found in earlier metaphysical poetry—the medieval work of Dante and Cavalcanti.[9] Whereas, he asserted, the sensibility of the medieval poets was "classical" and "ontological"—rooted in man's orientation toward absolute value—the sensibility of the Renaissance metaphysicals was "romantic" and "psychological":[10] Donne, instead of contemplating metaphysical ideas for their intrinsic value, diminished his intellectual seriousness by writing poetry that portrays a mind "entertaining" these ideas. As Eliot put it in his second lecture, "Instead of pursuing the meaning of the idea, letting it flow into the usual sequence of [medieval] thought, [Donne] *arrests* it, in order to extract every possible ounce of the emotion suspended in it."

In contrast to this "romantic" subordination of thought to feeling, Eliot endorsed the medieval wisdom of Richard of St. Victor, Aquinas, Cavalcanti and Dante. These writers, he said, were interested only in the impersonal value of feeling and thought. They extended the frontiers of the mundane world by the intellectual path of contemplation, "the development and subsumption of emotion and feeling through intellect into the vision of God." Poetry or prose, their work represented an ontological inquiry into the nature of existence. This was true even in the erotic verse of Dante and Cavalcanti, where a statement of the effect of the beloved upon the lover in contemplation served "solely . . . to suggest the beauty and dignity of the object contemplated." Consequently Trecento love poets used both images and language more rigorously and more seriously than Donne.[11]

As suggestive as these comments are in relation to *The Hollow Men,* Eliot's explanation of their source is even more so. In the introduction to his lectures, he announced that the pivot on which "the whole of my case turns" was his reading and interpretation of the *Vita Nuova.*[12] And some of the most revealing of Eliot's observations are those in which he used examples of the *Vita Nuova*'s handling of erotic material to criticize the degenerate "modern" sensibility. For example, in the third lecture he accused Donne of conflating the human and the divine aspects of love, and went on to say:

> Donne, the modern man, is imprisoned in the embrace of his own feelings. There is little suggestion of [Dante's] adoration, of worship. And an attitude like that of Donne leads naturally to one of two things: to the Tennysonian happy marriage—not very different from Donne's own—which is one sort of bankruptcy; or to the collapse of the hero of Huysmans' *En Route: Mon dieu, que c'est donc bête:* It leads in fact to most of modern literature; for whether you seek the Absolute in marriage, adultery or debauchery, it is all one—you are seeking in the wrong place.

In the fourth lecture Eliot continued his argument in relation to lines from Donne's "The Blossome":

> There is a great deal of the modern "recherche de l'absolu," the disappointed romanticism, the vexation or resignation at finding the world other than one wanted it to be. The literature of disillusionment is the disillusionment of immaturity. It is in this way that I have ventured to affirm that Dante is more a man of the world than is Donne.

Eliot obviously has someone besides Donne in mind when he writes of the "disillusionment of immaturity." His remarks are self-admonishing. He criticizes Donne for writing the kind of poetry he himself had recently admired and imitated. Any doubt of this is erased when he goes on to include Laforgue in his line of attack—the principal model of his early poetry and the poet who provided him access to Donne. According to Eliot's eighth lecture, Laforgue's writings had the same metaphysical origin as Donne's: Laforgue "had an innate craving for order: that is, that every feeling should have its intellectual equivalent, its philosophical justification, and that every idea should have its emotional equivalent, its sentimental justification." Laforgue also shared with Donne the need for "a *Vita Nuova* to justify, dignify and integrate his sentiments toward the jeune fille in a system of the universe." Instead, what Laforgue wrote, Eliot said in his third lecture, was a "poetry of adolescence" unintegrated into an adult view of the world: he thus "remains, for us, imprisoned within his adolescence, with a philosophy which should have been mature. . . . For Laforgue to have passed into a larger life would have necessitated a violent struggle, too violent for so delicate a constitution."

It was Dante, not Laforgue, who had "passed into a larger life" and then embodied the experience in the *Vita Nuova.* Eliot pointed out that the *Vita Nuova* used the same material as Laforgue's verse: "the material of adolescence; but it is handled by a mature man with a philosophy which assigned a place to such experience." To Eliot's mind, therefore, the *Vita Nuova* came to constitute a "record of the method of utilizing, *transforming instead of discarding, the emotions of adolescence;* the record of a discovery analogous to those concerning the use of the waste products of coal-tar in industry. The result of this discovery was a real extension of the area of emotion, and an attitude both more 'spiritual' and more 'worldly' than that of Donne or that of Tennyson or that of Laforgue" (from the third and fourth lectures; emphasis mine).

The relation of these remarks to Eliot's introduction to Valéry is striking. "The *Vita Nuova*," Eliot said in the third Clark lecture, "is to my thinking a record of actual experience reshaped into a particular form." If we put equal weight on both the phrases "actual experience" and "reshaped into a particular form," we begin to see what he was getting at. The *Vita Nuova,* "transforming instead of discarding" Dante's experience of adolescence, "reshapes" it by later reflection. The thought is clearer in Eliot's 1929 essay on Dante:

> The attitude of Dante to the fundamental experience of the *Vita Nuova* can only be understood by accustoming ourselves to find meaning in *final causes* rather than in origins. It is not, I believe, meant as a description of what he *consciously* felt on his meeting with Beatrice, but rather a description of what that meant on mature reflection upon it. The final cause is the attraction towards God (SE, 234).

This essay also hints at what Eliot thought the "particular form" of the *Vita Nuova* really was. "The system of Dante's organization of sensibility," he adds, is embodied in "the contrast between higher and lower carnal love, the transition from Beatrice living to Beatrice dead, rising to the Cult of the Virgin" (SE, 235).

Eliot's reading of the *Vita Nuova* would become more common as the twentieth century wore on. Beginning with the assumption that Trecento poetry gives an "exact statement of the visual impression made by the beloved upon the lover,"[13] Eliot assumes that the poems in the *Vita Nuova* present stages in the growth of a young man's feelings "from Beatrice living to Beatrice dead," which is to say from the early poems that express the selfish love-struck emotions of an adolescent to the last sonnet, which shows a "pilgrim spirit" directed heavenward and blessed with "a new perception born of grieving Love."[14] Appropriately, in the Clark Lectures Eliot cites a long passage in which Dante addresses a group of ladies and announces that the quality of his feelings for Beatrice has changed.[15] In this emphasis, as in so much else, Eliot anticipates Charles Singleton, who described the *Vita Nuova* as a movement "from love to caritas."[16]

The best way to understand Eliot's new praise for the *Vita Nuova,* however, is not to compare it to the remarks of other Dantisti but to see it in the context of the forces that had energized his own poetry. Eliot's thematic center of gravity, the problem and the opportunity of his poetry, had always been the dilemma of how to reconcile an emotional inclination toward romantic material and an equally strong distrust of the romantic view of the world. The *Vita Nuova*, Eliot now saw, handled the claims of heart and head in a way that reconciled instead of aggravating the destructive tension between them; it illustrated a way to emphasize "not our feelings, but the pattern which we may make of our feelings." Accepting that model, he rejected Laforgue and Donne, whose ironies now seemed to him merely the "disillusionment of immaturity." From the first poems he wrote for *The Hollow Men* to the completion of *Ash Wednesday*, Eliot set out to make Dante's "method of utilizing, transforming instead of discarding, the emotions of adolescence" his own. His career had reached one of those turning points that he later described in "American Literature and the American Language":

> Some of my strongest impulse to original development, in early years, has come from thinking: "here is a man who has said something, long ago or in another language, which somehow corresponds to what I want to say now; let me see if I can't do what he has done, in my own language—in the language of my own place and time" (TCC, 56).

The question of whether adapting what Dante had "done" in the *Vita Nuova* led to an improvement or a decline in Eliot's poetry, of course, is another matter. The new poems did not attempt anything like *The Waste Land*'s psychological portraiture, and they avoided *The Waste Land*'s dramatic intensity. Unquestionably, though, Eliot was no longer able to yoke the conflicting impulses that had sustained his earlier work. His poetry advanced in the only direction it could go. And, as we shall see, Eliot's adaption of the *Vita Nuova*'s "method" encouraged as much stylistic experimentation as it foreclosed: Dante provided a suggestive but general strategy for handling romantic material, and Eliot had to "make it new" not only with "the language of [his] own time" but with new poetic forms. To understand how, consider the development of *The Hollow Men*.

2

Doris's Dream Songs

I

Eyes that last I saw in tears
Through division
Here in death's dream kingdom
The golden vision reappears
I see the eyes but not the tears
This is my affliction

This is my affliction
Eyes I shall not see again
Eyes of decision
Eyes I shall not see unless

At the door of death's other kingdom
Where, as in this,
The eyes outlast a little while
A little while outlast the tears
And hold us in derision.

II

The wind sprang up at four o'clock
The wind sprang up and broke the bells
Swinging between life and death
Here, in death's dream kingdom
The waking echo of confusing strife
Is it a dream or something else
When the surface of the blackened river
Is a face that sweats with tears?
I saw across the blackened river
The camp fire shake with alien spears.
Here, across death's other river
The Tartar horsemen shake their spears.

III

This is the dead land
This is cactus land
Here the stone images
Are raised, here they receive
The supplication of a dead man's hand
Under the twinkle of a fading star.

Is it like this
In death's other kingdom
Waking alone
At the hour when we are
Trembling with tenderness
Lips that would kiss
Form prayers to broken stone.

The earliest-written of the fragments that led to *The Hollow Men* was
"Song to the Opherian," a lyric that Eliot published by itself in 1921
and then included in the *Waste Land* manuscript.[17] Rejected for *The
Waste Land,* "Song" provided a useful bridge to the twentieth-century
Vita Nuova Eliot wanted to write: not only did it sound the theme of
tormented sexual desire, but (at least in the *Waste Land* manuscript ver-
sion) it envisioned a change of life "after thirty years." In the *Chapbook*
for November 1924, Eliot recast "Song" as the second of "Doris's Dream
Songs," a suite of three poems that opened with an explicit nod toward
Dante in the form of a poem that began, "Eyes that last I saw in tears."

Given Eliot's notion that the *Vita Nuova* describes the "reshaping" of
adolescent feelings by "mature reflection," it is not surprising that his
point de départ should have been the chapters after Beatrice's death.
Starting in chapter XXXII, the *Vita Nuova* recounts how Dante's tears

and the salvation they promise are endangered by the attentions of a compassionate lady at a window. Dante almost succumbs to the temptation of this new and more worldly love, but recovers in time to rebuke himself and chastise his eyes for their treason. Inspired in part by the canzone that begins "The eyes that weep for pity of the heart/ Have wept so long that their grief languisheth,/ And they have no more tears to weep"[18] and in part by the poems that follow it, Eliot's "Eyes that last I saw in tears" accomplishes two things. It adapts Dante's self-rebuke to his own purposes. And, retaining its communications with the *Vita Nuova*, it places what might have been a self-pitying episode of poetic psychobiography within the "ontological" co-ordinates of an eternal moral universe—what Eliot refers to in the poem as "death's kingdom."

In order to understand Dante, Eliot wrote, we must "conceive of an age (of many ages) when human beings cared somewhat about the salvation of the 'soul,' but not about each other as 'personalities'" (SE, 233). Thus the "I" of "Eyes that last I saw in tears" is less a psychologically complex personality than a type of the general spiritual life. The poem presents that moment in the "attraction toward God" when the soul becomes aware that by itself it may not have the capacity to sustain a spiritual attachment to a loved one who is no longer present. (For Dante, the dead Beatrice; and, I suspect, for Eliot the wife from whom he had become emotionally estranged.) Eliot makes use of modernist concision to suggest the instant when an awareness of something outside the self becomes fused with a moment of self-recognition. From the opening lines ("Eyes that last I saw in tears/ Through division"), it is impossible to tell whether the eyes and the tears are the speaker's or the beloved's, and thus impossible to determine whether the "division" is a division between the speaker and his beloved or a figure of the speaker's internal division. The poem's suggestion, of course, is that the division is *both* physical and psychological, and that the combination of the two has caused the speaker's fall from wholeness and meaning into the unreality of "death's dream kingdom."

For the speaker to heal the division and enter "death's other kingdom," he must have the aid of penitential tears, which he can no longer summon. The speaker's "affliction" is to "see the eyes but not the tears." At first this seems to mean he sees his beloved's eyes but not her tears. In the second stanza, though, it becomes clear that most of his horror arises because in "this" kingdom *his* eyes outlast his tears:

> At the door of death's other kingdom
> Where, *as in this,*
> The eyes outlast a little while
> A little while outlast the tears. . . .

The speaker's awareness that his inadequacy has caused his fall from a former state of contrition is what really gives the beloved's eyes their power to "hold us in derision."

It is worth noting that "Eyes that last I saw in tears" presents a moment of self-accusation differently from the way Eliot treated the same subject in his earlier poetry. His earlier practice had been to couch such a moment in a double-edged irony that both lashed and excused his subject. Now Eliot simply presents it as a quiet moment of awareness. Compare "Eyes that last I saw in tears" with these lines from "Prufrock":

> And I have known the eyes already, known them all—
> The eyes that fix you in a formulated phrase,
> And when I am formulated, sprawling on a pin,
> When I am pinned and wriggling on the wall,
> Then how should I begin . . . ?

"Prufrock" is a psychological portrait of the anxieties of egocentric confinement, and Eliot presents the rising intensity of Prufrock's uneasiness through Laforguian ironies of diction: an unexpected latinate usage suggests sudden discomfort and psychological constraint; the indecorous but energetic present participles render Prufrock's increasingly uncomfortable, though ambivalent, response to the idea of becoming something less than the fastidious idealist of his self-image. In contrast, "Eyes that last I saw in tears" is what Eliot called "ontological." It emphasizes the elements of a speaker's vision and not the speaker himself and so is not directed toward presenting the psychological mannerisms of a dramatic posture. Revealingly, Eliot's polysyllables are no longer ironic. The stanzas of "Eyes that last I saw in tears" give the impression of opening and closing with polysyllabic words, but Eliot does not use the unexpected formality of the words to mock the seriousness of their meanings. When the word "derision" chimes the second stanza closed, the effect is to underline the justness and authority of a learned word and to communicate a self-rebuke that is not lightened by a sense of playfulness. (Compare the decision/derision rhyme here with the play on "decisions" and "revisions" in "Prufrock.")

The second of "Doris's Dream Songs" was a revised version of "Song to the Opherian" called "The wind sprang up at four o'clock." In "Doris's Dream Songs," the poem advances the speaker's fall from contrition and from union with his beloved. "The wind sprang up" spatializes a feeling of division by situating the speaker across the river from what he is watching, and suggests a feeling of impoverished alienation by locating fire and action on the *other* side of the divide. Meanwhile, the river of tears, parodying the river Lethe in *Purgatorio* XXXIII, effects the speaker's separation and becomes "a face that sweats with tears." As in "Eyes that last I saw in tears," these tears are an image of the speaker's own tears telescoped with those of his beloved, but here the image is darker—a demonic reminder that without contrition tears have no more healing power than sweat.

The conclusion of "Doris's Dream Songs" occurs in "This is the dead

land," a poem that would eventually become *The Hollow Men,* part III.
Although the poem's desolate imagery and sense of futility have led
readers to assume it was an extension of *The Waste Land,* it too seems
to be an outgrowth of Eliot's study of the *Vita Nuova.* In the *Vita Nuova,*
after Beatrice dies, Florence becomes for Dante an empty vessel, and
he alludes to the city of Lamentations in his cry of grief: "the whole
city came to be as it were widowed and despoiled of all dignity."[19] In a
moment of recognition, then, Dante implicitly identifies Florence with
the city of Lamentations and comes to understand the significance of
his native city through the symbolic pattern of its Biblical antitype. This
is precisely the action of "This is the dead land," which presents the
impression of suddenly identifying a familiar landscape with a pattern
remembered from the Old Testament. Hence the poem's repeated and
emphatic use of demonstratives, as in a moment of blinding recognition:[20]

> *This* is the dead land
> *This* is cactus land
> *Here* the stone images
> Are raised, *here* they receive
> The supplication of a dead man's hand
> Under the twinkle of a fading star. . . .

The familiar landscape of "This is the dead land," later amplified in
The Hollow Men, part II, is the landscape of romantic feeling and romantic poetry. In attempting to "utilize" and "transform" instead of
"discarding" the "emotions of adolescence" in his new poetry, Eliot returned to the poets of his own adolescence—especially Shelley.[21] Eliot's
essay "Swinburne as Poet" (1920) had compared Shelley and Dante to
Swinburne (SW, 146-48), and his Clark Lectures contained an extended comparative analysis of Shelley's "To a Sky-Lark" and Crashaw's "The Weeper."[22] Though the latter was not kind to Shelley, it
indicated a contemporary rereading that can be detected in "This is the
dead land" and in *The Hollow Men.* Eliot's lightly-touched allusions
in these poems to Shelley's Sky-Lark, that unseen "star of heaven" whose
music is like "vernal showers/ On the twinkling grass,"[23] help him call
up the emotions of adolescence. More glances than allusions, they do
not enchant the reader with the charm of adolescent love as *The Waste
Land* enchants with Wagner's *Frisch Weht der Wind;* they merely recapitulate the characteristic note of adolescence as it is remembered in
the "mature reflection" of later life.[24] "This is the dead land," reflecting
Eliot's reading of the *Vita Nuova,* neither mocks adolescent emotion nor
regards it as the ultimate source of value: the speaker looks back at it
feelingly but with a sense of its final inability to put him at peace. "The
hour when we are / Trembling with tenderness" is apprehended not
with the irony of "Prufrock" nor with the exaggerated hope and de-

spair of *The Waste Land,* but with compassion and pity. The speaker remembers the seductiveness of such hours, but has come to realize that "the love of man and woman" can only be "explained and made reasonable by the higher love" (SE, 234–35). That he does not feel the stirrings of that higher love only increases the poem's sadness.

3

Three Poems

I

Eyes I dare not meet in dreams
In death's dream kingdom
These do not appear:
There, the eyes are
Sunlight on a broken column
There, is a tree swinging
And voices are
In the wind's singing
More distant and more solemn
Than a fading star.

Let me be no nearer
In death's dream kingdom
Let me also wear
Such deliberate disguises
Rat's coat, crowskin, crossed staves
In a field
Behaving as the wind behaves
No nearer—

Not that final meeting
In the twilight kingdom
With eyes I dare not meet in dreams.

II

Eyes that last I saw in tears
Through division
Here in death's dream kingdom
The golden vision reappears
I see the eyes but not the tears
This is my affliction

This is my affliction
Eyes I shall not see again
Eyes of decision
Eyes I shall not see unless
At the door of death's other kingdom
Where, as in this,
The eyes outlast a little while

A little while outlast the tears
And hold us in derision.

III

The eyes are not here
There are no eyes here
In this valley of dying stars
In this hollow valley
This broken jaw of our lost kingdoms

In this last of meeting places
We grope together
And avoid speech
Gathered on this beach of the tumid river

Sightless, unless
The eyes reappear
As the perpetual star
Multifoliate rose
Of death's twilight kingdom

The hope only
Of empty men.

Eliot began to tinker with "Doris's Dream Songs" almost as soon as the suite was published. But at least at first, he made no radical changes in its shape. In a sequel called "Three Poems," published in the January 1925 *Criterion,* he experimented with different moments in what is recognizably the same spiritual journey. The emotional curve of "Doris's Dream Songs" had moved from an awareness of the spiritual inadequacy of natural affection ("Eyes that last I saw in tears") to a sense of alienation from reality ("The wind sprang up at four o'clock") to a final recognition that the landscape of romantic love is the landscape of Lamentations ("This is the dead land"). Retaining only "Eyes that last I saw in tears," "Three Poems" begins at an even earlier point on the same emotional curve and ends at a point beyond "This is the dead land."

The first of the "Three Poems" (and later *The Hollow Men,* part II) is a poem that begins "Eyes I dare not meet in dreams." It presents a speaker resisting self-knowledge during the psychic interval between a first dim awareness of his own spiritual inadequacy and a full consciousness of it. The speaker "dares" not meet the eyes of his beloved, for he is sufficiently aware of what they would make him formulate about himself. He struggles to maintain the pretense that his responsibility can be evaded by effacing his soul behind "deliberate" but less than human "disguises": "Rat's coat, crowskin, crossed staves." And he implies that the eyes and voice of his beloved have been transfigured and now exist only in the aesthetic landscape of his imagination in the forms of "Sunlight on a broken column" and "voices . . ./ More distant and more solemn/ Than a fading star." But all the while his guilt draws him toward a confrontation with his beloved's eyes and with his own spiritual insufficiency. And as we hear in the inflections of his internal monologue, the pull is strong enough to overcome considerable psychic resistance ("No nearer— / Not that") and bring him home to the self-knowledge of "that final meeting/ In the twilight kingdom" where he will meet the eyes last seen in tears.

After that meeting, "Three Poems" enters an emotional landscape even more desolate than the one in "This is the dead land." Eliot's method of suggesting this new desolation, moreover, embodies the peculiar poetic virtue of this phase of his career. The third song, "The eyes are not here," reproduces the landscape of the previous songs but reproduces it as seen from a changed angle of spiritual vision: whereas the speaker of "Eyes I dare not meet in dreams" was *reassured* that his beloved's eyes were drowned in sunlight and "do not appear," now he is preoccupied and near despair because "There are no eyes here." The landscape is apprehended, in other words, as a manifestation of the *lack* of something essential. And the speaker's attitude toward the landscape is no longer merely aesthetic appreciation: the aura of romantic sublimity has been purged from the objects of his perception, and what he once saw as a "fading star" he now sees as just one of the "dying stars / In this hollow valley."

Although *The Hollow Men* has been compared to "minimalist" art, the stylistic provenance of the poems we have been discussing is hardly so avant-garde. Eliot indicates shifts in the spiritual orientation of his speaker by allowing the speaker's emotional apprehension of the objects of his perception to change while the objects themselves remain the same. This procedure is a variation of the techniques that Ezra Pound had used a decade before to write less religious but equally subtle dramatizations of shifting consciousness. Without digressing too much from the text of "Three Poems," it is worth noting that the "songs" not only show Eliot retreating from the ironic procedures of *The Waste Land,* they also show him re-immersing himself in other, non-ironic techniques he wished to preserve.

The ending Eliot wrote for "Three Poems" anticipates the way he would end *The Hollow Men.*[25] When the spiritual orientation of the suite's speaker becomes so divorced from worldly vision that his internal landscape is transformed into a Biblical emblem of broken pride ("This broken jaw of our lost kingdoms"), he begins to sense that the missing eyes of his beloved may have been the representatives of divine light. In his now-moral imagination the eyes of his beloved are telescoped with the eyes of the Virgin Mary, Dante's "perpetual star" and "multifoliate rose."[26] But since this has occurred only after romantic passion has been found wanting, the intuition can paradoxically be "The hope only/ Of empty men": after the heart's desires have been concentrated on one object and that object disappears, the heart cannot return to lower desires. Its love for the world is over, a condition that feels like the emptiness of death but may lead to the spiritual love. If it does, the lesson of the *Vita Nuova* has been learned: "not to expect more from *life* than it can give or more from *human* beings than they can give; to look to *death* for what life cannot give" (SE, 235). The ambiguity between death and birth at the end of "Three Poems" anticipates the same ambiguity in the "whimper" that concludes *The Hollow Men*—the whimper that, Helen Gardner pointed out, was both the "whimper of defeat" and also "the whimper of a little creature drawing its first breath."[27]

The combined fragments of "Doris's Dream Songs" and "Three Poems" thus compose a single spiritual drama having what we may call a double movement. Psychologically, the drama moves downward from resistance to submission, but spiritually it moves upward from proud isolation through humility to a thirst for divine love. Eliot hinted at this doubleness when he sent Ottoline Morrell some of the *Hollow Men* manuscripts in late 1924.[28] More precisely, he told her that he had laid down the principles of what he was doing in a lecture he had just given at Cambridge on Chapman, Dostoevsky[29] and Dante. And although the lecture has not survived, Eliot's description of it connects it with the arguments of his 1925 essay on Chapman,[30] passages in the Clark Lectures on Dostoevsky and Chapman[31] and a long section of Eliot's 1934 essay on John Marston.[32] I quote from the last, which is the most accessible:

> What distinguishes poetic drama from prosaic drama is a kind of doubleness in the action, as if it took place on two planes at once. In this it is different from allegory, in which the abstraction is something conceived, not something differently felt, and from symbolism (as in the plays of Maeterlinck) in which the tangible world is deliberately diminished. . . . We sometimes feel, in following the words and behaviour of some of the characters of Dostoevsky, that they are living at once on the plane that we know and on some other plane of reality from which we are shut out. . . . More fitfully, and with less power, this doubleness appears in the work of Chapman. . . .
> . . . as we familiarize ourselves with [Marston's *Sophonisba*] we perceive a pattern behind the pattern into which the characters deliberately involve themselves; the kind of pattern which we perceive in our own lives only at rare moments of inattention and detachment, drowsing in sunlight. It is the pattern drawn by what the ancient world called Fate; subtilized by Christianity into mazes of delicate theology . . . (ED, 161–62, 165).

These are the terms, then, that in 1924 Eliot had begun to use for understanding his own life (perhaps as a result of some "rare moment . . . drowsing in sunlight" like the one that reappears at the end of "Burnt Norton"). And these are the terms he applied to the suite he was writing. No less than one of Chapman's or Dostoevsky's characters, the speaker of Eliot's "Songs" lives out different patterns of life on different planes of existence. Thereafter, of course, this kind of doubleness becomes one of the constants of Eliot's verse. *Sweeney Agonistes,* "The Journey of the Magi," "A Song for Simeon," "Marina," *Ash Wednesday* and each of the *Four Quartets* all turn on the perception that the way up and the way down are the same. And though Eliot is usually said to have discovered this perception in St. John of the Cross, it is far more likely that he found elaborated in St. John what he had already proven on his pulses and encountered in the pages of the *Vita Nuova.*

4

Sometime between the composition of his suite of "Three Poems" and its publication, Eliot wrote "We are the hollow men," a fragment significantly unlike any of its immediate predecessors. For one thing, it reintroduces an edge of self-mockery into Eliot's verse.

> We are the hollow men
> We are the stuffed men
> Leaning together
> Headpiece filled with *straw. Alas!*
> Our dried voices, when
> We whisper together
> Are quiet and *meaningless*
> As wind *in dry grass*
> Or rats' feet over *broken glass. . . .*

The poem's broken rhythms and disconcerting half-rhymes prepared for the lines of *The Hollow Men* we all remember, the still-to-be-written last poem, in which Eliot took the bounce of a nursery rhyme and suggested a feeling of conscious and intense futility:

> *Here we go round the prickly pear*
> *Prickly pear prickly pear. . . .*

The poetics of "We are the hollow men" are as different from any of the "Songs" as its tone. Instead of "presenting" a psychic event from the inside, the poem consists of a group of speakers voicing a single emotional mood, as a Greek chorus might voice the prevailing mood at the end of a tragedy. Hence the shift in point of view from the impersonal "I" that had dominated the "Songs"[33] to an insistent use of "we."

Moreover, the members of Eliot's new chorus were not anonymous. When he affixed the Guy Fawkes Day epigraph to "We are the hollow men," Eliot gave one of his voices the rudiments of a local habitation and a name, and conferred on his new poem a relation to the outside world that was more straightforward than that of the "Songs." Being presentations of timeless spiritual conditions, the "Songs" used allusions only to formulate certain general states of the imagination—the adolescent romantic imagination of Shelley, say, or the religious imagination of Dante and the Bible. "We are the hollow men," though, refers to the Guy Fawkes story and invites readers to use historical information to make sense of what the poem is about. The poem is consequently less rarefied than the "Songs," more "objective," more like the dramatic monologue of a historical figure. It runs the risk, though, that readers will lose sight of its emotional subject in the process of pursuing its historical references.

Eliot clearly did not write "We are the hollow men" to fill a predetermined space in the "Songs." He typed the poem out without indicating on the typescript that it was part of a larger sequence, and he published it alone in the French periodical *Commerce* as "Poème inédit."[34] Only afterwards did he decide where the poem belonged. (Decide, in fact, that he would have to rearrange everything.) Between sometime in mid-November 1924, when he typed out the fragment, and November 30, 1924, when he sent the typescript to Ottoline Morrell, Eliot penciled in a new sequence title—*The Hollow Men*—and a roman numeral one. It was at that point that "We are the hollow men" became the opening poem in an entirely new suite.

What Eliot had in mind for *The Hollow Men* becomes apparent from the shape he gave to the sequence as it grew into its final form. In the *Dial* for March 1925 he published a three-part version that consisted of an opening choral chant ("We are the hollow men") and two dramatic episodes ("Eyes I dare not meet in dreams" and "The eyes are not here"). Then in November 1925 he reintroduced a third dramatic episode ("This is the dead land"), and framed the suite by the addition of a concluding choral ode (*"Here we go round the prickly pear"*). His very last act was to append the epigraph "Mistah Kurtz—he dead."

Eliot's changes gave *The Hollow Men* its symmetrical frame and its controlling narrative. In making them, he recapitulated the last stages of composing *The Waste Land*. The title of *The Waste Land* and what now seems to be its controlling myth (the Grail legend) had been late additions to the poem: Eliot used them to frame and unify his fragments, and in the process introduced a "spurious plot" that long obscured *The Waste Land*'s lyrical center.[35] Reworking *The Hollow Men* for book publication, Eliot repeated the same operations. Once again he wanted to overlay the formal and ethical shapeliness of a clear narrative pattern onto material he was afraid had too little shape. So he layered the narratives of Guy Fawkes and *Heart of Darkness* over his drama of salvation. And once again he sent readers hunting through history and literature to reconstruct the skeletons of stories that at best suggestively mirror the action that is *there* on the page.

What was new in Eliot's revisions of *The Hollow Men* came from his interest in stage drama and his work on *Sweeney Agonistes*. He had since 1922 considered the creation of ritually stylized drama his most important project.[36] And in November 1924, when Eliot rearranged *The Hollow Men* around "We are the hollow men," that preoccupation was foremost in his mind. When he sent Ottoline Morrell the *Hollow Men* typescripts, he told her that his new sequence of poems was an avocation of his more revolutionary play, which he had been too weak to go on with. And the final form he gave *The Hollow Men* in 1925 was a form derived from the traditions of drama. Specifically, it was derived from Eliot's then strongly held view that "the drama was originally ritual" and that it was born in "the beating of a drum."[37]

Eliot chose one of *The Hollow Men*'s narrative or "mythical" overlays because it was a story still celebrated in popular ritual. The English people do not simply remember the fate of Guy Fawkes, they re-enact it every year. And the forms of their re-enactment partake of that primitive vitality of rhythm and style which, Eliot said in 1923, was the source of "*all* art," especially poetry.[38] We get some feeling for what Eliot was thinking of as he revised *The Hollow Men* when we consider his notion of how a music hall performance affects the average Englishman. A member of the music hall audience, Eliot once wrote, participates in a give-and-take with the larger-than-life figures on the stage and "transcends himself . . . unconsciously lives the myth, seeing life in the light of the imagination."[39] It was just such an unconscious fusion of life and meaningful shape that Eliot wanted to accomplish when he put Guy Fawkes at the center of the suite's new choruses, and when he composed them in the irresistible rhythms of popular verse.

Like *Murder in the Cathedral, The Hollow Men* begins and ends with a chorus. And as Eliot says of the old women of Canterbury, the voices of *The Hollow Men* reflect "in their emotion the significance of the action" that occurs around them (OPP, 86). Only in the case of *The Hollow Men,* the circumjacent drama is more delicately rendered. The framing choruses of *The Hollow Men* were meant to generalize the spiritual action of the poem into broad emotional statements of emptiness. Their nursery-rhyme rhythms act as resonators for the tentative accents of the middle lyrics. And their rehearsal of the yearly expiration and return of Guy Fawkes endows Eliot's central pattern of abasement and redemption with the strong coloring of the popular imagination. It is just a step, in fact, from "*Here we go round the prickly pear*" to the choruses of *Sweeney Agonistes,* written a short time later:

> Any old tree will do for me
> Any old wood is just as good. . . .

In all probability Eliot regarded the choruses of *The Hollow Men* as preparations for the more "revolutionary" choruses of *Sweeney.* Even thematically, the two works are counterparts. No less than Sweeney himself, the members of *The Hollow Men*'s chorus return "from the dead to tell the story of [their] horrible purgation, [their] divestment of the love of created beings. . . ."[40]

When he refashioned *The Hollow Men,* Eliot intended to inject the "Songs" with the kind of vigor his studies told him was at the heart of popular drama. Whether the poem succeeds as he intended, is another story. Certainly, although the formal unity of *The Hollow Men* is open to question, the success of the poem's choruses cannot be denied. As Elisabeth Schneider put it, "the final line has gained the currency of a proverb."[41] But in looking back at how the poem changed, we are entitled to ask at what price that particular success was achieved. When Eliot grafted his dramatic concerns onto his suite in progress, he altered its organic coherence and all but obscured its origins. I for one am inclined to regret that an exquisite miniature of the *Vita Nuova* was for decades obscured from view. And I suspect that, at one time or other, Eliot shared my doubts. Consider the pains he took to preserve "Eyes that last I saw in tears" and "The wind sprang up at four o'clock" in his *Collected Poems.*

5

After *The Hollow Men,* Eliot virtually abandoned the procedures of Imagism for a less concentrated and more discursive style. Like Joyce halfway through the composition of *Ulysses,* his interest in spare treatment dried up and was replaced by a fascination with musical elaboration. And although *The Hollow Men*'s stylized handling of popular material resurfaced in *Sweeney Agonistes* and played a small part in Eliot's (and Auden's) plays, it too now seems a backwater left behind by the tide of Eliot's late manner. Probably *The Hollow Men* is best thought of as an attempt to execute the matter of the *Vita Nuova* by means that proved unsuitable to the personal and poetic demands of Eliot's new style. As such it may be considered a thematic but not a formal forerunner of *Ash Wednesday.* There was one formal development in *The Hollow Men,* though, that did point forward instead of back.

Eliot, as we saw at the beginning of this chapter, became fascinated with the poetry of Paul Valéry and with the way Valéry had "classicized" the symbolist tradition. His introduction to "Le Serpent," moreover, commented particularly on the way Valéry gave a firm structure to the loose revery of symbolist verse. Valéry, Eliot said, appropriated the fluid meditations of the symbolists and, through the medium of strict versification, created something "static," something "which knows its end and has reached it; which can afford to stand, changeless, like a statue."[42] And implicit in Eliot's praise was something more, an admiration for the method behind Valéry's achievement. Although Eliot never got round to articulating it in the 1924 introduction, he was impressed with the way Valéry had been able to impose a static order on the rapid movements of symbolist verse without diminishing their expressiveness. In so doing, he created a meditative form in which succeeding phases of feeling and thought became impersonal and inevitable—a form whose movements resembled the elements of rigorous disquisition. This emerges later from one of Eliot's tributes to Valéry. On that occasion Eliot compared Gray's "Elegy," his personal touchstone for English meditative verse,[43] to Valéry's "Cimetière marin" and told his French audience: "Le poème de Valéry a, ce que j'appelle, la structure philosophique, une organisation non pas [here Eliot speaks of the "Elegy"] seulement de réactions successives à une situation donnée, mais de réactions à ses premières réactions." He went on to say that "[dans les poèmes de Valéry] le mode abstrait et le mode poétique, sont mieux unis que dans l'oeuvre d'aucun autre poète."[44]

In Eliot's observations about Valéry's "structure" and "mode," we see him admiring the kind of poetry he began to write in the mid-twenties and continued to write until the *Four Quartets.*[45] Whereas before *The Waste Land* Eliot had praised *vers libre* for its ability to isolate and emphasize the intensity of a theatrical moment,[46] here he praises the use of traditional versification as a medium in which such moments can be subsumed (as arguments are subsumed in philosophical discourse). Once he had praised Imagist poetry that "presents the object," that struggles "to digest and express new objects, new groups of objects, new feelings";[47] here the praises Valéry's use of "le mode abstrait." In *The Waste Land* he had tried to dramatize the prison of the individual ego. Now he voiced his appreciation of a meditative poetry in which structural pattern was more important than any individual voice, a poetry in which the ego of the poet is absorbed and nullified by an impersonally musical structure. (Arthur Symons had recorded "the enquiry pursued by Mallarmé" this way: "The pure work . . . implies the elocutionary disappearance of the poet, who yields place to the words, immobilised by the shock of their inequality; they take light from mutual reflection, like an actual train of fire over precious stones, replacing the old lyric afflatus or the enthusiastic personal direction of the phrase.")[48]

Eliot's inclination toward abstract language and symbolist impersonality was a novelty only in the sense that it was freshly charged with new thought and enthusiasm. The *Waste Land* manuscript shows occasional flashes of Augustan generality suitable to an admirer of Gray's "Elegy."[49] And Eliot's early tendency toward symbolist incantation[50] welled up powerfully as he wrote the fifth section of *The Waste Land.* After *The Waste Land,* Eliot, not surprisingly, again began to read the symbolists with care. The result: he reconsidered his relation to French poetry and came to admire figures he had known for half a lifetime as if he were reading them for the first time. Valéry was one of his first discoveries. It was he who permitted Eliot to renew the sources of his poetry just at a time when Eliot, as he told John Lehmann,[51] was afraid he would never write again.

To return to *The Hollow Men,* Valéry's impact on Eliot may be gauged and dated by the traces of Valéry we find in *"Here we go round the prickly pear."* Writing about "Le Cimetière marin" in his 1924 introduction to Valéry, Eliot remarked how "strongly though accidentally" the line "Entre le vide et l'événement pur"[52] suggested Brutus's:

> Between the acting of a dreadful thing
> And the first motion, all the interim is
> Like a phantasma or a hideous dream.

The lines are remarkably similar, but it is neither accidental nor surprising that Valéry's poem spurred Eliot to remember them. "Le Cimetière marin" is the quintessential expression of Valéry's melancholy skepticism, which Eliot attributed to "the agony of *creation*. . . . the mind constantly mocks and dissuades, and urges that the creative activity is vain. . . ."[53] Eliot was searching for a literary formula to suggest just such a note of skepticism in the conclusion of *The Hollow Men.* Although the lines Eliot wrote are usually glossed by reference to *Julius Caesar,* Eliot was thinking as much of Valéry as of Shakespeare when he wrote them.

Three stanzas of precisely used abstractions comprise the final stylistic development of *The Hollow Men:*

> Between the idea
> And the reality
> Between the motion
> And the act
> Falls the Shadow
>
>   *For Thine is the Kingdom*
>
> Between the conception
> And the creation
> Between the emotion
> And the response
> Falls the Shadow
>
>   *Life is very long*
>
> Between the desire
> And the spasm
> Between the potency
> And the existence
> Between the essence
> And the descent
> Falls the Shadow
>
>   *For Thine is the Kingdom*

These stanzas use Valéry's characteristic methods to convey his melancholy theme—"the agony of creation." In them a poetry of meditation takes its place in *The Hollow Men* alongside the Imagist drama of the middle lyrics and the ritual chants of the choruses.

There is "only one higher stage possible for civilised man," Eliot said about Valéry's philosophical skepticism, "and that is to unite the profoundest scepticism with the deepest faith."[54] The above stanzas of *The Hollow Men* attempt to unite the two by antiphony. With three different textures of speech—the meditative abstractions of "Between the idea/ And the reality," the grave elegance of the Lord's Prayer, and the *cri de coeur* "Life is very long"—Eliot counterpoints three moods. The moods cannot be said to reach a conclusion; they reflect a series of shifting ironies and sum up *The Hollow Men*'s double movement of death and rebirth. It would be a mistake to push the moods to any conclusion other than the ambivalence expressed in the ambiguity of "Shadow," which refers both to annihilation and to the shadow of the Holy Spirit in Luke, or to read into the lines an easy correspondence to the situation of Brutus in *Julius Caesar*. Once more Eliot's allusion merely juxtaposes a tangential and suggestive analogue to the experience presented in the action of the words on the page.

If noticing Eliot's association of Brutus's lines with "Le Cimetière marin" does nothing more, it should remind us again of how misplaced our usual assumptions are about the part borrowings from other writers play in his work. As chapter five demonstrated, in Eliot's poetry allusions for the most part do *not* appropriate the broad narrative contexts of larger works; they evoke what Pound called the "emotional equations" of the literary tradition. Eliot once wrote, "You cannot effectively 'borrow' an image, unless you borrow also, or have spontaneously, something like the feeling which prompted the original image. . . . You are entitled to take it for your own purposes in so far as your fundamental purposes are akin to those of the one who is, for you, the author of the phrase, the inventor of the image; or if you take it for other purposes then your purposes must be consciously and *pointedly* diverse from those of the author. . . ."[55] He intended glancing references like the ones we have been considering to suggest the "feeling" he wished to convey, and his allusions need to be interpreted with more tact than most of his readers have possessed. In the three abstract stanzas of *"Here we go round the prickly pear,"* Eliot clearly wanted to reinforce a mood of melancholy and philosophical skepticism, and he went about it by borrowing "equations" that were, *for him,* invented by Valéry and by Shakespeare. In this case the less obvious of the equations are the more important: not only do the lines beginning "Between the idea/ And the reality" express a theme from Valéry, they express it in formal procedures borrowed from Valéry as well. In the perspective of Eliot's stylistic growth his borrowing of those procedures was the most significant development of *The Hollow Men:* though he handled them in a tentative and halting manner, they composed the one formal innovation in the poem that points toward the music of the *Four Quartets.*

CHAPTER SEVEN

"Desire and control"

I lunched with Eliot, and Gordon George. . . . After the first course Vivian appeared, shivering, shuddering, a scarecrow of a woman with legs like jackstraws, sallow as to face. She examined me with furtive intensity through the whole meal: flung gobs of food here and there on the floor: eyed me to see if I had seen this: picked them up: stacked the dishes, scraping the food off each one in turn; and during everything constantly directed at T[om] a cold stream of hatred, as he did (so it seemed to me) toward her. George said something about pure intellect. Tom, giving his best pontifical frown, said there was no such thing. Vivian at this looked at me, then at Tom, and gave a peacock's laugh. Why what do you mean, she said. You argue with me every night in your life about pure intellect, don't you. —I don't know what you mean, says Tom. —Why don't be absurd— you know perfectly well that *every* night you tell me that there *is* such a thing: and what's more, that *you* have it, and that nobody *else* has it. —To which Tom's lame reply was You don't know what you're saying.

Conrad Aiken to Theodore Spencer, 31 October 1930

It were a wise inquiry for the closet, to compare, point by point, especially at remarkable crises in our life, our daily history with the rise and progress of ideas in the mind.

Ralph Waldo Emerson

After *The Hollow Men,* Eliot's development was in a way inevitable. He had been given a retrospective vision in which he saw his life as a chronicle of humiliation and spiritual growth, and his way of thinking about poetry changed accordingly. In the early thirties, he might fondly remember the "sincerity" of *Bubu of Montparnasse* and the book's record of "events as they happened, without irrelevant and disturbing comment."[1] But since by then he had affirmed that it was "not our feelings but the pattern which we may make of our feelings" that counted, he was, to say the least, ambivalent about the value of the buried life or a "sincerity" whose purpose was to divulge it. Eliot now wanted to order psychic events, not simply to "record" them, and to escape from the self rather than to excavate it. Thus, when he consulted French writing, it was more likely to be Valéry than Philippe. *Four Quartets,* apparently, was just over the horizon.

And yet, like so many of the literary historian's generalizations, the inevitability of Eliot's development exists largely in hindsight. It is true that he had had his vision. But it is also true that he had no idea how long it would last. It might change his life or it might disappear into the whirlpool of the next moment's crisis. What he made of it, how he nursed it and reinforced it was as important as the vision's extraordinary occurrence. The same can be said about the way Eliot constructed a new style. As with the way he recapitulated the nineties' quarrel with rhetoric, his new symbolist music was shaped as much by his character as by his reading. To quote from "Animula," which is perhaps the central poem of this decade, the "imperatives" of his development from 1922 to 1935 were no longer matters of "memory and desire" but of "desire and control."

From 1922 Eliot exerted all the control he could muster, and his results were considerable. His life changed so markedly, in fact, that an observer might be excused for thinking there had been some dramatic improvement at home. In fact, his relations with Vivien were as bad as ever. Eliot's new energy seems rather to have been liberated by two pieces of good fortune connected with his writing. Starting in late 1922 his self-esteem was strengthened by a strong (though not universally positive) reaction to *The Waste Land*.[2] By 1924 his fame had elicited an invitation to deliver the prestigious Clark Lectures. And well before then he had successfully launched his own journal. At the *Criterion*, Eliot might be captain. As he planned the first issue he felt he could affect the course of European sensibility. We can gauge what that renewed sense of mastery meant to him from the report of a perceptive witness. Virginia Woolf, whose diaries and letters provide our best picture of these years in Eliot's life, recorded that when Eliot told her he was "starting a magazine," he grew, unexpectedly, "supple as an eel . . . positively familiar & jocular & friendly. . . ."[3] Drawing on this renewed confidence, Eliot redoubled his efforts to impose an unshakable intellectual structure on his thinking and put his personal life in order.

The year 1923 saw the publication of "The Function of Criticism," the first of Eliot's essays to make an explicit connection between conservative ideology and literary criticism. In his argument, which appeared in the fourth number of the *Criterion*, Eliot attacked John Middleton Murry's dubious faith in man's "inner voice" and remarked that to "those of us who find ourselves supporting . . . Classicism," such a faith is as disagreeable as a political belief without "allegiance to principles, or to a form of government, or to a monarch"; as disagreeable as a religous belief without allegiance to a "Church"; as disagreeable, in short, as any belief that does not recognize the "principle of unquestioned spiritual authority outside the individual" (SE, 15).[4]

Only a year after the publication of *The Waste Land*, then, Eliot was already trying out the Maurras-like stance of his 1928 Preface to *For Lancelot Andrewes:* "classicist in literature, royalist in politics, and anglo-catholic in religion" (FLA, vii).[5] By 1924 he could write to Herbert Read that "we need more dogma."[6] And in the spring of 1925, when he was preparing the Clark Lectures, he began to integrate his new intellectual creed into his poetry. By that time, though, he had already made significant alterations in his non-literary affairs.

The first thing he changed was his job at Lloyd's bank. According to Frank Morley, one of the members of the *Criterion* circle, "it had become increasingly impossible for him to keep to banking hours in the City."[7] Before his breakdown Eliot had tried to fight off his discomfort, and even sang the praises of non-literary work. Yet in 1922 he allowed Ezra Pound and Virginia Woolf to float separate patronage subscriptions to help him. (The details got too complicated and the schemes were dropped.) Now, at least to some of his friends, he acknowledged how much he disliked the bank and tried to do something about it.[8] Finally Eliot's friends Charles Whibley and Frank Morley, along with Bruce Richmond, the editor of the *Times Literary Supplement*, lobbied Geoffrey Faber to make Eliot a director at the publishing firm of Faber and Gwyer, and Eliot began his new career in 1925.[9]

What to do about his marriage was more difficult. Even when Tom and Vivien were well, life was a constant battle. Robert Sencourt puts it coyly when he says, "It was evident that the strain from which my new friends were suffering was that they no longer lived together in deepest unity."[10] Virginia Woolf is more informative: "And Tom is in a great taking, with Vivien as mad as a hare, but not confined, and they give parties, where she suddenly accuses him of being in love with Ottoline . . . and Tom drinks, and Vivien suddenly says when talk dies down 'You're the bloodiest snob I ever knew.' "[11] We need not exonerate Eliot from responsibility for the unpleasantness of his marriage to acknowledge that he had to remove himself from it to go on. But his conscience would not let him think of leaving Vivien, and at first he tried a variety of half-measures. One was simply emotional detachment, something Virginia Woolf noticed as early as 1923: "That strange figure Eliot dined here last night. I feel that he has taken the veil, or whatever monks do. He is quite calm again. Mrs. Eliot has almost died at times in the past month. Tom, though infinitely considerate, is also perfectly detached. His cell, is I'm sure, a very lofty one, but a little chilly."[12]

But, though detachment was less extreme than a complete break with Vivien, Eliot came to feel that it too was unforgivable. He tried strenuously to keep from withdrawing, and in 1925 he made a "long gaslit emotional rather tremulous & excited visit" to Virginia Woolf. According to an entry in her diary, Eliot "has been thinking over his state these past weeks, being alone, with time on his hands. He has seen his

whole life afresh, seen his relations to the world, & to Vivien in particular, become humbler suppler more humane . . . accusing himself of
being the American husband, & wishing to tell me privately . . . what
store V. sets by me, has done nothing but write since last June, because
I told her to!" It was during this visit that Eliot announced his impend-
ing release from the bank and told Woolf that he and Vivien were
taking a house [in Chester Terrace] near Sloane Square. It was all an
attempt, he said, to "start fresh." [13] The attempt, however, proved only
a partial success. His move from the bank turned out to be permanent,
but in a few years money worries forced the Eliots back to their flat at
Clarence Gate Gardens and back to their old quarrels. No matter how
Eliot tried, he always had to try again. Robert Sencourt, though biased
toward Eliot, still convinces when he reports Eliot's efforts as late as
1930 to take Vivien abroad and try once more to "establish serenity
between them." [14]

But the most thoroughgoing of Eliot's attempts to "start fresh" had
nothing to do with Vivien or the bank. Between 1923 and 1928 he first
gravitated and then marched toward the Anglican church. In 1923 he
made the acquaintance of William Force Stead, an American who some
years previously had been ordained in the Church of England. Correspondence between the two men shows Stead becoming Eliot's spiritual
confidant, and in November 1926, when Eliot, after several months of
attending morning communion, decided to be confirmed, he asked
Stead for assistance. The ceremony was performed on June 19, 1927.
Nine months later Eliot made his first confession, an event he told Stead
made him feel as if he had crossed a wide and deep river. Whether he
got much farther or not, he felt, it was certain that he would not cross
back. And *that*, he told Stead, gave him an extraordinary sense of surrender and gain.[15]

Eliot's words make it clear that, whatever exhilaration he felt, at the
heart of his conversion was a much-desired escape from his former life.
And though he believed he was heading toward communion with
something larger than himself, his older sister Ada had her doubts. She
told Frank Morley that "she was both interested and concerned about
Tom's 'Way of contemplation,' which she was imagining might divorce
him from 'human' relationships and drive him into a shadow-world of
'dramatism,' into increasing tendencies of outward 'acting' and inward
'mysticism.' She saw two forces pulling apart, yet compensations of each
other." [16]

Doubtless based on a vision of the double pattern of his life, the
ecstacy of Eliot's conversion was short-lived. Following his breakdown,
he was more than ever suspicious of the "inner light" and able to assent
only after long bouts of intellectual skepticism. Eliot's experience seems
to have resembled the one he describes in his essay "The 'Pensées' of
Pascal":

The Christian thinker—and I mean the man who is trying consciously and conscientiously to explain to himself the sequence which culminates in faith, rather than the public apologist—proceeds by rejection and elimination. He finds the world to be so and so; he finds its character inexplicable by any non-religious theory: among religions he finds Christianity, and Catholic Christianity, to account most satisfactorily for the world and especially for the moral world within. . . .

. . . every man who thinks and lives by thought must have his own scepticism, that which stops at the question, that which ends in denial, or that which leads to faith and which is somehow integrated into the faith which transcends it. And Pascal, as the type of one kind of religious believer, which is highly passionate and ardent, but passionate only through a powerful and regulated intellect, is in the first sections of his unfinished Apology for Christianity facing unflinchingly the demon of doubt which is inseparable from the spirit of belief (SE, 360, 363).

Quite likely Eliot, as Lyndall Gordon observes, soon felt no religious excitement and "began to think of religion as a long-term regimen."[17] We can see the strength of his determination in a story Herbert Read tells. Staying over at the Eliot house on Chester Terrace, Read realized one morning that his host had departed, and learned later that it was to communion service.[18] Rising early and leaving without explanation, Eliot did not invite comment by his wife or his friends. He had decided his course and he would permit neither their arguments nor his lack of enthusiasm to sway him. Even in April 1928 he could write Stead that he did not expect to make great progress at present, only to keep his soul alive by prayer and regular devotions.[19] Regularity of all kinds, in fact, became the anchor of a life that still seemed as if it might come apart. In the mid-twenties, Eliot became fastidious about social and intellectual convention. Virginia Woolf's account is typical. She writes to Roger Fry in May 1923, "We have the oddest conversations: I can't help loosing some figure of speech, which Tom pounces on and utterly destroys. Never mind: I loose another. So we go on. But at my time of life, I begin to resent inhibitions to intercourse."[20]

In all of these circumstances—Eliot's undertaking of the *Criterion*, his wish to make a new start in his marriage, his dogged progress toward conversion and his increasing social fastidiousness—we can see him reacting against emotional disorder. It appears that he no longer had any faith in the power of his inner life to give shape to his experience. He now wanted to unify himself by force of will—by erecting a carapace of received and regular forms that would hold him together from the outside. His inclination toward greater control over his feelings and his heightened need for intellectual structure seem to have preceded and modified his religious submission. Only by recognizing that, I think, can the link between Eliot's conversion and his new poetry be understood. The style of Eliot's Christianity and the style of his new poetry are related to a personal style that conditioned them both.

2

"A Song for Simeon," published approximately a year after Eliot's confirmation, points to where Eliot's attempts at control were taking him and tells us something about how, without his stubborn honesty, Eliot's career might have evolved. The word "Song" in the title, an allusion to the "Nunc dimittis," one of the hymns of the Anglican service, also links the poem to the "songs" out of which Eliot fashioned *The Hollow Men*. Once more we are in a "dead land," measuring the movement of the sun and wind across an unpeopled landscape, and once more Eliot's figures are what the Clark Lectures had called "ontological." As in *The Hollow Men*, they do not dramatize the psychological frissons of experience but render a spiritual state. Simeon tells us "My life is light . . ./ Like a feather on the back of my hand." Then, augmenting the simile, he figures his life first by "Dust in sunlight" and then by "memory in corners," both of which wait "for the wind that chills toward the dead land." The feeling picks up from the end of *The Hollow Men*, but now includes a sense of anxious resignation. As in the fourth section of *The Hollow Men*, life is empty and yet paradoxically there is hope associated with vacancy: three incomplete fragments of a former unit, therefore—the feather, the dust and the memory—are the first objects to feel the wind's force.

The subject of "A Song for Simeon" corresponds to the recent events of Eliot's life. Anticipating *Ash Wednesday,* the poem reflects the "time of tension" after his first flickering vision of rebirth. At its beginning, it hovers between dust and blooming hyacinths, between the feeling of having outlived one's purpose and an anticipation of renewed vitality. Then, in the second stanza, the poem suggests the darker side of renewal. There, Simeon is suddenly aware that rebirth will mean that his old self (his "house") will be forgotten. At that moment, everything he once imagined as the future of "my children's children" will be dislocated and, from his old perspective, destroyed. It is only in the third stanza, struggling manfully against those thoughts, that Simeon accepts for his progeny the Christian course of "lamentation," and that he momentarily allows himself to be cheered by "the Infant"—the still unspeaking and unspoken Word. But he concludes the stanza with a heavy heart, burdened by a self that will not be so easily disowned.

The poem ends on that note, much magnified. In the last stanza, Simeon attempts to lighten somberness with an assertion that "they"—Israel, his children's children—will not be desolated but, as they mount the martyr's stair to "the ultimate vision," will in every generation suffer an affliction that is also a glory. Yet his dark mood remains. "The ecstacy of thought and prayer" is "not for me"—not for Simeon and not for the poet who speaks through him. In its place there is heartache, fatigue and the fear of death. He finishes with a plea for aid that is implicitly a statement of helplessness ("Let thy servant depart") and a stubborn statement of the minimum he knows or can expect. He has felt the possibility of rebirth. Having seen his salvation, he can neither forget it nor pretend that it remains for him more than a distant possibility.

Stylistically, two things distinguish the drama of Simeon's spiritual struggle from *The Hollow Men*. The first is the way this poem uses liturgical expression. Three years earlier, Eliot had integrated the phrase "Thine is the Kingdom" into the conclusion of *The Hollow Men*, but only to augment the poem's final ambivalence. The sequence "Grant us thy peace . . . Grant us thy peace . . . According to thy word . . . Grant me thy peace . . . Having seen thy salvation," which, on the evidence of the manuscript, Eliot imposed on a poem already conceived,[21] represents something more. It is not a counterpointed melody but an emotional bass. Note that the sequence does not correspond to Eliot's established habit of poetic borrowing, which he defines in "Philip Massinger" as the process of welding poetic "theft into a whole of feeling which is unique, utterly different from that from which it was torn" (SW, 125). When Eliot introduces the "Nunc dimittis" into "Simeon," it is *not* to weld it into a new and unique whole of feeling. Rather he uses it to sound a note that is anything but unique, a feeling which is impersonal not because it arises from the depths of the unconscious but because it belongs to many centuries of shared experience.

Also, by identifying himself with the continuous speech of a single character, Eliot breaks radically with the way his earlier poetry had projected the self. This is obvious as soon as we compare "Simeon" with Eliot's previous monologues, which either constructed a tentative, composite self ("Prufrock," "Gerontion") or entertained historical identities with great hesitation and suspicion (the "characters" in *The Waste Land*). "Simeon" is in fact less "modern" than any of these and more like a poem of Browning's. (Later Eliot would hold up Browning as the model for all non-theatrical dramatic verse.)[22] In "Simeon," Eliot willingly assumes the unity and substantiality of the self just as he rejects the notion that public speech is unable to convey inner truth. His entire sense of reality, it seems, has changed. But before asking how, or for how long, a last word should be said about the relation of "Simeon" to Eliot's psychological profile.

With "Simeon," we are no longer dealing with poetic composition that verges on automatic writing. When Eliot composed *The Waste Land*, he started with a plan but what he actually wrote grew out of his exploration of what I have called *images trouvailles*. Thinking about this or a similar experience he said in "The Three Voices of Poetry" that in writing lyrics the poet "has something germinating in him for which he must find words; but he cannot know what words he wants until he has found the words" (OPP, 106). He added that in the same kind of poetry "the 'psychic material' tends to create its own form," or rather that "what happens is a simultaneous development of form and material; for the form affects the material at every stage; and perhaps all the material does is to repeat 'not that! not that!' " (OPP, 110).

However Eliot also pointed out in the same essay that there were other ways to write and that in them "the form is already to some extent given. . . . if I set out to write a play, I start by an act of choice: I settle upon a particular emotional situation . . . and I can make a plain prose outline of the play in advance. . . ." (OPP, 110–11). It is precisely this *other* sort of poetry that in "Simeon" and the poems that come after it Eliot attempted to write, and his phrase "an act of choice" speaks eloquently about what he tried to change after *The Waste Land.* Starting with "Simeon," Eliot's poetry is "chosen" or *willed.* In the best of it there is a harmony between will and psychic pressure so that, like "Simeon," it strikes us with double force of personal and traditional utterance. Quite often, however, the element of will dominates and (a possibility Eliot acknowledged in "The Three Voices of Poetry") the poetry turns into rhetoric. What can be especially disconcerting is that this kind of rhetoric often infects poetic procedures we ordinarily associate with pure poetry. In *Ash Wednesday,* for example, it is Eliot's incantation that is strained and willful. And though "Simeon" is a less flawed (and a less ambitious) poem, it is tainted by the same willfulness, as one of its lines makes unmistakably clear:

> Now at this birth season of decease. . . .

3

The altered thrust of a poem like "Simeon" corresponds to the way Eliot reversed some of his literary judgments in the mid-twenties. His change of mind about Donne is a case in point. A related and equally striking example concerns Lancelot Andrewes, whom Eliot now read with new eyes.

Generations of preachers in his family had sensitized Eliot to the sermon as a form of literature, and Andrewes's place in that tradition was indisputable. But when Eliot first wrote about "The Preacher as Artist" in the 1919 *Athenaeum,* the sermons of Donne and not Andrewes provoked his warmest praise. Though Eliot admits that Andrewes was "a writer of genius," he laments that he "had nothing to say which could not be put into a very good sermon, no feelings which the sermon could not satisfy." Donne, more "mature" and more "introspective" than Andrewes, was able to "break, now and again, through the close convention of Elizabethan-Jacobean speech" and achieve *"a direct personal communication."* [23]

Yet, as we have seen, by 1925 Eliot had begun to wonder about the "virtues" he had seen in Donne and whether Donne's "psychological" immediacy might be such a good thing. In 1925 Eliot had for two years been writing to William Force Stead, who, according to Robert Sencourt, "from their first meeting in 1923, steadily drew [Eliot] towards the writings of seventeenth-century Anglicanism, and especially those of Lancelot Andrewes."[24] When he wrote his famous leader about Andrewes for the *Times Literary Supplement* in 1926, then, Eliot was no longer the man who wrote "The Preacher as Artist." In "Lancelot Andrewes," which he later made one of the keystones of *Selected Essays*, Eliot cast out Donne and much of what he had meant to him. Referring to a since-rejected younger self, and repeating some of the things he said in the Clark Lectures, he told his readers that Donne is "dangerous only for those who find in his sermons an indulgence of their sensibility, or for those who, fascinated by 'personality' in the romantic sense of the word . . . forget that in the spiritual hierarchy there are places higher than that of Donne" (SE, 309–10). One of those higher places Eliot assigns to Andrewes, whose "emotion is purely contemplative; it is not personal, it is wholly evoked by the object of contemplation, to which it is adequate. . . . Donne is a 'personality' in a sense in which Andrewes is not: his sermons, one feels, are a 'means of self-expression.' He is constantly finding an object which shall be adequate to his feelings; Andrewes is wholly absorbed in the object and therefore responds with the adequate emotion" (SE, 308–9).[25]

Being "wholly absorbed in the object" will be Eliot's aim in life and in art from this time on, and at least through *Ash Wednesday*, the object he seeks will be a traditionally sanctioned form of thinking and feeling. He describes the state as "not personal," but as "A Song for Simeon" suggested, this impersonality only superficially resembles the one Eliot described in *The Sacred Wood*. There Eliot said a world of objects was merely the representation of a "complex tissue of feelings and desires" (SW, 119). After "Lancelot Andrewes," the "object" in which he wishes to be absorbed is an ideal of form or feeling in the name of which the sensibility is to be left behind. The former impersonality belongs to what Eliot once called "the order of nature" or at best "the order of mind"; the latter to "the order of charity." But since the three orders are "*discontinuous* [and] the higher is not implicit in the lower" (SE, 368), there can be no question of distilling one kind of impersonality from the other. In life and in art the demands of the emotional self are to be regarded as part of the lower end of the "spiritual hierarchy." Only by losing that self in a higher order of contemplation can one attain a condition of wholeness or reality. In life this means "thought, study, mortification, sacrifice" (SE, 329). And since for Eliot poetry is always a more complete and more honest extension of life, the act of composition becomes yet another form of moral discipline.

"Ritual" and "convention" now become key words of Eliot's criticism, since both provide inflexible structures in which the artist's tendency toward self-expression might be disciplined. Thus Eliot asserts in one essay that the drama must be based on convention, which "may be some quite new selection or structure or distortion in subject matter or technique; any form or rhythm imposed upon the world of action" (SE, 94). Making essentially the same point he says elsewhere: "The drama was originally ritual; and ritual, consisting of a set of repeated movements, is essentially a dance."[26] The discipline of the dance, in fact, becomes one of the preoccupations of his prose.[27] This may be, as Audrey T. Rogers has suggested, because his wife was a dancer.[28] But it was also because dancing provided a wonderful example of an activity that seems to involve instinctual release but actually requires discipline and restraint. In his most revealing comments on the dance Eliot writes, "What is the strength of the ballet? It is in a tradition, a training, an *askesis*. . . . any efficient dancer has undergone a training which is *like a moral training* . . . it is a system of physical training, of traditional, symbolical and highly skilled movements. It is a liturgy of very wide adaptability" (SE, 34–35; emphasis mine).

Substitute "poetry" for "dance" in Eliot's call for "askesis," "moral training" and "liturgy" and we begin to understand something about the new "impersonality" of "A Song for Simeon." To lose oneself in an impersonal form which has behind it the authority of secular or religious tradition now appears to be the artist's task. But once Eliot redefined his notion of poetic impersonality he also had to revise his understanding of poetic sincerity. In the period of *The Sacred Wood*, sincerity had to do with identifying and recapturing the source of one's most authentic attitudes, and involved acknowledging the "simple, terrible and unknown" passions that underlie "the surface of existence."[29] Thus Eliot in his 1920 essay on Blake defines sincerity as seeing "from the centre of [one's] own crystal" (SW, 154). But in the twenties "sincerity" came to mean for him less a reference to the impulses behind thought and feeling than a looking outward toward the contours of reality.[30] Thus in the fourth of his Clark Lectures Eliot allows Donne one kind of sincerity only to deny him claim to a second and more valuable kind. Although the feeling behind Donne's thought "is perfectly sincere," Eliot comments, it is possible to call the thought insincere by another criterion: Donne's "immediate experience passes into thought . . . [but] this thought, far from attaining *belief*, is immediately the object of another feeling. If you like you may call the thought 'insincere,' because it does not reach belief."

Nor is Eliot content to connect sincerity with just any stance, any belief. In "Donne in Our Time," an essay that grew out of the Clark Lectures, Eliot implies that the highest kind of "belief" in which sincerity might culminate is one which involves a unity of experience. "In the poetry of Dante, and even of Guido Cavalcanti," he writes, "there is

always the assumption of an ideal unity in experience . . . the subsumption of the lower under the higher, an ordering of the world more
or less Aristotelian. But . . . there is in [Donne's] poetry hardly any
attempt at organisation; rather a puzzled and humorous shuffling of
the pieces. . . ."[31] Even a poem as moving as "A Valediction Forbid-
ding Mourning" fails ultimately to be sincere, because in it Donne retains a number of images that, however ingenious, are irreconcilable
with any coherent experience of reality.

Beginning in 1927, the problem of poetry and belief was very much
on Eliot's mind.[32] The subject is ordinarily discussed, as Eliot himself
discusses it, primarily as a matter of how a reader's convictions affect
his responses.[33] A more interesting question, however, is: how much
did these considerations affect the texture of Eliot's own work? The
answer seems to be a great deal. Not only did Eliot's reorientation affect his attitude toward the formal conventions of poetry, it seems to
have reshaped his attitudes toward technical matters like diction and
syntax. In short, toward precisely those matters which constitute the
idiom or *style* of a poet—his indelible signature and voice.

Eliot once wrote that "without doubt, the effort of the philosopher
proper, the man who is trying to deal with ideas in themselves, and the
effort of the poet . . . cannot be carried on at the same time" (SW,
162). Nevertheless he was always intrigued by the apparition of philosophical poetry. According to John Soldo, his interest in Dante began
as a fascination with the discursive cantos of the *Purgatorio.*[34] In his
1920 essay on Dante he tried to argue that, properly understood, philosophical poetry is as valid in our time as any other. And, as the last
chapter demonstrated, in 1924 his developing hunger for intellectual
order turned him toward the philosophical poetry of Valéry. We see
this interest in philosophical poetry transformed in the mid-twenties
into a conviction that poetry should dramatize the struggle of belief. In
"Shakespeare and the Stoicism of Seneca" (1927), for example, he introduces a discussion of the theory of belief with a series of remarks
about the relation of poetry to thought. Philosophical and religious poetry are here linked in his mind as variations of a kind of writing that
presents the phenomenological context of experience.[35] In 1929 he
elaborates what he meant in 1927 with the term "belief attitude" (SE,
219), but his most illuminating explanation is to be found in an early
version of "The Social Function of Poetry":

> [Virgil's *Georgics*, Lucretius's *On the Nature of Things*, Dante's *Divine Comedy*]
> were not designed to persuade the readers to an intellectual assent, but to
> convey an emotional equivalent for the ideas. What Lucretius and Dante
> teach you, in fact, is *what it feels like* to hold certain beliefs; what Virgil
> teaches you, is to feel yourself inside the agrarian life.[36]

To dramatize "what it feels like" to hold Christian belief in an age of
skepticism became Eliot's object in the poems he wrote around the time

Eliot—third from left, top row—as a student of Milton Academy ("the ghost of myself at the age of seventeen or thereabouts").

Eliot among the ladies: Eliot with his mother and sisters after a tornado had driven them out of their St. Louis home.

"The earliest personal influence I remember, besides that of my parents, was an Irish nursemaid named Annie Dunne, to whom I was greatly attached."

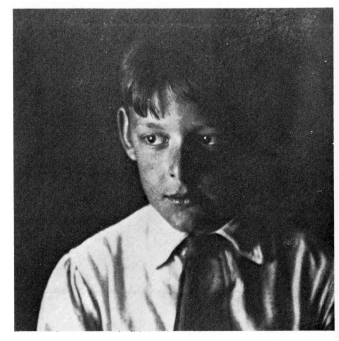

Eliot, aged ten.

Eliot, his mother and sister in the summer of 1921 ("eyes that fix you").

Eliot, back from his "romantic year" in France (1910–11).

Eliot and his mother at Hampton Court in the summer of 1921. (Eliot had written that he would never be happy again unless he saw her once more.)

Vivien Eliot.

Eliot in the eyes of Wyndham Lewis (1922). The sketch suggests something of the mask Eliot would assume as captain of the *Criterion* and later of the London literary world.

The young man of letters: publicity photo of Eliot in the early 1920's.

Eliot outside Faber's in 1926 (a time of "desire and control").

The garden that separated the Eliot home in St. Louis from the Mary Institute ("there was . . . a . . . picket fence . . . [and] a high brick wall").

Two passport photos speak of the changes in Eliot's life. The first dates from the 1910's. The second was taken in 1932, on the eve of Eliot's eventful return to America.

Eliot with Frank Morley's children at Pikes Farm in the mid-thirties ("he talked . . . about childhood days").

Eliot at a Faber's editorial board meeting in 1939 ("the immediate future is not bright").

A young Eliot, on Cape Ann ("We had the experience but missed the meaning").

Eliot at his typewriter in Sweden in the spring of 1942. After a year of revising "Little Gidding," he was afraid he would have to let the poem disintegrate.

of "Simeon." And achieving it required a different order of discourse from the pre–*Hollow Men* poems. To describe the movements of the intellectual and spiritual life, Eliot no longer needed the psychological resonance of his former verse. What he did need, he began to see, was to master words that rigorously denote ideas even as they reveal the bias of the thinking mind. He would also have to master the kind of syntax that, without malforming the intellectual arguments it advances, suggests inflections of hesitation, sudden conviction and last-minute doubt.

Both Eliot's new diction and his new syntax involve the denotative aspects of language in a way that far exceeds the concerns of his earlier poetry. And both point him away from a poetry of pure or dramatic lyricism and toward a poetry of meditation. (In "The Three Voices of Poetry" [1953], the essay which contains his most searching discussion of lyric verse, Eliot refuses to speak of the lyric at all; commenting on Gottfried Benn's *Probleme der Lyrik,* he speaks of "meditative verse" [OPP, 106].) We can see Eliot thinking out the needs of this new style in essays of the mid-twenties and implementing his thought in the poems that accompanied them.

In "Lancelot Andrewes," for example, he suggests that Andrewes's sermons form one of the few literary monuments of the English church that can be set alongside Dante; in Eliot's words, "the intellectual achievement and the prose style of Hooker and Andrewes came to complete the structure of the English Church as the philosophy of the thirteenth century crowns the Catholic Church" (SE, 301). The justifications he offers for this praise, moreover, link it to his search for the lineaments of a poetry of belief. Among "the most conspicuous qualities of [Andrewes's] style," Eliot asserts, are his "precision in the use of words" and his "relevant intensity" (SE, 302). In that remark, one might deduce the two not always complementary forces that controlled Eliot's later work. On the one hand, a way of proceeding that suggests the soul's "intense" struggle for sincere belief. On the other, a precise use of the denotative powers of language. Thus on one hand Andrewes's sermons are the meditations of a poetic soul. They have an "internal structure. . . . His single thoughts are no doubt often suggested by the words he borrows, but the thoughts are made his own, and the constructive force, the fire that fuses them, is his own" (SE, 303). On the other, the sermons are machine-like impersonal constructs, designed to squeeze important words until they yield "a full juice of meaning":

> Reading Andrewes on such a theme is like listening to a great Hellenist expounding a text of the *Posterior Analytics:* altering the punctuation, inserting or removing a comma or a semicolon to make an obscure passage suddenly luminous, dwelling on a single word, comparing its use in nearer and in the most remote contexts, purifying a disturbed or cryptic lecturenote into lucid profundity. To persons whose minds are habituated to feed

> on the vague jargon of our time, when we have a vocabulary for every-
> thing and exact ideas about nothing—when a word half-understood, torn
> from its place in some alien or half-formed science, as of psychology, con-
> ceals from both writer and reader the meaninglessness of a statement . . .
> Andrewes may seem pedantic and verbal. It is only when we have satu-
> rated ourselves in his prose, followed the movement of his thought, that
> we find his examination of words terminating in the ecstasy of assent. An-
> drewes takes a word and derives the world from it; squeezing and squeez-
> ing the word until it yields a full juice of meaning which we should never
> have supposed any word to possess. In this process the qualities which we
> have mentioned, of ordonnance and precision, are exercised (SE, 304–5).

What Eliot describes here are the inflections of seventeenth-century
religious meditation. But, significantly, he characterizes Andrewes as if
he were an ancestor of Mallarmé, another writer who "takes a word
and derives the world from it." Like Andrewes, Eliot was to develop
the implications of words until his sequences terminated in the ecstacy
of assent. But his first concern would be a preoccupation with verbal
and syntactic precision: a wish to purify the dialect of the tribe. And to
that end he now began to read ancient and modern examples of the
type of poet whose work, as Arnold said, belongs to the classics of our
prose, not our poetry. Writing especially about Dryden, Eliot sought
out a style that was alive to the histories of words and the function of
"a comma or a semicolon."

4

Eliot opened and closed the decade of his poetic transformation with
major essays on Dryden. In the 1921 *TLS*, he qualified an obvious lack
of enthusiasm for Dryden's poetry with a fascination with Dryden's prose
precision, and anticipated some of the difficulties he would encounter
achieving that precision himself. Though Eliot admits that Dryden
"lacked what his master Jonson possessed, a large and unique view of
life . . . insight . . . profundity," yet he praises the way in which "Dryden's words . . . are precise," how "they state immensely." And he ends
by prophesying a new direction in twentieth-century writing: "In the
next revolution of taste it is possible that poets may turn to the study
of Dryden. He remains one of those who have set standards for English
verse which it is desperate to ignore" (SE, 274, 273, 274; Eliot's "desperate," I think, highlights the motivation behind his own "turn to the
study of Dryden").

By 1930, when he delivered a series of five talks on Dryden for the
BBC [in 1932 three were collected in *John Dryden: The Poet, The Dramatist, The Critic*], Eliot's distaste had largely evaporated and he speaks
of Dryden not as a guardian of the future but as one of the assured
masters of English poetry. According to these essays, "good sense" and

"sobriety" are qualities "poetry cannot afford for very long to do without."[37] Consequently, the way Dryden "justly" keeps in place "the part of inspiration (or free association from the unconscious) and the part of conscious labour"[38] comes in for the highest praise. Eliot's remarks indicate how successfully he had willed the days of *The Sacred Wood* and *The Waste Land* behind him. Still intuitively a romantic poet, he would forswear the truths of the unconscious for a Drydenesque fidelity to "good sense" and "sobriety." *Murder in the Cathedral* and the *Four Quartets* hover over the text when Eliot quotes from "Religio Laici" and "The Hind and the Panther" and comments, "Anyone who today could make such an exact statement in verse of such nobility and elegance, and with such originality of versification and language, might well look down upon his contemporaries."[39]

The preoccupations that provoked Eliot's praise of Dryden also led him to praise Marianne Moore. Eliot first read Moore's work in the 1917 *Others* and became a tireless supporter. The honor of publishing her first collection belongs to H.D. and Bryher, the women writers who brought out *Poems* (1921) without Moore's knowledge, but Eliot had encouraged her to collect her poems even before, and had told her that her work interested him more than that of anyone writing in America.[40] In the 1923 *Dial* he was effusive about Moore's *Poems* and *Marriage,* and in his capacity as director of Faber and Gwyer he persuaded her in 1935 to let him publish her *Selected Poems,* which contains his own introduction. More pertinently, in a letter of 1925 Eliot wrote how gratified he was that she had appreciated his Dryden essay.[41] Of all his contemporaries she was the one who had successfully appropriated the virtues he now wanted to make his own. As early as 1918 he had praised the way she suffused her ideas (usually "imageless") with feeling and had pointed out how she presented the movements of thought with "a sort of Latin shapeliness."[42] In 1935 he was more explicit. In his introduction to *Selected Poems* he wrote that "she seems to have saturated her mind in the *perfections of prose, in its precision* rather than its purple; and to have found her rhythm, her poetry, her appreciation of the individual word, for herself. . . . To the moderately intellectual the poems may appear to be intellectual exercises; only to *those whose intellection moves more easily* will they immediately appear to have emotional value. . . . [her poems] might be classified as 'descriptive' rather than 'lyrical' or 'dramatic.' Descriptive poetry . . . is really one of the permanent modes of expression. . . . For a mind of such agility, and for a sensibility so reticent, the minor subject, such as a pleasant little sand-coloured skipping animal, may be the best release for major emotions."[43]

As in his essays on Dryden Eliot here points to the way a precise and prosaic representation of thought may move us as poetry. Responding to Moore's disciplined use of images and to her natural speech, he praises her ability to write poems that are perilously close to being "intellectual" exercises. Following the remarks just cited, he also observes her ability to articulate emotionally charged thoughts through the subtleties of syncopated rhymes and careful lineation. Along with the intellectual variety of Moore's "descriptive" verse, these distinctions will mark his own later verse. Blessed by nature with a taste for poetry not only of description but of statement, Marianne Moore mastered a style that pivots on the transition points of expository syntax. The result, as Eliot saw it, was an example he could not but emulate if he was to compete with Andrewes or Dryden. Her descriptiveness would condition the landscape poems he was soon to write. And in a swatch of her verse that he includes in his introduction we notice inflections common to "Journey of the Magi" and "Burnt Norton":

> I recall their magnificence, now not more magnificent
> than it is dim. It is difficult to recall the ornament,
>   speech, and precise manner of what one might
>   call the minor acquaintances twenty
>   years back. . . . .

More significant than Eliot's fascination with Dryden or Moore, though, was his long-standing appreciation of the great middle cantos of the *Purgatorio*. Curiously enough, in "Dante" (1929), though he asserts that "from the *Purgatorio* one learns that a straightforward philosophical statement can be great poetry" (SE, 213–14), he does not explain how. He cites at length from *Purgatorio* XVI and XVII, and he exhorts his readers that the citations are to be appreciated not as philosophy but as poetry. For an elaboration of what he means, however, the reader must look elsewhere—to the essay "Sir John Davies," for example, where Eliot, writing about an inferior Dante of the Elizabethan period, suggests the importance of the philosophical sections of the *Purgatorio* in his own work.

Eliot's 1926 essay on Davies concludes with an extended citation from *Purgatorio* XVI, but he begins by discussing another philosophical poem, *Nosce Teipsum*. Davies's vocabulary, he writes,

> is clear, choice and precise. . . . the thought is continuous. . . . The style appears plain, even bald, yet Davies's personal cadence is always there. Many critics have remarked the condensation of thought, the economy of language, and the consistency of excellence; but some have fallen into the error of supposing that Davies's merit is of prose. . . . with a taste in language remarkably pure for his age, Davies had that strange gift, so rarely bestowed, for turning thought into feeling (OPP, 152–53).

What Eliot then adds says a great deal about why the "gift" of "turning thought into feeling" should now be so precious to him. Linguistic precision and intellectual coherence, according to Eliot, are guides to the sincerity of a poet's feeling. As with Dante, Davies's "thought is not exploited for the sake of feeling, it is pursued for its own sake; and the feeling is a kind of by-product." The cause is Davies's "capacity for belief," which is almost "mediaeval." Thus the prose precision of Davies's poetry certifies both his belief and his real but narrow range of feeling—the only kind of feeling, Eliot now argues, which is appropriate to great poetry.

This is, it hardly needs saying, almost a complete about-face from Eliot's earlier view that poets must be obscure, "difficult," "indirect," "to force, to dislocate if necessary, language into . . . meaning."[44] According to "Sir John Davies," a poet must disregard the immediate experience which antecedes thought and pursue only that feeling which is the direct result of thought, of "a man reasoning with himself in solitude."

There are, I think, few better formulae for Eliot's later poetry than "a man reasoning with himself in solitude." And interestingly, leading up to the phrase, Eliot revived a subject which had once caused him acute psychic distress. As the first part of this study demonstrated, *The Waste Land* may be seen as a (finally inadequate) response to anxieties called up by Eliot's own inclination toward rhetoric. Now, as Eliot was groping toward a second style, the issue reappears:

> The type of his thought, and consequently the tone of his expression, separates him from the Senecals. His thought, as we have said, is inferior as philosophy, but it is coherent and free from eccentricity or pose. He thinks like a scholastic, though the quality of his thought would have shocked a scholastic. Chapman, Daniel, and Greville, so far as they can be said to have thought at all, thought like Latin *rhetoricians*. Like the other dramatists, they imbibed from Seneca a philosophy which is essentially a *theatrical pose*. Hence their language, even when pure and restrained—and Daniel's is astonishingly pure and restrained—is always orotund and *oratorical;* their verse is *as if spoken in public,* and their feelings as if felt in public. *Davies's is the language and the tone of solitary meditation;* he speaks like a man reasoning with himself in solitude, and he never raises his voice (OPP, 154; emphasis mine).

The revulsion animating Eliot's use of phrases like "theatrical pose" and "felt in public" suggests he had still not resolved his old tensions. Having given up his faith in the power of the emotional self, Eliot yet continued to resist the pull of oratory, of public speech, of rhetoric. And that resistance, I think, helps to explain why the pressures that tore him apart in 1921–23 would soon re-emerge in his poetry.

Despite what would seem a necessary connection between the discourses of philosophy and public speech, in Eliot's later work they will be put in constant opposition. As the words I just quoted suggest, Eliot fastened upon philosophical precision not as a mode of public speech but as a way of avoiding it. Though he prasies the illusion of "a man reasoning" in Davies's poetry, he has in mind a man reasoning not with his fellow men but with himself. He has adopted the virtues of reason, coherence and precision, it seems, for the same purpose his *images trouvailles* once served: as a way to avoid rhetoric. But according to Eliot, not only is philosophical meditation "intent on its object" and free from "pose," it is also free from "eccentricity"—that is, free from the individual flavor he had once been at such pains to cultivate. Thus, in "Sir John Davies," Eliot lays out a blueprint for a poetry not, as "Burnt Norton" would have it, of "concentration / Without elimination," but of a concentration which eliminates both the outer and the inner worlds to aid in the contemplation of the divine. This poetry will deal in the logic of meditation and will be centered upon what in "Lancelot Andrewes" he calls the difficult "ecstacy of assent."

Once that is apparent, it is not hard to see why Eliot's later poetry always seems hard-won. Whereas his early verse had at least acknowledged the romantic and anti-romantic elements of his personality, the later poetry will exhibit a fierce concentration on "a man reasoning with himself in solitude." Its intellectual and denotative precision, however, will be imperiled by two psychic forces—from below by excluded feelings, and from above by defensive anti-romantic postures Eliot is at pains to resist. It is no wonder that in the *Four Quartets,* where the difficulty of maintaining linguistic precision becomes one of his reiterated themes, Eliot thinks of clarity in terms of resisting temptation. In "Burnt Norton," for example, his discipline is a way to conquer the horrors of *The Waste Land:* "decay," "mockery," and "tempting voices":

> Words strain,
> Crack and sometimes break, under the burden,
> Under the tension, slip, slide, perish,
> Decay with imprecision, will not stay in place,
> Will not stay still. Shrieking voices
> Scolding, mocking, or merely chattering,
> Always assail them. The Word in the desert
> Is most attacked by voices of temptation,
> The crying shadow in the funeral dance,
> The loud lament of the disconsolate chimera.

Eliot ends "Sir John Davies" with three tercets from *Purgatorio* XVI, tercets which he says are "vastly finer" than anything in *Nosce Teipsum* "for two quite different reasons": First, "Dante was a vastly greater poet." Second, "the philosophy which he expounds is infinitely more substantial and subtle":

> *Esce di mano a lui, che la vagheggia*
> *prima che sia, a guisa di fanciulla*
> *che piangendo e ridendo pargoleggia,*
>
> *l'anima semplicetta, che sa nulla,*
> *salvo che, mossa da lieto fattore,*
> *volentier torna a cio che la trastulla.*

Di picciol bene in pria sente sapore;
quivi s'inganna, e retro ad esso corre,
se guida o fren non torce suo amore.

From his hands who fondly loves her ere she is
in being, there issues, after the fashion of a little
child that sports, now weeping, now laughing,

the simple, tender soul, who knoweth naught save
that, sprung from a joyous maker, willingly she
turneth to that which delights her.

First she tastes the savour of a trifling good; there
she is beguiled and runneth after it, if guide or curb
turn not her love aside.

Eliot speaks as if he would be greatly pleased to see this "substantial and subtle" thinking rendered into contemporary philosophical verse. Three years later he himself tried to do just that. In many ways "Animula" (1929) represents the intentions of the middle phase of Eliot's career in their purest form. At the same time, it suggests some of the pitfalls that were to plague Eliot to the end of his life.

5

"Animula" is a meditation on the text with which it begins: " 'Issues from the hand of God, the simple soul.' " Reflecting on Dante's exposition of life as a pilgrimage generated by desire, Eliot absorbs Dante's parable into one of his own. The poem is what Eliot had called phenomenological. Each of its four movements illustrates "what it feels like" to view the world from a different platform. Lines one through fifteen, for example, envisage the difficulties of a child-like state of sensation. Although a child takes strong and genuine pleasure "In the fragrant brilliance of the Christmas tree, / Pleasure in the wind, the sunlight and the sea," his sensation alone cannot distinguish between "the actual and the fanciful." Consequently, the child comes to feel everything is fanciful, trivial, unreal—matter no more substantial than "What the fairies do and what the servants say." Sensation, in other words, is not enough. A man needs intellectual convictions to give his world value and solidity. But, as the next section (ll. 16–23) suggests, convictions alone are bound to be felt as unreal "burdens." Without faith, they are nothing but the "imperatives of 'is and seems' / And may and may not, desire and control." To found moral judgment upon them is an act of immaturity, an immaturity Eliot figures in the synechdoche of the small soul's naive trust in the *Encyclopaedia Britannica*. Finally, the soul's inability to distinguish between what is real and what is not results in an anxious paralysis of the will. The third section of "Animula" (ll. 24–31) anatomizes that inevitable condition from the standpoint of an awareness already beyond it, and the fourth, having rejected the various postures of unbelief, turns to prayer.

Paraphrasing "Animula," of course, ignores the poem's "concrete imagery" which, as Eliot's best readers have pointed out, makes "the spiritual visible" and creates the "charm" of its "picture of childhood."[45] It does, however, suggest why Eliot's style seems to be so unstable. Bracketing out the poem's central figure, we are left with Eliot's efforts to fix the way stages of consciousness feel. And since he is now interested in "the salvation of the 'soul' " rather than in " 'personalities' " (SE, 233), Eliot dramatizes "the way it feels" in generalized terms ("the imperatives of 'is and seems' "). In Eliot's earlier verse, generalizations had been subordinated to a cluster of concrete images:

> April is the cruellest month, breeding
> Lilacs out of the dead land, mixing
> Memory and desire, stirring
> Dull roots with spring rain.

But in "Animula," generalized phrases depend for their impact not on dramatic or symbolic heightening but on a kind of attention-getting precision. Thus configurations like "the offered good" are intended to avoid emotional distractions and reinforce our concentration on universal truths. So "Animula" finally reminds us of Eliot's admiration for Dryden, a writer who he said "became a great poet . . . because he had that uncorruptible sincerity of word which at all times distinguishes the good writer from the bad, and at critical times such as his, distinguishes the great writer from the little one."[46]

But "Animula" bespeaks more than an "uncorruptible sincerity of word." It also conveys something else that Eliot said on the same occasion: "It is harder to be natural than to be artificial; it requires a great deal more work, and is painful and unpleasant, because sincerity is always painful and unpleasant. Dryden did the work, and experienced, no doubt, the pain and unpleasantness, and he restored English verse to the condition of speech."[47]

An honest reading of "Animula," I think, uncovers a great deal of labor, pain and unpleasantness. Through intense concentration on philosophical implication and denotative precision, the poem softens the resonance of its emotional subject. And though it sometimes succeeds on its own terms, this exclusion comes back to haunt it in the form of an all-but-palpable resistance, an awkwardness of expression that seems to require a considerable effort to overcome. One might even say that it is precisely the poem's occasional achievement of true precision, either of statement or image or cadence, that makes us aware of its countervailing tension. Such moments highlight phrases that have the precision of neither good poetry nor good prose ("flat world") and make us aware of effects that can only be called lugubrious (the rhyming of "arm and knee" with "and the sea").

To appreciate what Eliot's style excludes, consider the source of his illustrative detail. In an extraordinary manner "Animula" fashions philosophical generalization out of the raw material of personal confession. The poem's childhood by the sea, its "imperatives of 'is and seems,'" its will "Unable to fare forward or retreat, / Fearing the warm reality, the offered good, / Denying the importunity of the blood" are recognizably Eliot's own. They remind us of the summers of his growing years he spent on Cape Ann, of the intellectual crisis of his adolescence, and of his marriage. (In 1929 Eliot with characteristic agony was trying to decide whether to leave Vivien or make another new start.) But though "Animula" looks back at his life, its manner and its diction try to exclude his inner experience, only to provoke in their turn an intrusive resistance in lines like "Unable to fare forward or retreat."

One index to how much resistance is at work in "Animula" is the extent to which the poetry is disfigured by mannerism, and in particular, by Eliot's long-time weakness for parallel constructions. Earlier, Eliot had lived with this tic and had used it to open his poems up to the apparent contradictions of subconscious ambivalence ("I looked for the head of Mr. Apollinax rolling under a chair./ *Or* grinning over a screen"). Once Eliot ceased to care about representing the unconscious, however, his old habit fell under the sway of other impulses. In "Animula" it is rampant:

> . . . dry or damp, chilly or warm;
>
> . . . .
> Rising or falling. . . .
>
> . . . .
> Content with playing-cards and kings and queens,
> What the fairies do and what the servants say.
>
> . . . .
> Perplexes and offends more, day by day;
> Week by week, offends and perplexes more
>
> . . . .
> Unable to fare forward or retreat,
>
> . . . .
> Shadow of its own shadows, spectre in its own gloom. . . .

Unmistakably, this collection of parallelisms signals a lapse in Eliot's poetic "touch." Willfully rejecting his romantic temper, he permits his style to waver, and, his instincts disabled, the lines are allowed to stand. But Eliot's decision to overlook those flaws was overdetermined, and it is a second field of determination that makes "Animula" so valuable an indicator of Eliot's development.

If the pattern of mannered parallelisms I have pointed out weakens "Animula," it no less clearly also bolsters it from an unexpected direction. Whatever the poem's aspiration to present "a man reasoning with himself in solitude," its characteristic rhythms have less to do with a philosopher's thought than with a certain kind of poetic lyric. Eliot's syntactic liberties create an incantatory rhythm that effaces the poem's affinity with, say, Marianne Moore, and charges it with the repetitive power of a charm or a litany:

> Shadow of its own shadows, spectre in its own gloom. . . .

We have seen Eliot drifting into incantation before, of course, and for similar reasons. In the water-dripping song of *The Waste Land,* he overlaid Imagist concentration with incantatory effects to ward off the menace of feelings his images had unexpectedly dislodged. Now, although his style has changed, the same kind of thing recurs. In "Animula," Eliot approaches his life through the mediation of philosophy but he nonetheless disturbs feelings he is not prepared to confront. These feelings, which his new discursive style excludes from direct representation, seek release in two ways. As I have suggested, they create a resistance in what the French practitioners of *la nouvelle critique* would call Eliot's languaging, turning composition into a constant struggle with awkwardness. And they achieve a more positive expression in the form of an incantatory rhythm that has little to do with the poem's principal subject. No less than the incantatory style of Poe, which Eliot would later disparage, the rhythmic shape of "Animula," "because of its very crudity, stirs the feelings at a deep and almost primitive level" (TCC, 31).

However similar the function of the incantatory sequences in "Animula" and *The Waste Land,* though, the way Eliot responded to them was very different. Although he admired his water-dripping song, the accumulated weight of his early procedures made it difficult to incorporate its principles into his poetic practice: his next project, *The Hollow Men,* was still a recognizably Imagist work. By the time of "Animula," he was not only ready to approve what he had made but to remake himself around it. We see this beginning to happen in "Sir John Davies" (1926), where Eliot comments that philosophical poetry must clarify belief. The poem's "entertainment," then, falls to rhythm: the "variation is in the metrics" (OPP, 154). That is, the rhythms of discursive poetry need not be part of a "unique whole of feeling" but may instead be a means of pleasing "variation." They are, in other words, a vehicle to bring out the truth not of a poet's mood but of his philosophy. Yet, divorced from mood, they lose their hold on the only solid anchor in Eliot's world. It is not surprising, then, that the more earnestly Eliot strives toward philosophical concentration, the more he seems to veer toward loosened syntax, musical elaboration of ideas and incantatory rhythms. Such was the power of his emotional life to resist the requirements of purely intellectual analysis.

As the quotation from the essay on Poe at the end of chapter five suggested, in moments of self-consciousness Eliot would be appalled by the attractions of incantation and denounce a "syntax . . . determined

by the musical significance" as meretricious "rhetoric."[48] Nevertheless,
from the mid-twenties on precisely those procedures became the key-
stone of what he understood by "the magic of verse" (TCC, 31). Out
of character in *The Waste Land,* and tentative and halting in the fifth
section of *The Hollow Men,* these procedures became during the period
of the *Ariel* poems part of his *stil novo.* In a remarkable passage in the
choruses from *The Rock* (1934), Eliot even hails incantation as the very
"soul" of poetry, foreshadowing "Burnt Norton":

> The soul of Man must quicken to creation.
> Out of the formless stone, when the artist united himself with
>   stone,
> Spring always new forms of life, from the soul of man that is
>   joined to the soul of stone;
> Out of the meaningless practical shapes of all that is living or
>   lifeless
> Joined with the artist's eye, new life, new form, new colour.
> Out of the sea of sound the life of music,
> Out of the slimy mud of words, out of the sleet and hail of ver-
>   bal imprecisions,
> Approximate thoughts and feelings, words that have taken the
>   place of thoughts and feelings,
> There spring the perfect order of speech, and the beauty of
>   incantation.
>
> (CPP, 111)

How pronounced Eliot's desire to emerge "Out of the slimy mud,"
and how unlike the high modernist contention "that life would be intolerable except for the fact that one has, from the top, such an exceptional view of the public dump."[49] Detectably in "Animula" and unde-
niably in *The Rock,* Eliot was being drawn out of the orbit of Pound and
Joyce and back into the orbit of the symbolists. And as his first gestures
toward a music of ideas in *The Hollow Men* had corresponded to a reading of Paul Valéry, so now his growing passion for incantation attracted
him into the world of Valéry's master, Mallarmé. That movement, which
culminated in the *Four Quartets,* would reinforce Eliot's tendency to devalue his earlier poems, and affect the way he performed them. When
asked in 1949, for example, why he tended to chant his verse, Eliot
replied that he found "the incantatory element is very important. So far
as possible, the reciter should not dramatize. It is the words that matter, not the feeling about them. When I read poetry myself I put myself in a kind of trance and move in rhythm to the rhythm of the piece
in question."[50] It is an answer that goes a long way toward explaining
why his recordings of the dramatic lyrics he wrote before *The Hollow
Men* so often disturb their admirers.

The full story of Eliot's encounter with Mallarmé is best postponed,
however. Although Eliot began to reread him in 1925, his fullest re-

sponse came in the early thirties—the period of "Landscapes" and "Burnt Norton." Closely related, however, is a more contemporary rapprochement.

6

The way Eliot's notion of poetic figuration altered during the nineteen twenties is apparent from remarks already considered in this chapter. In the distinction he drew in 1926, for example, between Donne (who finds "an object which shall be adequate to his feelings") and Lancelot Andrewes (who is "wholly absorbed in the object and therefore responds with the adequate emotion"), we see Eliot move away from Pound ("the proper and perfect symbol is the natural object") and toward Yeats, who argued that poetic figures may be shadows as long as "long association" gathers around them.[51] From there it was but a small step to affirm the value of self-conscious poetic symbols. If, as Eliot wrote in *The Rock,* the life of poetry exists in the "new forms" that the poet generates from "the meaningless practical shapes of all that is living," then clearly the value of an image depends less on its original context than on the context the poet gives it. As Eliot elaborated in 1931, it is the destiny of all the words in a poem to approach the status of symbols—a status which has a counterpart in religious tradition:

> Symbolism is that to which the word tends both in religion and in poetry; the incarnation of meaning in fact; and in poetry it is the tendency of the word to mean as much as possible. To find the word and give it the utmost meaning, in its place; to mean as many things as possible, to make it both exact and comprehensive, and really to *unite* the disparate and remote, to give them a fusion and a pattern with the word, surely this is the mastery at which the poet aims. . . . [and] no extravagance of a genuine poet can go so far over the borderline of ordinary intellect as the Creeds of the Church.[52]

Little wonder that Eliot would later characterize Imagism as a minor offshoot of French symbolism that concentrated on "purification of language and the creation of new metaphor" but which developed a theory "inadequate" to the school that produced and survived it.[53]

As with so many of Eliot's stylistic transformations, his enthusiasm for symbolic incarnation grew up around an encounter with another poet. In 1931, in the midst of praising Harry Crosby's "search for a personal symbolism," Eliot described his own "progressive imitation" of a symbolist predecessor, an imitation which is actually, he said, "a finding of [ourselves] by a progressive absorption in, and absorption of, and rejection (but never a total rejection) of other writers."[54] In this case the predecessor in question was the poet and diplomat St.-John Perse, whose *Anabase* Eliot translated between 1926 and 1930.[55] In the preface to this translation, Eliot made his famous pronouncement that "there is a logic of the imagination as well as a logic of concepts."[56] But this remark, often quoted in introductions to modern literature, is something less than the encapsulation of his career it is sometimes said to be. Made a year before Eliot's defense of Harry Crosby's "concentrated and exact . . . sequence and arrangement of image and rhythm,"[57] and accompanying lavish praise for what would become *Finnegans Wake,* Eliot's *pronunciamento* affirms an aspect of poetry that had become central to his work only recently.

Anabase is a poem whose haunting beauty is impossible to describe to anyone who is not acquainted with it. Combining concrete detail with narrative indefiniteness, it achieves the "jeu, très allusif et mystérieux . . . à la limite du saisissable" that Perse said he had aimed at.[58] The poem was inspired by Xenophon, but, as Eliot points out in his introduction, it has "no particular reference" to the external world—neither to the historical journey of the Ten Thousand nor to the map of Asia Minor.[59] Instead it renders what Perse called "la solitude dans l'action. Aussi bien l'action parmi les hommes que l'action de l'esprit envers autrui comme envers soi-même. J'ai voulu rassembler la synthèse non pas passive mais active de la ressource humaine."[60] To do so it assembles, to again use Eliot's terms, a sequence of images, ideas, stresses and pauses. And this sequence, concentrated to evoke an eternal moment of the human soul, helped Eliot find himself once again. At least, his effort at translation made an impact such that recalling it in 1949 he confessed, "On voit son influence dans quelques-uns des poèmes que j'écrivis après avoir achevé la traduction: influence des images et peut-être aussi du rythme. Ceux qui examineront mes derniers ouvrages trouveront peut-être que cette influence persiste toujours."[61]

Perhaps the best way to demonstrate what translating *Anabase* meant to Eliot is to look at a particularly influential section along with Eliot's translation. I give the beginning of Canto VI.

> TOUT-PUISSANTS dans nos grands gouvernements militaires, avec nos filles parfumées qui se vêtaient d'un souffle, ces tissus,
> nous établîmes en haut lieu nos pièges au bonheur.
> Abondance et bien-être, bonheur! Aussi longtemps nos verres où la glace pouvait chanter comme Memnon . . .
> Et fourvoyant à l'angle des terrasses une mêlée d'éclairs, de grands plats d'or aux mains des filles de service fauchaient l'ennui des sables aux limites du monde.
> Puis ce fut une année de souffles en Ouest et, sur nos toits lestés de pierres noires, tout un propos de toiles vives adonnées au délice du large.
>
> OMNIPOTENT in our great military governments, with our scented girls clad in a breath of silk webs,
> we set in high places our springes for happiness.

Plenty and well-being, happiness! For so long the ice sang in
our glasses, like Memnon . . .
And deflecting a crossing of lights to the corners of terraces,
great chargers of gold held up by the handmaidens, smote the
weariness of the sands, at the confines of the world.
Then came a year of wind in the west and, on our roofs
weighted with black stones, a whole business of bright cloths
abandoned to the delight of wide spaces.[62]

In this excerpt, Perse conjures up a state of mind ("nos filles parfu-
mées qui se vêtaient d'un *souffle, ces tissus,*") and then alters the coloring
of the images to suggest a shifting mood ("Puis ce fut une année de
souffles en Ouest et, sur nos toits lestés de pierres noires, tout un propos
de *toiles* vives, adonnées au délice du large"). His combination of concreteness and suggestiveness reminded Eliot of the extended myth-
ological passages in Pound's *Cantos*,[63] but that association is as deceptive
as it is helpful. Whereas in Pound's *Cantos* images are allowed to assert
their own claims, here they are amplified with the apparatus of bardic
chant. Perse shares with Pound an incantatory parataxis and an ability
to suggest the visionary present through participial constructions ("Et
fourvoyant à l'angle . . ."). But his breathlessness and his weakness for
imprecise metaphor ("l'ennui des sables aux limites du monde") suggest
not the *Cantos* but Dylan Thomas's "Fern Hill." Eliot's translation,
moreover, emphasizes precisely this element of rhapsodic fluidity. In
Eliot's hands "se vêtaient d'un souffle, ces tissus" loses its caesura and
becomes "clad in a breath of silk webs." He also alliterates "tout un
propos de toiles vives" as "a whole business of bright cloths."[64] Eliot is
concerned, in other words, to heighten the opacity of the verse and
emphasize the exoticism and otherworldliness of Perse's central images.
In the original, and even more in the translation, Perse's substantives
approach the status of musical themes and combine with what Eliot's
preface calls the poet's *"declamation,* the system of stresses and pauses,"
to transform a passage of natural description into a self-conscious poetic confection. (Perse in fact complained to Eliot about his liberties,
but his protest had no effect.)[65]

The sixth canto of *Anabase* is particularly significant because it inspired a section of "Journey of the Magi":[66]

'A cold coming we had of it,
Just the worst time of the year
For a journey, and such a long journey:
The ways deep and the weather sharp,
The very dead of winter.'
And the camels galled, sore-footed, refractory,
Lying down in the melting snow.
There were times we regretted
The summer palaces on slopes, the terraces,
And the silken girls bringing sherbet.

> Then the camel men cursing and grumbling
> And running away, and wanting their liquor and women,
> And the night-fires going out, and the lack of shelters,
> And the cities hostile and the towns unfriendly
> And the villages dirty and charging high prices. . . .

I am not the first to notice that Perse was the source of Eliot's serving girls, or that the syntax and the figurative thrust of *Anabase* give Eliot's lines their idiosyncratic flavor.[67] "Journey of the Magi" begins by borrowing from Lancelot Andrewes's 1622 Christmas Day nativity sermon and like the sermon sharpens the gospel's detail. But the developing incantatory power of the passage transforms Andrewes's liturgical repetition and creates a Persean world of imagination. It is true that Eliot is more precise about his images than Perse, and that we find nothing in his poem that resembles "adonnées au délice du large." But no less obviously Eliot establishes and repeats his images to suggest a series of delicate emotional shifts. (Notice for example the way "we regretted . . . the silken girls bringing sherbert" is repeated in another key as "the camel men . . . wanting their . . . women"). As in Perse or Pound, Eliot's syntax suspends images in a world of enclosed vision. Thus the incantatory series "And the camels . . . And the silken girls . . . And the night-fires going out" makes us almost forget the gritty realism of the scene. As Perse had admonished him on the draft of his translation of *Anabase,* the purpose of such poetry is not to call up a single journey in the mind's eye but to suggest the significance—at once geographical and spiritual—of a journey toward the interior.[68]

But these reminiscences in the poem's first stanza only begin to suggest its debt to Perse. Its most distinctive Persean elements emerge in what is to follow, and turn it into a more difficult kind of poem than it first appears. A companion piece to "A Song for Simeon," "Journey of the Magi" dramatizes the period in Eliot's life that followed his official conversion, when his old ways of thinking and feeling seemed irrevocably alien and his new life as a Christian existed more in intention than fact. Like Simeon's recognition of the Christ child in the temple, its Christmas epiphany corresponds to Eliot's own fleeting conversion experience. "Journey of the Magi," however, transcends its fiction in a way that "A Song for Simeon" does not. In it, Eliot undermines the dramatic monologue form almost as soon as he announces it. Instead of cultivating the illusion of an objective speaker, for example, Eliot suggests that the events of the monologue are convenient but inadequate representations of an experience that lies outside the dramatic frame. In doing so he calls into question the continuity of the private experience to which the frame corresponds. Thus though composed a year earlier than "Simeon," "Journey" is a less conventional work. It is also a better guide to where Eliot was going.

Like "Animula," "Journey of the Magi" begins with a self-conscious

citation, signaling that the following account is not a dramatic monologue but a meditation that centers around the assumption of a role.
As stanza two begins, this becomes clearer and Eliot's setting turns
problematic. Departing from the story of the Magi, he introduces images from two unexpected sources—from accounts of the Passion and
from his own storehouse of private imagery. ("Why, for all of us . . .
do certain images recur, charged with emotion, rather than others? . . .
six ruffians seen through an open window playing cards at night at a
small French railway junction where there was a water-mill: such memories may have symbolic value, but of what we cannot tell, for they
come to represent the depths of feeling into which we cannot peer.")[69]

> Then at dawn we came down to a temperate valley,
> Wet, below the snow line, smelling of vegetation;
> With a running stream and a water-mill beating the darkness,
> And three trees on the low sky,
> And an old white horse galloped away in the meadow.
> Then we came to a tavern with vine-leaves over the lintel,
> Six hands at an open door dicing for pieces of silver,
> And feet kicking the empty wine-skins. . . .

Noticing that the story's frame of reference has been broken, most
readers feel compelled to do one of two things: either they invoke the
authority of Christian allegory and gloss the entire section by reference
to the traditional commentaries about the Passion; or they emphasize
the pressure of Eliot's own inner life.[70] But to do either is to ignore the
fact that the poem flaunts its indeterminacy. Eliot's symbolic configuration conflates three realms of reference—the fictional frame, the correspondences of Christian typology, and his own deepest and most
troublesome feelings. And far from asserting the dominance of any of
them, the poem opens up a field in which the question of reference is
deliberately deferred.[71]

What allows Eliot to perform this act of prestidigitation, of course, is
the effects he had appropriated from Perse. In the incantatory magic
of stanza two, the boundaries between the dramatic and the allegorical
blur and the unexpected Biblical allusion to Calvary's "three trees on
the low sky" jars but a little. Thus when we try to interpret a detail like
the valley's redolent vegetation, it is good to keep in mind Eliot's opinion of *Anabase:* writing to Virginia Woolf from Los Angeles once, he
told her that in America, to use the words of *Anabase,* "doubt is cast on
the reality of things."[72] The same holds for everything Eliot introduces
in the second stanza of "Journey of the Magi." The vegetation, the
running stream, the water mill, the three trees, the old white horse and
the rest come from two different worlds of significance—the world of
pre-conscious experience and the world of Christian exegesis. "Doubt
is cast" by the poem on the significance of both. Both worlds represent

different ways of apprehending the decomposition and death that Eliot inevitably associates with spring and the natural world. (Along with other things, it is certainly death that lies at the bottom of the "depths of feeling into which [Eliot] cannot peer.") But in stanza two, Eliot is willing to bestow the name of reality on neither his private fears nor Christianity's promises. Both put the solidity of his natural setting in question, but the Perse-like ambiance in which both are introduced puts them in question as well.

The context of Eliot's ambiguity, of course, is a retrospective testing of epiphanic experience. Very much as in the Hyacinth garden episode of *The Waste Land,* Eliot's speaker (in this poem, he is only the focus of Eliot's meditation) asks in the final stanza: Was I "led all that way for / Birth or Death?" (Did I look "into the heart of light" or the "silence?") Here, though, the question, no less insistent and no less tortuously sincere, is explicit, and the "heart of light" has a name. If Eliot, speaking equivocally through the mask of the Magus, cannot credit the Christian explanation of things, he is at least willing to entertain it, and to bring the Passion, the cross, and the resurrection into his trance-like world.

In *Ash Wednesday* and some of the shorter pieces that follow it, Eliot will experiment further with the possibility of a symbolism that is not simply the correlative of powerful feeling. He will, proceeding from a desire to assimilate philosophical discourse, allow poetry to be more than the expression of states of feeling that antecede it. And yet his eventual achievement will only superficially resemble the discursiveness of the *Purgatorio.* In fact, he will allow his poetry to become more of a game. In Perse's words, he will create "un jeu, très allusif et mystérieux,"[73] in which feelings lead the self beyond *what is* to *what might be.* In it, things are called into question and even natural scenery is as immaterial as a ghost—no more substantial than religious icons and as abstract as the artificial dance of philosophy. These poems will be dreams, but not in the manner of *The Waste Land.* Their dreams will be hallucinatory fields, open areas where the attractions of the ideal are as pressing as sorrow. They will, in short, be fields of crossing between one system of "belief attitudes" and another—or as the conclusion of *Ash Wednesday* would have it, places "of solitude where three dreams cross." To quote something Eliot said about Poe and Mallarmé in 1926, they will be worlds which expand sensibility *"au-delà des limites du monde normal"* and discoveries of "nouveaux objets propres à susciter de nouvelles émotions."[74]

Finally, as he strives in these poems to liberate himself from the oppressive world of his tortured psyche, Eliot will pay the price of frequent failure. Like the incantatory techniques that help call them into being, his poetic fields will venture beyond the condition of immediate experience and fall victim to a number of different kinds of falseness. At first the attempts will be forced and unsupple, but as Eliot becomes more sure of himself the willfulness of the mid-twenties will fall away. Looking ahead, his progress from "Journey of the Magi" to "Burnt Norton" will be a development in which Eliot forces himself to introduce new modes of discursiveness, symbolism and incantation, tests their limits and finally reimposes the control of an expended authenticity. *Ash Wednesday* will have its blemishes, but without them, "Burnt Norton" is inconceivable. As Eliot himself said with reference to the poems of Harry Crosby, "Except in directions in which we can go too far there is no interest in going at all; and only those who will risk going too far can possibly find out just how far one can go." [75]

CHAPTER EIGHT

"Explaining to himself": *Ash Wednesday*

Between the usual subjects of poetry and "devotional" verse there is a very important field still very unexplored by modern poets—the experience of a man in search of God, and trying to explain to himself his intenser human feelings in terms of the divine goal. I have tried to do something of that in "Ash Wednesday."

T. S. Eliot to William Force Stead, 9 August 1930.[1]

Ash Wednesday, then, is not devotional poetry, which Eliot disdained because of its *"special* and limited awareness" of human passion (SE, 345). Religious attitudes play a part in the poem, they do not control it. Instead, the poem presents a struggle between secular and religious ways of Eliot's "explaining to himself" his own "intenser human feelings." Testing the validity of his religious calling, he sways between different visions of life. And it is precisely in the sway—in the dizzying disengagement from old organizations of the self, mirrored in poetry that at times comes very close to nonsense—that a new self is born. As the poem's conclusion puts it, borrowing the word "dream" from *The Hollow Men,*

> This is the time of tension between dying and birth
> The place of solitude where three dreams cross. . . .

Eliot's poetry, of course, had always been a place of solitude where amorous dreams crossed, and *Ash Wednesday* registers some of the poet's oldest crossed purposes. But this place of solitude also reflects a specific moment in Eliot's life. Written and published piecemeal during 1928, 1929 and 1930, the fragments of *Ash Wednesday,* like the *Ariel* poems, give us the inner landscape of Eliot's protracted and difficult conversion—his awareness of its costs and his fear that even after he had publicly committed himself to the Anglican church, his profession of belief would never ripen into spiritual fulfillment. Attempting to solidify his new-found faith, the poem explores the apprehensions of one who all too consciously "affirms before the world and denies between the rocks." As Elisabeth Schneider has said, "Though its theme is appropriate enough for the day that marks the beginning of Lent, [it] is not merely the self-examination and repentance prescribed for the occasion. It contains these, but they fall within . . . a history and in the end a meticulously honest examination of one man's inner change and a weighing of that change to know how great it is, how genuine, how small."[2]

We are struck by the personal quality of Eliot's *Ash Wednesday* regimen when we recognize the confessions that, unwilling to elaborate, he takes small pains to conceal. "Desiring this man's gift," he acknowledges the chronic unproductiveness that continues to worry him even as he prays to leave secular concerns behind. Later, he sees below him a shape (on the typescript he wrote "my own shape")[3] that mirrors "the devil of the stairs who wears / The deceitful shape of hope and of despair" and embodies the doubts that inhabit his essay on Pascal. More poignantly he remembers the failures of his marriage and his discomfort when, over Vivien's strenuous objections, he disengaged himself from her expectations and entered the church:

> Let these words answer
> For what is done, not to be done again
> May the judgement not be too heavy upon us. . . .

(Eliot originally dedicated *Ash Wednesday* "To My Wife," and it is difficult not to suspect that he offered the poem that she might understand what he previously had not been able to put into words.)

Nor are *Ash Wednesday*'s connections to Eliot's life limited to the painful circumstances that haunt its opening. The origins of the happy state by which the suite assesses the claims of religious devotion are no less private. From "what is done, not to be done again," the poem leads us, just before its final recapitulation, to a "gate" where children gather. In the terms of "Animula," having found himself "irresolute and selfish, misshapen, lame, / Unable to fare forward," Eliot retraces his steps to a time and a state when the ultimate happiness, luminous in the first awareness of love, seemed just on the other side of an unassuming threshold. On the autograph manuscript of "Because I do not hope to turn again" and on the typescript of the same poem he sent Ottoline Morrell in 1928, Eliot entitled his poem "All aboard for Natchez, Cairo and St. Louis."[4] Heeding that call, the poem returns to the sight of a St. Louis schoolyard gate that Eliot recalled vividly in an address he gave in 1959 to the Mary Institute in his old neighborhood. (The gate will reappear in "Burnt Norton.") The Mary Institute was a sister to the school he had himself attended (both were founded with his grandfather's help), and in the address Eliot remembers how the Mary schoolyard

abutted on my father's property. There was at the front of our house a sort of picket fence which divided our front yard from the schoolyard.

This picket fence merged a little later into a high brick wall which concealed our back garden and also concealed the schoolyard from our back garden. There was a door in this wall and there was a key to this door. Now when the young ladies had left the school in the afternoon and at the end of the week, I had access to the schoolyard and used it for my own purposes of play. . . . I remained extremely shy with girls. And, of course, when they were in the schoolyard I was always on the other side of the wall; and on one occasion I remember, when I ventured into the schoolyard a little too early when there were still a few on the premises and I saw them staring at me through a window, I took flight at once.[5]

With its echoes of this moment, *Ash Wednesday,* exploring the sincerity and value of religious response, confirms the persistence of childhood in Eliot's imagination of happiness. And though even childhood intimations will prove inadequate to "explain" his most intense feelings—only "the divine goal," he thinks, will do that—their recovery is powerful enough to invalidate other urgent explanations. With this in mind, we begin to understand *Ash Wednesday*'s literary ancestry. Apparently modeled on Dante's tumultuous reunion with Beatrice in the *Purgatorio,* the poem has more to do with the emotional coloring of the *Vita Nuova*—Dante's progress "from love to caritas"—a work in which the poet's joyful return to beatitude is as important as his renunciation. Eliot was aware of the correspondences between the works, and once wrote that "we cannot understand fully Canto XXX of the *Purgatorio*" until we know the *Vita Nuova*" (SE, 223). Composing *The Hollow Men,* he began with the *Vita Nuova* but made use of passages that recalled Beatrice's rebuke of Dante in the *Purgatorio. Ash Wednesday* reverses the emphasis and transforms Dante's meeting with Beatrice into an idealized vision, very much like the ones at the beginning of the earlier work. As Eliot seems to have personally identified with those visions, it was a way of touching home. (In his 1929 essay on Dante he testified to the *Vita Nuova*'s parallels in experience: "The type of sexual experience which Dante describes as occurring to him at the age of nine years old," he said, "is by no means impossible or unique. My only doubt [in which I found myself confirmed by a distinguished psychologist] is whether it could have taken place so *late* in life as the age of nine years. The psychologist agreed with me that it is more likely to occur at about five or six years of age" [SE, 233].)

In short, though *Ash Wednesday* acknowledges that the reality of adult relations can never be "adequate to human desires" (SE, 379), it also celebrates the effects of uncorrupted desire, both as we encounter it through a glass darkly in childhood and as we understand it "in terms of the divine goal."

"Celebrate," though, is perhaps too strong. It would be more accurate to say a celebration of desire is the polestar toward which *Ash Wednesday* moves. In fact the suite is only marginally more successful in celebrating the life of the heart than were Eliot's earlier poems. At first dramatizing the pattern of the *Commedia*, where an attempt at self-reformation by power of will is thwarted and gives way to a gradual reorientation of the will, *Ash Wednesday* retreats from the oppression of what is actual (I) to a theatre of memory and fantasy (II). In its climax, in the middle of section IV, vision seems to transform both memory and the here and now. But from that point on, Eliot's struggle to cling to the vision is as difficult as ever. Culminating the line of young girls whom Eliot approached in his earlier poetry, the silent sister of *Ash Wednesday*'s vision is partly an object of religious devotion and partly an object of sexual passion. Colored by Eliot's childhood memories of his adored older sisters and their friends as well as by more motherly figures, she appears to provide a focus for a variety of longings without provoking his usual ambivalence. And yet in the fifth section of the poem, which attempts to transform a moment of unimpeded love into a permanent affirmation of faith, Eliot discovers that nothing has changed. He still "cannot surrender," and he turns away from the lady's face. In doing so he re-enacts the tableau of "La Figlia Che Piange": on one side an ardent but self-conscious swain, on the other a young girl whose "fugitive resentment" implies the lover's complicated ambivalence about love. That resurgent image, remaining just below the surface of the poem, charges Eliot's confession of religious inconstancy with its peculiar power. Though he now believes he is only one of many who "chose and oppose"—in other words, that his recalacitrance is not something peculiar to himself but a matter of original sin—his aspirations remain crossed by all the old contorted impulses of his character.

2

Eliot's ambivalent attitude toward desire animates *Ash Wednesday* from its opening lines. Though he recounts private experience and speaks as "I," he wants to emphasize the universality of his experience. Thus he takes pains not to dramatize the personal flavor of his voice. Like Andrewes he would efface his personal feelings and fashion an impersonal medium to squeeze his material "until it yields a full juice of meaning." But with a romantic temperament as strong as Eliot's, a truly impersonal treatment is impossible: the same pressures that had generated irony in Eliot's earlier poetry continue to make themselves felt in his *stil novo*. Consequently, when the "I" tenuously posited by the first poem of *Ash Wednesday* disintegrates into different voices, it does so along fault lines implicit in the opening style of the verse.

As *Ash Wednesday* begins, we overhear Eliot, to use his words in "Sir John Davies," "reasoning with himself in solitude" (OPP, 154). At least, he tries to reason. As we overhear him, he is, with considerable agitation, attempting to persuade himself of the justice of turning from the world. But though his persuasion originates on the level of rational discourse, the pressures working against it (and against the rational self it presumes) are considerable. Before the end of the first verse paragraph, a Shakespearean phrase ("Desiring this man's gift and that man's scope") signals how difficult it is to keep dispassionate self-analysis from lapsing into *The Waste Land*'s neurotic circle of self-conscious rhetoric and reflex self-disgust.[6] Like the twitch of an obsession that has almost been outgrown, the lapse is fleeting, but it serves to underline how much energy Eliot has to expend to maintain a surface of lucidity and directness.

The internal resistance that disturbs Eliot's reasoning is in fact so strong that new readers are shocked when they realize how straightforward the syntactic skeleton of the first part of *Ash Wednesday* is. Eliot begins with a piece of self-exhortation organized around two statements of the form "since I am X, therefore I must do Y":

> (I) Because I do not hope to turn again
>
> . . . .
>
> I rejoice that things are as they are and
> I renounce the blessèd face
>
> . . . .
>
> And I pray that I may forget
>
> . . . .
>
> (II) Because these wings are no longer wings to fly
>
> . . . .
>
> Teach us to sit still.

Against the resolution generated by these syllogisms, however, almost everything else in the poem pulls. The lines I have omitted, by themselves, are hardly obscure; mostly qualifications, they restate the lines they follow with more, or more precise, emphasis:

> Because I do not think
> [No,] Because I *know* I shall not know. . . .

Together, though, they give the discourse a direction of their own, which is not the direction of Eliot's resolve. Given entry by the rules of logic, the subterranean impulses of the poem resist proceeding from "since" to "therefore" into the future and instead regress, logically and temporally, from "because" to "because" to "because":

> Because I do not hope to turn again [Pause]
> *Because* I do not hope
> *Because* I do not hope to turn. . . .

Pushing himself back from because to because upon the origins of his present crisis, Eliot reminds himself of feelings which, though he judges them incapable of producing happiness, are part of him still. And so as we read the poem the syntax we notice is not "Because I do not hope . . . I renounce the blessèd face," but

> Because I do not hope to turn again
>
> . . . .
>
> Why *should* I mourn
> The *vanished* power of the usual reign?

—a sequence which bears the implication "I still *do* mourn."

Similarly, in the following, we do not feel the phrase "I do not hope" as the consequence of something Eliot has freely chosen to do but as the outcome of something he cannot do, though he still yearns to:

> Because I do not hope to know again
>
> . . . .
>
> Because I *cannot* drink
> There, where trees flower, and springs flow, for there is nothing again. . . .

The same is true in:

> Because I know that time is always time
>
> . . . .
>
> I renounce the blessèd face
> And renounce the voice
> Because I *cannot* hope to turn again. . . .

Because of this internal resistance, then, the first section of *Ash Wednesday* becomes not the account of one who has judged his weaknesses and turned his back on them, but the *cri de coeur* of one who would turn his back and yet cannot keep from continuing to lament.

Nor is the counter-stress of which I speak connected simply to the double syntactic movement of the poem's declarative statements. An equal part of it undermines the forms of the statements themselves. Even beyond its insistence on logical procedure ("because," "consequently"), the surface of Eliot's address is measured, qualified, controlled. With two exceptions—his slighting evocation of "wings" to suggest former romantic aspirations[7] and a momentary vision of a place "where trees flower, and springs flow"—he rejects the possibilities of figuration in favor of an abstract, generalizing style that keeps emotion in the grip of judgment. In this style, the emotional concreteness of remembered love becomes in latinate, summary description, "the infirm glory of the positive hour."

Eliot's subject, though—a questioning of "intenser human feelings" almost too painful to recall—exerts an emotional pressure that is not so easily contained. Phrases like "the infirm glory of the positive hour" or "the vanished power of the usual reign" evade as much as they define and, even judged by the standards of prose, will not bear close scrutiny. Striving for prose-like precision, they achieve neither emotional nor discursive clarity, only sonority. The energy of this sonority, however, along with the extraordinary power of the truncated vision that escapes the censure of Eliot's discipline, suggests something has been repressed that will not stay repressed for long. When we look back at the first section of *Ash Wednesday*, we notice an undercurrent of emotional resistance that can be felt not only in the unsatisfactory nature of Eliot's grandiloquent abstractions, but throughout. The lineation, diction and syntax of his address at first suggest the oppressive conscientiousness of concentrated purpose, but the minute we read the poem out loud, we realize they can also serve a very different function. In harmony with Eliot's rhymes, which are as insistent as they are unexpected, his repetition of phrase from statement to qualified restatement acquires a life of its own and makes it extremely difficult to read the poem with the halting deliberation it seems to require. We are forced to read the poem, as Eliot himself reads it in recordings, as an incantation. And the nearer Eliot's internal dialogue comes to the resolute conclusion required by its organizing syntax, the stronger the power of that incantation becomes, and the greater the dominance of rhythm and feeling:

> Because these *wings* are no longer *wings* to fly
> But merely vans to beat the *air*
> The *air* which is now thoroughly *small* and *dry*
> *Smaller* and *dryer* than the *will*
> *Teach us* to *care* and not to *care*
> *Teach us* to sit *still*.

When we hear this, even without glancing forward to the last section, where "unbroken wings" are still "seaward flying," the energy of Eliot's rhymes tells us that his heart's wings are anything but vans. Dislocated from the words that announce his purpose, his yearning dissolves into the rhythm of his address. He tells us he would renounce his wings. He even tries to turn the image into a figure of the striving of conscience. (Writing about Henry Adams, Eliot compared conscience to "wings . . . beating vainly in a vacuum jar.")[8] But in vain. The image of "vans to beat the air," once called into being, comes to objectify a despair connected with the act of limiting the self to a notion of "will" which is synonymous with conscious determination.

Thus the first part of *Ash Wednesday* ends not with solidified resolve but in a moment of radical instability. The impulse behind Eliot's echoing rhymes all but overwhelms the wall of prudence his language tried to erect around his feeling. As the fragment of *Ave Maria* that he added in revision[9] brings the movement to a close, the controlled and rational "I" of the poem dissolves in prayer. Unable to identify itself with the conscious will, and unable to suppress both emotion and outside connection, the self begins to disintegrate under the pressures of a deeper will, which does not heed the constraints of reason, and will not "sit still."[10]

The second poem of *Ash Wednesday* opens in the middle of that disintegration. We overhear Eliot speaking in the first person and remain to observe his voice splinter into several voices, each corresponding to a subterranean current of section I. In the resulting counterpoint, "I" continues to articulate the impulses of the conscious will and continues to speak of renunciation—a desire to be forgotten and to forget. Again it marshals the tools of logical persuasion and speaks with the measured precisions of prose:

> Let the whiteness of the bones atone to forgetfulness.
> There is no life in them. As I am forgotten
> And would be forgotten, so I would forget,
> Thus devoted, concentrated in purpose.

But from the start of this second poem, it is clear that this voice and the impulses behind it are losing control. For one thing, Eliot, previously alone and self-absorbed, now begins speaking in rapt contemplation of something outside himself. He addresses his "Lady" as if to explain an experience she is part of, and in words that have been wrung out of him:

> Lady, three white leopards sat under a juniper-tree
> In the cool of the day, having fed to satiety
> On my legs my heart my liver and that which had been contained
> In the hollow round of my skull.

"Salutation," the title of this poem when it appeared in the 1927 *Saturday Review of Literature,* is fully appropriate. The piece adapts the *Vita Nuova*'s account of Dante's response to Beatrice's salutation. It presents a moment of being called out of oneself, of sensing "the natural functions of [the] body . . . vexed and impeded," of a vision in which a "lord of terrible aspect" holds one's heart burning in his hands.[11] As in the Italian original, Eliot's adaptation demonstrates the power of a lady's salutation to shatter the equilibrium of the self and to release the energies of growth. In 1926 Eliot said he admired Nathaniel Wanley's vivid note on the partial resurrection of legs and arms on Good Friday in Cairo, and quoted Wanley's account of a man who had "touched divers of these rising members."[12] In *Ash Wednesday* II, he fuses the detail of Wanley's note with the *Vita Nuova* and the story of the dry bones in Ezekiel to suggest a resurgence of parts of the psyche which had been fastidiously excluded from the self. In a dream-like sequence in which parts of the body quicken in an involuntary motion charged with sexual overtones, Eliot suggests an experience in which the ego gives way to what lies beneath it. What follows is a debate between the primitive voices of an internalized judge,[13] who challenges:

> Shall these bones live? shall these
> Bones live?

and who mocks the purposiveness of conscience:

> Prophesy to the wind, to the wind only for only
> The wind will listen

—and the judge's antagonists, the bones, who assert their own logic ("Because . . . and because . . . and because,") and who break into a full-fledged song that fulfills the incantatory yearning of the first poem.

Let us, though, double back and compare the dream-like sequence which introduces these primitive voices with the section of *The Waste Land* it so much resembles:

> Lady, three white leopards sat under a juniper-tree
> In the cool of the day, having fed to satiety
> On my legs my heart my liver and that which had been con-
>   tained
> In the hollow round of my skull.
>
> A rat crept softly through the vegetation
> Dragging its slimy belly on the bank
> While I was fishing in the dull canal
> . . . .
> White bodies naked on the low damp ground
> And bones cast in a little low dry garret,
> Rattled by the rat's foot only, year to year.

In both, Eliot proceeds by projecting feeling into the objects of a landscape. He is, by means of his projection, both the rat and the bones, the leopards and the leopards' feast. But where the feelings associated with the rat and its victim had been repulsion and furtive terror, the keynote of the passage from *Ash Wednesday* is "satiety": relief from the heat of the day and freedom from the demands of appetite (demands which are seated, as Dante believed, in the legs, the heart, the liver and the skull).[14]

There are also other, more significant departures from *The Waste Land*. An awareness on the part of "I," for example, that the voices it unearths are "mine," and consequently an implied belief, not felt in *The Waste Land*, that something in the self is substantial and will survive dismemberment. Consider the passage just quoted. It seems to take place *not* in a dream world where things are, for better or worse, out of the dreamer's control, but in a kind of half-way station between dreaming and waking. It has both the immediacy of a dream and a certain remoteness, "as if the speaker were seeing a distant though vivid and hallucinatory vision" of something "rather than experiencing it" as either dream or reality.[15] In it the speaker is ready to play with other selves but not quite ready to give up his own. Eliot gives us a touchstone for the state with the odd word "dissembled":

> And I who am here dissembled
> Proffer my deeds to oblivion, and my love
> To the posterity of the desert and the fruit of the gourd.

The primary meaning of "dissembled" here is, of course, "dismembered," but its secondary meaning, "feigned," suggests that the "I" consciously allows its boundaries to sidestep the restrictions of "things as they are." This dissembling, permitted by a will which has not dissolved, has neither the satisfaction nor the anxiety of *The Waste Land*'s dramatization of immediate experience. Never completely out of control of the will, the dissembling does not reach the deeps of the unconscious. It is more like tentative play than psychic exorcism. As such it anticipates certain characteristics of the chant of the bones, which surfaces despite the efforts of the first voice of the poem to suppress it:

> Lady of silences
> Calm and distressed. . . .

The song of the bones has links both to the Catholic liturgy's Litany of the Blessed Virgin[16] and to instances of liturgical imitation in the religious verse of Gourmont[17] and Verlaine.[18] But its tone is distinctive, and it requires us to treat it on its own terms. Like the vision of the leopards, it represents part of what happens to the poet when he responds to his Lady (who now is addressed again). It is, that is to say, prophetic: it voices what is intuited but not yet understood, and its voice is filled with wonder. We hear the wonder in the energy of the dimeter chant, which is doubly effective because we recognize it as the fulfillment of feeling formerly held in check. But we also hear it in the poem's recurrent use of paradox. Together, incantation and paradox insinuate a voice from beyond the self, releasing us from the here and now into a mood of unearthly tranquility. And this voice seems to identify itself by playing with words for their own sake:

> End of the endless
> Journey to no end. . . .

At the heart of this play, however, stands a serious riddle, emanating from a will deeper than consciousness. After seven lines of apostrophe, the poem declares:

> The single Rose
> Is now the Garden
> Where all loves end. . . .

When we read these lines, we tend to discount the fact that their subject is a "single Rose," plucked, as the first line tells us, from memory. Nevertheless it is true. This rose was once an object of worldly affection, a fact which would be even clearer had Eliot not dropped four lines from his first draft, including these two:

> Rose of memory
> Rose of forgetfulness
> *Spattered* and *worshipped*

. . . .
The single Rose
With worm-eaten petals
Is now the Garden
Where all loves end. . . .[19]

The assertion "The single Rose / Is now the Garden" brings the single Rose, whose spattering Eliot remembers and wishes to forget, into conjunction with the "Garden" which is the poem's controlling image of desire. It was the figure of a garden, remember, which was alone strong enough to break through the guarded rationalism of the suite's first poem, causing its speaker to lament, "I cannot drink / There, where trees flower, and springs flow, for there is nothing again." The same garden, according to the manuscripts, provided the seed of the sequence as a whole[20] and graced its original conclusion.[21] In the published version of *Ash Wednesday*, the "spirit of the fountain, spirit of the garden" receives the suite's final appeal. When we are told, therefore, that "the single Rose / Is now the Garden," we are close to the poem's central mystery. "Things are as they are," and yet, in the transfigurations of *au-delà*, a "worm-eaten" rose may be the locus of paradise, and produce a chant from beyond the grave.

It is the nature of this garden to be suggested by conflicting perspectives, though, and even after their conjunction both rose and garden are teasingly mysterious:

End of the endless
Journey to no end
Conclusion of all that
Is inconclusible
Speech without word and
Word of no speech. . . .

The paradoxes make this clear, but Eliot's use of paradox is only part of a larger pattern. By means of procedures not very different from the ones Pater used to call up his iridescent Gioconda or—more pertinently—Yeats used to call up his own "Secret Rose," Eliot creates a rose garden not out of a single paradox but out of a penumbra of suggestion:

She is older than the rocks among which she sits;
. . . .
And, as Leda,
Was the mother of Helen of Troy,
And, as St Anne,
Was the mother of Mary;
And all this has been to her but as the sound of lyres and
    flutes. . . .

(Pater)[22]

Red Rose, proud Rose, sad Rose of all my days!

(Yeats)[23]

Rose of memory
Rose of forgetfulness. . . .

(*Ash Wednesday*)

But it will not do to assign literary parentage to this garden too casually. Aside from Pater and Yeats, figures from Baudelaire to Valéry might be used to account for Eliot's sleight of hand. The most useful, it seems to me, is St.-John Perse. As in Eliot's homage to *Anabase* in the second verse paragraph of "Journey of the Magi," the referents of "the Garden/Where all love ends" are both literal (the schoolyard in St. Louis) and allegorical (the garden of Dante's earthly paradise, and of Christian commentary). Yet the garden on the page is more: a field of crossing, one of the poet's "nouveaux objets propres à susciter de nouvelles émotions."[24] It is therefore appropriate that the chant should be framed by juniper trees, which Eliot took from his (as it turned out) misguided 1930 translation of the seventh canto of *Anabase*. (*Jujubier*, he later learned, is French not for "juniper" but for "Jujuba," which correction appears in all editions after 1930.)[25]

The point I am getting to is this: the chant of the bones, the foundation stone of the later parts of *Ash Wednesday*, is serious in the way that *Anabase* is serious, and not in the way *The Waste Land* is serious. Compared with the concrete representation of experience in *The Waste Land*, the chant of the bones is, to use Perse's words, "un jeu, très allusif et mystérieux" in which the visionary realization of immediate experience is forgone for a kind of verbal playfulness. Building on immediate experience, it expands it "au-delà des limites du monde normal."[26] It is easy to be impatient with this lack of felt reality, of course, which can seem no more than incantatory nonsense—nothing more than "words of no speech." And yet the song is strangely effective in suggesting an experience of liberation. In context it provides a medium in which the oppression of the real, narrowly conceived, can be temporarily lifted, and in which the growth of the self can be induced by allowing it to dissemble attitudes that would appear absurd were the demands of sense not removed. The Rose of Eliot's chant is lover, sister and mother, and at the same time the Blessed Virgin and the logos of which the Virgin is the sign. It points toward all these things, but, in the sense of Eliot's earlier poetry, it is a fraud. A name capable of accommodating a number of feelings, many of them contradictory, it serves as a construct capable of embodying none of them. Yet, ultimately, it will permit a new will and with it a new self to emerge.

That metamorphosis, however, is not to occur in the second section of *Ash Wednesday*, where the chant of the bones represents merely the harbinger of impulses felt at a distance, a mysterious voice promising louder songs to come. In the remainder of the section, the urgency of the verse diminishes as Eliot's incantatory dimeter gives way to a long narrative line. As the visionary presence of the rose and the garden fades, an observer reports in the past tense that "under a juniper-tree the bones *sang,* scattered and shining."

This is the resolute voice of "I" again, and its alienation from the chant is clear from two of its observations: first that the bones, though singing in unison, are scattered. Then, more disquieting, that even scattered they (but—painfully—*not* "I") are *"united/*In the quiet of the desert" and are able to *forget* "themselves and each other." This alienation of "I," first an undertone, becomes clearer as section II draws to a close, and as "I" associates God's instruction to Ezekiel about the future division of the land of milk and honey with the ominous silence of the desert. It culminates with a recognition announced, as so often in Eliot, with a demonstrative pronoun:

> *This* is the land. We have our inheritance.

Confirming the note of "assurance and content" described by E. E. Duncan Jones as well as the frisson of death registered by Grover Smith,[27] this conclusion suggests both the exuberance of song and the lament of one who can know the song only as a product of dissembling.

The third poem of *Ash Wednesday,* entitled "Som de L'Escalina" in its 1929 publication, speaks like its predecessor of renuniation but effects a release. In *Purgatorio* XXVI, Arnaut Daniel salutes Dante from the seventh terrace of Mount Purgatory, and urges: *"Ara vos prec, per aquella valor / que vos guida al som de l'escalina, / sovegna vos a temps de ma dolor."* ("Now I pray you, by that Goodness which guideth you to the summit of the stairway, be mindful in due time of my pain.") His phrases had echoed through Eliot's writing, usually with emphasis on *ma dolor.* Now, although the pain is not forgotten, Eliot's stress falls on other kinds of memory, which begin in pain but lead out to growth. To get to Beatrice from the last terrace atop Mount Purgatory, Dante must step though a wall of flame so hot that he imagines immersion in boiling glass to be cool by comparison. In large part this fire encapsulates the canticle's recurrent purgatorial experience, but it also draws from more immediate surroundings. The pilgrim's entry into Paradise requires not only the correction of his will but also the restoration of his emotional capacity to the wildfire intensity of adolescence. His restored feeling needs to be redirected, which will prove an experience of no little humiliation, but the discomfort of the sequence extends beyond humiliation. Stepping through the wall of flame figures at least in part the pain of an experience that, though the stuff of paradise, is not re-embraced easily by anyone who has been wounded by love.

In the third poem of *Ash Wednesday* a man speaks who has screwed up his courage and prepared himself for drastic deprivation but not for engaging his sympathies anew. Liberated by the dislocation we have just witnessed and yet still not conscious of the liberation, he begins to speak as "I" with some of the resolution with which the suite began (listen to the insistent internal rhymes):

> At the first turning of the second stair
> I turned and saw below
> The same shape twisted on the banister
> Under the vapour in the fetid air
> Struggling with the devil of the stairs who wears
> The deceitful face of hope and of despair.

The matter of his speech, however, is not the strengthening of the conscious will but its transcendence. It is as if Eliot had gathered his energy once more to reject the temptation to "turn again" only to have "These matters that with myself I too much discuss" fall away. "The same shape . . . struggling with the devil of the stairs," like the "double part" of "Little Gidding" or the "you and I" of "Prufrock," represents the doubled image of a self in the midst of change. And not unexpectedly, this stage of Eliot's experience has two parts—two turnings of a single stair. In the first, the old self is experienced as other—caught in "hope and despair" of concerns that now appear part of another world: "under the vapour in the fetid air." In the second, commanding a separate verse paragraph, the spiritual reality of that former self emerges out of the dark of unconscious revelation. Suddenly Eliot apprehends the significance of his old life and recoils from a vision of appetite and decay. In that instant, he ceases to feel the familiar devil as kin, and perceives his old self and its spiritual reflection together as two halves of a monstrous hinge—something "Damp, jaggèd, like an old man's mouth drivelling, beyond repair, / Or the toothed gullet of an agèd shark." (In revision, Eliot added the epithet "agèd" to recall the "agèd eagle" of the first section.)[28] The passage is particularly striking because, with the erotic vision that follows, it provides one of the few reminiscences in *Ash Wednesday* of Eliot's old concreteness. Unlike anything in sections I or II, the repulsive image of the drivelling mouth belongs to the world of immediate feeling—of "is" and not *au-delà*. And so, to readers brought up on Eliot's earlier verse it is likely to take on the importance of the most authentic moment in the suite.

Beyond this recognition we find the climactic moment of the third poem, which is usually misread as a temptation surmounted. Significantly we no longer hear of "I." And rather than having the section's opening note of self-conscious resolution confirmed, we watch as it is dispersed by powerful images which suggest not increased care but the liberation of successive areas of repressed being: first sexuality in the figure of a "slotted window bellied like the fig's fruit" (a token both of the satisfactions of the vagina and of a window out on the world); then

beyond that the peaceful earthiness of a rural landscape and the intimation of something more: a deliberately mysterious "broadbacked figure" surrounded by an aura of childhood pastoral. In section IV, this
figure will give way to "the silent sister." But before he gives way (or
she—there is no way of telling here and the associations, such as they
are, are feminine), a desire erupts that is neither of the barnyard nor
the "antique flute":

> Blown hair is sweet, brown hair over the mouth blown,
> Lilac and brown hair. . . .

The resurgence of desire and pain evoked by this reprise of "Prufrock" is the fire at the top of Eliot's *escalina* and the precursor of the
vision immediately to come. But although the strong desire threatens,
we are not justified in identifying it alone as the "distraction" of the
next line. If in the complexity of Eliot's syntax desire may be a distraction, so may be the resistance that tears the speaker away from it.[29] We
have no way of telling, that is, whether Eliot is being moved by the
resolution of his ego or according to "the music of the flute." The poem
is deliberately ambiguous, and gets more so. Does Eliot receive "strength
beyond hope and despair" from renunciation or recovery? The phrase
is inescapably difficult, implying that in Eliot's *Vita Nuova*, "climbing the
third stair" is a matter of both purgation and liberated desire. Hence
section III's concluding cry—"but speak the word only"—finds its way
not only to the Lord of the liturgy but to *la donna*.[30] Deep in Eliot's
psyche the sudden cry quickens her image, and what in one instant was
a fleeting unrepressed desire explodes to become in the next the ruin
of all space, all time.

Out of the spark of section III grows a fire of recovery, restoration
and redemption. In it, the tormented years stretching back to Eliot's
childhood return with benevolent aspect, and he can no longer believe
that time is "always time" or that what is actual is "actual only for one
time / And only for one place." What occupies "the time between sleep
and waking" now seems actual for all time, in the place "where trees
flower, and springs flow," and where she walks "who made strong the
fountains and made fresh the springs." The point is not that this is a
place in time undiscovered until now but that it is a place long known
which a new apprehension, a new "reading," has illuminated. ("Reading" here should be taken in the sense of interpreting one area of experience in terms of another, of a man "trying to explain to himself his
intenser human feelings." It should not, however, be glossed with a
simple Christian paradigm. The way in which Eliot reads the leaves of
the past is not straightforward, and involves a mingling of old feelings
with the new in a manner not necessarily encompassed by Christian
symbols.)

Eliot's working title for section IV, "Vestita di Color di Fiamma," points to the mature Beatrice of *Purgatorio* XXX, "clad . . . in colour of living flame."[31] But as "we cannot understand fully Canto XXX of the *Purgatorio* until we know the *Vita Nuova*" (SE, 223), it also points back into the past. In the *Commedia*, Dante's vision on Mount Purgatory brings back not only his adolescent ardor but the first sight of his beloved, when he was nine and she was dressed in "goodly crimson."[32] Like Dante Eliot alters what might have been an erotic situation with the presence of a girlish figure, here dressed in the white of virginity. And like Dante he superimposes yet another presence—a motherly figure with complex ties to the world of childhood.[33] "In ignorance and in knowledge of eternal dolour," this third presence is of course an emanation of the Virgin Mary, but that is only part of her significance. What seems more important is that the verses in which she appears are charged with private associations flooding back from Eliot's pre-school years. Shortly after he drafted the fourth section of *Ash Wednesday* he wrote to Marquis Childs of the St. Louis *Post-Dispatch*:

> The earliest personal influence I remember, besides that of my parents, was an Irish nursemaid named Annie Dunne, to whom I was greatly attached; she used to take me to my first school, a Mrs. Lockwood's, which was a little way out beyond Vandeventer place. The river also made a deep impression on me; and it was a great treat to be taken down to the Eads Bridge in flood time. . . .
>
> I find that as one gets on in middle life the strength of early associations and the intensity of early impressions become more evident; and many little things, long forgotten, recur. The occasion on which my nurse took me with her to the little Catholic church which then stood on the corner of Locust street and Jefferson avenue, when she went to make her devotions; the *spring violets* and the rather mangy buffalo which I photographed in Forest Park; the steamboats blowing in New Year's day, and so on.[34]

Sovegna vos: remember. And Eliot does remember, all too painfully, "the years that walk between," the "lilac and brown hair" and even the "fig's fruit." But along with them he also remembers the idealistic stirrings of childhood. He remembers, for instance, Annie Dunne in the spring.

> Who walked between the *violet* and the *violet*
> Who walked between
> The various ranks of varied *green*. . . .

Like so many key moments in Eliot's poetry, however, this is more than memory; it is recognition—a recognition that, as section IV begins, is already underway. Behind every line of the first verse paragraph stands the discovery that it was not Annie Dunne but a mysterious *she* who walked,[35] and in the syntax that follows, the light grows stronger:

> *Here* are the years that walk between. . . .

Consider the conclusion to Eliot's first draft of section IV, with its suggestion of childhood intimations long "hidden" in memory:

> White light folded, sheathed about her, folding the flame and
>   green
> Clothes that now clothe her, while the flowers rejoice
> In the blessed face
> And the blessed voice
> Of one who has heard the unheard, seen the unseen.
> Desire chills, and the hidden thoughts outrace
> The way of penance to the means of grace.
>
> *Poi s'ascose nel foco* and
> After this our exile.[36]

Grounded in a boy's perception of his nursemaid's devotion in a church he never entered, the poetry concerns the Anglo-Catholic's experience of "grace." But it involves more (and less) than that. Like the chant of the bones earlier in the suite, the fourth part of *Ash Wednesday* is self-consciously literary, in the manner of St.-John Perse or the Perse-related sections of "Journey of the Magi." Its incantatory repetitions and paradoxes, its mixture of natural and allegorical imagery ("blue of larkspur, blue of Mary's colour"), its personification of the years evoke an experience beyond the powers of Imagism. And like the chant of the bones, the poetry once again suggests an experience of consciousness disengaged from the burden of memory and for a moment susceptible to alternate realities and alternate selves. For a moment, impulses beckon which had been suppressed in life by a dominant self and in poetry by its counterpart, the poetry of experience. This beckoning is focused around a response to a figure with origins in Annie Dunne. Once liberated, though, the impulse calls up a new figure, who is part nurse, part mother,[37] part lover, part sister. Mostly sister, in fact, if we take the sense of that word from Baudelaire's "L'Invitation au voyage," where, according to Eliot, *soeur* has associations with "that sublimation of passion toward which Baudelaire was always striving"—a form of *"désir contemplatif qui n'a besoin que de la présence, et qui ne possède vraiment que parce qu'il ne possède pas"* ("Contemplative desire which is satisfied merely by the presence of its object and which truly possesses only because it refuses to possess"; FLA, 100). And as in *The Hollow Men*, in *Ash Wednesday* this figure emerges through the agency of the contrition that accompanies a cloud of tears.

To sum up, then, although less moving and less dramatic than the occurrences of *Purgatorio* XXX, the climax of *Ash Wednesday* gestures in its own disembodied way toward Dante's "conflict of the old feelings with the new; the effort and triumph of a new renunciation, greater than the renunciation at the grave, because a renunciation of feelings that persist beyond the grave" (SE, 224). It gives Dante to us, in fact, reflected in the mirror of a Lewis Carroll or a Mallarmé. As Elizabeth

Sewell noticed, Eliot, in his 1929 essay on Dante, advises that to enter the world of the *Purgatorio* we have to "pass through the looking-glass into a world which is just as reasonable as our own. When we have done that, we begin to wonder whether the world of Dante is not both larger and more solid than our own."[38] Partly Dante, partly *Alice in Wonderland,* both here and nowhere, the garden of *Ash Wednesday* foreshadows the bizarre garden of "Burnt Norton," which is announced by "the deception of the thrush" and where "we" *are,* but

> *they were,* dignified, invisible,
> Moving without pressure, over the dead leaves,
> . . . .
> And the bird called, in response to
> The unheard music hidden in the shrubbery,
> And the unseen eyebeam crossed. . . .

And so if Eliot approaches "grace" in *Ash Wednesday,* it is by entering a paradoxical world which may be Christian and Dantesque but only as we look back on it from the other side. Like Alice (or for that matter Marianne Moore), we enter this world by choosing nonsense over sense, and when we return from it, as Eliot does in the fifth paragraph of section IV, things look different and more malleable, and we feel suddenly charged with new purpose and energy. As section IV draws to a close, Eliot discovers that the silent sister is not merely a figure in the "higher dream" but had been part of the landscape in front of him, seated "behind the garden god," unrecognized. And after twenty lines of being lost in the charm of memory and vision, something now happens: she "*bent* her head and *signed* but *spoke no word.*" The event is trivial, but to Eliot it is like a thunderstroke. Bridging the gulf from the *au-delà* to the here and now, the sister's motion provokes a surge of prophetic self-exhortation. As in Canto LXXXI, where Ezra Pound's vision causes him to announce to himself and whoever else will listen that "what thou lovest well remains," so Eliot now cries:

> Redeem the time, redeem the dream
> The token of the word unheard, unspoken. . . .

Were *Ash Wednesday* a devotional poem of the kind Eliot was first said to have written, we would undoubtedly now be given an account of how the word unspoken by the devoted sister and unheard by the wondering boy is one and the same as the Word uttered by the Creator and celebrated by Christians since the time of St. John . But, as Eliot insisted, *Ash Wednesday* is not a devotional poem. Like *The Waste Land* in the moment of "the heart of light, the silence," or "La Figlia Che Piange" when it registers "Her hair over her arms and her arms full of flowers," the poem cannot sustain its vision. As "a thousand whispers" are shaken from the ever-present yew of an old and oppressive life, the fourth section of the suite ends with a chilling moment of doubt and with an ambiguous liturgical fragment. A part of the *Salve Regina*'s prayer of intercession, the phrase "and after this our exile" may imply that Eliot, having found the light, seeks strength to hold to it for the remainder of his earthly life. But like the end of "Journey of the Magi," it may also have a darker implication. Succeeding the wind's rattle, it suggests Eliot's progressive alienation first from the unreality of the material world and then from the unreality of the immaterial.[39]

Section V, certainly, is as dark and despairing as Eliot's earlier postludes to vision, and more bluntly confessional than most. The section's unrelieved somberness is especially striking when we are aware that it was originally conceived as balanced between self-accusation and hope. In a draft he read aloud to Leonard and Virginia Woolf in 1928, Eliot intended to conclude *Ash Wednesday* after five movements and appended to the present opening verse paragraph of section V a variant of what is now the third verse paragraph of section VI.[40] In this version, *Ash Wednesday* ended with:

> In this pool all the waves are silent
> In this pool all the seas are still
> All the waves die against this island
> Our life is in the world's decease
> Our peace
> In His will.
> Suffer me not to be separated
> O my people.

It is true that the mood of this conclusion is even less buoyant than that of the conclusion Eliot finally wrote. If, with a landscape Eliot will reuse in "Marina," it presents an island calm, the calm has about it a claustrophobic feeling, causing us to believe that Eliot dreads the peace he seeks. Even with that dark undertone, however, and with the last word given over to Christ rebuking his traitorous people (it is appropriated here to function as a self-rebuke), there is nothing in this early conclusion as dark as the self-accusations Eliot added when he expanded the fifth section and added a sixth.

Stylistically, section V of *Ash Wednesday* recoils from the practices of the poetry immediately preceding it. As the vision of the silent sister fades and Eliot bemoans his inability to sustain it, he also begins to question the procedures which heralded its birth. The charmed circle of the silent sister had depended on poetic assumptions in perfect accord with the poem's religious subject. Just as the Word—the vanished Christ—can neither be heard nor spoken but must be "read" from its pale traces, so in symbolist practice the word—any linguistic form—is only a poor token of the reality it shadows. Though the things at which words point are real, words themselves are only pointers. It is true they

may suggest reality beyond the gulf of silence even as events in the
material world may suggest the once and future reality of the Incarnation. And in fits of optimism, the poet may believe literature may
even construct a reality that corresponds to, if it cannot mirror, the
ultimate reality that lies beyond silence. But when the optimism fails,
the constructions begin to look like arrangements of ciphers, just as
worldly signs of the Word, taken too literally, mock us with their mythic
inadequacy.

As section V begins, Eliot attempts to sustain the magic of symbolist
incantation amid his awareness that it will never yield certainty, and to
assert a reality beyond words even though his inability to express it
makes the project seem hopeless. If the lost word of prayer, spoken
once by Annie Dunne or another, in Eliot's memory or in his imagination, can no longer be heard; or even if the word was never spoken—
or never could be spoken—still, Eliot insists (and from the desperation
of his insistence gains a claim on our attention) that the word—and the
Word—exists:

> Still *is* the unspoken word, the Word unheard,
> The Word without a word, the Word within
> The world and for the world. . . .

How, though, to comprehend it when even incantation betrays what
it attempts to express? As Eliot loses faith in his own manner of speech,
not only his recent vision but its literary ground starts to crumble, and
the reader confronts a chant gone sour. With fallen man as he is, how
can we be surprised that no place is fit for grace or that no word will
accommodate the logos? *In* context, the lifeless rhymes that follow tell
of deflated hope. *Out* of context they are egregious: to alter Conrad
Aiken's words, not even beautiful "gibberish": [41]

> Where shall the word be found, where will the word
> Resound? Not here, there is not enough silence
> Not on the sea or on the islands, not
> On the mainland, in the desert or the rain land,
> For those who walk in darkness
> Both in the day time and in the night time
> The right time and the right place are not here. . . .

The chant ends with a recognition that there can be no grace, either
for the self who once rejoiced that "things are as they are" and renounced "the blessèd face" *or* for the self who now inclines to return
to that disposition. Dissolved in his incantation, Eliot classes even his
penitent self among the fallen:

> No place of grace for those who avoid the face
> No time to rejoice for those who walk among noise and deny the
>   voice. . . .

At this point, however, an impulse of personal confession begins to complicate Eliot's incantatory impersonality. After all but accepting the sinning self of his judgment as his own, he asks the question, "Will the veiled sister pray for . . . ?" But the line breaks before he adds "me," and by the start of the next line he refers to his fallen self as an other, one of those whom he perceives in his own situation even as his disgust casts them at a distance. Like a similar passage in "Gerontion," his question, at least at first, is rhetorical; it assumes for its answer a thunderous no. Will the veiled sister pray for those who, like Eliot, knew her and "chose" her and yet continue to "oppose" her? Will she pray for those, who, like Eliot, had become children again in a schoolyard whose gate borders paradise and yet even there "cannot pray"? "What," Gerontion asked, "will the spider do, / Suspend its operations, will the weevil / Delay?" We are back in the situation of the early poems, with the lover looking back to a special moment and rebuking himself for being unable to revive it.

The final verse paragraph of section V increases the intensity of this questioning but also alters the emotional impulses behind it. Once again Eliot tries to unite his *cogito* and the sinning self to be judged by the sister, this time by entering more deeply into the situation of "those who offend her." Seen now from the inside, "they" are presented as "terrified" beings who (the phrase is more vivid than "chose and oppose") "affirm before the world and deny between the rocks." But even as he has made the connection between "them" and his own public self inescapable, Eliot shifts the terms of his discourse so that "they" are no longer generalized images of himself but elements in Christian history and Christian allegory. Whatever hope there was for a reconciliation of ego and self-image fades as it becomes clear that their act of betrayal takes place in "the desert / Of drouth." As the poem's response to the fallen state of man modulates from loathing to pity, some hope emerges. Unfortunately, however, the introduction of the apple-seed, an iconographic detail unconnected to the poem's world of vision, spoils the conclusion, and makes what might have been a moving surge toward Eliot's acceptance of his humanity sound managed and insincere.

Whatever the technical problems of the transition, however, there is no doubt that section VI begins on a note of tranquility. Speaking now in the first person again, Eliot, "wavering between the profit and the loss," no longer distances himself from the other sufferers—"those who are torn on the horn between season and season." The suite returns to its beginnings and, although Eliot's conflicting attractions to God and the world remain, the poet's original orientation toward that conflict does not. His syntax, we notice, continues to indicate opposing inclinations but no longer disguises the inclinations in a false rhetoric of concentrated purpose. The relative clause which announces his turn to-

ward God, for example, echoing section I with a difference, now receives
a straightforwardly opposing response:

> Although I do not hope to turn again
> . . . .
> The white sails still fly seaward. . . .

Similarly an acknowledgment of the continued strength of his worldly
desire ("the lost heart stiffens") is answered by an assurance that another world remains near: "But . . . / Let the other yew be shaken
and reply."

As I read it, the buried emotional center of section VI is an implied
allusion to St. John of the Cross, who acknowledged that "to banish
and mortify [the natural and first movement of the will] completely is,
in this life, impossible."[42] Hence the section's first verse paragraph ends
with a calm recognition that the wings of worldly desire can never, in
this world, be broken. To rephrase section I, such wings are "always
wings to fly." Though our desires enmesh us with unkillable strength
in worldly things, allowing ourselves to loathe them is both impossible
and counterproductive.[43] It is this note of acceptance that differentiates
the conclusion of *Ash Wednesday* from the conclusion Eliot originally
wrote. In the first ending, Eliot implies that one can guard the peace
of His will but only in the sanctuary of "this pool," and is understand-
ably ambivalent about the prospect of remaining within its confines.
The published ending, in which Eliot has understood that no sanctuary
is possible short of death, asserts a willingness to carry on the battle
between God and the world indefinitely. And the ebulliance of this assertion, I believe, keeps *Ash Wednesday* from being, in A. D. Moody's
description, "just as life-denying as it can be."[44]

The last verse paragraph of *Ash Wednesday,* however, presents a problem. Though he has acquired some equanimity about life in a "dream-
crossed twilight," Eliot yet turns once more toward the "blessed sister."
Knowing that he can in this life never hear the Word without uncertainty, he still cannot scotch an instinctive hope that "even among these
rocks" some kind of transcendence is possible. In the closing apostrophe he reinvokes the charm he had created out of childhood memory and symbolist chant. Then he uses it to express enormous yearning
for the Absolute, figured, as in so many of his poems, as a reunion with
the sea. This *cri de coeur,* chimed to a close by an appropriate pair of
liturgical fragments, is as moving as it is agitated, and says a great deal
about the failure of Eliot's Lenten quest for peace. Though it is not the
last appeal to the Virgin in Eliot's poetry it is the last time he will struggle to free himself of the human dilemmas "between blue rocks" with
quite so much passion. Henceforth he will acknowledge the pull and

power of the sea but will turn from it (as he will turn from the giddiest flights of poetry) to find, as "The Dry Salvages" puts it,

> (Not too far from the yew-tree)
> The life of significant soil.

3

Ash Wednesday was published in April 1930. At the end of that year Eliot told G. Wilson Knight that he was working on a poem inspired by Beethoven's *Coriolan* overture and that he wished to see Knight's recent essay on Shakespeare's *Coriolanus*.[45] The two-part fragment that grew out of Eliot's effort, moreover, shares more than chronology with *Ash Wednesday*. A nagging worry about bad faith suffuses both poems, which present opposite sides of the same spiritual coin. Whereas *Ash Wednesday* dramatizes how it feels to "affirm before the world and deny between the rocks," *Coriolan* tells of those who are *in* the world but beginning to stir: it is a poem about what it means to affirm the world and burn within the breast.

Like many passages in *Ash Wednesday*, *Coriolan* seems to owe a great deal to Eliot's work on *Anabase*, from which its opening lines borrow shamelessly.[46] Augmenting Perse's fascination with the leader, Eliot adds his own memories of the rallies of the *camelots du roi* and of a book written by the *chef du cadre*, Charles Maurras.[47] Fusing with Eliot's awareness of the rise of fascism, in 1931 these concerns led him to write the first fragment, "Triumphal March," whose flat dialogue suggests a *Sweeney Agonistes* turned toward politics. Eliot, it is clear, started writing it to dramatize how political belief may become "a substitute for religion, and therefore a muddle."[48] But as had happened before, the more he directed his attention to matters outside himself, the more the objects of his gaze became expressive of his own private preoccupations. To quote from a passage from the philosopher Edmund Husserl's *Ideas* that Eliot uses in "Triumphal March," only the average man understands experience as "an empty looking of an empty 'Ego' towards the object itself which comes into contact with it in some astonishing way"; the more sophisticated understand that consciousness cannot be separated from that "of which we are conscious."[49] Which helps, I think, to explain why Eliot, who intended to make "Triumphal March" a piece of political satire, ended by producing something that borders on the private nightmare of *The Waste Land*.

As Elisabeth Schneider has observed, though Eliot once said he intended to present stages in the growth of a young man named Cyril, the heart of the *Coriolan* fragments is not the satirical dialogue between Cyril and his mother but a discourse "between poet and spectators" and then between the poet and a tormented Coriolanus.[50] In "Triumphal March," this discourse begins with Cyril's mother's account of how she and Cyril waited for the military procession to pass by them on "the way to the temple." Beginning as the object of his satire, the life-killing materialism of Cyril and his mother starts to remind the narrator of himself, and he transfers his dissatisfaction with their inauthenticity to his own. When Cyril, not thinking why it matters, asks "is he coming," the narrator replies with a précis of Husserl's critique of how the man in the street thinks. Only instead of putting it in a way that excludes himself, he says: "The natural wakeful life of *our* Ego is a perceiving." And this establishes the keynote of "Triumphal March": the more the narrator contemplates the overweeningly public life of Rome, the more uncomfortably he feels the inauthentic nature of his own rhetoric, and the more satiric his narrative becomes. And so the line just quoted is followed by a second involving "our stools and our sausages" and soon by a list whose quotidian inappropriateness says volumes about not just the public worlds of Rome, England and Germany but also about the way the narrator thinks about his own world. This, then, is what life (his own as well as Europe's) has become:

> 5,800,000 rifles and carbines,
>   102,000 machine guns,
>   28,000 trench mortars. . . .

When the leader, Coriolan, appears, the narrator interjects himself for a second time:

> There is no interrogation in his eyes
> Or in the hands, quiet over the horse's neck,
> And the eyes watchful, waiting, perceiving, indifferent.

Once again, the subject of his account makes the narrator think of himself (there *is* interrogation in the narrator's eyes), and at first the response he implies is part fascination, part revulsion. As the revulsion wins out (the third line ends on "indifferent"), the narrator's thoughts fly to what this public life lacks, and what he, recognizing all too much of himself in this public figure, desperately desires. Only images will serve him, as he calls up a medley of religious associations that confect a new object of desire even as *Ash Wednesday* had confected "the silent sister":

> O hidden under the dove's wing, hidden in the turtle's breast,
> Under the palmtree at noon, under the running water
> At the still point of the turning world. O hidden.

As inaccessible as the Word of *Ash Wednesday,* that which is hidden has a devastating effect on him. What is unrelated to it seems but

> Dust
> Dust
> Dust of dust. . . .

And the common life looks no less vulgar. "Triumphal March" ends with a statement of contempt which is apparently directed at the figure of Coriolanus but in fact sums up Eliot's own self-disgust. In *L'Avenir de l'intelligence,* Charles Maurras had described his amazement at a stranger's account of how a literary personage was saluted on parade one day:[51] And you actually mean the soldiers stood at attention, for him? For that poetic charlatan? *"Et les soldats faisaient la haie?* ILS LA FAISAIENT."

By the end of "Triumphal March," then, we are back in the psychic drama that dominated Eliot's poetry from "Prufrock" through *The Waste Land.* As in the earlier poems, as contemplating a social identity leads to horror, Eliot recoils from common life. And once again an impulse to fulfill the Eliot family vision, combined with an opposing impulse to fly public life, leads to self-accusations and a sense of being an unmasked fraud. If anything, Eliot's recent religious activity seems to have increased the the pain and bitterness of this reversion. The only element still lacking is the pressure of his mother's eyes, and that will not be lacking for long.

Coriolanus, the play that gives life to "Difficulties of a Statesman"— the second part of *Coriolan*—had turned up previously in Eliot's "A Cooking Egg," his suppressed "Ode,"[52] and in *The Waste Land.* Nor is it difficult to understand why. In the words of Wyndham Lewis's *The Lion and the Fox,* a commentary on Shakespeare that Eliot admired,[53] it treats of a

> rigid and hypnotized schoolboy influenced in his most susceptible years by a snobbish and violent parent and urged into a course of destruction which, the machine of an idea, he mesmerically pursues.[54]

Eliot, who was as snobbish as he was self-conscious, and as fixated on his mother as he was eager to escape her, understood the character all too well. And when he undertook to continue his "Cyril" sequence in 1931, the passing of his own mother (she had died in 1929) inevitably intruded. The result is a full-scale treatment of personal problems he had often rehearsed and to which he would soon give theatrical life in *The Family Reunion.* "Difficulties of a Statesman" gives us Eliot's horror of both conforming and rebelling from the self contained in his mother's eyes. Its internal tensions are brought to great intensity by a mis-en-scène of Roman public life and it is punctuated by self-doubts of elementary force ("Resign Resign Resign"). Starting at full steam ("Cry what shall I cry") it centers around a reprise of Eliot's *Gerontion* persona. "A tired head among these heads," this Gerontion-like narrator confesses, in a dramatic sequence Eliot was never to surpass:

> What shall I cry?
> Mother mother
> Here is the row of family portraits, dingy busts, all looking re-
>   markably Roman,
> Remarkably like each other, lit up successively by the flare
> Of a sweaty torchbearer, yawning.
> . . . .
> O mother (not among these busts, all correctly inscribed)
> I a tired head among these heads
> Necks strong to bear them
> Noses strong to break the wind
> Mother
> May we not be some time, almost now, together,
> If the mactations, immolations, oblations, impetrations,
> Are now observed
> May we not be
> O hidden. . . .

That the poem should have been treated for so long as a minor piece of political satire is a mystery only the success of Eliot's self-marketing will explain.

CHAPTER NINE

"Beyond music"

[Now] I turn more often the pages of Mallarmé than those of Laforgue, [and] those of . . . Shakespeare than of his contemporaries and epigoni. This does not necessarily involve a judgment of relative greatness: it is merely that what has best responded to my need in middle and later age is different from the nourishment I needed in my youth.

From "To Criticize the Critic" (1961)

Enter Autolycus, *singing*.

The Winter's Tale IV:iv

Between *Ash Wednesday* and "Burnt Norton" Eliot returned to Harvard, started to face his family ghosts, and separated from his wife. As the next chapter will suggest, it was a time of forced maturation. But writing in the early forties, Eliot did not see all the changes that would turn his youthful self into another person, and he referred to the recent past as time "largely wasted." He regarded his life as a mess, and he took heart only from the fact that his poetry, though it came in unpredictable surges, seemed to be near a second flowering. In January 1934, he wrote Marianne Moore that he only needed a bit more new work to bring out an expanded *Collected Poems* or a second volume of it. *The Hollow Men* ended a period, he told her, and he would have to wait until the next period had enough weight (not necessarily bulk) to balance the first.[1]

Hugh Kenner has written that to unite in *Four Quartets* "a *Symboliste* heritage with an Augustan may have been Eliot's most original act." Which is one way of saying that the poetry of Eliot's *second* period honors the cultural roots of language at the same time as it seems to loosen words from their referents and places discursive syntax in the service of music. In Donald Davie's words, it "swings to and fro between the sonorous opalescence of Mallarmé and . . . a prosaicism so homespun as to be . . . positively 'prosey' or 'prosing.' "[2] Eliot fashioned a program to justify this tortured stance between 1930 and 1935, but for the most part he was concerned not with poetics but with the pain of growing. Living most authentically in his work, he strove to create space for enlarged experience. He wished, to use Hamlet's expression, that his old self, with what he feared was its inescapable history of cruelty and obsession, might melt, thaw and dissolve itself into a dew. His implicit paradigm for this new poetry was the pilgrim's experience at the beginning of the *Purgatorio,* where the light of dawn and the singing of a boatload of liberated souls serve to draw Dante out of his sinful self and make him aware of the glory of the created world. In what Eliot wrote, however, this brightening realm is resistant. It rings with alien sounds and allows entry only to the disembodied. Children's laughter mocks Eliot in "New Hampshire" and "Burnt Norton," and, in "Lines to a Persian Cat," he finds that "The songsters of the air repair / To the green fields of Russell Square," but "Beneath the trees there is no ease / For the dull brain, the sharp desires /And the quick eyes of Woolly Bear." As Eliot was about to discover once again, for him to take to the air he had to deny the world's sense of "what is actual" and become the ghost of himself.

We can, as Eliot encourages us to do, explain the pattern of the poems that precede "Burnt Norton" in religious terms and say that in the poetry of his second period Eliot followed the course of St. John of the Cross and renounced his " 'mere will' " in favor of " 'the will of the Divine' " (SE, 402). But that, I think, would be a mistake. Eliot stopped writing the poetry of experience after he stopped thinking about experience as a struggle between the inauthenticities of convention and the suppressed vitality of a buried life. And if we seek a religious guide to his reversal, it is not, I believe, only to St. John of the Cross that we should turn. In the theological explorations of the *Quartets,* we find a Heideggerian insistence that, in this life, spiritual being is not a timeless authenticity but a project, forever in play.[3] Here we are

> Caught in the form of limitation
> Between un-being and being.
>
> ("Burnt Norton")

Four Quartets, in other words, is not a new *Purgatorio,* and does not dramatize the way the heart's core opens out to an environment for which it was created. There is now no heart's core to dramatize. There is instead life in time, whose completion and whose meaning is achieved only in death.

Substituting Heidegger for St. John, though, brings us little closer to understanding the stylistic texture of the *Quartets.* For that, Eliot's encounters with his fellow poets provide a surer commentary. His experiments with Valéry and St.-John Perse, already mentioned, tell part of the story. The rest belongs to his commerce with a greater master. Stéphane Mallarmé's achievement, Eliot wrote in "Note sur Mallarmé et Poe" (1926), "constitue une brillante critique de Poe: *donner un sens plus pur aux mots de la tribu.*"[4] Mallarmé, that is to say, gave a new language to our experience: new in the sense of being a newly refreshed and newly efficient language. But more than that, a new language in that it evokes genuinely new experience. Yet Mallarmé's gift had a price, which Eliot was now to pay in his turn. The Eliot of the *Quartets* and the Mallarmé of the following passages generate new experience by questioning the ground of the old. They create by eliminating. Or, to elaborate Mallarmé's hint, they transform Dante's journey to Beatrice from a story about God's grace and man's reconciliation with nature into a tale of the poet and his angel of destruction:

> Je n'ai créé mon oeuvre que par élimination, et toute vérité acquise ne naissait que de la perte d'une impression qui, ayant étincelé, s'était consumée et me permettait, grâce à ses ténèbres dégagées, d'avancer plus profondément dans la sensation des Ténèbres Absolues. La Destruction fut ma Béatrice. . . .
>
> . . . Toute naissance est une destruction, et toute vie d'un moment l'agonie dans laquelle on ressuscite ce qu'on a perdu, pour le voir, on l'ignorait avant. . . . Je crois pour être bien l'homme, la nature en pensant, il faut penser de tout son corps, ce qui donne une pensée pleine et à l'unisson comme ces cordes de violon vibrant immédiatement avec sa boîte de bois creux. . . . Je suis véritablement décomposé, et dire qu'il faut cela pour avoir une vue très—une de l'Univers! Autrement, on ne sert d'autre unité que celle de sa vie.[5]

2

It would be an error, though, to link the *Quartets* with Mallarmé too quickly. For one thing, Eliot gave his own idiosyncratic coloring to Mallarméan notions like "silence" and "music." For another, there is the issue of Eliot's Augustan heritage. In his 1958 introduction to Paul Valéry's *Art of Poetry*, Eliot summed up three decades of opposition to the symbolists' desire to sever language from speech and from society. "The words set free by Valéry," Eliot wrote, "may tend to form a separate language. But the farther the idiom, vocabulary, and syntax of poetry depart from those of prose, the more artificial the language of poetry will become. . . . the *norm* for a poet's language is the way his contemporaries talk. In assimilating poetry to music, Valéry has, it seems to me, failed to insist upon its relation to speech."[6]

In this view, the poet, if he is a poet, cannot turn language inside out for his own purposes. Though not a creature of journalism, he is bound to the journalist: the poet's duty is to rehabilitate and renew the language they share. To quote "Little Gidding," which resists Mallarmé even as it translates him, poetry must "purify the dialect of the tribe." Or, as Eliot puts it elsewhere, "the social function of poetry in its largest sense . . . [is to] affect the speech and the sensibility of the whole nation." And, if the nation's speech and sensibility are "deteriorating, [the poet] must make the best of it. Poetry can to some extent preserve, and even restore, the beauty of a language" (OPP, 12).[7]

In one voice of his late maturity, then, Eliot asserts an ideal in which Swift would have delighted (cf. Eliot's remark "I am averse to simplified spelling which destroys all traces of a word's origin and history" [TCC, 46]). It is this Augustanism that would give the *Quartets* their remarkable gravity. But it is the same quality that leads the Eliot of the thirties and forties perilously close to a lifeless traditionalism.[8] As St.-John Perse observed when asked whether he would compare Eliot's use of unusual words with his own, "Eliot's interest in words was literary and etymological; he learned about words by reading the Oxford dictionary; whereas [my] own vocabulary comes from [my] knowledge of many skills and crafts. . . . [My] descent is from Conrad and W. H. Hudson: *poetry, but not 'literature.'* "[9] (And Perse's observation can be easily confirmed. Eliot himself acknowledged that "I find, in trying to write poetry still more than in writing prose, that I constantly refer to the largest English dictionary available; and still more for words, if they are key words, the current use of which I fully understand, than for words of the meaning of which I am not sure; and the reason for using the biggest dictionary, is to study the examples of the meanings of the word, the ways in which it has been used, by English authors since it was first around. The more of these meanings that can be suggested in one's own use of the word, the better. Of course, the dictionary . . . cannot include all the uses of that word as a symbol, that is to say . . . the emotions it aroused.")[10]

The danger in Eliot's quickened interest in the language of the tribe, then, was plain to his contemporaries. It inclined him to the production of "literature" rather than "poetry." What was clear to others was not always apparent to Eliot, though, and the reason why goes a long way toward explaining his attitudes' psychological source. Certainly, Eliot's Swiftian feeling for words harmonizes with the ideas about impersonality, sincerity and tradition he adopted near the time of his conversion. But a letter of 1934 suggests that there were also other, less obvious, determinants. Comparing notes with Marianne Moore about what it felt like for a poet's first critic to be his or her mother (Moore's mother was her confidante and constant companion, and Eliot's was an amateur poet of some pretension), Eliot remarked that whenever he was disposed to be vainglorious, he reminded himself of a remark his mother once made to Sally Bruce Kinsolving of Baltimore. "Mrs. Kinsolving," she said, "I like your poetry, because I can understand it, and I don't understand my son's." There was, Eliot told Moore, something in that.[11]

Apparently, though her remembered glance seemed to signify different things than it had in the teens and twenties, in 1934 Eliot's mother was still looking over his shoulder. She told him: you cannot write simply for yourself. And her representative inside him agreed. The imperative and the assent may be said to have been the penultimate exigencies of Eliot's New England self, and they were far-reaching. Not only did they help to generate the sophisticated notion of the social function of poetry just discussed; with interesting implications, they also inspired a cruder but more influential variation of it, a variation concerned not so much with the precision of words as with how easily words could be understood. As this passage near the end of "The Music of Poetry" indicates, Eliot's New England vulnerabilities were still painfully evident. Impelling him toward a loosely conversational idiom, they reinforced his drift toward the theatre and helped change his thinking about how poetic texture and poetic meaning are related.

> I suppose that it will be agreed that if the [verse] of the last twenty years is worthy of being classified at all, it is as belonging to a period of search for a proper modern colloquial idiom. We have still a good way to go in the invention of a verse medium for the theatre, a medium in which we shall be able to hear the speech of contemporary human beings, in which dramatic characters can express the purest poetry without high-falutin and in which they can convey the most commonplace message without absurdity (OPP, 32).

An impulse to *himself* express a "commonplace message" in a language any educated person's mother could understand was one of the dominant aims of Eliot's late work. It supported the writing of *The Rock, Murder in the Cathedral* and *The Family Reunion*. And as Eliot later recalled, writing those plays "made a difference to the writing of the *Four Quartets*. I think that it led to a greater simplification of language and to speaking in a way which is more like conversing with your reader. I see the later *Quartets* as being much simpler and easier to understand than *The Waste Land* and 'Ash Wednesday.'"[12]

3

One component of Eliot's final style, then, was nothing more than a reformulation of the New England side of himself. His old need for clarity and order, first transformed into a thirst for philosophical precision, now demanded that he develop the conscience of a philologist and a journalist's eye for the commonplace. But, as always in Eliot's quarrel with himself, the metamorphosis of one set of psychic impulses brought about the metamorphosis of the other. If Eliot's preoccupation with the social function of poetry and his involvement with the popular theatre allied him with the pedant and the hack, his antinomian impulses were already struggling to control his new preoccupations for themselves. Throughout Eliot's second period we find him concerned not only with the cultural roots of words but also with the hermetic possibilities of language. At the same time as he championed the "com-

monplace message" of the theatre, he also elaborated a conception of
the theatre which was far from commonplace and had little to do with
what we ordinarily think of as its message. The complexities of Eliot in
middle age and the consequent complexities of the *Quartets* are embed-
ded in this passage from his Norton Lectures of 1932–33. Recalling the
experiment of *Sweeney Agonistes,* he points to the poet's desire to be
"something of a popular entertainer"—to create a medium that will
appeal to all:

> The ideal medium for poetry, to my mind, and the most direct means of
> social "usefulness" for poetry, is the theatre. In a play of Shakespeare you
> get several levels of significance. For the simplest auditors there is the plot,
> for the more thoughtful the character and conflict of character, for the
> more literary the words and phrasing, for the more musically sensitive the
> rhythm, and for auditors of greater sensitiveness and understanding a
> meaning which reveals itself gradually. . . . At none of these levels is the
> auditor bothered by the presence of that which he does not understand,
> or by the presence of that in which he is not interested. I may make my
> meaning a little clearer by a simple instance. I once designed, and drafted
> a couple of scenes, of a verse play. My intention was to have one character
> whose sensibility and intelligence should be on the plane of the most sen-
> sitive and intelligent members of the audience; his speeches should be ad-
> dressed to them as much as to the other personages in the play—or rather,
> should be addressed to the latter, who were to be material, literal-minded
> and visionless, with the consciousness of being overheard by the former.
> There was to be an understanding between this protagonist and a small
> number of the audience, while the rest of the audience would share the
> responses of the other characters in the play (UPUC, 153).

In the theatre, he is saying, it is all right to be plain. It is all right for
plays to have an accommodating surface, a way of not being "high-
falutin." But it *is* all right because the theatre is its surface and more
than its surface. Though drama might be addressed to the "material,
literal-minded and visionless," it is also intended for the musically sensitive, and Eliot's stress on music is crucial. The theatre is a place, in
his view, where the commonplace is absorbed into pattern and where
language maintains its social function and yet points toward a silent
"meaning which reveals itself gradually."

Such thoughts have an obvious bearing on the *Quartets,* a poem which,
like Eliot's account of Valéry, would sometimes have "la force d'un lieu
commun exprimé dans des mots que personne n'a encore employés;
comme pour certains vers de Gray, je sens une sorte d'étonnement et
d'admiration comme devant un miracle de résurrection de morts."[13]
The seed of Eliot's speculation, moreover, is as interesting as its fruit.
His thoughts about the theatre can in part be traced to the writing of
G. Wilson Knight, whose early work on Shakespeare Eliot read a few
years before he returned to Harvard.

As Knight remembered it, Eliot was so impressed with Knight's 1929 essay "Myth and Miracle" that he "offered to recommend, and even himself personally take, my other Shakespearian essays . . . to the Oxford University Press, where they were published as *The Wheel of Fire,*" for which Eliot wrote the introduction. Eliot's response to "Myth and Miracle," Knight adds, was "more than courtesy," for in 1930 Eliot sent Knight "his 'Marina,' inscribed 'for' me as 'with, I hope, some appropriateness.' " Eliot had composed in "Marina," Knight suggests, "a perfect poetical commentary on those Shakespearian meanings which I had unveiled. His full critical acceptance was witnessed further by his 1932 reference to them in his essay on John Ford."[14]

When he wrote his reminiscence, however, Knight did not realize how much his work had gathered up and extended Eliot's own intuitions. The novelty of Knight's point of view in "Myth and Miracle," later worked out in a number of book-length studies, may be summed up under three headings: first, it approached the plays through their poetic fabric of theme and imagery and, as Eliot said in his introduction to *The Wheel of Fire,* searched "for the pattern below the level of 'plot' and 'character.' . . . [the] subterrene or *submarine music.*"[15] Secondly, it related the pattern of Shakespeare's late plays to the pattern of the bard's own spiritual progress from "pain and despairing thought through stoic acceptance to a serene and mystic joy."[16] And finally it put special stress on the last group of romances, particularly *Pericles,* whose experience was colored by music and whose myth reflected "that mystic truth from which are born the dogmas of the Catholic Church . . . the temptation in the desert, the tragic ministry and death, and the resurrection of the Christ."[17] When Eliot encountered these assertions, he himself was "mulling over some of the later plays, particularly *Pericles, Cymbeline,* and *The Winter's Tale* . . . reading the later plays for the first time in my life as a separate group, [and becoming] impressed by what seemed to me important and very serious recurrences of mood and theme."[18] His response to Knight's parallel investigations was immediate, and generated several chains of thought.

One of the things Eliot concluded from his study of Shakespeare gave Elisabeth Schneider the thesis for her 1975 book *T. S. Eliot: The Pattern in the Carpet.* According to Schneider, Eliot, prompted by Knight's reading of Shakespeare, affirmed that what " 'matters most' in weighing the greatness of a poet is . . . 'unity in a lifetime's work,' [and] that the whole of Shakespeare's work 'is *one* poem . . . united by one significant, consistent, and developing personality.' "[19] Acting on that belief, Schneider argues, Eliot tried to impose the same kind of unity on the development of his own work. According to *The Pattern in the Carpet,* Eliot took "material from his earlier poems and suitably [altered] it to reflect the changing or 'developing personality' of the present poet as he conceived him to be. The result is sometimes happy,

sometimes frigid; but in either case the effect of the deliberateness itself upon the texture of his writing, noticeably different from that of
unconscious or half-conscious recurring patterns in the work of most
poets, is marked."[20]

The problem with this is that it does not sufficiently acknowledge the
other supports of Eliot's new work. For one thing, when Eliot, in an
essay of 1932 that Schneider does not quote, speaks of "a poet in his
maturity working up into better form some image or rhythm which was
an inspired flash of his youth,"[21] he has not only Shakespeare but Mallarmé in mind. As we shall see at the end of this chapter, much of the
deliberateness and frigidity that Schneider discovers in the *Quartets* can
be traced to the way Mallarmé's poems repeat and recapitulate themselves. Knight's procedures, after all, had largely served to open Eliot's
eyes to the way the most quotidian theatrical plot might be illuminated
by regarding it with a symbolist's eye.

The more important instigation in Knight's discussion of Shakespeare was not so much his contention that Shakespeare reworked his
themes, but his description of how Shakespeare's romances reworked
tragic themes into something more than tragedy. In "Myth and Miracle," Knight glances at the way Shakepeare's middle tragedies are "obsessed with love's impurity and death's hideousness," only to turn, in
the late romances, to the truth of "miracle" and to the lesson of the
Book of Job: "after endurance to the end the hero has a mystic vision
of God and then, in spite of reason and experience, we are told that
his original wealth and happiness are restored to him tenfold."[22]

Reading this in 1929, Eliot could not have been more receptive. As
Ash Wednesday, "Journey of the Magi" and "A Song for Simeon" had
recently confessed, Eliot's life had reached that point of diminution
when, as Knight describes Lear, he could hope for nothing more than
"death . . . the sweet ender of suffering."[23] Increasingly conscious of
the stiff carapace of his accumulated experience and the limitations of
his earlier work, Eliot's speakers yearn for a way of "restoring / Through
a bright cloud of tears, the years, restoring / With a new verse the ancient
rhyme" (*Ash Wednesday* V). But before he began to "mull over"
Shakespeare's romances, that seemed all but impossible. Because of
"what is done, not to be done again," Eliot lived in an "air which is now
thoroughly small and dry" (*Ash Wednesday* I). And as of 1929 his poetry
offered little more. Aside from the intermittent play of "Journey of the
Magi" and *Ash Wednesday*, his verse had contracted to a confessional
sincerity which could acknowledge guilt, sin and error but not transcend them. Invoke as he might the redemptive vision of the *Vita Nuova*,
he could not effectively conjure up the experience of rebirth. Like
Shakespeare's Pericles, he was a man "who for this three months hath
not spoken / To any one, nor taken sustenance. / But to prorogue his

grief" (*Pericles* V.i.24–26). And like Leontes in *The Winter's Tale,* he could not "do as the heavens have done; forget your evil; / With them forgive yourself" (V.i.5–6).

As iron to a magnet, then, Eliot was drawn to Shakespeare's parables of rebirth and to the spectacle of Shakespeare enacting his own rebirth in plots whose "predominating symbols are loss in tempest and revival to the sounds of music."[24] In a sequence of essays dating from the late twenties to the late thirties, Eliot rehearsed the Shakespearean progress as a mantra for his own spiritual metamorphosis. "John Ford" (1932), "John Marston" (1934) and especially Eliot's unpublished 1937 Edinburgh University lectures, "Shakespeare as Poet and Dramatist," trace his persistence and urgency. In the latter, Eliot writes that "what Shakespeare seems to ask me to do, and when I am in a sensitive enough mood makes me do, is to see *through* the ordinary classified emotions of our active life into a world of emotion and feeling beyond, of which I am not ordinarily aware. What he makes me feel is not so much that his characters are creatures like myself, but that I am a creature like his characters, taking part, like them, in no common action, of which I am for the most part quite unaware."[25]

Eliot, we are reminded, had felt these possibilities before. About the time he wrote *The Hollow Men* and spoke in the Clark Lectures about the "doubleness" of life in Chapman and Dostoevsky, he had had a vision that he could see through to a transcendent plane where his life made sense. At the end of the decade, however, the vision was still incomplete. In 1929, six years after he had first thought of conversion, Eliot still saw himself as one of those who "affirm before the world and deny between the rocks" (*Ash Wednesday* V). And inevitably, his frustration made him more exercised about the reality of spiritual vision. As he confronted *Pericles* around 1930, he seemed once more haunted by the thought of a double universe—a universe where our inevitable humiliation is also the source of our salvation. And by the time of his Edinburgh lectures, it was his constant theme—the discovered crown to Shakespeare's art and humanity:

> It seems to me to correspond to some profound law of nature, that in the work of such a man as Shakespeare you should find a point in which he touches the imagination and feeling of the greatest number of people to the greatest possible depth, and that thereafter, like a comet continuing its course away from the earth, he should gradually disappear into his private mystery. . . .
>
> The personages in *Cymbeline, The Winter's Tale, The Tempest* and *Pericles* are the work of a writer who has finally seen *through* the dramatic action of men into a spiritual action which transcends it. . . . Dramatic action, in the ordinary sense, is inadequate for making these emotions perceptible. Shakespeare tends, therefore, to simplify his characters, to make them ve-

hicles for conveying something of which they are unaware. It is in these
late plays that one becomes most conscious of the fact that we know neither
what we do nor what we feel. . . .

    . . . after *Hamlet*. . . . as the emotion tends to become something which
exists only in the whole play, so the author perhaps comes to find that he
is interested in expressing emotion which is beyond the primary "dramatic." This is not *un* dramatic or *non* dramatic: it is another plane of
dramatic reality. . . .

    . . . in poetic drama . . . we are lifted to another plane of reality, and
a hidden and mysterious pattern of reality appears as from a palimpsest.
. . . [The pattern needs an ordinary plot of] immediately acceptable and
recognisable human emotions. . . . [but there is] something over and above
plot, development of character, and conflict of character. . . . speech expressing more than what the characters know or know they feel. Something is exhibited of which we have only rare glimpses in our daily life.

These remarks give us our major entry into Eliot's plays, about which
this study will have little to say. But they also stand behind his 1930
lyric "Marina," and gloss the poem that once and for all took his writing beyond the boundaries of the dramatic lyric into what the Edinburgh lectures call the " 'ultra-dramatic.' " "Marina" was published the
same year as *Ash Wednesday*, but between them Eliot underwent a rite
of passage.

The moment dramatized by "Marina" is the Shakespearean one to
which we have just seen Eliot obsessively return, with this difference.
Rather than the experience of *seeing* through "the ordinary classified
emotions of our active life into a world of emotion and feeling beyond," or *seeing* through "the dramatic action of men into a spiritual
action which transcends it," Eliot's speaker in "Marina" *smells* the scent
of pine and *hears* "the woodthrush singing through the fog." The shift
has to do with Eliot's reading of *Pericles*, in which he found "a pattern
in which all the senses are used to convey something beyond sense"
and "a pervading smell of seaweed throughout."[26] And it tells us something about what it was that Eliot thought Shakespeare pierced through
to, and what was about to happen to Eliot's poetry. As J. Hillis Miller
remarks, because Eliot's hold on the world outside him is so slack, there
is little recognition in Eliot's early poetry "that men have other senses
beside eyesight." It is only in the later poetry that he returns from an
"idealist isolation to a physical world," and his return supplies "one
dimension, and not the least moving, of 'Marina.' "[27] In "Marina,"
crystalized or figured by the recognition of his daughter, the experience of Eliot's speaker corresponds to a sudden assurance of the solidity of the world outside him. The poem enacts a miraculous dissolution
of his diseased self-consciousness, which he had shared with "those who
sharpen the tooth of the dog," but which is now "by this grace dissolved

in place." Finally convinced of the world's reality, he is on the point of recognizing his own.

That said, however, it must also be said that the poem is not simply "a 'privileged moment' . . . of serenity and transfiguration."[28] Like the three *Ariel* poems that precede it—"Journey of the Magi," "A Song for Simeon," and "Animula"—"Marina" presents the feeling of a man in the process of dying to one life and unable to be born into another. The ambivalence, it is true, is authorized by Shakespeare, or more particularly by the terror Pericles feels in his moment of bliss:

> O Helicanus, strike me, honour'd sir;
> Give me a gash, put me to present pain,
> Lest this great sea of joys rushing upon me
> O'erbear the shores of my mortality
> And drown me with their sweetness.
>
> (*Pericles* V.i. 192–96)

But our truest guide to the ambivalence dramatized in the poem is probably one of Eliot's own remarks. Asked what he meant by the poem, Eliot pointed to his epigraph, which evokes the story of Hercules awaking to find he has slaughtered his children. "I intend," he said, "a crisscross between Pericles finding alive, and Hercules finding dead—the two extremes of the recognition scene."[29] Which is to say that *his* Marina brings with her an aching sense of the fragility of old age, and his Pericles recalls the surprise of the Boatswain in *The Tempest* that an old ship, once split, could be restored:

> The best news is that we have safely found
> Our king and company; the next, our ship,
> Which, but three glasses since, we gave out split,
> Is tight and yare and bravely rigged as when
> We first put out to sea.
>
> (*Tempest* V.i.221–24)

Thus in Eliot's poem, the same speaker who admonishes himself to "let me/ Resign my life for this life" also registers an ominous premonition of what the submission will cost him:

> What seas what shores what granite islands towards my timbers. . . .

We are not yet, apparently, out of the world of "Journey of the Magi," where birth feels more than a little like death.

Still, if Eliot's faith in the endurance of "a world of emotion and feeling beyond" is problematic in "Marina," the vividness of the moment for once is not. Figured by an intuition of the uncontrollable resurgent energy which exists at the source of things ("Whispers and small laughter between leaves," "hurrying feet / Under sleep, where all the

waters meet"), a daughter calls to his speaker across the quotidian surface of life. More than in any of his representations of Dante, Eliot's
homage to Shakespeare invests the experience of rebirth with poetic
authority. A comparison with *Ash Wednesday* is instructive. In section IV
of *Ash Wednesday*, Eliot uses the elaborate hieratic apparatus of Dante's
"higher dream" to evoke the rhythms of rebirth. For an instant, his
speaker regains the memory of a moment when the energies of renewal were activated, when "the fountain sprang up and the bird sang
down." But the agent of that renewal, the "silent sister," is a figure as
intimidating as she is efficacious. Wrapped in stillness, she "signed, but
spoke no word." And in section V of *Ash Wednesday*, Eliot wonders
whether she will "pray for those who offend her." She is linked to the
world of eros, and despite Eliot's evident will to do so, he cannot make
her permanently one with the place "where trees flower, and springs
flow." In his imaginative effort to realize that place, she is as much his
impediment as his guide.

In "Marina," thanks to the music of Shakespeare, Eliot finds a way
to fuse woman and fountain, eros and agape. The image of the beloved
never appears, but we sense her in tremblings of the speaker's recognition and in the urgent music of Eliot's verse:

> And scent of pine and the woodthrush singing through the
> fog. . . .

Eliot's representation of the instigations of love thus has the flavor of
his description of Shakespeare's: it is "beyond good and evil" in the
common sense, so that the laws of its morality are "as 'natural' as any
discovered by Einstein or Planck."[30] Shakespeare's vision of love begins
with a music which flows from the sources of the universe. It involves
energies which exist in God's willingness to forgive, and which lie beyond the reach of sin or error. It is a vision connected to the irrepres-
sible force of "spring incarnate" that Knight was later to associate with
Autolycus, that "figure of absolute comedy" in *The Winter's Tale*.[31] In
Knight's view, which became Eliot's, this power achieves its consummate expression in the love which pulses and orders what Pericles calls
that "heavenly music" that "nips me into listening" (*Pericles* V.i.234-35).

As it was conditioned by his reading of Shakespearean romance, then,
Eliot's attraction to "the music of poetry" has Platonic and Christian
overtones—it has as much to do with the miraculous instigations of love
as it does with the imaginative patterns of poetry. And so, for the Eliot
of the *Quartets*, music is not simply a formal property of verse; it is the
emanation of a spiritual fountain. As Eliot explains it in his Edinburgh
lectures, after *Hamlet*, "there appears dimly another plane of emotion,
apprehensible through the *music* of the play—coming from the depths
of Shakespeare himself." It is this music, this plane of emotion, which

Eliot says in his Edinburgh lectures is responsible for the "ultra-dra-matic" effects of the romances—the phenomenon we sense when a character in the plays is speaking "beyond character" so that his speech "has the impersonality of something which utters itself, which exists in its own life."

Finally, Eliot's Edinburgh lectures suggest why in the poems Eliot wrote under Shakespeare's spell, the rhythms of children's songs should be joined with the elaborate patterns of verbal symphony. The "wood-thrush singing" and the "whispers and small laughter" of "Marina," the "children's voices" of "New Hampshire" and the "dance / Of the gold-finch" of "Cape Ann" are all related to the island music of *The Tempest* and give us the ground bass of the philosophical and personal medita-tion of "Burnt Norton." In "Burnt Norton," we hear the "hidden mu-sic," the "mysterious pattern of reality" that the Edinburgh lectures tell us emerges from the romances "as from a palimpsest." It is the same music that Ferdinand hears in *The Tempest:*

> Sitting on a bank,
> Weeping again the King my father's wrack,
> This music crept by me upon the waters,
> Allaying both their fury and my passion
> With its sweet air.
>
> *(Tempest* I.ii.390–94)

4

Between "Marina" (1930) and "Burnt Norton" (1935), Eliot found ways to re-create Shakespeare's hidden music in the possibilities of a twentieth-century meditative lyric. There was first of all his groping use of the chorus in *The Rock* and *Murder in the Cathedral.* To Eliot, who had expressed interest in it as early as the late teens,[32] the chorus was an obvious way for the playwright to suggest the "ultra-dramatic" con-dition of "something which utters itself." More than any other resource of the dramatist, it permits speech to be uttered "beyond character," somewhere between dramatic speech and music. Traditionally associ-ated with philosophical material, it also articulates the rhythms of an-tique tragedy. And, at least as Eliot envisioned it, the chorus directs drama toward "gnomic" utterance and helps bring out the hidden di-mensions of realistic action. "The choruses of Sophocles," he wrote, "as well as the songs of Shakespeare, have another concern besides the hu-man action of which they are spectators, and without this other concern there is not poetry."[33] One could say the same about the chorus-like passages of "Burnt Norton," which are both the utterance of a middle-aged man and part of the amassing harmony of a whole that is beyond his compass. It is not for nothing that "Chard Whitlow," Henry Reed's infamous parody of "Burnt Norton," should remind us of a potted translation of Sophocles or Aeschylus:

> As we get older we do not get any younger . . .

No less connected to the music of "Marina," however, were Eliot's experiments with landscape. Beginning with what in *Collected Poems 1909–1935* he called "Five Finger Exercises," Eliot began to write short, melodically sophisticated evocations of landscape. These verses, the most successful of which are the five "Landscapes" ("New Hampshire," "Virginia," "Usk," "Rannoch, by Glencoe," and "Cape Ann"), continue a trend that had started in the mid-twenties. Like "Journey of the Magi," they represent the meditations of a voice contemplating some phenomenon external to itself. As Nancy Hargrove observes, the titles of the poems indicate the shifting focus of Eliot's career: no longer the names of symbolic characters or internal landscapes, they refer to particular settings, which provide the poems' primary "means of objectifying [their] emotional/spiritual content."[34]

The evolving status of speech in the "Landscapes" provides another clue to Eliot's intentions. In "New Hampshire" and "Virginia," there is a speaker who calls attention to himself as "me" and interjects himself into his speech. In both poems, he contemplates a landscape and then imposes his own mood upon it. However, in the third poem, "Usk," an imperative voice enters (a voice which will dominate the *Quartets*). In "Usk," this voice commands, "do not spell / Old enchantments"; "Lift your eyes" to the reality around you, "Where the roads dip and where the roads rise." Afterward, the speaker of "Rannoch, by Glencoe" follows the advice of that imperative voice, and confirms its wisdom. The road he discovers "winds in / . . . Clamour of confused wrong." And, contemplating the history of our fallen world, he becomes oblivious to his own iron thoughts. The only response to this revelation is the response of "Cape Ann," and the only voice which can deliver it is as impersonal as a saint's or an old song's: "But resign this land at the end, resign it / To its true owner."

As should be obvious from the above, "Landscapes" form a suite which anticipates the orchestration of the *Quartets*.[35] While suggesting stages in the emotional or spiritual progress just described, the parts of the suite are arranged in seasonal order: spring, summer, fall, winter and renewed spring. They also exhibit Eliot's inclination, soon to grow even stronger, to associate a feeling for nature with strong personal emotions that for him inevitably have their source in Missouri and New England.[36] So "Landscapes" call up scenes from his childhood ("New Hampshire" and "Cape Ann") that had been recently restored by a forty-year-old's return. Or, in the case of "Virginia," they memorialize a trip that could not help but recall memories of the Mississippi.

But the personal resonance of "Landscapes" is not exhausted by their local color. "Rannoch, by Glencoe" also presents old preoccupations re-configured in unfamiliar geography. Once, obsessed with Donne's vision of passion surviving the grave, Eliot had imagined the senses transcending their function to register the secrets of being. According to the conceit of "Whispers of Immortality," Donne was

> Expert beyond experience,
>
>> He knew the anguish of the marrow
>> The ague of the skeleton;
>> No contact possible to flesh
>> Allayed the fever of the bone.

Then, in *The Hollow Men,* Eliot's perception changed. What persisted beyond death, he recognized, were old desires and the proud self that sustained them—the self which, in Biblical idiom, became "This broken jaw of our lost kingdoms." For *that* self, humiliation is the only road to a new life. The catch was that, as Eliot's subsequent life confirmed, the old self, even broken, will not let go. "Rannoch, by Glencoe" recognizes that truth in the story of old stones, and Donne's lines return to him with a grim irony. Not the passionate glow of bright hair, but the force of an old life is what retains power over us, even when we think we have entered a better one:

> Memory is strong
> Beyond the bone. Pride snapped,
> Shadow of pride is long. . . .

However much Eliot associates them with his private experience, however, his "Landscapes" are not just the expressions of his mood. In fact, only because he keeps himself distinct from his settings do their revelations persuade us. It should be noted, though, that the settings are not anchored in elaborate description. As Eliot said about "Cooper's Hill" in 1928, "the importance of the view or scenery contemplated [in descriptive poetry] is slight."[37] What is more important is the suggestion of some knotty truth. In "Landscapes," Eliot dramatizes the difficult effort of registering a quiddity imperceptibly suggested by our surroundings. In "Usk," it is a matter of focusing the sight, of lifting our eyes to "where the roads dip." In the other poems, his hearing is in question—in "New Hampshire" hearing "children's voices"; in "Virginia," "the mocking-bird / Heard once"; in "Cape Ann":

> O quick quick quick, quick hear the song-sparrow. . . .

And in "Rannoch, by Glencoe," the

> Clamour of confused wrong, apt
> In silence.

At the heart of each of the "Landscapes," there is the "note" of a stylized scene. Together, these notes come to imply a pattern of existence beyond the speaker, so that listening for them becomes an exercise in "sincerity"—an exercise in separating each man's tune, as Seamus Heaney has it, in "that moment when the bird sings" from "the music of what happens."[38] The outcome, of course, as it is in "Rannoch, by Glencoe," can be a suggestion of the reality of our own lives. But when it is, it will be in the form of a music we would not at first have recognized as our own.

From this perspective, the stylized rhythmic and imagistic music so often noted in the suite makes sense. Just as Eliot would connect the disturbing presence of music in key scenes of the romances to Shakespeare's larger pattern of musical orchestration and ultimately to "the music of the spheres" (*Pericles* V.i.231), so in his own poems he embeds distant notes that form part of an elaborate musical frame. The difference is that in "Landscapes," the frame has a French rather than an English model. Not plays but post-symbolist lyrics, "Landscapes" look back to nineteenth-century France and to Eliot's earliest manner, so that the connections between individual notes in the suite are allowed to emerge, as Eliot once said, "like Anadyomene from the sea" (UPUC, 147). Forgoing the implied theatrical frame of "Marina," Eliot creates a poetic field whose poles are on one hand commonplace speech and on the other the barely visible, barely audible "music of what happens." It is the same field that he will exploit with greater confidence in "Burnt Norton," where it will allow him to voice his own everyday self without implying that it is either fully adequate or contemptibly shallow. Like the drama Eliot had already started to write, "Burnt Norton" confesses the "material, literal-minded and visionless" component of his awareness, and yet, by its musical pattern, also implies the coexistence of a silent "meaning which reveals itself gradually." Once more Eliot's observations on Elizabethan drama are worth quoting. This is a passage from "John Marston" (1934) which fulfills the musings of the Clark Lectures as "Burnt Norton" fulfills the suggestions of *The Hollow Men*:[39]

[Marston's] is an original variation of that deep discontent and rebelliousness so frequent among the Elizabethan dramatists. He is, like some of the greatest of them, occupied in saying something else than appears in the literal actions and characters whom he manipulates. . . .

In poetic drama a certain apparent irrelevance may be the symptom of this doubleness; or the drama has an under-pattern, less manifest than the theatrical one. We sometimes feel, in following the words and behaviour of some of the characters of Dostoevsky, that they are living at once on the plane that we know and on some other plane of reality from which we are shut out: their behaviour does not seem crazy, but rather in conformity with the laws of some world we cannot perceive. . . . In the work of genius of a lower order, such as that of the author of *The Revenger's Tragedy*, the characters themselves hardly attain this double reality; we are aware rather of the author, operating perhaps not quite consciously through them, and making use of them to express something of which he himself may not be quite conscious.

It is not by writing quotable "poetic" passages, but by giving us the sense of something behind, more real than any of his personages and their action, that Marston established himself among the writers of genius (ED, 161–62).

Before we take up "Burnt Norton," though, there is yet one subject to consider. As I have suggested, although the discourse of the *Quartets* registers the "submarine music" of the Elizabethans, it does so only by way of the codes of post-symbolist poetry. And so, though it was inspired by a reading of Shakespeare, the poem in fact acquires its shape by rehearsing the somber, difficult music of Mallarmé.

5

Already mentioned twice in this study, Eliot's "Note sur Mallarmé et Poe" signaled the kindling of an enthusiasm that was by 1926 six years old. Earlier than that, Eliot had been skeptical. In the late teens, he had praised Pound's sharp images at the expense of Mallarmé's "mossiness" (TCC, 170), and he had suggested that beside the "sincere" prose of Rimbaud, the "laboured opacity of Mallarmé fades colourless and dead."[40] By 1920, though, Eliot's opinion began to change. In the *Athenaeum* for that year, he directed his readers to Dujardin's study of Mallarmé,[41] and two years later he was commending Mallarmé along with Dryden "for what he made of his material" (SE, 269). Writing in the 1921 *Chapbook*, he elaborated:

Verse is always struggling . . . to take up to itself more and more of what is prose, to take something more from life and turn it into "play." Seen from this angle, the labour of Mallarmé with the French language becomes something important; every battle he fought with syntax represents the effort to transmute lead into gold, ordinary language into poetry; and the real failure of contemporary verse is its failure to draw anything new from life into art.[42]

Having anticipated so much of the emphasis of his later poetry, in 1921 Eliot went no further. Busy with other things (the summer of 1921 was the summer of *The Waste Land*), he did not begin to study Mallarmé for several years. According to what Eliot told Edward Greene, it was 1925—at the time he was preparing the Clark Lectures—when he began to reread him seriously.[43] It is conceivable, in fact, that Eliot's interest was quickened as he wrote the eighth of the lectures, which treats Laforgue and Corbière as "metaphysical" poets because their verse acquires emotional coloring by entertaining metaphysical beliefs.[44] It was only the limitations of the occasion, I suspect (the lecture on Laforgue was the last in the series), that prevented him from speaking of Mallarmé. We know, at any rate, that Eliot published his "Note Sur Mallarmé et Poe" a few months later, and that he introduced it as an appendix to a "suite d'études encore incomplète [sur] . . . *la poésie métaphysique.*"[45] Accordingly, Eliot wrote, he wished to consider a poet who relied on philosophy "pour raffiner et pour développer [son] puissance de sensibilité et d'émotion." The work of Donne, Poe and Mallarmé, Eliot explained, "était une expansion de leur sensibilité *au-delà des limites du monde normal,* une découverte de nouveaux objets propres à susciter de nouvelles émotions."

This, of course, is the kind of achievement Eliot soon would recognize in Shakespearean romance. Yet what first intrigued him about the work of Mallarmé was not the sort of gradual effect he found in Shakespeare, but local matters of lineation and syntax. Matters, in other words, closer to his own métier. Though Eliot wrote in his "Note" that he did not wish to explore the subtleties of Mallarmé's craft, he did ascribe Mallarmé's "nouveaux objets propres à susciter de nouvelles émotions" to a syntax so difficult that it "empêche le lecteur *d'avaler d'un coup* [son] phrase ou [son] vers." Through mastery of syntax, Mallarmé transmutes "de l'accidentel en réel." How, though, does Mallarmé achieve this reality if he, like Poe and Donne, "ne *croient* pas aux théories auxquelles ils s'intéressent"? By means, according to Eliot, of "*incantation* . . . qui insiste sur la puissance primitive du Mot.*"

At the center of Eliot's argument, and justifying his future experiments with incantation and indeterminacy, is "le Mot"—the Word. By 1926 Eliot had seen that in Mallarmé's incantatory syntax, every word dislocates the expectations of discourse with a new beginning and liberates the reality behind speech from our conditioned sense of it even as the dislocations of Shakespeare's plays liberate us from the conventions of "character" and "action." Installed in its "puissance primitive," the word can conduct us from "[le] monde tangible" to a world beyond: "[le] monde des fantômes."[46]

Having written a statement as strong as the "Note sur Mallarmé et Poe," Eliot seemed to be in the grip of a new master. And it is true, Eliot acknowledged the powers he had attributed to Mallarmé in his soon-to-be-written translations of St.-John Perse. Even more, he suggested the powers of incantation and "le Mot" in *Ash Wednesday,* where "Against the Word the unstilled world still whirled /About the centre of the silent Word." Yet for several years, Eliot resisted any closer approach. In *Ash Wednesday,* his emphasis still falls on personal salvation, not, as in the *Quartets,* on a quest that "impelled *us* / To purify the dialect of *the tribe.*" As late as 1930, the example of Mallarmé, though tantalizing, remained alien.

Then in January of 1933, Eliot interrupted his stay at Harvard to give the Johns Hopkins Turnbull Lectures, which he called "Varieties of Metaphysical Poetry." They were in fact an abbreviated version of the Clark Lectures of 1925–26. Cutting and rearranging his original eight lectures into three, though, Eliot enlarged his text to accommodate a single subject—French symbolism, especially the poetry of Mallarmé.[47]

The third Turnbull lecture is particularly interesting, for it contains one of the autobiographical asides that gave particular poignancy to Eliot's addresses of that year. "I doubt," Eliot told his audience, "whether, without . . . Baudelaire, Corbière, Verlaine, Laforgue, Mallarmé, Rimbaud—I should have been able to write poetry at all. Without them, the Elizabethan and Jacobean poets would have been too remote and quaint, and Shakespeare and Dante too remote and great, to have helped me." Yet as Eliot went on to talk about his present notions of poetry, he made it clear that his debt had if anything increased over the years. Using phrases adapted from his "Note sur Mallarmé," he said that the ideal literary critic should "primarily be concerned with the word and the incantation; the question whether the poet has used the right word in the right place, the rightness depending upon both the explicit intention and an indefinite radiation of sound and sense." By very much the same criteria, the "important poets" will be "those who have taught the people speech . . . the function of the poet at every moment is to make the inarticulate folk articulate; and as the inarticulate folk is almost always mumbling the speech, become jargon, of its ancestors or of its newspaper editors, the new language is never learnt without a certain resistance, even resentment. *Donner un sens plus pur aux mots de la tribu,* Mallarmé said of Poe; and this purification of language is not so much a progress, as it is a perpetual return to the real."

And if the third Turnbull lecture demonstrated that Mallarmé was playing a greater part in Eliot's thinking about poetry and poets, the second lecture said something more specific about how he had entered Eliot's technique. Speaking of Crashaw and defending a kind of figuration that had found little place in his early verse, Eliot advised:

> It is a mistake to suppose that a simile or a metaphor is always something meant to be *visible* to the imagination; and even when it is meant to be visible, that all its parts are meant to be visible at once. Examine a sonnet by a modern poet—I say modern because I have a friend who was a friend of his—Stéphane Mallarmé; *M'introduire dans ton histoire,* and you will find in the fourteen lines four or five images which it is quite impossible to imagine or conceive simultaneously, and at least one which cannot be visualised at all:

> > Dis si je ne suis pas joyeux
> > Tonnerre et rubis aux moyeux
> > De voir en l'air que ce feu troue

Avec des royaumes épars
Comme mourir pourpre la roue
De seul vespéral de mes chars

"Thunder and rubies up to the wheel hub" is just as difficult to figure out as the career of Crashaw's tear; and it is only when you have an impression of the sonnet as a whole that it comes into place, and has meaning. The poet's business is to know what effect he intends to produce, and then to get it by fair means or foul. There is the element of rationality, the element of precision, and there is also the element of vagueness which may be used; and we must remember that one distinction between poetry and prose is this, that in poetry the word, each word by itself, though only being fully itself in context, has absolute value. Poetry is *incantation,* as well as imagery. "Thunder and rubies" cannot be seen, heard or thought together, but their collocation here brings out the connotation of each word.

Focused on lines he later absorbed into "Burnt Norton,"[48] this is clearly one of those discriminations Eliot made to "prepare the way for his own practice" (TCC, 33). As in his "Note sur Mallarmé," he ends by affirming the radical potential of "each word." But here he is thinking his insight through, and along the way he connects his claim to several subsidiary notions he had been toying with since he finished *The Waste Land.* For the poet to preserve the "absolute value" of each word, for example, Eliot recognizes that he must rely on the "impression of the sonnet as a whole," on "collocation," on "context." In the early twenties, feeling himself into his second period, Eliot had put it baldly: "a creation, a work of art, is autotelic" (SE, 19); "it is essential that a work of art should be self-consistent, that an artist should consciously or unconsciously draw a circle beyond which he does not trespass" (SE, 93). Now the implications of those remarks for a new kind of poetry began to make themselves felt.

Several other ideas Eliot brings to bear in this passage are also elements of his recent work. Chapter seven, for example, observed the importance of "vagueness," "connotation," and "incantation" for *Anabasis* and "Journey of the Magi." Here Eliot connects the terms in a near-comprehensive neo-symbolist statement of the *musical* characteristics of poetry. In part, the statement corresponds to what Eliot later said in his 1958 essay on Valéry: that the essence of music as the symbolists understood it was a striving "towards an unattainable timelessness . . . a yearning for the stillness of painting or sculpture."[49] This is, of course, something like the "musical design" (OPP, 80) Eliot had attributed to Shakespearean romance. "Burnt Norton," shading the word "silence" as Mallarmé does in his essay "The Crisis of Poetry,"[50] would put it this way:

Words, after speech, reach
Into the silence. Only by the form, the pattern,

Can words or music reach
The stillness, as a Chinese jar still
Moves perpetually in its stillness.
Not the stillness of the violin, while the note lasts,
Not that only, but the co-existence,
Or say that the end precedes the beginning,
And the end and the beginning were always there. . . .

Yet the music of Eliot's poetry goes beyond stillness, and these lines represent only one mood of "Burnt Norton." As we shall see, in the first of the *Quartets,* as in the Turnbull Lectures, Eliot's heaviest weight falls on a *jangle* of dissonant words—phrases and images that are, Eliot says, "impossible to imagine or conceive simultaneously," and which together suggest resurgent energy. The thought is elaborated in "The Music of Poetry," where Eliot advised that the phenomenon of his title was at least as much a matter of tension as of resolution. For one thing, Eliot said, poetic structure demands it: "Dissonance, even cacophony, has its place: just as, in a poem of any length, there must be transitions between passages of greater and less intensity, to give a rhythm of fluctuating emotion essential to the musical structure of the whole" (OPP, 24–25). For another, the music of an individual word occurs "at a point of intersection: it arises from its relation first to the words immediately preceding and following it, and indefinitely to the rest of its context" (OPP, 25).

Nor, given the coloring of his religious dispositions, is Eliot's emphasis on dissonance unexpected. Consider what Eliot's friend Joseph Chiari wrote in an essay Eliot introduced as "the first book in English on Mallarmé and his art of poetry":

[Mallarmé] came to realise that the *logos*—God's expression—was beyond the human, and could not be heard or apprehended, for it was silence—the absolute, source of all things—and the poet, if he were absolutely logical, could only remain silent. . . . In Mallarmé's poetry, each word anticipates and merges into the next, therefore only exists in its dual capacity of projection backward and forward axled on a state of virtuality which is the continuous becoming of the word. . . . the words [that is to say] are used as much as possible like musical notes or signs; they have been deprived by various syntactic distortions of their logical meaning so that they never produce a static picture in the Parnassian style; their aim is to give life by continuity and movement. . . . Language is used both symbolically and also musically as a kind of magic aimed at creating a state of trance whence will rise the unheard music, the vision of the absolute. . . . Yet such an ideal is condemned to failure, for the words, part of creation, can never be rid completely of the contingent, and therefore they cannot destroy *le hasard.*[51]

As Chiari allows us to infer by his reference to the logos, Mallarmé's symbolist aesthetic fits Eliot's Anglican beliefs like a well-made glove.

How better to convey the Christian's humble awareness of his inability to apprehend or characterize the logos—what *The Rock* was to call the "Light invisible . . . / Too bright for mortal vision" (CPP, 112)—than through a poetry yearning toward "silence" yet conscious that failure is inevitable?

But the medium Eliot fashioned for the *Quartets* did not simply depend on religious principle. It had other components, components which were rooted in the rebellious impulses of Eliot's psychic economy. For Eliot to affirm poetry's fundamental inadequacy was also to affirm its open-endedness. On the one hand, this points toward a deplorable condition close to Eliot's life-long sense of inadequacy. It means that every attempt to use words

> Is a wholly new start, and a different kind of failure
> Because one has only learnt to get the better of words
> For the thing one no longer has to say, or the way in which
> One is no longer disposed to say it.
>
> ("East Coker")

But it also means something more positive, something that had been asserted by Eliot's earlier struggle against convention. It implies that the self, which stands in no less provisional a relationship between man and God than speech does between words and an ideal language, cannot be fixed. As man is forced constantly to revise his speech, so he is forced constantly to revise himself. He is permanently in question, but he is also *free* to recast his history of unhappiness and guilt; he can, in the play of "a world of speculation" ("Burnt Norton"), at any moment renew himself. Curse or blessing, that is his lot. And to Eliot, who was approaching middle age burdened with the psychic load of an old man, at times it seemed a very great blessing indeed—one that more than compensated for the difficulties it made for his Flaubertian ideals of shapeliness, harmony and finish. For a moment, Shakespeare and Mallarmé conjoining, it seemed possible to attempt a kind of writing in which "we are lifted for a moment beyond character" (OPP, 81)—to aim, as Eliot wrote in 1933,

> to write poetry which should be essentially poetry, with nothing poetic about it, poetry standing naked in its bare bones, or poetry so transparent that we should not see the poetry, but that which we are meant to see through the poetry, poetry so transparent that in reading it we are intent on what the poem *points at,* and not on the poetry, this seems to me the thing to try for. To get *beyond poetry,* as Beethoven, in his later works, strove to get *beyond music.*[52]

Still, the poetic consequences were considerable. As is apparent from the trouble Eliot had tying up the *Quartets,* to follow Mallarmé down this road meant abandoning the hope of poetic closure. If the poem, like the self, is condemned never to reach wholeness or stillness, if it exists in a state of continuous becoming, if "the word by itself," like each successive act of choice, "has absolute value," then literature is always in play and closure is always self-conscious and arbitrary.

I wonder, though, whether Eliot ever put the proposition to himself as nakedly as that, and I suspect he did not. The logical extension of endorsing the importance of open-endedness in the self and in poetry is a movement that horrified Eliot: the literature of Dada. Yet Eliot, drawing so close to Mallarmé and Perse, was also aligning himself with Rimbaud's *Illuminations,* Apollinaire's *Calligrammes* and their successors in the tradition of what Marjorie Perloff has called "the poetics of indeterminacy."[53] Insisting on "la puissance primitive du Mot," Eliot invites comparison with a post-modernist like John Ashbery and with the American who most anticipates Ashbery, William Carlos Williams in his Dadaist phase. In fact, if we seek a contemporary guide to the premises of Eliot's late work, we could do worse than to turn to Williams's *Spring and All.* The affinities are close enough that when Williams's best critic, James Breslin, instructs us how to read Williams, he does so in phrases haunted by the *Four Quartets.* The poems of *Spring and All,* Breslin writes, should be read "in a voice that is more flat than dramatically expressive—giving equal weight to each of the words." He adds that to approach Williams properly is "to discover a new world, one that is open, fluid, and shifting. . . . Ends dissolve into beginnings. Each poem . . . becomes a series of lines, each of which . . . pulls toward isolation, independence, at the same time that it is pulled back by syntax, by recurrences, toward all the other lines. At the edge of chaos, containing the pressure of its pushing and pulling, the poem trembles with force."[54]

PART THREE

"Costing Not Less Than Everything"

CHAPTER TEN

"Our first world":
"Burnt Norton"

The international situations, the elaborate complications in which many of Henry James's problems involve themselves, now seem remote; what is not remote is his curious search, often in the oddest places, like country houses, for spiritual life.

From Eliot's "Commentary" in the *Criterion,* April 1933.

"It was because I loved them so," she said at last, brokenly. *"That* was why it was, even from the first—even before I knew that they—they were all I should ever have. And I loved them so!"

She stretched out her arms to the shadows and the shadows within the shadow.

"They came because I loved them—because I needed them. I—I must have made them come. Was that wrong, think you? Did I wrong any one?"

Kipling, "They"

The defect of ["Little Gidding" as opposed to the other *Quartets*], I feel, is the lack of some acute personal reminiscence (never to be explicated, of course, but to give power from well below the surface). . . .

Eliot to John Hayward, 5 August 1941[1]

Eliot delivered his Milton Academy address on June 17, 1933. One week later, he sailed on the *Tuscania* to an England where he would see his wife again only a handful of times. After a year when, according to his brother, family reminiscences had provided one of the happiest periods he had known since childhood, he entered the last third of his life stripped of any family save the siblings he was leaving behind. And filled with the currents of wistfulness, anxiety and melancholy that feed "Burnt Norton," he concluded his undergraduate lectures at Harvard by comparing himself to two minor poets at the end of an era, Fletcher or Tourneur in 1633.[2] Eliot's mood was probably closest to the Coleridgean nostagia for lost joy on which, that March 31, he had closed the Norton Lectures:

I fear that I have already, throughout these lectures, trespassed beyond the bounds which a little self-knowledge tells me are my proper frontier.

If, as James Thomson observed, "lips only sing when they cannot kiss," it may also be that poets only talk when they cannot sing. I am content to leave my theorising about poetry at this point. The sad ghost of Coleridge beckons to me from the shadows (UPUC, 155–56).

On May 3, Eliot wired his friend Frank Morley, on whose English country place, Pikes Farm, he had pre-arranged to stay. Morley was to make final arrangements, with "carte blanche to commit me to anything." The words convey a desperation which was not lost on Eliot's host. In Morley's view, Eliot had reached "a moment of crisis, and a turning-point." Whatever doubts he had about this were erased over the next several months by Eliot's frequent allusions to "childhood days in St. Louis."[3] In the Norton Lectures Eliot had asked, "Why, for all of us, out of all that we have heard, seen, felt, in a lifetime, do certain images recur, charged with emotion, rather than others? . . . We might just as well ask why, when we try to recall visually some period in the past, we find in our memory just the few meagre arbitrarily chosen set of snapshots that we do find there, the faded poor souvenirs of passionate moments" (UPUC, 148). Now not sure whether he wanted to relive the past or forget it, he was troubled by both possibilities. He was still deep in the ambivalence of his Milton Academy remarks, which had wavered between relief that he was no longer "myself at the age of seventeen or thereabouts" and an uncomfortable feeling that the "ghost" of his seventeen-year-old self would disdain the men he had become. In the next months he would review memories long wrapped for storage, including the glories of Paris in 1910.[4]

What was particularly painful about all this was that, more than any time in the last twenty-eight years, Eliot was free to revamp who he was. While in Cambridge, he had been proposed a professorship of literature at Harvard.[5] Eliot had refused, almost reflexively, but the proposal suggested how quickly he could alter the course of his life. Back in England, he threw himself into a number of decisions which, with their anxious emphasis on control, recall the years after *The Waste Land*. The foremost of these decisions concerned the theatre and the Anglican church. About six weeks after Eliot installed himself at Pikes Farm, Morley returned from a holiday to find Eliot recovering from his crisis and entertaining a request that he write a church pageant for the producer, Martin Browne.[6] On September 22, Browne received permission from his sponsor to offer Eliot the project, and by October 6 Eliot had accepted.[7] Later, Eliot compared the effect of his decision to "the effect that vigorous cranking sometimes has upon a motor car when the battery is run down" (OPP, 98). And although he meant the car to be taken as "my meagre poetic gifts" (OPP, 98), the figure also applies to his general state. Committing himself to the pageant gave not only his writing but his life a direction and a shape, and thus dissolved some of his uncertainty about what future role he was to play. He meant emphatically to put his skills to public use for the good of the church, and the thoroughness of his self-effacement suggests how much he feared the freedom of a life suddenly open to redefinition. It also testifies to how strongly he needed to justify his continued existence in a way that no one—not Vivien, not his grandfather nor his mother in his mind's eye—could dispute. Having made his decision, moreover, Eliot followed through. After another month at Pikes Farm, he moved to 33 Courtfield Road, London, "partly to get into theatre," partly to be near the church of St. Stephen's, Gloucester Road, known for its Anglo-Catholic services.[8] In the months following, while he helped *The Rock* into production (May–June 1934) and worked on *Murder in the Cathedral* (commissioned May 1934, performed June 1935), he also gained the confidence of Father Eric Cheetham, the pastor of St. Stephen's. Eliot became Cheetham's Vicar's Warden (the highest lay position in the parish) and then shared lodgings with him. In the midst of this willed activity, however, he continued to suffer paroxysms of melancholy and indecision. Robert Sencourt tells the story of a friend who took note of Eliot's sadness and remembered his sitting listlessly, repeating to himself, "I wonder, I wonder."[9]

Part of the reason Eliot took so long to recompose himself after he returned to England was a cherished friendship his year in America had renewed. Before he left Harvard in 1914, Emily Hale had been more than companion, less than fiancée.[10] The two had corresponded at length in the years between his marriage and his Norton lectureship, and their letters, now sequestered, were undoubtedly full of pointed silences. The letters, however, also must have resonated with that special kind of indulgent tenderness that two people assume when they can be attentive without deception.[11] Yet that kind of tenderness has its dangers. For someone suffering the pains of a marriage like Eliot's, the mannered intimacy of such letters can come to acquire the allure of a fantom that seems to need only a little extra attention to make it come alive. That feeling or something like it seems to have impressed itself on Eliot after he broke with Vivien in America. Even before that, in 1932, we know, he exerted considerable effort to visit Emily Hale in Los Angeles, where she was teaching at Scripps College. We also know that Emily Hale arranged to spend the summer after Eliot's return with her aunt and uncle at Chipping Campden in the Cotswolds, and that Eliot visited her there that summer and the following summer. And we know that in September 1935, he accompanied her to the deserted gardens of Burnt Norton[12] and afterwards thanked Emily's aunt for her hospitality, adding: "I had come to feel 'at home' in Campden in a way in which I had not felt at home for some twenty-one years, anywhere."[13]

The presence of Emily Hale, then, forced Eliot to confront one of his most firmly repressed wishes. In a manner more insistent than the offer to teach at Harvard, she beckoned him to start over again, and the thought intoxicated him. (Virginia Woolf describes him in her diary as "10 years younger: hard, spry, a glorified boy scout in shorts & yellow shirt. He is enjoying himself very much. He is tight & shiny as a wood louse. . . . he wants to live, to love; even seeing Rochester is an event to him. He has seen nothing, nobody for the last 10 years.")[14] Driven by an old impulse, he felt the power of childhood desire, and for an instant a desire for childhood itself. Eliot said that in writing "Burnt Norton" he meant to tie it back to "New Hampshire,"[15] and we can see why. Part of the experience the poem explores is the nostalgia and the nostalgic grief of its predecessor:

> Children's voices in the orchard
> Between the blossom- and the fruit-time:
> Golden head, crimson head,
> Between the green tip and the root.
> Black wing, brown wing, hover over;
> Twenty years and the spring is over. . . .[16]

Nor does this nostalgia argue against Eliot's fear of change. That fear, after all, would not have been so strong had not part of Eliot welcomed change with something like equal strength. We can see Eliot's yearning flicker even in the rolling, weighty philosophical dialogue he wrote for *Murder in the Cathedral*. In the spring of 1935, Martin Browne requested that Eliot thicken the play's emotional texture by dramatizing the priest's reaction to the tempters' speeches. Eliot complied in part by writing a passage of thirteen lines to be inserted after the exit of the second tempter. Thomas's second temptation is, in Helen Gardner's description, "to try to go back to the moment when a choice was made and make a different choice." And the priest, as Eliot conceives him, makes the temptation vivid with a movingly poetic articulation of the theme of "what might have been and what has been." Eliot afterward excised these lines, only to alter them for the beginning of "Burnt Norton." Even by themselves, they invoke the story of Alice, who hears the white rabbit's footsteps but cannot get through the door into the rose garden. In Helen Gardner's words, the lines refer Thomas's temptation "to the most poignant 'might have been' of our lives: the rose-garden at the end of 'the passage we did not take' ":[17]

> Time present and time past
> Are both perhaps present in the future.
> Time future is contained in time past. . . .
> What might have been is a conjecture
> Remaining a permanent possibility
> Only in a world of speculation. . . .
> Footfalls echo in the memory

Down the passage which we did not take
Into the rose-garden.[18]

Worse, what flickered when Browne forced Eliot to elaborate this
episode of *Murder in the Cathedral* became incandescent when Eliot again
addressed what had been the dark embryo of the play. Sometime in
September 1935, after walking through the grounds of Burnt Norton
with Emily Hale, Eliot's need to disturb romantic memories became
imperative. The upshot, however, which took all of "Burnt Norton" to
express, was not simply a marshaling of possibilities renewed or possibilities forgone.

A poem of melancholy desire, "Burnt Norton" is also a poem of recognition and release. Whatever else happened as memory afterward
struggled with that afternoon in Chipping Campden, in at least the
enlarged experience of his verse Eliot gave up many of the half-sup-
pressed desires he had harbored for so long. Veiled in "Burnt Norton,"
the situation is transparent in *The Cocktail Party,* where a husband who
has been carrying on a clandestine affair suddenly has the chance to
marry his mistress. At that moment, he realizes that he does not want
to, that he has been nursing a desire which has kept him from truly
living but which cannot sustain a life of its own. The passage where he
explains himself is suffused with the characteristic rhythms of the *Quartets,* but enacts only a minor component of "Burnt Norton"—the sadness which precedes release, but whose shadow lingers. Edward Cham-
berlayne, puzzling things through for himself, says to Celia Coplestone:

The one thing of which I am relatively certain
Is, that only since this morning
I have met myself as a middle-aged man
Beginning to know what it is to feel old.
That is the worst moment, when you feel that you have lost
The desire for all that was most desirable,
And before you are contented with what you can desire;
Before you know what is left to be desired;
And you go on wishing that you could desire
What desire has left behind.

(CPP, 325)

An illumination of this kind lies at the center of "Burnt Norton," but
makes itself felt indirectly. "Burnt Norton" is haunted by a story Eliot
remembered from his childhood—Kipling's "They," which, he told John
Hayward, had "stuck in my head" for thirty years.[19] The story tells of
a blind woman who has never had offspring of her own, but whose
maternal affection attracts the ghosts of others' children. Thus in "Burnt
Norton," the figures whose presence Eliot senses as he moves through
the garden suggest his personal "might have been," evoked by an unbearable desire to live more fully than he had lived before. At the side

of an unnamed companion, he feels the happiness that might have been his, become more intense than if he had actually lived it. In Lawrence Lipking's words, "All the missed opportunities of life assemble in *Four Quartets*. Now that life is almost past, the time that was wasted reproaches the poet with all that he has not done."[20]

Yet, like Edward's melancholy recognition in *The Cocktail Party*, the piercing sadness of "Burnt Norton" is a prelude to growth. Ultimately it is a poem about what it means to enter "our first world." It points to Eliot's turning away from a longtime, poisonous attempt to realize his buried self—a search which, he now saw, for him really represented an *idealization* of "what might have been." According to "Burnt Norton" "our first world" has nothing to do with that striving. Our true authenticity lies rather in expanding our sensibilities beyond the limits of "what we really are and feel." Doing so, we encounter a harmony outside us. The final effect of the poem, though, is not effervescent. Its intense concentration tells us we cannot live in this expanded world without special grace, for we are doomed to the "natural sin of language."[21]

2

As F. R. Leavis observed, the gloom of the beginning of "Burnt Norton" does not come simply from regret for "what might have been": "The [word] 'unredeemable' . . . suggests . . . something that is to be expiated."[22] Like so much else in "Burnt Norton," the word leads us to a harsher moment in Harry Monchensey's family reunion and to a sense of the awful inescapability of "what has been":

> I am the old house
> With the noxious smell and the sorrow before morning,
> In which all past is present, all degradation
> Is unredeemable. As for what happens—
> Of the past you can only see what is past,
> Not what is always present. That is what matters.
>
> (CPP, 234)[23]

Thus "Burnt Norton" starts at the point where *Ash Wednesday* had started, only lower:

> If all time is eternally present
> All time is unredeemable.
>
> ("Burnt Norton" I)

> Because I know that time is always time
> . . . .
> And what is actual is actual only for one time
> . . . .
> Because I cannot hope to turn again. . . .
>
> (*Ash Wednesday* I)

Once again near despair, Eliot confronts the unpleasant actualities of his past and the gloomy portents of his future. And as in *Ash Wednesday,* he does so in the psychic vicinity of that gate behind his house in St. Louis which "concealed the [Mary Institute] schoolyard from our back garden" and where Mary Institute girls were "always on the other side of the wall."[24] However, if we expect to find the penumbra of romantic associations *Ash Wednesday* had discovered in "the Garden/ Where all loves end," the poem draws us up short. It is true we soon feel the presence of a looking-glass world and suspect we are involved in some scene from Eliot's *Vita Nuova.* But instead of a "silent sister" we encounter the disturbing and problematic presence of a mysterious "they." This rose garden has a certain coldness. It lacks the feverish romanticism of the gardens of "La Figlia Che Piange" or *The Waste Land* or *Ash Wednesday,* all of which Eliot recalls. Instead, it suggests the garden of Vaughan's "The Retreat," from which Eliot had quoted a few years before:

> Happy those early days! when I
> Shined in my Angel-infancy.
> Before I understood this place
> Appointed for my second race,
> Or taught my soul to fancy ought
> But a white, celestial thought,
> When yet I had not walked above
> A mile or two, from my first love,
> And looking back (at that short space)
> Could see a glimpse of that bright face;
> When on some gilded cloud, or flower
> My gazing soul would dwell an hour,
> And in those weaker glories spy
> Some shadows of eternity. . . .

On that occasion, Eliot cautioned:

This does suggest, of course, both Wordsworth's "Ode on Intimations of Immortality" and his primrose by the river's brim, his daffodils, etc. But I think it represents something both different and more specific. . . . the eternal life dimly revealed through nature is still the eternal life of Christianity; therefore, he never runs the risk of deifying nature itself. . . .[25]

And with Eliot's warning in mind, I propose we attend to the rose garden of "Burnt Norton" and note what, hurrying to approach the "heart of light," most readers overlook.[26] For one thing, the episode involves two reversals, the first of which disappoints romantic expectations and implicates Eliot in something more disturbing. Impelled "into the rose-garden," Eliot expects to find the news that Mary brings to Harry in *The Family Reunion:*

                            news
        Of a door that opens at the end of a corridor,
        Sunlight and singing; when I had felt sure
        That every corridor only led to another,
        Or to a blank wall. . . .

                                                (CPP, 252)

In fact, he finds what *displaces* this news in Harry's mind:

        That apprehension deeper than all sense,
        . . . .
        From another world. I know it, I know it!
        . . . .
        Come out! Where are you? Let me see you,
        Since I know you are there, I know you are spying on me.
        Why do you play with me, why do you let me go,
        Only to surround me?—When I remember them
        They leave me alone: when I forget them
        Only for an instant of inattention
        They are roused again, the sleepless hunters
        That will not let me sleep. . . .

                                (CPP, 252–53, emphasis mine)

These are the lines from "Burnt Norton":

        There they were, dignified, invisible,
        Moving without pressure, over the dead leaves,
        In the autumn heat, through the vibrant air,
        And the bird called, in response to
        The unheard music hidden in the shrubbery,
        And the unseen eyebeam crossed, for the roses
        Had the look of flowers that are looked at.
        There they were as our guests, accepted and accepting.
        So we moved, and they, in a formal pattern,
        Along the empty alley, into the box circle,
        To look down into the drained pool.
        Dry the pool, dry concrete, brown edged,
        And the pool was filled with water out of sunlight,
        And the lotos rose, quietly, quietly,
        The surface glittered out of heart of light,
        And they were behind us, reflected in the pool.
        Then a cloud passed, and the pool was empty.

Obsessively returning to the mysterious "they," "Burnt Norton" puzzles out the meaning of an intrusive memory. Thus we are told that
the bird *"said* find them, find them." As always in such experience,
though, what the memory means is not at first apparent; the poem,
therefore, cannot specify who "they" are. Figures of "what might have
been," "they" are capable of assuming different emotional valences. As
a matter of fact, what turns out to be most important is a *shift* in emotional valence. Eliot announces "there they were" as if he had come

upon them before, and his repetitive "they" dramatizes an attempt to understand what they signify. His chief surprise is that "they" were *in the rose garden* and that their attitude toward him was *different* from the one he had expected. Once again it is clear that the moment has affinities with *The Family Reunion*. In the garden of "Burnt Norton," Eliot has some of Harry's apprehensions the first time he sees his hunters:

> In the Java Straits, in the Sunda Sea,
> In the sweet sickly tropical night, I knew *they* were coming.
> In Italy, from behind the nightingale's thicket,
> *The eyes* stared at me, and corrupted that song.
> Behind the palm trees in the Grand Hotel
> *They were always there.* But I did not *see* them.
> Why should they wait until I came back to Wishwood?
> There were a thousand places where I might have met them!
> Why here? why here?
>
> (CPP, 232; emphasis mine)

The first reversal of the episode, then, involves the fact that Eliot had found "them" in so pleasant a place. The second reversal makes itself felt in Eliot's subordinate clauses. Not only were "they" in the garden, they were "dignified," they were "accepted and accepting," they moved "in a formal pattern." Eliot, like Harry, had been dreading their appearance. In his fear, he had expected the dead leaves, the autumn heat. But now he finds that "they" have the power to produce "unheard music" and to attract the bird's response. And when he moves with them "in a formal pattern," "they" lead him to look down into the dry brown-edged pool of his life and see the pool "filled with water out of sunlight." It is only when its surface glitters "out of heart of light," it turns out, that he can see them behind him "reflected in the pool." And as in *The Family Reunion*, the sight is both reassuring and shocking. The bird chastises Eliot to go because, having sensed "them" in the garden, he had tensed against their accusations. But no, the bird calls (its call is its message),

> the leaves were full of children,
> Hidden excitedly, containing laughter.

Note that the emotional tenor of these lines is not ecstatic. No bird here

> sang down
> Redeem the time, redeem the dream. . . .
>
> (*Ash Wednesday* IV)

Here, reacting to Eliot's inability to recognize that his long-feared ghosts reside in a world of laughter, the bird admonishes,

> Go, go, go . . . human kind
> Cannot bear very much reality. . . .

Thus in a preliminary summing up, we might characterize what transpires as Eliot sorts out his memory this way: first the ghosts of "what
might have been" appear—figures both of a wished-for future Eliot
never had and of the now-stifled self which once might have produced
them. Eliot had long ago left these possibilities behind, but not without
reservation. Some of his uneasiness had intimated itself as the ghost of
his Milton Academy address. The rest would explode in the nightmarish homecoming of *The Family Reunion,* where Harry, evoked through
phrases taken from "Burnt Norton,"

> will find another Harry.
> The man who returns will have to meet
> The boy who left. Round by the stables,
> In the coach-house, in the orchard,
> In the plantation, *down the corridor*
> That led to the nursery, *round the corner*
> Of the new wing, he will have to face him—
> And it will not be a very *jolly* corner.
> When the loop in time comes . . .
> The hidden is revealed, and the spectres show themselves.
>
> (CPP, 229; emphasis mine)

Expecting excoriation for having deserted his childhood self and its
offspring even as he secretly coveted their memory, in "Burnt Norton"
Eliot is dismayed by how long "they" have accompanied him. Like Harry
he realizes how long he had feared their inevitable rebuke. In the same
moment, however, he has a vision of his ghosts welcoming him and his
companion into a circular dance of love—a vision that brings home the
providential order of his life. Though he hardly expects it of them,
"they" turn out, in the terms of *The Family Reunion,* to be "bright angels"—Eumenides.

The problem Eliot then has is to maintain the conviction of what he
has experienced—a problem, it turns out, that has as much to do with
affirming the validity of his way of writing as it does with that writing's
particular kind of truth.

3

I have been speaking of the first movement of "Burnt Norton" as if it
were an event in Eliot's inner life, and, as part of that expanded life he
lived in his poetry, it was. But because poets "gotta use words when
they talk to you," it is not possible to leave things there. The presentation of what happens in the poem's rose garden is stylized, literary. As
Eliot confessed, one of his models in this was the world of *Alice in Wonderland,* that masterpiece of linguistic strangeness.[27] Even more than
Carroll's, though, Eliot's "first world" lives along the line. Nor is this
unexpected from Eliot. From the beginning of his poetic career Eliot

had dislocated syntax to discover the ambivalent impulses of a life be-neath, a buried self; now, even more self-consciously, he arranges his words to cajole a less oppressive existence out of "dissonances," "caco-phanies," "intersections" (OPP, 24–25).

Consider: Eliot enters the garden of "Burnt Norton" not through one of the apparently unsought epiphanies of his earlier poetry but by means of willed negation—his attention-getting introduction of the *au-delà* (call it nonsense or call it never-never) opens a hole in the despair-ing expanse of "what is actual." This is obvious in the provocative con-tradictions of a movement "Down the passage which we did not take/ Towards the door we never opened." It is less obvious in the imaginary "footfalls" we are told "echo in the memory." These non-existent but ever-expected footfalls in fact call up ominous associations in Eliot's work from "Gerontion" to *The Family Reunion*—associations of the fron-tier of death.[28] But they also recall another occasion on which Eliot had spoken of footfalls in a way that hinted at death, yet suggested the death of the familiar—the death of the unreality that we had assumed was real. This regenerative kind of de-creation involves the spirit, but begins with language. Thus in his 1926 "Note sur Mallarmé et Poe," Eliot said that the two poets' "effort pour restituer la puissance du Mot," which inspired their special difficulties of syntax, also produced their finest effects. "Il y a aussi," Eliot concluded, *"la fermeté de leur pas lors-qu'ils passent du monde tangible au monde des fantômes."*[29]

As much as any external citation can, I think, this statement points to the special quality of "Burnt Norton"'s linguistic world. Hollowing out our habitual semblance of reality, this poem's "passages" are made through effects that construct a new reality out of language. And though D. W. Harding and F. R. Leavis early on emphasized the way the poem achieves its "creation of [the] concepts" of "eternity" and "reality"[30] by its concretizing skill, they might with equal justice have pointed to what Eliot remarked in Mallarmé: his ability to give "the word, each word by itself . . . absolute value."[31]

To read "Burnt Norton" without awareness of its multiple levels of discourse is to misunderstand it. There is first the poem's status as a philosophical treatment of time, a status which, as Helen Gardner has written, is largely illusory.[32] Then there is its rendering of what F. R. Leavis called the "imperative personal concern" which commands the poem's "abstract argument."[33] Finally, though, the poem's presentation of personal concern exists in a larger context. This is apparent at the heart of the garden episode, in the sentence:

> There they were, dignified, invisible,
> Moving without pressure, over the dead leaves,
> In the autumn heat, through the vibrant air,
> And the bird called, in response to
> The unheard music hidden in the shrubbery,

> And the unseen eyebeam crossed, for the roses
> Had the look of flowers that are looked at.

The uncanny delicacy of these lines comes from a self-conscious attention to the related values of prosody and syntax.[34] Like most of the *Quartets,* the verses eschew Mallarmé's central syntactic strategy, which Hugh Kenner has described as establishing a kernel sentence and then supplanting it "by a mutant version composed of words that open lines."[35] Eliot is apparently more indebted to Whitman, who gets his power by repeating the same grammatical structure from line to line while he varies the lines' rhythmic emphases.[36] But like William Carlos Williams at his best, Eliot supplements Whitman with Mallarmé's preternatural sensitivity to the openings made possible by ambiguous etymology and word order.

The first two lines of the sentence I have quoted are dominated by a strong stress norm which at first seems to correspond to the natural emphases of a speaking voice. The syntax of the lines, in step with their accentuation, expands Eliot's simple declaration of what he had seen ("There they were") in an incremental series of appositions:

> There they were, // dignified, invisible,
> Moving without pressure, // over the dead leaves. . . .

Then, almost imperceptibly, the concentration intensifies in the third line; the emphases of two cretic feet mark the advent of a breakthrough in perception:

>   / ⌣   /   / ⌣ /
> In the autumn heat, // through the vibrant air. . . .

Thus anticipated by a variation in stress, the real quickening is accomplished by a shift in syntax. In the first hemistitch of the next verse, Eliot reinforces the force of a spondee by the first active verb of the sentence, a verb that pressures us into a weak, single-stressed hemistitch and a run on into the following line:

>   /   /   /
> And the bird called, // in response to
>   /   /   /   /
> The unheard music / hidden in the shrubbery. . . .

Finally, a similar pattern builds on the first. The first hemistitch of the next line also introduces an active verb, this time emphasized by five consecutive strong stresses. Characteristically, Eliot's ghosts make their presence felt by the intensity of their gaze as they reach out to the bird whose music was a response to their own:

>   /   /   /   /   /   /
> And the unseen eyebeam crossed, // for the roses
>   /   /   /   /
> Had the look of flowers / that are looked at.

Here again we are impelled by a shortened second hemistitch into the conclusion. But if we go too quickly, we miss one of the passage's most significant effects. Counterpointing syntax with line break here, Eliot puts extra emphasis on the last phrase in the line. The rhythmic momentum of the sentence's first three lines insists we now stop where the inflections of imperative personal concern do not stop—on the word "roses." And once we do, the line rearranges itself in a manner inconsistent with the movements of a dramatic voice. So we read, "And the unseen eyebeam crossed [. . .] *for the roses,*" and a connection between the eyes and roses takes place, never to be withdrawn.

At this point, the poetry has crossed a line. Using Donald Davie's distinction, it has ceased to be "a syntax like music," miming the undulations of unfolding experience, and has approached "a syntax like mathematics," where syntactic transformations acquire an interest of their own.[37] But Davie's discrimination, which associates "the syntax of mathematics" with a certain aridity, does not really apply here. The fact, as Davie recognizes in a later essay, is that "Burnt Norton" trusts in a written linguistic pattern to suggest what no voice, however faithfully registered, could.[38] In the counterpointing in which the poem is most fully actualized, Eliot holds being in time in tension with the echoes of the ideal. In the lines we have been considering, this tension is almost invisible, since the poem's dramatized voice is close on an apprehension of the harmonies emanating from "the unheard music." But "before and after," where Eliot is further away from that apprehension, the effect is more salient, and the ghostly aura around Eliot's meditation more apparent.

Reconsider the poem's opening lines, where the doubleness of Eliot's medium establishes the pattern of what will follow in the characteristic moments of "Burnt Norton":

> Time present and time past
> Are both perhaps present in time future,
> And time future contained in time past.
> If all time is eternally present
> All time is unredeemable.
> What might have been is an abstraction
> Remaining a perpetual possibility
> Only in a world of speculation.
> What might have been and what has been
> Point to one end, which is always present.

Registering only the notation of what Eliot had called "a man reasoning with himself in solitude" (OPP, 154), this is as masterful as it is melancholy, a clear advance over even *Ash Wednesday.* The lines present a meditation on the continuities of experience and begin on a note of anxious optimism. The first gives not only the subject of the meditation but the norm of its music: the concerns of present and past are symmetrically balanced in an evenly divided six-syllable line:

> ╱ ╱ ◡   ◡ ╱ ╱
> Time present // and time past. . . .

Surely the second line will add an eight-syllable equivalent—

> ◡   ╱ ╱ ◡   ◡ ╱ ╱ ◡
> Are both present // in time future. . . .

But in fact, the line alters the expected, intruding the word "perhaps"—the locus of both Eliot's optimism and his uneasiness, and the strongest metrical unit in either line:

> ╱ ◡ ╱ ╱ ◡   ◡ ╱ ╱ ◡
> Are both perhaps present // in time future. . . .

The effect of this displaced balance is then repeated in the third line. Taking off from the object of Eliot's darkest concern—time future—the line's unexpected extra syllables are here augmented by the strength of an active verb to suggest an assertion of the self's continuity:

> ◡   ╱ · ╱ ◡ ◡ ╱   ◡ ╱ ╱
> And time future *contained* // in time past.

Trying to compound its assurance, the syntax then builds a second sentence on the first. In line four, the emphases are gathered at the beginning of the line like weight gathered to hurl; and the caesura, anticipating the run on into the next line, is all but effaced:

> ◡   ╱ ╱ ◡ ◡ ╱ ◡◡ ╱ ◡
> If all time is eternally present. . . .

But for nought. The only alternative to the fragmentation of the self in time, it seems, is even worse: an unchanging self inescapably oppressed. This time a spondee followed by a caesura at the beginning of the line registers suspense and delay, and a series of iambics announces dejection like tumbling bricks:

> ╱ ╱   ◡ ╱ ◡ ╱   ◡ ╱
> All time // is unredeemable.

And so it goes in the next five lines, which duplicate the first five not only in their sentence arrangement but in their symmetries. Once again Eliot starts with a subject for anxious hope ("what might have been"), precariously sustains it through one sentence and then dashes it by returning to bleak actuality in a second sentence's last word:

> What might have been // is an abstraction
> Remaining // a perpetual possibility
> Only in a world // of speculation.
> What might have been // and what has been
> Point to one end, // which is always present.

And yet, because the lines are haunted by the kind of doubleness I have tried to suggest, no second-time reader of the poem hears them like that. The reasons are connected to what Eliot learned from the symbolists. Although here he depends little on syntax to open a line or a group of lines up to new patterns of feeling,[39] Eliot acknowledges the lesson of the French in another way. Consistent with his praise of the way Mallarmé's "incantation" insists on "la puissance primitive du Mot," he uses an incantatory Old English strong stress meter which insists on the priority of individual words and individual syllables. In combination, the self-conscious precision of his diction keeps the etymological ambiguities of his words alive, and allows words and word fragments, not lines, to open up alternative emotional directions.

In fact, adapting the spirit of Mallarmé, Eliot was incorporating the practice of Marianne Moore. In 1935, the year he wrote "Burnt Norton," Eliot remarked on Moore's ability "to make a pattern directly in contrast with the sense and rhythm pattern [of her poetry], to give a greater intricacy." In particular, he said, her light rhymes have the effect of "giving a word a slightly more analytical pronunciation, or stressing a syllable more than ordinarily." And as examples he gave these:

> al-
> ways has been—at the antipodes from the init-
> ial great truths. "Part of it was crawling, part of it
> was about to crawl, the rest
> was torpid in its lair." In the short-legged, fit-
> ful advance. . . .

and:

> an
> injured fan.
> The barnacles which encrust the side
> of the wave, cannot hide . . .
> the
> turquoise sea
> of bodies. The water drives a wedge. . . .[40]

Exploiting techniques like these through the harmonic possibilities of a more subtle metrical grid, the first movement of "Burnt Norton" aims with Marianne Moore to give words "a slightly more analytical pronunciation." To name only the obvious, in the variable stress patterns of its opening ten lines, Eliot's poem suggests an awareness that "present" means more than "here and now"—it also means "apparent to the imagination." Similarly, we are made to sense the contradictory roots of "eternally" (which can mean both "perpetual" and "timeless"), "abstraction" and "speculation."[41] As opposed to Moore's practice, though, the secondary meanings of these words point to a consistent other dimension: they join in suggesting the ideal. Implied by effects Moore had used simply to underline the agility of consciousness, Eliot's "pattern directly in contrast with the sense and rhythm pattern" sounds the footsteps of a being that can have no more concrete manifestation. The result is that after ten lines, we are conditioned. By the time we follow Eliot "Down the passage which we did not take / . . . Into the rose-garden," his words have indeed "echoed" in our minds—echoed with multiple overtones that prepare us for "unheard music hidden in the shrubbery." And afterward, when the bird tells us "the leaves are full of children, / . . . containing laughter," we are not nonplussed. Has not a secondary sense of "contained" (a sense implying energy suppressed) already done its ghostly work in line three?

> And time future // contained in time past.

Along with time future and time present, it seems, the ineffaceable history of culture in the words we use points to ends which are no longer recognized by a twentieth-century sensibility. As Eliot had written two years before,

> There are also people who, while recognizing the interest of the work of literature as a document upon the ideas and the sensibility of its epoch, and recognizing even that the permanent work of literature is one which does not lack this interest, yet cannot help valuing literary work, like philosophical work, in the end by its transcendence of the limits of its age; by its breaking through the categories of thought and sensibility of its age; *by its speaking, in the language of its time and in the imagery of its own tradition, the word which belongs to no time.* Art, we feel, aspires to the condition of the timeless. . . .[42]

4

What remains to be said is that there are poetic problems connected with the doubleness just described. If a line contains both a human voice and the ghost of a larger sensibility, for example, how are we to read it? Reciting the poem, how do we intone *these* words, which conclude ten lines of oppressiveness?

> Point to one end, which is always present.

Do we recite them the same as, or differently from, the words of line 46, which bring twenty-nine lines of growing illumination to a close?

> Point to one end, which is always present.

Eliot, we know, would himself allow no special emphasis, no dramatic swell or fall. With reference to "Burnt Norton," he said that "so far as possible, the reciter should not dramatize. It is the words that matter, not the feeling about them."[43] And following his own advice, he read the *Quartets* in a way that provoked Leavis to call his "command of inflexion, intonation and tempo—his *intention,* as performer . . . astonishingly inadequate."[44]

But according to Eliot's principles, there was no choice. Following "Journey of the Magi" and *Ash Wednesday,* the first movement of "Burnt Norton" is an extended field of crossing. Even more than with the two earlier poems, to read it is to feel the pull of two elaborate belief systems. Miming the inflections of a meditation conditioned by twentieth-century skepticism, we also pass through the linguistic echoes of a sensibility which has no authentic twentieth-century voice. And as in the central passage of "Journey of the Magi," the two sensibilities belong to two different worlds of reference, worlds which admit of no easy reconciliation. Here though, the larger sensibility speaks of more than the system of Christian iconography—it provides the linguistic traces of two thousand years of cultural maturation. As before, the two worlds of utterance are entertained by the verse in what Perse called a "jeu, très allusif et mystérieux."[45] But in a way more programmatic than even *Ash Wednesday*'s song of the bones, the verse is essentially indeterminate. Taut, disciplined, musical, it is poetry whose "intentions" cannot be prescribed.

Upon reflection, then, the opening movement of "Burnt Norton," which at first appears to be the speech of a man puzzling out the pattern of his life, turns out to be less straightforward. At its fullest it is an interaction between two forces: the echoes of a written music that cannot be ignored and the fragments of a speech that cannot be completed. Word by word, the movement's music puts individual and traditional statements of belief in question before their periods finish. And it is that insistent questioning that gives us the impression of hearing two discourses at once: the voice of a man searching for the meaning of his life, and intimations from a ghost who has passed beyond our hesitations. As Eliot hoped, if we take poetry to be a variety of dramatic speech, these forty-six lines produce the effect of getting "*beyond* poetry, as Beethoven, in his later works, strives to get *beyond* music."[46] And they get beyond poetry by continually de-creating speech, by giving each new word the power to disrupt dramatic continuity. To alter Denis Donoghue's phrases, in the first movement of "Burnt Norton," Eliot's poetry becomes graphi-writing rather than epi-writing. Neither a self nor a dramatic voice is implied *behind* the writing. Here, as Eliot said, the voice *is* the writing, because the writing is "beyond character" (OPP, 81).[47]

Yet finally we must ask if these lines do actually get "*beyond* poetry" and even whether they *are* poetry, at least the kind of poetry the younger Eliot had tried to write. Converting the "dissembling" of *Ash Wednesday*'s moments of dissolution into a consistent "deception" ("shall we

follow / The deception of the thrush?"), are they not merely a literary
game? Don't they, as Leavis grudgingly admits, lead Eliot just a little
too easily to something that no longer has a connection to even the
innermost chambers of experience?[48]

> Yet the enchainment of past and future
> Woven in the weakness of the changing body,
> Protects mankind from heaven and damnation
> Which flesh cannot endure.

These questions are real, and they establish the ground for any final
accounting of "Burnt Norton." To use a discussion of Elizabeth Sewell's
against her own application of it, is not the first movement of *Four
Quartets* really more like one of the reveries of Edward Lear than the
tremendous dream of *The Waste Land*? *Four Quartets*, Sewell says in a
widely read essay, escapes pure nonsense only by emphasizing "unitive
subjects, particularly love and religion."[49] Yet given the discussion where
she first established this term, her assertion is less than convincing. In
The Field of Nonsense, Sewell writes that "Nonsense is a game." It seems
fanciful, but plays by strict rules. It is therefore unlike dreams, which
involve distortions of syntactic relations in their imaginative syntheses.
In nonsense, "syntax and grammar are not disordered. . . . [It] takes
the form of [that kind of] verse, which by its organization is the reverse
of disordered. There is only one aspect of language which Nonsense
can be said to disorder, and that is reference, the effect produced by a
word or group of words in the mind."[50]

By these criteria, the rose-garden episode of "Burnt Norton" is much
closer to pure nonsense than *The Waste Land*. Entering the rose garden,
we are continually aware of an intrusive arrangement of words that
resists the pull of dream. Although the syntax is elaborately controlled,
unlike that of *The Waste Land*, it is never allowed to break down. Instead, as in the *Alices*, its disorder is simply a disorder of reference.
That is why its language constantly asks us to cast a cold eye on experience and why we never have the sense of becoming part of a drama.

Consequently, looking back to the Hyacinth garden episode of *The
Waste Land*, it no longer seems we are dealing with the same species of
writing. Eliot has achieved an illusion of enchantment, an intimation,
as in a childhood game, of existing in a world charged with order and
meaning and yet also unaccountably free. But he has lost *The Waste
Land*'s ability to render the nerve endings of a sensibility, the illusion
that he has penetrated the masks of the self and arrived at the source
of the buried life. If *The Waste Land* gives us our definitive example of
modernist poetry, "Burnt Norton" must be called something else: like
Finnegans Wake, Between the Acts or *The Plumed Serpent*, it is already post-
modern.

5

Does the above go too far? Is it misleading to suggest that the first movement of "Burnt Norton" is more game than art, more nonsense than modernist vision? Possibly. And yet the bulk of "Burnt Norton," in its uneasiness with the precarious balance of part I, seems to imply a similar misgiving. The first movement of the poem asserts that a moment of authentic vision must be communicated through the music of an indeterminate structure, because only that kind of unvoiceable music is attuned to "the music of what happens." Only in play can words approximate the harmony of the spheres, whose reality human speech can never mime. The implications of children's laughter or the call of the thrush, untranslatable, may yet be simulated by a shimmering sequence of nonsense.

Yet even after all this has been demonstrated, Eliot resists. Despite the enormous sense of liberation achieved by the first movement's negations, neither half of his temperament can easily accept an artistic or epistemological stance that allows itself to be characterized as play. Eliot's romantic impulses yearn for something more concrete, more lasting, and his New England conscience would have things more unequivocally defined. Waking at intervals through the rest of "Burnt Norton," both insist on giving the incertitudes of the first movement a false outline. Finally, it is only Eliot's indomitable honesty, strained to the breaking point, that desists. Pulled by the attractive finality of a fixed musical arrangement, the poem's central impulse to get "*beyond* music" is constantly in danger of reifying. Only in the last movement does it triumph, enabling ("Sudden in a shaft of sunlight / Even while the dust moves") the "hidden laughter" of children to rise in the foliage.

But I am getting ahead of myself. The transition from part I to part II of "Burnt Norton" is signaled by the archness of a new lyric style and announced by a call to

> Ascend to summer in the tree. . . .

Even without the call, the formality of the verse tells us how eager Eliot is to ascend from the provisional balance of part I to some place where his dualisms are "reconciled among the stars." Yet the truest note of the lyric—the one which leads to the too-fervent assertions of the next verse paragraph—sounds in its third and fourth lines:

> The trilling wire in the blood
> Sings below inveterate scars. . . .

It was the intransigence of these scars that had resisted the inhuman gaiety of children's laughter, and had prompted the first shift in the poem's style. Now the same intransigence will not permit the verse to

ascend too far from the here and now. It requires still another way of
putting things, in which unheard music is said to be

> At the still point of the turning world. Neither flesh nor flesh-
> less;
> Neither from nor towards; at the still point, there the dance is,
> But neither arrest nor movement. And do not call it fixity,
> Where past and future are gathered. Neither movement from nor
> towards,
> Neither ascent nor decline. Except for the point, the still point,
> There would be no dance, and there is only the dance.
> I can only say, *there* we have been: but I cannot say where.
> And I cannot say, how long, for that is to place it in time.

More successful than the lyric immediately preceding, these lines yet
have problems of their own—faults that can best be described with reference to *Ash Wednesday*. Like the song of the bones in the earlier poem,
the lines live in paradoxes and progress by the notion of contradiction.
Their cadence, therefore, is incantatory. A little as in the first movement of *Ash Wednesday*, we feel in this incantation a contradiction between the self that wills and the impulses of something deeper. But
here the contradiction has been stage-managed—it does not correspond to a drama of consciousness. For one thing, the impulse toward
prose precision is not thoroughgoing. It is diluted from the beginning
by metaphor ("the still point"), and its intensity is weakened by the
gesture of an aside ("And do not call it fixity").

The aside is a tipoff. It signals that the verse is not what it seems.
Instead of a strenuous attempt at philosophical rigor, the line speaks
of a smugness on the other side of struggle. It cautions us that philosophy will never get to the root of reality's conundrums. And so, for all
the apparent deliberateness of their seeking and the hidden art of their
arrangement,[51] these lines ultimately lack the only kind of strength that
matters. Not surprisingly, the verse paragraph they introduce builds an
edifice out of unqualified certainties—a pile of precisions untested in
the fires of emotional honesty:

> The inner freedom from the practical desire. . . .

Addressing the question of flux and permanence as it pertains to the
little world of the psyche, these lines achieve some marvelous defini-
tions ("concentration / Without elimination"), but finally prove mere enthusiasm. There is, after all, no intellectual precision which can justify
the religious terms they propose (a "heaven and damnation / Which flesh
cannot endure"). And alive to their own dishonesty, the lines break off
by themselves. After a hiatus, which is marked both by a line break and
a "but," we find a different kind of assertion, characterized by halting
self-qualification, and a more modest return to the limitations of life in
time:

> Time past and time future
> Allow but a little consciousness.
> To be conscious is not to be in time
> But only in time can the moment in the rose-garden,
> The moment in the arbour where the rain beat,
> The moment in the draughty church at smokefall
> Be remembered; involved with past and future.
> Only through time time is conquered.

There is an implicit rebuke in that last line, a rebuke that calls up the third movement of the poem. Recoiling from an unsuccessful attempt to consolidate the delicate illumination of part I, the poem is forced back into contemplating the probabilities of the quotidian. It has not given up the possibility of further illumination (it speaks of "time before and time after," no longer of "time present and time past"), but it has given up an easy assurance that art can preserve or prepare that possibility. Thus we find ourselves in a situation very like the one in the fifth section of *Ash Wednesday*—in a "twittering world" where, in the words of the earlier poem, the word cannot resound because "there is not enough silence." And even more than in *Ash Wednesday*, there is a sense here that no shapeliness of art will cause the word to be heard or spoken.

In part III, then, after the glow of part I has faded and as it becomes clear that the exertions of part II will not suffice, Eliot is left with the anxieties of his present life and one or two practical methods to charm them away. The pressure of his life, his desires and his fears, is present, as it had been in *Ash Wednesday* and "Animula," in the few images that emerge through the verbalism of the charm: "the strained . . . faces," the "bits of paper, whirled by the cold wind," the roll-call of tube stops which Eliot passed traveling to and from his Kensington flat:

> the gloomy hills of London,
> Hampstead and Clerkenwell, Campden and Putney,
> Highgate, Primrose and Ludgate.

But struggling against these, we find two kinds of intellectual defense: first the latinate generalizations, distancing life even as they try to master it:

> Emptying the sensual with deprivation
> Cleansing affection from the temporal.

Then, added to the abstracting drive of this charm, the impersonal authority of a saint. In July 1934 one of Eliot's editorial colleagues, Thomas McGreevy, told the readers of the *Criterion* that a certain edition of St. John of the Cross was small enough to put in one's pocket "when leaving for a weekend or the summer holidays."[52] And it seems that, traveling to the Cotswolds, Eliot took McGreevy's advice; the lines below paraphrase that translation's *Dark Night of the Soul:*

> Descend lower, descend only
> Into the world of perpetual solitude,
> World not world, but that which is not world.
> Internal darkness, deprivation
> And destitution of all property,
> Desiccation of the world of sense,
> Evacuation of the world of fancy,
> Inoperancy of the world of spirit. . . .

[In the second, or passive, night of the spirit, which] disposes the soul to the highest union with God. . . . God now denudes the faculties, the affections, and feelings, spiritual and sensual, interior and exterior, leaving the understanding in darkness, the will dry, the memory empty, the affections of the soul in the deepest affliction, bitterness and distress. . . . All this our Lord effects in the soul by means of contemplation, pure and dark.[53]

By part IV, his intellectual maneuvering having served only to extend his despondency, Eliot's mood has sunk as far as it will go. Venting the melancholy against which parts II and III had wrestled, the lyric gives full voice to the poem's deepest subject—an anxiety about death that had emerged as early as "the dust on a bowl of rose-leaves." Though part III had bravely implied that there was a higher permanence which the illusions of "daylight" could only "with slow rotation" suggest, now the prospect of a life deprived of light provokes profound somberness. Deprived of daylight's assurance of permanence by an intuition of death, Eliot senses his diminished place in the world. It falls to him to ask by indirection a series of questions that recall the poem's epigraph: though each of us apprehends himself the enduring center of his universe, when the light fades, does nature agree? "Will the sunflower [whose obeisance acknowledges the source of light] turn to *us*"? Will "the clematis [which is so difficult for gardeners to shape] / Stray down, bend to *us*"? Not likely. What attention we get will come only when "tendril and spray / Clutch and cling" in the cemetery and "Fingers of yew be curled / Down on us."

At this point, from the nadir of this horror, Eliot turns outward to a nature purified of his presence. Yet he turns only to note with melancholy what part II had so confidently asserted, too early and with too much complacency:

> After the kingfisher's wing
> Has answered light to light, and is silent, the light is still
> [*There*, not here] At the still point of the turning world.

One of nature's creatures—the kingfisher—does indeed provide what Eliot elsewhere calls a "visible reminder of Invisible Light" (CPP, 112).

But by his very recognition that what he sees is only a reflection of that Light, the moment contains as much sadness as exultation. In part II Eliot had cried, "at the still point, there the dance is." Here the object of his contemplation is the same, but his felt knowledge of it has increased and his mood has darkened. There is now no mention of the dance. Instead there is awe and fear as he registers the stillness, and his fear grows with the mention of a word used (it hardly seems possible) for the first time in the poem: "silent." That silence, indicating the impossibility of man ever recovering the Word, repeats the end of *The Rock* in a chastened and subdued key. One year before, Eliot's choruses had proclaimed that even in the utmost executions of art or music, or in the ultimate symbol which is the church, man must never hope to capture the divine reality. At the most, art can create an iridescent structure of indeterminacy, whose disciplined openness, the analogue of spiritual humility, makes it available to moments of grace. The concluding prayer of *The Rock* puts it this way:

> O Greater Light, we praise Thee for the less;
>
> . . . .
> Our gaze is submarine, our eyes look upward
> And see the light that fractures through unquiet water.
> We see the light but see not whence it comes.
> O Light Invisible, we glorify Thee!
>
> . . . .
> And we must extinguish the candle, put out the light and relight
> it;
> Forever must quench, forever relight the flame.
> Therefore we thank Thee for our little light, that is dappled
> with shadow.
> We thank Thee who has moved us to building, to finding, to
> forming at the ends of our fingers and beams of our eyes.
> And when we have built an altar to the Invisible Light, we may
> set thereon the little lights for which our bodily vision is made.
> And we thank Thee that darkness reminds us of light.
> O Light Invisible, we give Thee thanks for Thy great Glory!
>
> (CPP, 113–14)

Which leads us to a reading of the last section of "Burnt Norton" in which the emphasis of its first thirteen lines falls not on stillness but on silence:

> Words move, music moves
> Only in time; but that which is only living
> Can only die. Words, after speech, reach
> Into the silence. Only by the form, the pattern,
> Can words or music reach
> The stillness, as a Chinese jar still
> Moves perpetually in its stillness.
> Not the stillness of the violin, while the note lasts,

> Not that only, but the co-existence,
> Or say that the end precedes the beginning,
> And that the end and the beginning were always there
> Before the beginning and after the end.
> And all is always now.

And in fact, the full passage, struggling to exclude "specious possibilities, seizing on the essentials that remain,"[54] recapitulates the poem as a whole. Trying to consolidate a second hard-won apprehension of "stillness," it disintegrates after nine lines into paradox and four lines later into anguished confession of failure. The ten verses that follow are the ones quoted in chapter seven to suggest the fundamental fault-line of Eliot's second style. In "Burnt Norton," Eliot owns up to the fissure and exposes it as an aspect of man's fate. It is impossible for art to do more than "reach / Into the silence," for within every precision, every pattern,

> Words strain,
> Crack and sometimes break, under the burden,
> Under the tension, slip, slide, perish,
> Decay with imprecision, will not stay in place,
> Will not stay still. Shrieking voices
> Scolding, mocking, or merely chattering,
> Always assail them. The Word in the desert
> Is most attacked by voices of temptation,
> The crying shadow in the funeral dance,
> The loud lament of the disconsolate chimera.

The poem therefore ends neither by despairing of the pattern which comprehends Love, music, light and Word, nor by triumphantly reproducing it. In the assured triple stress rhythm of the final lines, there is a more humble assertion that, though the pattern exists, we cannot know it, caught as we are

> in the form of limitation
> Between un-being and being.

The humility of that position then gives rise to a reprise of part I, a reprise which has been earned by an extended effort to say more which was finally too honest to persist. The improbable rearrangement of the dust of past life in memory, the unforeseen sounds of children's laughter, are simply accepted as

> Quick now, here, now, always. . . .

And if the reappearance of these words reminds us of the kind of music that gathers its motifs into a triumphant conclusion, we should not too quickly be taken in. Yes, the suggestion of that kind of conclusion is there. But, true to the systematic doubleness which constitutes the sincerity of this poem, so is something else. The last two lines begin with a gesture that seems to look back at life as a comedy, much like the comedy that Chaucer's Troilus looks down upon from the heavens:

> Ridiculous . . .

But the words that stay with us point to what can never with honesty in this life be hymned over:

> the waste sad time
> Stretching before and after.

CHAPTER ELEVEN

"A new and shocking valuation": *Four Quartets*

I am relieved to hear that Tom has picked up his tablets again after all these months—almost a year—of silence. . . . He now writes to say that he is making a little progress with a new poem in succession to "Burnt Norton"—the second of three quatuors. . . . "It may be quite worthless," he adds, "because most of it looks to me like an imitation of myself. . . ."

John Hayward to Frank Morley, February 1940

You ask me about Tom's progress with "Little Gidding". . . . His chief fear was that he was simply repeating himself and so running into the risk of producing an elegant parody of the earlier poems in the group.

the same, July 1942[1]

Ubi saeva indignatio ulterius cor lacerare nequit.

Swift, *Epitaph*

Swift has sailed into his rest;
Savage indignation there
Cannot lacerate his breast.
Imitate him if you dare. . . .

W. B. Yeats, from "Swift's Epitaph"

Recollected a dozen years after the fact, Eliot's account of how he came to write *Four Quartets* tells only part of the story: " 'Burnt Norton,' " he said, "might have remained by itself if it hadn't been for the war, because I had become very much absorbed in the problems of writing for the stage and might have gone straight on from 'The Family Reunion' to another play. The war destroyed that interest for a time: you remember how the conditions of our lives changed, how much we were thrown in on ourselves in the early days? 'East Coker' was the result—and it was only in writing 'East Coker' that I began to see the Quartets as a set of four."[2]

Eliot's "absorbed" has the ring of truth. Away from Vivien, Churchwarden at St. Stephen's, a valued voice at Faber's, he was now free to become absorbed in his literary endeavors. And being so absorbed, for him the second half of the 1930's passed like a dream. True, his reputation had become something of a problem, and he served on too many committees. But his life seemed of a piece. More and more he was able to bring his growing religious and cultural preoccupations into his editorial work at the *Criterion,* which he had come to share with a group of like-minded thinkers. And, almost exclusively now, he socialized with the *Criterion* circle, moving from the conviviality of the editorial room to boisterous evenings on the edge of *le beau monde* with his friends Frank Morley and John Hayward.[3] Even in the late thirties, though, something in Eliot's Puritan conscience made him mistrust his prosperity, and his mistrust was reinforced by events across the Channel. Along with the dreams of many other Englishmen, Eliot's burst in 1939. But for Eliot it happened with a special jolt, as if a long-expected bill collector had arrived at his door.

In 1939, Eliot's play *The Family Reunion,* the product of four years' work[4] and the vehicle for Eliot's remaining literary ambitions, opened at the Westminster Theatre in London. Greeted by lukewarm reviews, it closed after five weeks. How much its failure disheartened Eliot even he never admitted, but there is some sense of it in a letter he wrote Virginia Woolf. Many times in the past he had feared that his career was over, and he had recently confessed to Bonamy Dobreé that "he was abandoning the writing of poems because . . . he did not want to repeat himself."[5] Now his old fear returned, and was augmented by despair about the value of what he had already written. Thinking especially of his recent work, in 1939 he asked Woolf what profession was more trying than an author's. After one finishes a piece of work, he told her, it only seems good for a few weeks; or if it seems good at all you are convinced that it is the last you will be able to write. And he added that if it seems bad you wonder whether everything you have done is not poor stuff really. It is one kind of agony when you are writing, and another kind when you are not.[6]

Forced to reassess the merits of *The Family Reunion,* Eliot also recognized, possibly for the first time, what the play had to say about his life. Very likely he knew that in portraying Harry Montchensey's crisis he had retold "Burnt Norton"'s story of spiritual renewal. But it is hard to believe that, writing *The Family Reunion,* he was conscious of the bitter flavor he had given the retelling. When, near the end of the play, Harry departs to "follow the bright angels" (CPP, 281), the departure takes place amid the gloom of an unreconciled mother's death and a deserted sweetheart's concern. That gloom, called out of Eliot in the process of constructing a workable piece of theatre, now faced him from the boards of the Westminster stage and resonated with other events of a somber year.

There was for one thing the fact of Vivien's institutionalization just before the war.[7] Whatever peace Eliot had been able to make with himself about their separation was fragile at best. Since 1933 it had been threatened a number of times by Vivien's efforts to arrange a reconciliation, or at least to stage one more scene. In the words of Eliot's friend Robert Sencourt, "If he could have forgotten [her], she could not forget him. She would return to his office in Russell Square and try to waylay him on the stairs. . . . There are stories of her coming to his lectures wearing on her back a placard bearing the words 'I am the wife he abandoned,' and she was to be a regular attender of his plays."[8] After Vivien's nervous breakdown, the wound was rubbed raw yet again. Eliot could no longer hope that Vivien would make a new start, as she had several times promised to do. He knew now that her life was ruined, and he would bear the responsibility till he died. How could "hidden laughter" redeem the time "stretching after" a fact like that?

Nor was there any shortage in 1939 of public events to amplify Eliot's gloom. He had spent the thirties trying to steer a middle course between economic and political solutions to the worsening world crisis. At the *Criterion,* which he had founded to promote European cultural communication, he involved himself in economics and politics, all the while insisting that a revivified Christianity was the only path to genuine practical reform.[9] By 1939 even Eliot saw that although his crusade had diverted the *Criterion*'s literary energies, it had done nothing to advance his ends. Despite the combined powers of pen and cross, the collective life of Europe had dissolved. Nine months before Germany invaded Poland, Eliot disbanded the journal which had been the rock of his London existence, and in his last "Commentary," he mixed sorrow with self-flagellation. With his old sense of inadequacy rising, he gave his readers his "Last Words":

> With this number I terminate my editorship of *The Criterion.* I have been considering this decision for about two years. . . . During the autumn, however, the prospect of war had involved me in hurried plans for suspending publication; and in the subsequent *détente* I became convinced that my enthusiasm for continuing the editorial work did not exist.
>
> Sixteen years is a long time for one man to remain editor of a review; for this review, I have sometimes wondered whether it has not been too long. A feeling of staleness has crept over me, and a suspicion that I ought to retire before I was aware that this feeling had communicated itself to the readers. . . .
>
> Literary symptoms of decline. . . . are only symptoms . . . the demoralization of society goes very much deeper. . . . It will perhaps need more severe affliction than anything we have yet experienced, before life can be renewed. . . . But in any case, the immediate future is not bright.
>
> For this immediate future, perhaps for a long way ahead, the continuity of culture may have to be maintained by a very small number of people indeed. . . .
>
> In the present state of public affairs—which has induced in myself a depression of spirits so different from any other experience of fifty years as to be a new emotion—I no longer feel the enthusiasm necessary to make a literary review what it should be.[10]

In that mood in late 1939 or early 1940 and "thrown in on himself," Eliot began to feel the pull of another meditative poem. His thoughts ran back to a pilgrimage he had made in 1937 to East Coker, the village where his ancestor Andrew Eliot had lived before striking out for America in the seventeenth century. Perhaps in 1937 Eliot had made the trip to provide a setting for a poem he might one day write. Perhaps he had gone out of non-literary motives and had been inspired by the place to elaborate "Burnt Norton" into a vision of seventeenth-century communal life. That ur-version of "East Coker," had it been written, would have given us Eliot returning to his roots and solidifying personal vision by the force of English tradition.

By January 1940 Eliot's life had altered too much to write that poem. His contemporary readers assumed that he had intended *Four Quartets* as a whole from the beginning.[11] Their assumption is belied both by the facts and by the *Quartets'* emotional texture. Radically different in mood from "Burnt Norton," the last three of the *Four Quartets* were never intended to enlarge upon a private vision of grace. Eliot's continuation of the suite was instead the product of "a new and shocking / Valuation" ("East Coker" II) of all he had felt and been.[12] And as soon as we begin "East Coker," we know how bitter that revaluation was. In Kristian Smidt's words, "East Coker" "expresses a strong feeling of disappointment and disillusionment."[13] If anything, Smidt understates the case. More than disillusioned, Eliot was furious that he could have written a poem like "Burnt Norton," which took so little account of Vivien's (and Europe's) suffering and which so easily spared him the pain of self-reproach.

In consequence, "East Coker" ends not by affirming a moment of harmony but with the exhortation that "Old men ought to be explorers." Its keynote is the shocked tone, the pain and anger that sounds in the first lines of part II:

> What is the late November doing
> With the disturbance of the spring. . . .

The poem, to be sure, begins with the motto "In my beginning is my end"—begins, that is, as if Eliot had found a piece of earth to embody the "end" he had reached in the last lines of "Burnt Norton" I ("What might have been and what has been / Point to one end, which is always present"). But even at the start, Eliot's optimism does not stand unquestioned. Long before the verse formally announces time's power to "shake the tattered arras woven with a silent motto," the poem undercuts the assurance of its opening with the rhythms of Ecclesiastes. As Eliot returns in his mind to the yearnings he had brought to East Coker, he is forced to recognize that his ancestors' lives were no less difficult than his own. Far from returning Eliot to a lost spiritual community, the first movement of "East Coker" probes a terror that admits of alleviation neither in private vision nor in the historical past. In it, Eliot faces the truth that there never has been a community whose customs could redeem "the void that I find in the middle of all human happiness and all human relations. . . . [the void which] tends to drive [me] towards asceticism or sensuality, [and to Christianity, without which] life . . . is otherwise disgusting."[14] In the words of part I, the end of all human effort is a return of ashes

> to the earth
> Which is already flesh, fur and faeces,
> Bone of man and beast, cornstalk and leaf.

Little wonder that the old terror of *The Waste Land* creeps in, and the wind that once "crossed the brown land" now breaks "the loosened pane" and shakes "the wainscot where the field-mouse trots."

In the emotional logic of "East Coker," by the time the second verse paragraph repeats the words "In my beginning is my end," their effect is heavily ironic. In the lines that follow, the word "end" once again points to terminus, death, and extinction, and the poem all but retracts "Burnt Norton"'s vision of the "heart of light." Once more we are in the heat, and once more the sun is central. But whereas in "Burnt Norton" the heated air had been "vibrant," now it is "sultry." Where the silence had been full of "unheard music," now it is "empty." Where the "moment in the rose-garden" had been full of provocative reflection, now the "light / Is absorbed, not refracted, by grey stone." So much, then, for the providential value of "the little lights for which our bodily vision is made" (CPP, 114).

In "that open field," Eliot's vision of seventeenth-century life appears. For a moment, he makes us feel as he once felt—that the torpid silence of his age is on the point of shattering. Unexpectedly, the oppression of the heat is relieved by an antique epithalamium. And after recording the "empty silence," he tells us that if we "do not come too close," we can sense the local spirits, the unheard music, the dance. Surely, he has found his way back to a ritualized communal life in which the precarious experience of the garden does not depend simply on an individual moment of grace.

However, suggesting what Eliot had foolishly felt himself, the poem's first movement only leads to further disillusionment. Yes, Eliot introduces the wisdom of his distant and famous forbear, Sir Thomas Elyot, with a display of solemn dignity. He even maintains Elyot's spelling, as if reluctant to violate Renaissance wisdom with the inflections of his own age or voice:[15]

> The association of man and woman
> In daunsinge, signifying matrimonie. . . .

But, as A. D. Moody points out, Eliot's reverence is not what it seems.[16] Unexpectedly, Sir Thomas's humanism starts looking as quaint

as its spelling, conveying to his descendent only the pastness of the
past. Thus "East Coker" 's melancholy deepens, ushering Eliot into a
moment which has the lure of harmony but is anchored in darkness:

> Round and round the fire
> Leaping through the flames, or joined in circles,
> Rustically solemn or in rustic laughter. . . .

Up to here, the poem leads us to expect a fairy-tale as we ordinarily
conceive of it—a vision of fulfilled desire. But the truth of Eliot's vision
is not that. It is instead

> Earth feet, loam feet, lifted in country mirth
> Mirth of those long since under earth
> Nourishing the corn.

Time in "East Coker," which, from afar, seemed unlike the "waste sad
time" of "Burnt Norton," now reveals itself as it has always been, a

> time of the coupling of man and woman
> And that of beasts. Feet rising and falling.
> Eating and drinking. Dung and death.

Yet this too recalls a fairy-tale, of another kind. Eliot confessed that
when he wrote the first section of "East Coker," his imagery had "been
influenced by recollections of 'Germelshausen,' "[17] the Friedrich Gerstärker story of a town which, caught in time by the decree of a Pope,
"resumes for the space of one day [every hundred years] its ghostly
revelry, and then sinks again under the earth."[18] In the Gerstärker
story, the curse and the ghostly revelry disturb a time-traveling observer. And although Helen Gardner protests that "the implications of
the story and the poem are entirely different,"[19] "East Coker" does not
bear her out. The town Eliot imagined in 1937 *was* under a curse, as
was the man who imagined it. In the grip of what the younger Eliot
had called the romantic's "short cut to the strangeness without the reality" (SW, 31), the pilgrim of 1937 transformed the town of his ancestors into a land of his desire. It was only three years later that he saw
the changeless community of his fantasy was as lifeless as it was unreal.
And as always when Eliot's romantic dreams dissolved, a hangover followed. In the latter half of the verse paragraph we have been considering, what has seemed a timeless dance turns into a circle of vanity
and recurrence. Sixteen lines into the stanza a lugubrious rhyme
("mirth"/"earth") announces the end of Eliot's effortless revery. Then
the mood of Ecclesiastes resurfaces and along with it the full force of
Eliot's disgust and horror ("dung and death").

It is then that part II of "East Coker" begins with the lines already
quoted: "What is the late November doing / With the disturbance of the
spring . . . ?" As Eliot said was Valéry's practice in "Le Cimetière
marin," the lyric represents a species of "réactions à . . . premières

réactions."[20] Brought up short after five years of false tranquility, Eliot awakes to find himself alive and raw. Suddenly, it comes to him that "Burnt Norton" solved nothing, that all the old desires and all the old scars still hurt. That is the burden of his first seven lines, which remind us that "April is the cruellest month" with the painful directness of old age. Even the much weaker lines that follow display some of the same urgency. The phrase, a "vortex that shall bring," recalls the anxious cadences of Prufrock and Mrs. Porter, and the final image of an "ice-cap" communicates Eliot's horror of emotional torpor.[21]

Then, with the lyric of part II fading, "East Coker" proceeds systematically to repeat and revise "Burnt Norton." Compensating for the earlier poem's naivete, Eliot now emphasizes how difficult it is to hear the music of the spheres, and how much it costs. His concern is explicit in part IV, a somewhat precious lyric written, he said, in imitation of "the style of Cleveland or Benlowes."[22] But it also informs the more successful lyric interlude of part III:

> Whisper of running streams, and winter lightning.
> The wild thyme unseen and the wild strawberry,
> The laughter in the garden, echoed ecstasy
> Not lost, but requiring, pointing to the agony
> Of death and birth.

Still acknowledging that "the laughter in the garden" is deeper than suffering, Eliot here adds that to hear the laughter "requires" suffering, "points to" agony and the death of our old selves. Without that necessary prelude, ecstasy has no meaning. It is a matter, in the words of part II, of giving up ourselves "to another, or to others, or to God."

Finally, with a last echo and definitive revision of "Burnt Norton," "East Coker" concludes with a somber evocation of the Word. Eliot's part V meditation on the paradoxes of communication is bleaker and more distressing than its predecessor's and so is his symbolic restatement. Whereas "Burnt Norton" ended by figuring the truth on the other side of the void as the call of a bird ("Quick now, here, now, always—"), "East Coker" suggests the same idea in a different emotional register. Reaching back to the "grey stone" of part I, Eliot retrieves the one element of his ancestral village that had withstood the blur of his enchantment. The poem ends with his perception of "pattern more complicated," a perception which is based on "old stones that cannot be deciphered." Like the bird's song, these stones, the gravemarkers in the little yard beside the town church, disclose "what has been lost" in a language that cannot be translated. But unlike the bird's call, the stones speak of pain, isolation and death.

Nevertheless the poem at its conclusion does not despair. Having seen the emptiness of "time present and time past," and of "what might have been and what has been," Eliot responds with black elation. His way clear, there is nothing now for him to do but, in Conrad's words, "into the destructive element immerse." And so he dares the flood, "Through the dark cold and the empty desolation, / The wave cry, the wind cry, the vast waters / Of the petrel and the porpoise." Praying for new life after death by water, Eliot concludes "East Coker" with a programmatic reversal. Inked late onto his typescript, the poem's last phrase rights its opening by restoring a borrowed motto to its original form: "In my end is my beginning."

Nor did Eliot transcribe that restoration lightly. Having drafted and polished "East Coker" in February of 1940, he published it in March and went immediately on. Its successor—"The Dry Salvages"—was in mind by April, in Hayward's hands by the end of the year and in press by the following September.[23] And true to Eliot's word, the successor began where "East Coker" ended.

In "The Dry Salvages," Eliot devotes himself with disconcerting exhilaration to elaborating the reality that "prevents us everywhere" ("East Coker" IV). Still angry, still intent on puncturing the mood of "Burnt Norton" (and on punishing himself for having believed in it), he turns his anger toward a celebration of death and eternal judgment. Thus, having everything to do with "East Coker" 's "old stones that cannot be deciphered," the "salvages" of his title touch on both savagery and salvation: in the terms of "East Coker," they are the adversity which is our highest good, the curse which is our spiritual redemption.

But the salvages of the poem are more than a religious icon, and "The Dry Salvages" is a richer and more interesting poem than the Christian implications of its title might suggest. Along with their primary symbolism, the rocks also represent the seat of some of Eliot's strongest childhood memories. Mantra-like, they seem to have helped him release a complex vision of his early life. Writing the poem, Eliot addressed a longstanding part of his private mythology (an ancestor of his, he suspected, had been shipwrecked there, and he and a friend were once storm-bound on a neighboring island).[24] And in so doing, he seems to have suddenly seen the coherence ("We had the experience but missed the meaning") in a childhood he had regarded as unbridgeably divided. ("My family were New Englanders," he once wrote, "who had been settled—my branch of it—for two generations in the South West—which was, in my own time, rapidly becoming merely the Middle West. The family guarded jealously its connexions with New England; but it was not until years of maturity that I perceived that I myself had always been a New Englander in the South West, and a South Westerner in New England; when I was sent to school in New England I lost my southern accent without ever acquiring the accent of the native Bostonian. In New England I missed the long dark river, the ailanthus trees, the flaming cardinal birds, the high limestone bluffs where we searched for fossil shell-fish; in Missouri I missed the fir trees, the bay

and goldenrod, the song-sparrows, the red granite and the blue sea of
Massachusetts.")[25]

Consider the way Eliot arrived at the poem's controlling image. The
rough schema he started with said nothing about the river, only the
sea:

Notes

1. Sea picture —general
2.   —particular
                  problem of permanence
                  of past pain
3. Past error can only be reconciled
   in eternity. Arjuna & Krishna.
4. Invocation to the B.V.M.
   meaning of "mother" and "father".
5. *Generalisation:* Liberation from
   the past is liberation from the
   future. To get beyond time &
   at the same time deeper into
   time. the Spirit & the Earth[26]

But by the time Eliot had finished his first draft, the sea and the river
were related in one venerable figure: the river of an individual life
flowing into the sea of eternity. Moreover, each half of that figure had
acquired a particularly American coloring—one might even say a double wash. The river, for instance, emerges in Whitmanesque lines that
recall more than Whitman:

> I do not know much about gods; but I think that the river
> Is a strong brown god—sullen, untamed and intractable. . . .
> His rhythm was present in the nursery bedroom,
> In the rank ailanthus of the April dooryard,
> In the smell of grapes on the autumn table,
> And the evening circle in the winter gaslight.
>
> ("The Dry Salvages" I)

Steeped in the Emersonian notion that the American self is a process,
the lines remind us that Whitman envisioned the river of life as an
open road, and that after him Mark Twain put the river road at the
center of *Huckleberry Finn.* That openness of self was part of Eliot's
birthright, and he would later give us a landmark description of Twain's
achievement:

> The River gives the book its form. . . . We come to understand the River
> by seeing it through the eyes of the Boy, but the Boy is also the spirit of
> the River. . . . [Huck Finn's independence is] the independence of the
> vagabond. . . . Like Huckleberry Finn, the River itself has no beginning
> or end.[27]

Yet if the river in "The Dry Salvages" suggests a peculiarly American self, it also has a deeper resonance, no less American. Eliot wrote in his essay on Twain that

> the river with its strong, swift current is the dictator to the raft or to the steamboat. It is a treacherous and capricious dictator. At one season, it may move sluggishly in a channel so narrow that, encountering it for the first time at that point, one can hardly believe that it has travelled already for hundreds of miles, and has yet many hundreds of miles to go; at another season, it may obliterate the low Illinois shore to a horizon of water, while in its bed it runs with a speed such that no man or beast can survive in it. At such times, it carries down human bodies, cattle and houses. At least twice, at St. Louis, the western and the eastern shores have been separated by the fall of bridges, until the designer of the great Eads Bridge devised a structure which could resist the floods. In my own childhood, it was not unusual for the spring freshet to interrupt railway travel; and then the traveller to the East had to take steamboat from the levee up to Alton, at a higher level on the Illinois shore, before he could begin his rail journey. The river is never wholly chartable; it changes its pace, it shifts its channel, unaccountably; it may suddenly efface a sandbar, and throw up another bar where before was navigable water. . . .
>
> Mark Twain is a native, and the River God is his God. It is as a native that he accepts the River God, and it is the subjection of Man that gives to Man his dignity. For without some kind of God, Man is not even very interesting.[28]

Here, if the river is a self, it is that "untamed and intractable" portion of the self that makes itself available to the passions of God and of the devil. It is what Eliot's ancestors had called the immortal soul, and it reminds us both of Massachusetts Bay and of one of Eliot's favorite cantos in the *Purgatorio,* where Buanconte di Montefeltro "ended my words upon the name of Mary" on the stream called Archiano, and where angel and devil struggled as Buanconte's body "the raging Archian found, and swept it into the Arno . . . [rolling it] along its banks and over its bed, then covered and wrapped [it] with its spoils."[29]

Likewise, the sea as it appears in "The Dry Salvages" is both American and double-dyed. Recalling Melville's and Dickinson's visions of the sublime, it reaches beyond them to the sea in the mind of the Puritans, for whom America was a "rock and a shelter for his righteous ones to run unto," and yet a rock only for those who knew that "none are fitter for comfort than those that think themselves furthest off."[30] It is possible that these associations, implied and unstated, had helped preserve the power of Eliot's Cape Ann memories over the years. What is unquestionable is that as he now peered back in his memory to "the experience of a child of ten, a small boy peering through sea-water in a rock-pool, and finding a sea-anemone for the first time" (UPUC, 78–79), the vividness of his recall had as much to do with an intuition of mortality as with the joy of childhood.[31]

Thus, in "The Dry Salvages," Eliot's record of the sea and the shore of Cape Ann combines boyhood gentleness with the steely precision of a journalist at the scene of a disaster. Yet what Eliot most emphasizes is not sight but sound. As in his Landscapes and "Marina," in the first movement of "The Dry Salvages" Eliot searches for a reality beneath the changing world of visual impressions. Beyond the fragments the sea has thrown up, beyond the fog and beyond the Tennysonian voices of the romantic sublime, he strains to hear the music of what happens. But when he does, it is distinct and terrifying—not as in "Marina" the "woodthrush singing through the fog," but a "tolling bell."

Interestingly, however, we sense the greatest emotional depths of the poem's imagery not in the lines of the first movement but shortly after them. Having followed the great river of his childhood down to a sea it never met, Eliot might have dwelt for the rest of the poem on the sea's associations with eternity and eternal suffering. And indeed, he does sustain his marine landscape into the sestina which opens "The Dry Salvages" II. In the prosy section immediately following, however, he unexpectedly turns back to the river. Or rather, as Helen Gardner observes, after having schematically connected the river and the sea, he seems suddenly to have felt the connection's significance, and doubled back. Unmentioned in the drafts of part II, the river appears in revision to make the final version unforgettable. In Gardner's words, the "two symbols from his childhood [come] together as symbols of the permanence of past agonies: the Mississippi and the reef of the Dry Salvages off Cape Ann": [32]

> Now, we come to discover that the moments of agony
> (Whether, or not, due to misunderstanding,
> Having hoped for the wrong things or dreaded the wrong things,
> Is not in question) are likewise permanent
> With such permanence as time has. We appreciate this better
> In the agony of others, nearly experienced,
> Involving ourselves, than in our own.
> For our own past is covered by the currents of action,
> But the torment of others remains an experience
> Unqualified, unworn by subsequent attrition.
> People change, and smile: but the agony abides.
> Time the destroyer is time the preserver,
> Like the river with its cargo of dead Negroes, cows and chicken
>   coops,
> The bitter apple and the bite in the apple.

Here, for its fullest expression of our unstable and fragmented life in time, the poem turns to Mark Twain's river and its debris. More disheartening than the unfathomable eternal ocean that tosses up its wreckage, the river figures the course of an individual life, moved by the pressure of fate and constrained within the levees of character.

There is no oceanic release in the movement of this current, nor is there any hope that the associated wreckage will be washed away. Perhaps the most moving in *Four Quartets,* the lines Eliot added in revision suggest what misery he now associated with the buried self he once so yearned to release—the self he had looked to for authenticity and wholeness but now saw as an irremediable source of sin and neurosis, pain and evil. After a veiled allusion to himself and Vivien ("the agony of others, nearly experienced, / Involving ourselves"), he makes the "river with its cargo of dead Negroes, cows and chicken coops" resonate with a horror of living with the ruin he has caused. And suffusing the lines is a horror that the impulses and cruelties of the self will never "with such permanence as time has" be outgrown. "People change, and smile: but the agony abides."

2

After that unexpectedly melancholy confession, "The Dry Salvages" returns to Eliot's plan. Following his schema, it moves from a "particular" example of the "problem of permanence of past pain" first to a philosophical examination of experience and then to an invocation of the Blessed Virgin and the subject of the Incarnation. At that point, however, the questions one wants to ask of it change. What becomes more interesting than what Eliot called "some acute personal reminiscence (never to be explicated, of course, but to give power from well below the surface)" is why the power sputtered.

Exploring the emotional pressures sustaining "East Coker" and "The Dry Salvages," the account just concluded does not mention two remarkable developments. The second and third *Quartets* are (as "Burnt Norton" was not) shaped by a structure larger than themselves. And, leaving riddling negations for a more direct, more prosaic and frequently more relaxed form of writing, they depart from the style of "Burnt Norton." The two developments, furthermore, stemmed from the same root: as Eliot's "new and shocking valuation" caused him to confront old doubts and fall into old patterns of self-accusation, it also triggered old defenses. The closer he got to the guilt and anger that had instigated "East Coker," the stronger he clung to order and generalization. And thus, ironically, having appended "East Coker" to "Burnt Norton" to open up that poem's facile harmonies, Eliot produced the most elaborate and constricting structure of his career.

Several years after the publication of Helen Gardner's definitive account, it is still shocking to remind ourselves that the four-part symmetries of *Four Quartets* have as little to do with the poem's original impulse as the grail legend has to do with the beginnings of *The Waste Land.* Yet the documents of the case are incontrovertible. According to Eliot's own statements, the symbolic correspondences were something he never foresaw. Produced by an itch for elaboration, at a certain point they just grew.

The impulse to prolong and revise "Burnt Norton" had taken Eliot to the end of "The Dry Salvages," and in the wake of that impulse he had made formal decisions as the necessity arose. As he looked back to "Burnt Norton" in "East Coker," it had seemed natural to repeat its five parts in what (circa 1940) seemed the more appropriate tones of earth. Then, perhaps in the midst of writing "East Coker," perhaps later,[33] repeating this structure suggested another pattern. In "The Dry Salvages," immersing the somber resolve of "East Coker" in currents of eternity, he repeated the five-part structure yet again. Probably only then did it strike him that he had rehearsed three parts of a Heraclitean grouping. We know at least that even after he had drafted "The Dry Salvages," Eliot led John Hayward to believe that it would be "the third poem of [his] trilogy."[34] And not until June 1941 did Eliot confirm he was working on a fourth poem. By then, apparently, he had convinced himself that his poems of air, earth and water required completion in fire.[35] However belated, the thought had its appeal. Eliot saw that, once completed, his quaternity of fives would (like the Landscapes) enact the cycle of yearly renewal. And so, as he explained to an American student, "perhaps only for convenience sake," the poem gradually began to assume "a relation to the four seasons and the four elements."[36]

Yet, "gradual" as it was, the development of the poem's formal relations was never merely "convenient." Reinforcing Eliot's incidental decisions was the weight of his recent poetics and behind that a great deal more. To begin with, the repetitive form of the *Quartets* satisfied Eliot's desire, examined in chapter seven, to write poems that conformed to traditional forms of shared experiences—poems that began with "an act of choice" and a "prose outline."[37] That thirst for order, a response to the anxieties of 1921–23, had all but been forgotten in "Burnt Norton." Now it returned as if it had never left. Alarmed at how his conscience had been anesthetized, Eliot forswore "Burnt Norton"'s supple play of voices and its impossible wish to capture the "music of what happens." Retaining "Burnt Norton"'s surface pattern as an act of self-discipline, he absorbed it into an extended but closed musical organization. The title *Quartets,* he told John Hayward in 1942, was a way of indicating that the poems were written "in a particular set form" with elaborations, a way of suggesting that they are woven out of "three or four superficially unrelated themes."[38] As he had written Anne Ridler the year before, "the poem as a whole ["East Coker"]—this five part form—is an attempt to weave several quite unrelated strands together in an emotional whole, so that really there isn't any heart of the matter."[39]

Then, a "set form" clear in his mind, Eliot set to work fabricating his "unrelated strands." And since it was wartime and he never knew when he would be called away from his desk, the moment fit the task. As he explained to Donald Hall, he worked on the three *Quartets* "written during the war . . . in fits and starts." "The form of the *Quartets*," he said, "fitted in very nicely to the conditions under which I was writing, or could write at all. I could write them in sections and I didn't have to have quite the same continuity."[40]

For better or worse, the *Quartets* bear out Eliot's recollections. What he gained from the procedure has long been celebrated by his commentators—a "brilliantly musical" organization "adapted to its creator's . . . desire to submit to the discipline of strict poetic laws, and at the same time to have liberty in the development of a verse capable of extremes of variation, and in the bringing together of ideas and experiences often divorced."[41] But what he lost is equally clear. Compare the following passages, taken from analogous sections of "Burnt Norton," "East Coker" and "The Dry Salvages":

> At the still point of the turning world. Neither flesh nor flesh-
> less;
> Neither from nor towards; at the still point, there the dance is,
> But neither arrest nor movement. And do not call it fixity,
> Where past and future are gathered. Neither movement from
>   nor towards,
> Neither ascent nor decline. Except for the point, the still point,
> There would be no dance, and there is only the dance.
>
> ("Burnt Norton" II)

> That was a way of putting it—not very satisfactory:
> A periphrastic study in a worn-out poetical fashion,
> Leaving one still with the intolerable wrestle
> With words and meanings. The poetry does not matter.
> It was not (to start again) what one had expected.
> What was to be the value of the long looked forward to,
> Long hoped for calm, the autumnal serenity
> And the wisdom of age? Had they deceived us
> Or deceived themselves, the quiet-voiced elders,
> Bequeathing us merely a receipt for deceit?
>
> ("East Coker" II)

> It seems, as one becomes older,
> That the past has another pattern, and ceases to be a mere se-
> quence—
> Or even development: the latter a partial fallacy,
> Encouraged by superficial notions of evolution,
> Which becomes, in the popular mind, a means of disowning the
>   past.
> The moments of happiness—not the sense of well-being,
> Fruition, fulfilment, security or affection,
> Or even a very good dinner, but the sudden illumination—

> We had the experience but missed the meaning,
> And approach to the meaning restores the experience
> In a different form, beyond any meaning
> We can assign to happiness.
>
> ("The Dry Salvages" II)

In "East Coker," the riddling tautness of "Burnt Norton," the sense of a mind rigorously striving toward some ghostly point beyond language, has relaxed. True, the lack has partly been filled by a vigorous directness ("Had they deceived us / Or deceived themselves . . . ?"), of which more later. But to an unfortunate degree, "East Coker" retains "Burnt Norton" 's manner only to dilute its spirit. The rhyme on "receipt" and "deceit," for example, has the heft of one of "Burnt Norton" 's paradoxical phrases ("Neither flesh nor fleshless . . . neither arrest nor movement") and more judgmental force, but nothing of its tense strength. (The same can be said of the difference between "Burnt Norton" 's organizing play on "Time present and time past" and "East Coker" 's mordant reversal of "In my beginning is my end.")

By the time we get to "The Dry Salvages," moreover, the problems all but leap off the page. In the words of Donald Davie's devastating critique, it is almost impossible to believe that the same poet is writing: "How," Davie asks, "can we explain that the same poet should now proffer, in such stumbling trundling rhythms, these inarticulate ejaculations of reach-me-down phrases, the debased currency of the study circle? And . . . [a]t the dismal jocularity of that 'very good dinner,' we throw in our hands." [42]

Nor is there any doubt but that the answer to Davie's question involves Eliot's acceptance of a set poetic structure of the kind he had always struggled to avoid. Like the more formal lyrics of the same poems, the passages quoted from "East Coker" and "The Dry Salvages" were written to "fit." Exchanging the authority of his own voice for the impersonality of an orchestra, Eliot frequently lost his touch. Sometimes, his simulated voices fail to convince. And sometimes, to quote Denis Donoghue, he cannot control "a piece which he scored for an unmanageable number of voices." [43]

Even when Eliot speaks in his own voice, moreover, he inclines toward a public speech for which he is temperamentally unsuited. Particularly in the last two *Quartets,* he speaks of the problem of pain not as "one man only" ("East Coker" V), but as an Englishman at war. It was, he felt, his solemn duty. As England's foremost poet, it was his obligation to unite his countrymen in their years of crisis, and, as he once remarked, "the last three of my quartets are primarily patriotic poems." [44] We therefore find not only references in "East Coker" to the Army in training, in "The Dry Salvages" to the experience of the Navy and in "Little Gidding" to the Blitz,[45] but also something else. Examining Eliot's uncollected prose of the period, it is clear he drew some of the most important images of the last two *Quartets* from his political journalism *entre deux guerres*. In an essay of 1937, for example, he had connected the figure of Arjuna to the dilemma of an uncommitted person contemplating the Spanish Civil War:

> Now an ideally unprejudiced person, with an intimate knowledge of Spain, its history, its racial characteristics, and its contemporary personalities, might be in a position to come to the conclusion that he should, in the longest view that could be seen, support one side rather than the other. . . . and even any eventual partisanship should be held with reservations, humility and misgiving. That balance of mind which a few highly-civilized individuals, such as Arjuna, the hero of the *Bhagavad Gita*, can maintain in action, is difficult for most of us even as observers, and, as I say, is not encouraged by the greater part of the Press.[46]

Set beside the passage of "The Dry Salvages" that they gave birth to, these remarks help explain a great deal of the poem's awkwardness. Writing of Krishna in 1941, Eliot wavers between emphasizing the private and public application of his text, and as in his journalism ends by emphasizing the public. This is the end of part III:

> ". . . O voyagers, O seamen,
> You who come to port, and you whose bodies
> Will suffer the trial and judgement of the sea,
> Or whatever event, this is your real destination."
> So Krishna, as when he admonished Arjuna
> On the field of battle.
> > Not fare well,
> But fare forward, voyagers.

Immediately beforehand, we remember, Eliot had been speaking of his own "moments of agony," and clearly the Arjuna passage is meant to steady his resolve to "fare forward" out of potentially paralyzing guilt. But just as clearly, the passage serves another purpose. Unable to rid himself of the thought of "the agony of others, nearly experienced, / Involving ourselves," Eliot submerges it in something larger: he links his private guilt to the collective guilt of Europe. First through Krishna and then as an anonymous prophet, he speaks of guilt in the great world and adopts the rhetoric of public wisdom. And before he knows it he has slipped into journalistic cliche:

> To explore the womb, or tomb, or dreams; all these are usual
> Pastimes and drugs, and features of the press:
> And always will be, some of them especially
> When there is distress of nations and perplexity
> Whether on the shores of Asia, or in the Edgeware Road.
> > ("The Dry Salvages" V)

Better than any poet of the century, Eliot knows the dishonesty of making poetry out of this kind of language. Yet, impelled by private evasion and patriotic duty, that is precisely what he does. In the lines just quoted, moreover, Eliot's worst offense is not just settling an old grudge with Freud. It is using the debased currency of this kind of rhetoric to speak of Chinese or English suffering as "distress of nations and perplexity."

But the relation of public and private language in "The Dry Salvages" cannot really be considered without reference to "Little Gidding," nor can the growing political emphasis of the suite be divorced from its insistently devotional stance. There had been little in "Burnt Norton" to predict "East Coker" 's Good Friday lyric upon the paradox of the fortunate fall or "The Dry Salvages" 's supplication of the "Queen of Heaven." Even they, however, hardly prepare us to be addressed by the voice of a saint:

> You are not here to verify,
> Instruct yourself, or inform curiosity
> Or carry report. You are here to kneel
> Where prayer has been valid. And prayer is more
> Than an order of words, the conscious occupation
> Of the praying mind, or the sound of the voice praying.
>
> ("Little Gidding" I)

Whatever its origins in "Burnt Norton," *Four Quartets* ends by approaching the status of religious meditation, a genre then much on Eliot's mind. In 1938, "asking for a revision of [George Herbert's] reputation," Eliot anticipated "Little Gidding" by suggesting that "we do not ask to know more of [Herbert] than what is conveyed in his utterance of his meditation on the highest spiritual mysteries."[47] A year later he went further still. "The probable direction of religious poetry in the immediate future," he wrote in an unpublished lecture, "is towards something more impersonal than that of [the nineteenth century]. . . . It will be much more interested in the dogma and the doctrine; in religious thought, rather than purely personal religious feeling." In a revival "deeply influenced by Thomism, and to some extent also by Karl Barth and Kierkegaard," it will be "concerned primarily with giving poetic form to theological thought." And in doing so it "will tend to have more kinship with that of the seventeenth century, than with that of the nineteenth." Like Herbert's own verse, it will be "content to meditate upon the central mysteries of the Incarnation and the Eucharist."[48]

Four Quartets, whatever else it might be, is Eliot's own meditation upon the "central mystery of the Incarnation." But, having been called up by "The Dry Salvages" ' recognition of evil at the center of his life, the subject of the Incarnation does not alone suffice. "Little Gidding," we discover, meditates upon a related but more intractable mystery. Its theme, as C. A. Bodelsen has pointed out, is the "theme of theodicy."[49]

With the fourteenth-century mystic Juliana of Norwich it acknowledges that "Sin is Behovely" (i.e., necessary or inevitable) while asserting that "All shall be well." In it, Eliot allows the Blitz to figure the full agony of life, yet he also asserts that "Love" is behind it all:

> The dove descending breaks the air
> With flame of incandescent terror
> Of which the tongues declare
> The one discharge from sin and error.
> The only hope, or else despair
>   Lies in the choice of pyre or pyre—
>   To be redeemed from fire by fire.
>
> Who then devised the torment? Love.
> Love is the unfamiliar Name
> Behind the hands that wove
> The intolerable shirt of flame
> Which human power cannot remove.
>   We only live, only suspire
>   Consumed by either fire or fire.

Here the *Quartets* reach a conclusion that had been inevitable since Eliot's first dismay that "Burnt Norton" had not acknowledged the fact of human suffering. Now, inexorably, having buttressed his pronouncement with every formal procedure at his disposal, Eliot concludes his suite with the most difficult possible affirmation of "the still point of the turning world"—the assertion that love and pain are inextricably intertwined, that "the fire and the rose are one." The entire authority of the poem stands behind that statement, the full power of its public rhetoric and the accumulated effects of its symbolic music.[50] Representing the poem's central truth, it is spoken in an impersonal voice that another "proud" and "haughty" man[51] had taught Eliot to believe was the product of humility: "We cannot," Eliot wrote, "as with Donne, read [Herbert's] poetry as a kind of cypher which will yield clues to a peculiarly interesting personality behind the poetry. . . . therefore, he achieves the greatest universality in his art; he remains as the human soul contemplating the divine."[52]

And yet, unable to find in it even "Burnt Norton"'s grounding in the authenticity of dramatized experience, with F. R. Leavis we may well ask whether Eliot's virtuoso conclusion is any more than "mere statement—statement so insistent as fairly to be called emphatic assertion?"[53] That question in its turn leads to others more troubling still. Since Eliot's "emphatic" conclusion seems to have grown out of an overwhelming need to punish himself, does it not have as much to do with anger as with an understanding of God's love for the world? And finally, is not Eliot's fierce and uncomfortable theodicy party to that same insensitivity to others' suffering that led Eliot to call the misery of

wartime China "distress of nations and perplexity / Whether on the
shores of Asia, or in the Edgeware Road?"

Given my admiration for Eliot, I raise these questions with great diffidence. However, two voices goad me on. The first is that of E. M.
Forster, who, disturbed by the insistence of Eliot's Christian certainties,
confessed that in his view, "Little Gidding," although a "wonderful"
poem, was also an "homage to pain. . . . endorsed by the school-
master and sanctified by the priest."[54] The second is, perhaps, anonymous. In 1936, acting as editor of *The Criterion,* Eliot chose to print an
unsigned review which displayed his own fastidious concern for language and his own conviction that life was a choice of "pyre or pyre."
In retrospect, the review seems to bare the displaced and disturbed
anger of "Little Gidding" 's terrible impatience with those who would
exaggerate the world's "claim on our compassion":

> *The Yellow Spot: The Outlawing of Half a Million Human Beings:*
> A Collection of Facts and Documents Relating to Three Years' Perse-
> cution of German Jews, Derived chiefly from Nationalist Socialist
> Sources, very carefully assembled by a Group of Investigators. With
> an Introduction by the Bishop of Durham. (Gollancz, 1936.) 8s. 6d.
> cloth; 5s. paper.

> There should be somebody to point out that this book, although enjoying
> a cathedratic blessing, is an attempt to rouse moral indignation by means
> of sensationalism. Needless to say, it does not touch on how we might al-
> leviate the situation of those whose misfortunes it describes, still less why
> they, among all the unfortunates of the world, have a first claim on our
> compassion and help. Certainly no English man or woman would wish to
> be a German Jew in Germany to-day; but not only is our title to the moral
> dictatorship of the world open to question, there is not the least prospect
> of our being able to exercise it. More particularly, it is noticeable that the
> jacket of the book speaks of the "extermination" of the Jews in Germany,
> whereas the title-page refers only to their "persecution"; and as the title-
> page is to the jacket, so are the contents to the title-page, especially in the
> chapter devoted to the ill-treatment of Jews in German concentration
> camps.[55]

3

Four Quartets, then, the child of a very dark embryo indeed, is shot
through with technical and emotional lapses that cannot be denied. Nor
is it easy to imagine the poem otherwise. The same impulses that thick-
ened Eliot's verse also led him to adopt a form that would not let him
face his demons honestly. And yet, in a way that Emerson would have
understood, even that disastrous choice had compensations. In 1942
Eliot underwent a sudden rebellion, the descendant of the anger he
had once turned on "Burnt Norton." And in the moment of that re-

bellion, he broke through into a genuinely new kind of writing, a rugged anti-figural style that crowned his three years' effort. The final stage in Eliot's long evolution, the great poetry of "Little Gidding" also represents the phoenix cry of modernist poetry; paired with the very different manner of "Burnt Norton," it announces the extremes of postmodernist verse.

Eliot never said much about his discomfort with the form of *Four Quartets* afterward, and he probably would have taken issue with anyone who did. Having completed the suite as his intellectual program dictated, he convinced himself that the *Quartets* were his "best work" and that "they get better as they go on."[56] That is not, however, what his poetic conscience told him in the heat of composition. From what can be gathered from Eliot's own remarks, while writing the *Quartets* he was at least as reluctant to wrap up his suite as he was eager to press on.

About Eliot's suspicion that repeating a set poetic form was a type of self-betrayal, his letters leave no doubt. First when he decided to subsume "Burnt Norton" in a larger work and then as he contemplated the suite's concluding poem, he was attacked by persistent hesitation. It could hardly have been otherwise for someone who believed that "there is almost no escape from [the darkness of moral obliquity and intellectual sloth]" for a poet who "has got to a stage in which he merely imitates himself."[57] Thus, after Eliot had drafted only two sections of "East Coker," he admitted to John Hayward that his continuation of "Burnt Norton" "may be quite worthless because most of it looks to me like an imitation of myself."[58] Then, still flushed with the satisfaction of having completed "The Dry Salvages," he wrote Hayward a letter that ended with a caricature of himself as an old minstrel, striking his harp with rheumatic fingers.[59]

Eliot's strongest resistance, though, erupted as he was bringing his sequence to a close. In July 1941, a week after sending the first draft of "Little Gidding" to John Hayward, he told Hayward, "I have pushed on with Little Gidding, and enclose provisional results. . . . My suspicions about the poem are partly due to the fact that as it is written to complete a series, and not solely for itself, it may be too much from the head and may show signs of flagging. . . . The question is not so much whether it is as good as the others (I am pretty sure it is not) but whether it is good enough to keep company with them to complete the shape."[60] A month later he added, "The defect of the whole [of "Little Gidding"], I feel, is the lack of some acute personal reminiscence (never to be explicated, of course, but to give power from well below the surface). . . ."[61] It was then that Hayward wrote Frank Morley that Eliot feared "he was simply repeating himself and so running into the risk of producing an elegant parody of the earlier poems in the group"[62] and that Eliot himself wrote Bonamy Dobrée that "I am afraid that I

have been overproducing, and at last trying to make poetry out of un-
seasoned material."[63]

Weighed down by these misgivings, Eliot inevitably dragged his feet.
At work by June 1941, he finished a draft of "Little Gidding" by July
7, which he sent off to Hayward with the comment "not sure." After
that, he found reason after reason to do something else. In October
1941, Hayward gloomily announced to Frank Morley that "Little Gidding" had been shelved until December. And eight months later, in
August 1942, Eliot was still tinkering dejectedly. He then told Hayward
that if his revision was still not good enough "I fear the poem must
simply be allowed to disintegrate." It was only in September that subsequent revisions softened his doubts, but even then he seemed more
weary than exhilarated. "After a time," he wrote Hayward on the seventeenth of September, "one loses the original feeling of the impulse,
and then it is no longer safe to alter. It is time to close the chapter."[64]
It was thus not until the end of 1942 that "Little Gidding" saw publication, and not until 1943 that it appeared as the fourth poem in *Four
Quartets*.

Eliot's resistance, though, would have been far less interesting had it
simply caused him to delay. In fact, as I have shown above, it had from
the beginning entered the dynamics of his writing with powerful results. Rereading *Four Quartets,* Eliot's impulse to subvert his own symmetries can be felt from the end of "East Coker," where it powers the
vociferousness of Eliot's self-admonition (coming just where we would
expect the harmony of some concluding chord) to "be still and still
moving." And from then on, as William Spanos points out, the more
the *Quartets* appear to seek the satisfaction of aesthetic and ontological
closure, the more stubbornly they assert the inescapeable openness of
experience. As "East Coker" had exploded the wisdom of the elders,
so "The Dry Salvages" destroys the myth of American progress and
"Little Gidding" an illusory faith in the sanctuary of sacred places. In
Spanos's words, when Eliot advises his readers that "what you thought
you came for / Is only a shell, a husk of meaning" ("Little Gidding" I),
he is only repeating a lesson the *Quartets* had dramatized several times
before—that the backward orientation of the past must be set aside as
a model "in favor of the projective present."[65] What Spanos does not
add is that this kind of resistance had played an important role in the
genesis of "East Coker," "The Dry Salvages" and "Little Gidding." I
have already spoken of how different "East Coker" was from the poem
it might have been and of how Eliot altered "The Dry Salvages" from
his original schema. The case of "Little Gidding" presents the same
phenomenon in a more striking way.

These are Eliot's first jottings for "Little Gidding," as Helen Gardner
reproduces them in *The Composition of Four Quartets:*

Winter scene. May.

Lyric. air earth water end & &
daemonic fire. The Inferno.

They vanish, the individuals, and
Our feeling for them sinks into the
flame which refines. They emerge
in another pattern & recreated &
    reconciled
redeemed, having their meaning together not apart, in a union
which is of beams from the central
fire. And the others with them
contemporaneous.

Invocation to the Holy Spirit.[66]

As Gardner comments, this is "a preliminary scheme, showing that [Eliot] had come to see the seasons and the four elements as an organizing element in the sequence of four poems, and that the underlying theme of the last poem was to be pentecostal." However, she goes on, there is "no indication [here] that the poem was to treat of attitudes to the historic past as well as of the poet's attitude to his personal history."[67] And yet it is just these omissions that reveal most about the poem's subterranean life. Eliot's first schema looks forward to "Little Gidding" I, IIa, IIIa and V, passages which view life from the perspective of the logos. It does not anticipate sections IIb, IIIb and IV, the ones in which we find the poem's most heavily charged material. Sections IIIb and IV, as I have already suggested, in addressing the subject of history, take up Eliot's anger against himself into a fierce and uncomfortable theodicy. Section IIb is more interesting still. Dramatizing what Gardner calls "the poet's attitude toward his personal history," Eliot's presentation of a wartime encounter with a "familiar compound ghost" was derived from the notation "Inferno" in the schema, but evolved into more than that. In fact, it never stopped evolving—after roughing it out in his earliest draft, Eliot was still worrying about individual words on his proofsheets. Spanning the more than a year that "Little Gidding" was in process, the passage became the focus for a subject whose existence the formal symmetries of "Little Gidding" had sprung up to mediate or obscure.

In a well-known statement of 1950, Eliot said that when he wrote the "compound ghost" passage, he meant it to be "the nearest equivalent to a canto of the Inferno or the Purgatorio, in style as well as content, that I could achieve. The intention . . . [was] to present to the mind of the reader a parallel . . . between the Inferno and the Purgatorio . . . and a hallucinated scene after an air-raid" (TCC, 128). He started, moreover, with a particular canto of Dante in mind. In his first manuscript drafts, he cries out to the "dead master" of his vision, "Are you here, Ser Brunetto?" and identifies his narrative with *Inferno* XV.[68] About a year later, though, Eliot's intentions became more ambiguous. Putting *Inferno* XV in the background, he decided to present merely "a canto of the Inferno or Purgatorio" with the emphasis on the latter.

Inferno XV had fascinated Eliot since his student days. It treats of a meeting between Dante and Brunetto Latini, a beloved master whose memory Dante has cherished without realizing he has outgrown his master's teaching. Coming upon Brunetto in hell shocks Dante almost as much as Beatrice's rebuke on the top of Mount Purgatory, and for the same reasons. In both cases, he is forced to see that he had misunderstood a relationship that had helped him to define himself and then is forced to give up a central part of his self-image. But of the two the meeting with Latini is more melancholy, for here there is no possibility of love's rehabilitation. Before he is quite ready to do so, Dante is forced to acknowledge the limits of his old master's aspirations and to bid him farewell. His poignant leavetaking emerges in the canto's last lines, which Eliot called specimens of the very greatest poetry. I give Eliot's (1929) translation:

> Then he turned, and seemed like one of those who run for the green cloth at Verona through the open field; and of them he seemed like him who wins, and not like him who loses (SE, 209).

The appropriateness of this particular story to the poem Eliot proposed is as obvious as his second thoughts are obscure. Eliot, after all, was preparing to write on Dante's central subject—the liberation of the will—and he saw that Dante's encounter with Latini was a crucial step in his progress toward what "Little Gidding" III calls "freedom":

> History may be freedom. See, now they vanish,
> The faces and places, with the self which, as it could, loved them,
> To become renewed, transfigured, in another pattern.

It is interesting, though, that in his 1941 drafts Eliot did not personalize his version of Dante's story by identifying the "compound ghost" with one of his own old masters, nor did he dwell on the part of himself he was leaving behind. At that early stage Eliot was busy tying up loose ends, and his emphasis fell on the future—on the sea change in his own life that he then devoutly wished. In the 1941 version, therefore, the master speaks the words of a kindly uncle. Instead of your theories or your language, he tells Eliot,

> Remember rather the essential moments
> That were the times of birth and death and change. . . .[69]

After a year of vacillation, however, Eliot's purposes suffered a sea change of their own. In a sudden burst of effort motivated by a felt lack of "power well below the surface" he removed his specific reference to Latini and explained to Hayward:

> I think you will recognise that it was necessary to get rid of Brunetto for two reasons. The first is that the visionary figure has now become somewhat more definite and will no doubt be identified by some readers with Yeats though I do not mean anything so precise as that. However, I do not wish to take the responsibility of putting Yeats or anybody else into Hell and I do not want to impute to him the particular vice which took Brunetto there. Secondly, although the reference to that Canto is intended to be explicit, I wished the effect of the whole to be Purgatorial which is much more appropriate.[70]

He also made a striking change in the passage's mood. Though intended as "Purgatorial," the verse is now charged with two kinds of bitterness—the ghost's bitterness about a life he never lived and his bitterness about the botched life he did. Also, Eliot's joining of student and master, rather vague in the original, has become real and unforgettable. When Eliot tells us in the revision, "I assumed a double part, and cried / And heard another's voice cry," the authority of his telling persuades us it is true. The following gives Eliot's final version and italicizes those lines which he retained or revised from the 1941 draft:

> *And he: "I am not eager to rehearse*
> *My thought and theory which you have forgotten.*
> *These things have served their purpose: let them be.*
> *So with your own, and pray they be forgiven*
> *By others, as I pray you to forgive*
> *Both bad and good. Last season's fruit is eaten*
> *And the fullfed beast shall kick the empty pail.*
> *For last year's words belong to last year's language*
> *And next year's words await another voice.*
> But, as the passage now presents no hindrance
> To the spirit unappeased and peregrine
> Between two worlds become much like each other,
> So I find words I never thought to speak
> In streets I never thought I should revisit
> When I left my body on a distant shore.
> Since our concern was speech, and speech impelled us
> To purify the dialect of the tribe
> And urge the mind to aftersight and foresight,
> Let me disclose the gifts reserved for age
> To set a crown upon your lifetime's effort.
> First, the cold friction of expiring sense
> Without enchantment, offering no promise
> But bitter tastelessness of shadow fruit
> As body and soul begin to fall asunder.

> Second, the conscious impotence of rage
>   At human folly, and the laceration
>   Of laughter at what ceases to amuse.
> And last, the rending pain of re-enactment
>   Of all that you have done, and been; the shame
>   Of motives late revealed, and the awareness
> Of things ill done and done to others' harm
>   Which once you took for exercise of virtue.
>   Then fools' approval stings, and honour stains.
> From wrong to wrong the exasperated spirit
>   Proceeds, unless restored by that refining fire
>   Where you must move in measure, like a dancer."

Here we find the heart of what Eliot felt he had excluded from "Little Gidding": an anger emanating from two ruined lives and from the waste that will never be made up for in the closures of understanding or art. But what are we to make of it? How, specifically, can Eliot have intended the effect of *this* whole to be "Purgatorial"? One can see why D. W. Harding would want to write that this is hell and that the ghost's grisly message is meant to provoke the reaction "there but for the grace of God go I."[71] Yet the sense the passage gives of a shattering enlargement of being and knowing (not to mention the way it deliberately alludes to Arnaut Daniel) prevents us from doing so. Somehow this *is* Purgatory, and for Eliot the ghost's outbreak of bitterness represents a moment of genuine liberation. But how?

The answer, almost certainly, has to do with W. B. Yeats, the primary presence behind Eliot's re-envisioned "compound ghost." Yeats, admittedly, was an unlikely candidate for the role, since his work had made "[no] deep impression" on the younger Eliot, and since there were many "aspects of [his] thought and feeling" which the mature Eliot found "unsympathetic."[72] His appearance at first makes sense only if we insist on the prominence of the Latini story and take the ghost to be a poet of limited spiritual capacity whose craft is acknowledged even as he himself is left behind. What makes the presence of Yeats so striking, though, is that Eliot thought of him only after he abandoned the Latini subtext. In fact, the same crisis that altered *Four Quartets* had led him several years before to look at Yeats through opened eyes.

In the spring of 1933 Eliot had reread all of Yeats for English 26, the undergraduate lecture course on "Contemporary English Literature" he gave during his Norton Professorship at Harvard. In those lectures Yeats played second fiddle to Joyce, and Eliot could at best remark upon his progress toward clarity and simplicity and the growing fineness of his metric.[73] But by 1935, Yeats's seventieth birthday and the appearance of his *Collected Plays* (1934) made him look different. In that year, Eliot wrote in *The Criterion* that "Mr. Yeats has been and is the greatest poet of his time," largely because of Yeats's continual development, which proved not merely his "genius" but his "character."[74] And by 1939, when Eliot prepared a lecture on "The Last Twenty Five Years of English Poetry" for an Italian lecture tour that never happened, the posthumous publication of Yeats's *Last Poems and Two Plays* (1939) had only reinforced that opinion. By this time Eliot's revaluation of Yeats had begun to form part of his own spiritual crisis, and he spoke with real passion of the way Yeats had made "a kind of purification of the language" which had become one of the major influences on younger men:

> In gaining simplicity and directness, in avoiding the poetical, in approximating to normal unaffected speech, [Yeats] has also gained intensity. . . . The change in his style . . . [is] due . . . most of all to right aims and to hard work. If, as I believe, one of the characteristics of a major poet is capacity for lifelong development, Yeats had this sign. And he must be mentioned, not only as a modern poet himself, but as one of the important influences upon the young men whose work began to appear about 1925.[75]

Finally, at the beginning of the war, wondering whether he himself would ever write again, Eliot marveled at the moral strength of the Irishman who had done his best work after sixty. Invited in 1940 to give the first Annual Yeats Lecture in Dublin, Eliot noted the "exceptional honesty and courage" that had been demanded of Yeats to grow as a poet through the years (OPP, 301). Comparing Yeats to Shakespeare, Eliot remarked upon the gumption it had taken for Yeats to recast his self-image according to the changing perspectives of successive decades of his life. Yeats, he said, had even maintained his courage when it was most difficult—in old age, with the final dissolution of death in full view. And he had resisted the temptation of public acceptance— "of becoming dignified, of becoming [a] public [figure] with only a public existence—[a coat-rack] hung with decorations and distinctions, doing, saying, and even thinking and feeling only what [he believes] the public expects of [him]" (OPP, 301–2). To Eliot, who was under so much pressure himself at the time to play the role of *maître*, this seemed an extraordinary demonstration of spirit, not less because he half suspected he could not live up to it himself.

Eliot, moreover, whether or not he realized that Yeats had in part arrived at his own ideal in the same manner, superimposed his portrait of Yeats on a portrait of Swift. Since at least the mid-twenties, Eliot had associated Swift with the realistic cynicism "of the mature and disappointed man of the world."[76] And he had habitually added that Swift's "great personality"[77] was of enormous benefit to his work. According to Eliot, Swift was one of the few figures in literature whose everyday self might enter his work without diminishing it, for his persona was but a more vivid representation of our universal condition. Swift alone could accuse mankind without celebrating himself, for he "had himself enough pettiness, as well as enough sin of pride, and lust of dominion, to be able to expose and condemn mankind by its universal pettiness and pride and vanity and ambition" (SE, 167).

But Eliot took his analysis of Swift one significant step further. Swift, he wrote, by centering his work around his "terrific personality,"[78] demonstrated a "terrible sincerity."[79] And having spent most of his life studying the meaning of sincerity, he did not use the word lightly. For him, Swift's sincerity was indeed extraordinary. Unlike Blake's, it was not egocentric, not just a vision from the center of one man's crystal. And unlike Herbert's or Lancelot Andrewes's, it was not self-effacing, not the product of a perhaps impossible contemplation of the divine. Instead of tranquility, it was full of fierceness and frenzy, and yet it was also vulnerable, with the vulnerability of a man who exposes his corruption to the world. Finally, it made it easier for us to accept the truth of Swift's ferocious moral judgments, for he always judged himself first. It was indeed a "terrible sincerity."

To return to 1942, it was *this* sincerity that seemed so lacking when Eliot re-examined "Little Gidding." He had, he sensed, smothered the anger of "East Coker" in an aesthetic structure more restrictive than "Burnt Norton" 's. And thinking both of Swift and Yeats, he felt how much he had impoverished his poem. "There are two forms of impersonality," he wrote in his Dublin lecture on Yeats, "that which is natural to the mere skilful craftsman, and that which is more and more achieved by the maturing artist. The first is that of what have have called the 'anthology piece.' . . . The second impersonality is that of the poet who, out of intense and personal experience, is able to express a general truth; retaining all the particularity of his experience, to make of it a general symbol. And the strange thing is that Yeats, having been a great craftsman of the first kind, became a great poet in the second" (OPP, 299).

"What," something in Eliot must have worried as he reread those words, "what about me?" Was it possible that he was writing the "anthology piece" of his career? In how much of his recent poetry had he become like the old men of his own Dublin lecture, who *"unless they are stirred* to something of the honesty with oneself expressed in [Yeats's] poetry, will be shocked by such a revelation of what a man really is and remains. They will refuse to believe that *they* are like that" (OPP, 302; emphasis mine).

At that moment or a moment like it, Eliot felt a desire to release himself from the expectations of his form and write like the Yeats he so much admired:

> You think it horrible that lust and rage
> Should dance attendance upon my old age;

> They were not such a plague when I was young:
> What else have I to spur me into song?[80]

Quoting those lines two years before, Eliot had claimed that Yeats's poetry is not the "personal confession of a man who differed from other men, but of a man who was essentially the same as most other men; the only difference is in the greater clarity, honesty and vigour. To what honest man, old enough, can these sentiments be entirely alien? They can be subdued and disciplined by religion, but who can say that they are dead?" (OPP, 302).

And remembering these words, Eliot made his model's voice his own. Reaching back to his original disillusion, he took strength from passages in the *Quartets* John Hayward had called "poignantly self-revealing":[81]

> Do not let me hear
> Of the wisdom of old men, but rather of their folly,
> Their fear of fear and frenzy, their fear of possession. . . .
>
> ("East Coker" II)

> So here I am, in the middle way, having had twenty years—
> Twenty years largely wasted, the years of *l'entre deux guerres*—
> Trying to learn to use words, and every attempt
> Is a wholly new start, and a different kind of failure
> Because one has only learnt to get the better of words
> For the thing one no longer has to say, or the way in which
> One is no longer disposed to say it.
>
> ("East Coker" V)

These, provoked by unflinching self-confrontation and devoid of metaphor (yet stopping short of personal confession), gave Eliot a starting point for refashioning the speech of his compound ghost. And from them he worked toward the cadences of Swift and Yeats. Swift's epitaph, *Ubi saeva indignatio ulterius cor lacerare nequit*, reverberates when the ghost speaks of "the conscious impotence of rage / At human folly, and the laceration / Of laughter at what ceases to amuse." And behind the ghost's "shame / Of motives late revealed" stands a passage of Yeats that Eliot had quoted in *After Strange Gods:*

> Things said or done long years ago,
> Or things I did not do or say
> But thought that I might say or do,
> Weigh me down, and not a day
> But something is recalled,
> My conscience or my vanity appalled.[82]

But so deeply immersed was Eliot in Yeats's work that it is probably pointless to enumerate the Yeatsian echoes here, or speak of imitation in an ordinary way. Eliot, giving us an emblem for his venture, scribbled part of the draft of "Little Gidding" on the reverse side of his Dublin lecture. At the beginning of his career, he had written of finding his poetic voice as if "under a kind of daemonic possession," [83] and now he knows how to show us what that means. Assuming "a double part," he cries and hears "another's voice cry" and speaks with the great spirit of Yeats.

What he speaks, however, bitter though it is, leads him out of the prison of himself. Confessing to his rage and his shame, he speaks with a note of personal honesty that he has found only by rejecting the problematic impersonality of most of "Little Gidding," and he speaks in the voice of a man more courageous than himself. It is thus that he is moved to see the tragedy of life with a pity not tainted with the coyness of self-pity, and, as he said about Swift's satire, to move from "pity . . . [to] a kind of purgation." [84] At that point, seeing his suppressed fury explode, feeling, even as he feels, that desiccation and guilt are not one man's alone, we understand the Purgatorial spirit of the passage. The voice of this ghost, however ferocious, is also tutelary, uplifting. And it is no accident that this is the only place in *Four Quartets* where Eliot speaks to someone else, or that someone else speaks to him. Here, in a way that the rest of "Little Gidding" refers to but never attains, we have the sense of a genuine communion—a meeting stripped of illusion and yet, "With the drawing of this Love and the voice of this Calling," filled with true generosity. How easy it would have been for Eliot to have included Yeats only to dismiss him, and how miraculous his impulse not to do so. Here truly one of the dead returns and brings Eliot with him.

Yet finally, the service is repaid in kind. Voicing the spirit of Yeats, Eliot's lines achieve an expressive power greater than anything he learned from "Vacillation" or "A Dialogue of Self and Soul" or "The Circus Animals' Desertion." Adding the rigor of Dante to the "clarity, honesty and vigour" of *Last Poems,* Eliot reaches the last pinnacle of his career, and there is no question but that the tribute he paid to Dante on the anniversary of the occasion applies to himself as well. Speaking of the trouble it cost him to produce his imitation canto, he testified that

> in this very bare and austere style, in which every word has to be "functional," the slightest vagueness or imprecision is immediately noticeable. The language has to be very direct; the line, and the single word, must be completely disciplined to the purpose of the whole; and, when you are using simple words and simple phrases, any repetition of the most common idiom, or of the most frequently needed word, becomes a glaring blemish (TCC, 129).

To this model of discipline and directness, the compound ghost of Swift, Yeats and Dante had brought Eliot in 1942. He would never surpass his success, nor, having achieved this plateau through Eliot's efforts, would twentieth-century poetry be the same. The modernist era had sung its swan song, and neither inflated dreams nor inflated despair would sound authentic again. Nor would post-modernist verse, coming back to "Little Gidding" and *Last Poems* when it was not engaged in dadaesque play, get (as of 1983) any further. For to get this far had required the sincerity of a lifetime. In the words of "Little Gidding," it was "A condition of complete simplicity / (Costing not less than everything)."

Notes

Preface

1. Introduction to *Ezra Pound: Selected Poems* (London: Faber and Gwyer, 1928; rpt. 1959), p. 19.
2. "Fifty Years of American Poetry," *The Third Book of Criticism* (New York: Farrar, Straus and Giroux, 1969), p. 314.
3. Henry James, *Partial Portraits* (1888; rpt. Ann Arbor: University of Michigan Press, 1970), p. 51.
4. "Mr. Lee Masters," *Manchester Guardian* 906 (9 October 1916), 3.
5. See, for example, the composition of *The Hollow Men* as described in chapter six, below.
6. See "Isolated Superiority," *Dial* 84.1 (January 1928), 6.
7. Letter of 10 April 1928, now in the William Force Stead Collection, Beinecke Library, Yale University.
8. *The Letters of Ezra Pound,* ed. D. D. Paige (New York: Harcourt, Brace and World, 1950), p. 40.
9. "For T. S. Eliot," *Harvard Advocate* CXXV.3 (December 1938), 17.
10. Sarah Lawall, *Critics of Consciousness: The Existential Structures of Literature* (Cambridge: Harvard University Press, 1968), pp. 267.
11. *The Arte of English Poesie,* ed. G. D. Willcock and A. Walker (Cambridge: Cambridge University Press, 1936), p. 148.
12. See Norman N. Holland, *The Dynamics of Literary Response* (New York: W. W. Norton, 1975), pp. 106, 226, 238.
13. For an anticipation of this approach, see George Bornstein, *Transformations of Romanticism in Yeats, Eliot, and Stevens* (Chicago: University of Chicago Press, 1976), pp. 132, 140, 153, 160.

1. Ghostly Selves

1. See Herbert Howarth, *Notes on Some Figures Behind T. S. Eliot* (Boston: Houghton Mifflin, 1964), p. 361.
2. See for example *The Family Reunion*, where Agatha tells Amy that Harry "will find another Harry":

> The man who returns will have to meet
> The boy who left. . . .
>
> . . . .
>
> And it will not be a very *jolly* corner.
>
> (CPP, 229)

The original manuscript made the reference even more striking by apologizing for having made an allusion.

3. *Milton Graduates Bulletin,* III.9 (November 1933), 5, 7, 6, 7.

4. Ibid., 8, 9.

5. For a jaundiced account of Eliot's difficult decision to remain in England as a poet rather than returning to Harvard's department of philosophy, see Richard Aldington's story "Stepping Heavenward" in *Soft Answers* (1932; rpt. Carbondale: Southern Illinois University Press, 1967), pp. 167–210, esp. pp. 183–85.

6. See Paul Valéry, *Le Serpent,* trans. Mark Wardle, Introduction by T. S. Eliot (London: published for the *Criterion* by R. Cobden-Sanderson, 1924), p. 12.

7. Milton address, pp. 7–8.

8. For Eliot's (often unreciprocated) admiration for Hemingway, see his "Commentary" in the *Criterion,* XII.48 (April 1933), pp. 466–73.

9. April 1910, cited in Lyndall Gordon, *Eliot's Early Years* (London: Oxford University Press, 1977), p. 33.

10. "The Post-Georgians," *Athenaeum* 4641 (11 April 1919), 171. Consciously or not, Eliot in remarking upon "the natural sin of language" was repeating Mallarmé in "Crisis in Poetry." See *Mallarmé: Selected Prose Poems, Essays and Letters,* trans. and with an Introduction by Bradford Cook (Baltimore: Johns Hopkins Press, 1956), p. 38.

11. On Emerson's search for authentic expression, see David Porter's *Emerson and Literary Change* (Cambridge: Harvard University Press, 1978), esp. chapter six: "A Breakthrough into Spaciousness."

12. For Eliot's memories of St. Louis and Annie Dunne, see the appendix, "The Eliot Family and St. Louis," to T. S. Eliot, *American Literature and the American Language* (St. Louis: Department of English, Washington University, 1953).

13. From "American Literature and the American Language" (printed without "The Eliot Family and St. Louis"), TCC, 44.

14. *My Friends When Young: The Memoirs of Brigit Patmore,* ed. with an Introduction by Derek Patmore (London: Heinemann, 1968), pp. 84, 87.

15. Conrad Aiken, *Ushant: An Essay* (Cleveland: World Publishing, 1952; rpt. 1962), p. 233.

16. "A Sceptical Patrician," *Athenaeum* 4647 (23 May 1919), 361.

17. Eliot to John Quinn, 6 January 1919, quoted in *Facs.,* xvi. On the subject of Eliot's fear of failure, see also his letter to Conrad Aiken of 30 September 1914 (in the Aiken Collection of Huntington Library, Pasadena, Calif.), where he laments that all his good stuff had been done three years previously, before he started to worry. According to the letter, Eliot sometimes thought it would be better to be just a clerk in a post office with nothing to worry about except the consciousness of having made a failure of one's life.

18. Letter of 26 January. See *Facs.,* xvi.

19. *A Sermon,* preached in Magdalene College Chapel, 7 March 1948 (Cambridge: Cambridge University Press, 1948), p. 5.

20. See Eliot's introduction to Josef Pieper, *Leisure: The Basis of Culture* (London: Faber and Faber, 1952).

21. "Style and Thought," review of *Mysticism and Logic* by Bertrand Russell, *Nation*, XXII.25 (23 March 1918), 768.
22. "A Contemporary Thomist," review of *Epistemology* by P. Coffey, *New Statesman* X.247 (29 December 1917), 312.
23. For more about Eliot and Bergson, see below, chapter two, p. 18.
24. See Gordon, *Eliot's Early Years*, pp. 40–41.
25. My paraphrase is a composite of Eliot's discussion of Laforgue in his 1926 Clark Lectures and a revised version of the same text delivered as the Turnbull Lectures at Johns Hopkins University in 1933. The second and a copy of the first can be found in the Houghton Library, Harvard University. Eliot repeated some of his remarks in a published essay on Baudelaire. See FLA, 95.
26. See KE, 15. After an introductory paragraph, the text begins, "Bradley uses the term 'experience' and the term 'feeling' almost interchangeably. . . ."
27. See above, p. 5. Also Eliot's distinction, made in *The Cocktail Party*, between "The self that wills—he is a feeble creature" and "the obstinate, the tougher self; who does not speak" (CPP, 326; quoted in full on p. 43 below).
28. UPUC, 34. The full citation reads as follows:

    [In adolescence] the poetry of a single poet, invades the youthful consciousness and assumes complete possession for a time. We do not really see it as something with an existence outside ourselves; much as in our youthful experiences of love, we do not so much see the person as infer the existence of some outside object which sets in motion these new and delightful feelings in which we are absorbed. The frequent result is an outburst of scribbling which we may call imitation, so long as we are aware of the meaning of the word "imitation" which we employ. It is not a deliberate choice of a poet to mimic, but writing under a kind of daemonic possession by one poet.

    Eliot later confirmed to Edward Greene that he was referring to himself and Laforgue. See Edward J. H. Greene, *T. S. Eliot et la France* (Paris: Boivin, 1951), p. 19.
29. "Reflections on Contemporary Poetry IV," *Egoist* VI.3 (July 1919), 39. Again, the whole passage is worth quoting:

    There is a close analogy between the sort of experience which develops a man and the sort of experience which develops a writer. . . . This relation is a feeling of profound kinship, or rather of a peculiar personal intimacy, with another, probably a dead author. It may overcome us suddenly, on or after long acquaintance; it is certainly a crisis; and when a young writer is seized with his first passion of this sort he may be changed, metamorphosed almost, within a few weeks even, from a bundle of second-hand sentiments into a person. . . . It is a cause of development, like personal relations in life. Like personal intimacies in life, it may and probably will pass, but it will be ineffaceable.

30. In a review of Edgar Lee Masters in 1916, Eliot told his readers that a successful dramatic poem must both be "detached" from its author and also "appear as an element in a supposed autobiographic situation." ("Mr. Lee Masters," *Manchester Guardian* 906 [9 October 1916], 3.) Later he confessed that "Prufrock" was even more autobiographical than that. In 1962 he said that "Prufrock" "was partly a dramatic creation of a man of about 40 . . . and partly an expression of feeling of my own." He added: "I

always feel that dramatic characters who seem living creations have something of the author in them." ("T. S. Eliot . . . An Interview," *Grantite
Review* XXIV.3 [1962], 17.)

31. Without risking the waters of psychoanalysis, it should be pointed out that
the way Eliot's amiably piercing gaze resembles his mother's in the snap-
shot of their 1921 reunion (she is next to him) suggests whose eyes (now
internalized) "fix you in a formulated phrase." This kind of self-
consciousness, moreover, seems to have run in the family. In an unpublished autobiographical memoir, now in the Washington University Archives (St. Louis), Eliot's father remembers how he felt "not . . . fear, but
reverential awe" for *his* father, "whose word was law and gospel," and how
his father's "eyes were magnificent, and one felt that he could read one's
inmost thoughts." (The memoir ends on another familiar note: "I have
spoken frequently of Father but have said little of My Mother. I could not
do so. Words fail to do her justice. I shall never get to heaven on my own
merit, but I know that I shall finally land there because she will never be
happy until I am with her.")

32. See Laforgue's "Pétition":

> Simple et sans foi comme un bonjour.

> (Simple and faithless as a "good day.")

A full discussion of the Laforguian elements of "La Figlia" can be found
in Greene, *T. S. Eliot et la France*, pp. 44–49.

33. "Beyle and Balzac," *Athenaeum* 4648 (30 May 1919), 393.

2. "The pathology of rhetoric"

1. The phrase "romantic year" comes from Eliot's reminiscence in the *Paris
Review*. See Kay Dick, ed., *Writers at Work: The Paris Review Interviews* (London: Penguin Books, 1972), p. 121.

2. See Lyndall Gordon, *Eliot's Early Years* (London: Oxford University Press,
1977) p. 38.

3. On Eliot and Dostoevsky, see John C. Pope, "Prufrock and Raskolnikov
Again: A Letter from T. S. Eliot," *American Literature* XVIII.4 (January
1947), 319–21. Also Eliot's remarks on Dostoevsky in "Beyle and Balzac,"
Athenaeum 4648 (30 May 1919), 392–93, and "London Letter," *Dial* LXXIII.3
(September 1922), 330–31—both discussed in chapter four. On Eliot and
the *camelots du roi*, see George Watson, "The State of Letters: Quest for a
Frenchman," *Sewanee Review* 84.3 (Summer 1976), 469–71. Watson quotes
Eliot's remark that "in 1910 I remember the *camelots* cheering the *cuirassiers*
who were sent to disperse them . . . all the time they were trying to
stampede their horses."

4. Letter of September 30, 1914, Aiken Collection, Huntington Library, Pasadena, California.

5. The first citation is from *Writers at Work*, p. 120. The second is from Eliot's
unpublished lecture "Tradition in the Practice of Poetry," now in the Eliot
collection of the Houghton Library, Harvard University.

6. See "What France Means to You," *La France Libre*, 15 June 1944, p. 94.

7. *A Sermon,* preached in Magdalene College Chapel, 7 March 1948 (Cambridge: Cambridge University Press, 1948), p. 5.

8. Eliot's own word, used about Bergson in the announcement to the last of his six Oxford Extension Lectures on Modern French Literature, delivered in the winter of 1916. See Ronald Schuchard, "T. S. Eliot as an Extension Lecturer, 1916–1919," *Review of English Studies* XXV.98 (1974), 167.

9. On the connections between Bergson and Bradley, see Sanford Schwartz, "The Relative Sublime: Pound, Eliot, Richards, and the Making of Modern English Poetics" (Ph.D. Diss., Princeton, 1977).

10. *The Diary of Virginia Woolf: Volume Two, 1920–1924,* ed. Anne Olivier Bell (New York: Harcourt Brace Jovanovich, 1978), p. 68.

11. See Gordon, *Eliot's Early Years,* p. 143.

12. See his letter of 4 March 1918 to John Quinn in the Manuscripts Division of the New York Public Library.

13. Arthur Symons, *The Symbolist Movement in Literature* (1899; rev. 1908). I quote from a 1958 reprint, ed. Richard Ellmann (New York: E. P. Dutton), pp. 5, 46.

14. Introduction to *The Oxford Book of Modern Verse: 1892–1935* (New York: Oxford University Press, 1936), pp. xii, ix.

15. From "Prolegomena" (1912). I cite from Pound's *Literary Essays,* ed. T. S. Eliot (New York: New Directions, 1968), p. 11.

16. From "Ezra Pound," originally published in *Poetry* LXVIII (September 1946). I quote from the reprint in Walter Sutton, ed., *Ezra Pound: A Collection of Critical Essays* (Englewood Cliffs: Prentice-Hall, 1963), p. 17.

17. For Yeats's notion of rhetoric, see Richard Ellmann, *The Identity of Yeats* (New York: Oxford University Press, 1954; rpt. 1968), pp. 132–45. For Pound's, see Ronald Bush, *The Genesis of Ezra Pound's Cantos* (Princeton: Princeton University Press, 1976), pp. 144–58.

18. Letter in the T. S. Eliot Collection of the Humanities Research Center, University of Texas, Austin. Undated, but possibly 8 October 1922. Eliot had more than once been reminded of his stiffness at Harvard. On an undergraduate essay he wrote about Kipling in 1908, for example, Charles Townsend Copeland had cautioned him to be "on your guard against becoming pompous, orotund, and voluminous." See J. Donald Adams, *Copey of Harvard: A Biography of Charles Townsend Copeland* (Boston: Houghton Mifflin, 1960), p. 163.

    Nor, as Eliot knew, was it only his writing that was at issue. In *Downhill All the Way,* Leonard Woolf remembers Virginia saying, "The odd thing about Eliot . . . is that his eyes are lively and youthful when the cast of his face and the shape of his sentences are formal and even heavy." Woolf adds on his own, "In conversation it was his brain that was disappointing, so much more rigid and less powerful than I had expected from the poems, and with so little play of mind. He was himself aware of this and disappointed in himself, for, in describing a week-end with Ottoline in Garsington, he said: 'And I behaved like a priggish pompous little ass.'" (*Downhill All the Way: An Autobiography of the Years 1919 to 1939* [New York: Harcourt Brace Jovanovich, 1967], p. 108.)

19. See TCC, 11; SE, 333; and p. xvii of Eliot's Introduction to G. Wilson Knight, *The Wheel of Fire* (London: Oxford University Press, 1930).

20. Eliot's figure comes from *Madame Bovary*. For a discussion of this passage and Eliot's "theme of articulate inarticulateness," see William Harmon, "T. S. Eliot's Raids on the Inarticulate," *PMLA* 91.3 (May 1976), 450–59.

21. "Reflections on Contemporary Poetry I," *Egoist* IV.8 (September 1917), 118.

22. "Reflections on Contemporary Poetry III," *Egoist* IV.10 (November 1917), 151.

23. See p. 8 of Eliot's Introduction to *Ezra Pound: Selected Poems* (London: Faber and Gwyer, 1928; rpt. Faber and Faber, 1959).

24. The phrases quoted are from "Some Notes on the Blank Verse of Christopher Marlowe," first printed in *Art and Letters* for 1919 and later collected in *The Sacred Wood* (see SW, 88). The interested reader can find discussions of rhetoric and Elizabethan literature in three other essays of the same year: "The New Elizabethans and the Old" (the April *Athenaeum*), "Whether Rostand Had Something About Him" (the July *Athenaeum*, reprinted with revision as "'Rhetoric' and Poetic Drama" in *The Sacred Wood*), and "Ben Jonson" (the November *TLS*, reprinted in *The Sacred Wood*).

25. From "A Romantic Patrician," first printed in the *Athenaeum* in May 1919 and reprinted with revision as "A Romantic Aristocrat" in *The Sacred Wood*, where the citation appears on pp. 30–31.

26. "Harold Monro," *Criterion* XI.45 (July 1932), 590; *Writers at Work*, 119.

27. See *A Survey of Modernist Poetry* (London: A. P. Watt, 1927).

28. For this and later citations, see "A Sceptical Patrician," *Athenaeum* 4647 (23 May 1919), 361–62.

29. Cf. Eliot's remarks about his response to Chapman's elevated language in UPUC, 147.

30. The most thorough treatment is probably still Robert F. Goheen's essay "Burbank with a Baedeker: The Third Stanza," *Sewanee Review* 61.1 (Winter 1953), 109–19.

31. From Eliot's lecture notes for English 26 ("English Literature from 1890 to the Present Day"), delivered at Harvard in the spring of 1933. The notes are now in the Harvard Archives.

32. See stanza 25.

33. I quote from Leon Edel's *Henry James: Selected Fiction* (New York: Dutton, 1964), pp. 330–31.

34. See above, note 24.

35. *Athenaeum* 4656 (25 July 1919), 665. Reading this passage, one associates Eliot with Coleridge in his debate with Wordsworth over the importance of natural speech. Eliot himself reflects on the controversy in UPUC, 71.

36. "Rostand," 665–66.

37. "Marivaux," *Art and Letters* II.2 (Spring 1919), 84.

3. "I would meet you upon this honestly": "Gerontion"

1. The citations in this paragraph are from Eliot's review of *The Education of Henry Adams* ("A Sceptical Patrician"), *Athenaeum* 4647 (23 May 1919), 361–62. On the evidence of letters in the Manuscripts Division of the New York Public Library, Eliot sent the manuscript of "Gerontion" to his friend and patron John Quinn in New York enclosed in a letter of 9 July 1919, and he instructed Quinn to put the poem at the head of the volume of poems

to be forwarded to Knopf. Eliot wrote the poem, then, in the same spring that he wrote "A Sceptical Patrician." He in fact mentions Adams in the letter accompanying the "Gerontion" manuscript, and tells Quinn that Adams is a type he *ought* to know better than any other.

2. This earlier version of "Gerontion" exists in the form of a typescript annotated by Ezra Pound in the Berg Collection of the New York Public Library.

3. *Inferno* XXXIII.122–23. Unless otherwise indicated, translations of Dante are from the Temple Classics edition (London: J. M. Dent and Sons, 1899) Eliot himself consulted.

4. Eliot's words appear in SE, 58. See Hugh Kenner, *The Invisible Poet: T. S. Eliot* (New York: Citadel, 1959), p. 140.

5. See CP, 263, and OPP, 142–43.

6. See CPP, 362, 360.

7. See A. D. Moody, *Thomas Stearns Eliot: Poet* (Cambridge: Cambridge University Press, 1979), pp. 68–69.

8. Sherna S. Vinograd, "The Accidental: A Clue to Structure in Eliot's Poetry," *Accent* 9.4 (Summer 1949), 234.

4. "The poet's inner world of nightmare"

1. The citations in this paragraph are taken from "Reflections on Contemporary Poetry I," *Egoist* IV.8 (September 1917), 118–19. (For an earlier discussion of this essay, see chapter two.)

2. T. S. Eliot, ed., *Literary Essays* (New York: New Directions, 1968), p. 5.

3. "Introduction" to *Marianne Moore: Selected Poems* (New York: Macmillan, 1935), p. xi.

4. See, for example, J. Hillis Miller, *Poets of Reality* (Cambridge: Harvard University Press, 1969).

5. For Eliot's own construing of these matters in Bradley, see KE, esp. pp. 146–52.

6. Hugh Kenner, *The Invisible Poet: T. S. Eliot* (New York: Citadel, 1959), p. 55.

7. Gourmont provided the epigraphs for and stood as the principal model for the opening essay of *The Sacred Wood*, "The Perfect Critic." In his preface to the 1928 edition, Eliot confessed that in writing *The Sacred Wood* he had been "much stimulated and much helped by the writings of Remy de Gourmont" (SW, viii). He confirmed the statement on several subsequent occasions. In *La Nouvelle Revue Française* for 1 May 1922, for example, he said that he personally could speak about the influence of France on his generation: "Je sais combien forte a été l'influence de Rémy de Gourmont. . . . Gourmont est l'un des guides qui nous firent étudier Flaubert" ("I know how strong the influence of Remy de Gourmont has been. . . . Gourmont is one of the guides who led us to study Flaubert"; "Lettre d'Angleterre," p. 260). In his 1963 introduction to UPUC, he made the same admission in a different mood: "My earliest critical essays, dating from a period when I was somewhat under the influence of Ezra Pound's enthusiasm for Remy de Gourmont, came to seem to me the product of immaturity" (UPUC, 10).

For previous discussion of the presence of Gourmont in Eliot's work, especially concerning the question of impersonality, see Edward J. H. Greene, *T. S. Eliot et la France* (Paris: Boivin, 1951); Glenn S. Burne, *Remy de Gourmont: His Ideas and Influence in England and America* (Carbondale: Southern Illinois University Press, 1963); Mowbray Allan, *T. S. Eliot's Impersonal Theory of Poetry* (Lewisburg, Pa.: Bucknell University Press, 1974); and Richard Sieburth, *Instigations: Ezra Pound and Remy de Gourmont* (Cambridge: Harvard University Press, 1978). An even more penetrating discussion of the subject can be found in Sanford Schwartz, "The Relative Sublime: Pound, Eliot, Richards, and the Making of Modernist Poetics" (Ph.D. diss., Princeton, 1977).

8. Pound's essay on Remy de Gourmont first appeared in the *Little Review* for 1919 and is reprinted in his *Literary Essays*, pp. 339–58. For the citation in question, see p. 353.

9. From Pound's 1915 obituary essay on Gourmont, collected in William Cookson, ed., *Ezra Pound: Selected Prose 1909–1965* (London: Faber and Faber, 1973). See p. 387.

10. From "Anonymity: An Inquiry" (1925), collected in *Two Cheers for Democracy* (1938). I cite from a republication (New York: Harcourt Brace and World, 1951), pp. 83–84. Forster's "anonymity" is actually closer to Emerson's "oversoul" or Shelley's "principle of poetry" than to what Eliot and Gourmont meant by "impersonality." ("Poetry," Shelley wrote, "and the principle of self of which money is the visible incarnation, are the God and Mammon of the world.") That is, while in Eliot and Gourmont the deeper self is radically individual, in Shelley, Emerson, Forster (and, for that matter, Lawrence) it is part of divine creative energy. Virginia Woolf gives still a third orientation when she contrasts the center of a novel to the "I" of self-reflection, the latter being "a convenient term for somebody who has no real being." See *A Room of One's Own*, 1929. I cite from the 1957 Harcourt Brace edition, p. 4.

11. Sanford Schwartz, for example, points out that Eliot's pejorative definition of "the undigested 'idea' or philosophy, the idea-emotion" (SW, 67) corresponds to Gourmont's remark in *Le Problème du style* that "if, instead of sensations, material memories, the brain retains only the imprint of emotion, or if the perception of the senses has been rapidly transformed into an abstract notion, or into an emotional idea, then art is no longer possible. . . . One can therefore generalize and divide writers again into two classes: the sensorials and the ideo-emotives; or in other words, the plastics and the sentimentals" ("The Relative Sublime," p. 121).

12. For discussion, see Sieburth, *Instigations*, pp. 54–55.

13. From "Eeldrop and Appleplex, I," *Little Review* IV.1 (May 1917), 7–11. For a counterpart in Gourmont's writing, see Glenn S. Burne, ed., *Remy de Gourmont: Selected Writings* (Ann Arbor: University of Michigan Press, 1966), p. 115.

14. *Dial* LXXII.5 (May 1922), 512. Cf. Gourmont, *Selected Writings*, p. 122.

15. Eliot is referring to the passage in *Paradiso* I he quotes in "Dante" (1929), in which Dante the pilgrim says (I quote Eliot's translation): "Gazing on her, so I became within, as did Glaucus, on tasting of the grass which made him sea-fellow of the other gods. To transcend humanity may not be told

in words, wherefore let the instance suffice for him for whom the experience is reserved by Grace" (SE, 225–26).

16. "Notes on the Way," *Time and Tide* XVI.3 (19 January 1935), 89. Glenn Burne translates Eliot's citation from Gourmont this way:

> Life is a process of sloughing-off. The proper end of man's activities is to scour his personality, to cleanse it of all the stains deposited by education, to free it of all the imprints left by adolescent admirations. . . .
>
> Flaubert incorporated all his sensibility into his works. . . . Outside his books wherein he transfused himself drop by drop to the dregs, Flaubert was not very interesting (*Gourmont: Selected Writings,* pp. 124–25).

17. *Selected Writings,* p. 124.
18. See Allan, *T. S. Eliot's Impersonal Theory,* pp. 61–66.
19. See above, note 7.
20. *Selected Writings,* pp. 181–82.
21. See KE, 112–40, esp. pp. 124–26.
22. My citations are taken from "The Noh and the Image," *Egoist* IV.7 (August 1917), 102–3.
23. "The New Elizabethans and the Old," *Athenaeum* 4640 (4 April 1919), 135.
24. See above, p. 43.
25. In "The Bible as Scripture and Literature" (1932), now in the Houghton Library, Harvard University.
26. Out of this connection between poetry and dreams, Eliot formulated a theory that would become, in the form of the "intentional fallacy," one of the doctrines of New Criticism: because poetry arises from an area of the self beneath will and intention, "there may be much more in a poem than the author was aware of. . . . the ambiguities may be due to the fact that the poem means more, not less, than ordinary speech can communicate" (OPP, 23).
27. "John Dryden—II. Dryden the Dramatist," *Listener* V.119 (22 April 1931), 681, emphasis mine.
28. "Beyle and Balzac," *Athenaeum* 4648 (30 May 1919), 392, emphasis mine. See also Eliot's "London Letter" in the *Dial* LXXIII.3 (September 1922), 331.
29. Allen Tate later took Eliot's hint and wrote a brilliant essay about the scene. See "The Hovering Fly," in *The Man of Letters and the Modern World: Selected Essays 1928–1955* (Cleveland and New York: Meridian, 1955), pp. 146–61.

5. "Unknown terror and mystery": *The Waste Land*

1. See above, chapter one, note 17.
2. *The Autobiography of Bertrand Russell: 1914–1944* (Boston: Little, Brown, 1968), p. 64.
3. Ibid., p. 61. The story of Eliot's "pseudo-honeymoon" is also Russell's, as recalled in Lyndall Gordon, *Eliot's Early Years* (Oxford: Oxford University Press, 1977), p. 76.
4. Cited by Richard Ellmann in "The First *Waste Land*," in A. W. Litz, ed., *Eliot in His Time* (Princeton: Princeton University Press, 1973), p. 61.
5. *Facs.,* xvi.

6. Ibid., xviii.

7. Ibid., xxi.

8. Ibid., xxii. On Vittoz, see Harry Trosman, "T. S. Eliot and *The Waste Land:* Psychopathological Antecedents and Transformations," *Archives of General Psychiatry* 30.5 (May 1974), 709–17.

9. *Facs.,* x (emphasis mine).

10. Letter of 21 September 1922, in the Manuscripts Division of the New York Public Library.

11. See the "Prefatory Note" to the reprinting of Aiken's 1923 "An Anatomy of Melancholy" in Allen Tate, ed., *T. S. Eliot: The Man and His Work* (New York: Delta, 1966), p. 195.

12. Review of *The Name and Nature of Poetry* by A. E. Housman, *Criterion* XIII.50 (October 1933), 154.

13. OPP, 107. For discussion, see above, chapter one.

14. See Grover Smith, "The Meaning of *The Waste Land,*" *Mosaic* 6.1 (1972), 127–41, and Hugh Kenner, "The Urban Apocalypse," in Litz, *Eliot in His Time,* pp. 23–49.

15. I cite from Eliot's typed version of a holograph manuscript. See *Facs.,* pp. 42–43 and 36–37. Lyndall Gordon dates the holograph 1917 or 1918 in *Eliot's Early Years,* p. 95.

16. This corresponds to the way Anthony Cronin remembers Eliot explaining the origins of the poem. As far back as 1918, Eliot told Cronin, he had been meditating "a certain sort of poem about the contemporary world." See "A Conversation with T. S. Eliot about the Connection Between *Ulysses* and *The Waste Land,*" in the *Irish Times* for 16 June 1972, p. 10.

17. See *Facs.,* 31.

18. SW, 58 (emphasis mine). Note that Eliot uses the word "personal" here in the special pejorative sense that Gourmont had dissociated (see above, chapter four).

19. See the discussion of *images trouvailles* in chapter four. Conrad Aiken goes further and suggests that Eliot, though he believed his work was "pure calculation of effect," was actually indulging himself in "selfdeception." See Joseph Killorin, ed., *Selected Letters of Conrad Aiken* (New Haven: Yale University Press, 1978), pp. 185–86.

20. Eliot first recorded many of these impressions (including his visit to Magnus Martyr on a dreary lunch hour, his living through a "hot rainless spring" and his witnessing an outbreak of flu that "leaves extreme dryness and a bitter taste in the mouth") in 1921 "London Letters" for the *Dial* and the *Nouvelle Revue Française.* A. Walton Litz discusses these letters and their provenance in "*The Waste Land* Fifty Years After" (see *Eliot in His Time,* pp. 13–17), but concludes that they are finally less important for the poem than the reading which shaped Eliot's imagination: Pound, Bradley, James, Conrad, Frazer and Joyce. I would agree that, in themselves, these impressions are only "raw materials," but hesitate to go further. From his first awareness of them to the time they assumed their place in his completed poem, Eliot's privileged moments were shaped as much by the sea-world of his non-literary sensibility as by any of his literary models.

21. As we know from Valerie Eliot's notes to the *Facsimile,* Eliot sketched "Marie" in "The Burial of the Dead" from a woman he had met and shaped some

of "The Game of Chess" from his own conversations with Vivien. See *Facs.*, 126.

22. See above, note 10. Another note in the *Facsimile* explains that the last dialogue of "A Game of Chess" was modeled after the words of Eliot's maid, Ellen Kellond (p. 127).

23. See the epigraphs to this chapter and SW, 115.

24. From "Learning from the Beatles," in *The Performing Self: Compositions and Decompositions in the Language of Contemporary Life* (New York: Oxford University Press, 1971), p. 137.

25. *Autobiography*, p. 7. The full passage is worth quoting: "After seeing troop trains departing from Waterloo, I used to have strange visions of London as a place of unreality. I used in imagination to see the bridges collapse and sink, and the whole great city vanish like a morning mist. Its inhabitants began to seem like hallucinations, and I would wonder whether the world in which I thought I had lived was a mere product of my own febrile nightmares. . . . I spoke of this to T. S. Eliot, who put it into *The Waste Land*."

26. See "Eeldrop and Appleplex I," originally in the May 1917 *Little Review*, reprinted in Margaret Anderson, ed., *The Little Review Anthology* (New York: Horizon, 1953), p. 104: "In Gopsum Street a man murders his mistress."

27. Manuscript in the Berg Collection of the New York Public Library.

28. See Hugh Kenner, *T. S. Eliot: The Invisible Poet* (New York: Citadel, 1959), pp. 161 ff.

29. See chapter two, note 18.

30. CPP, 342 (emphasis mine). For another discussion of this passage, see Gordon, *Eliot's Early Years*, p. 106.

31. My gesture toward *Finnegans Wake* is deliberate. As Margot Norris has argued, much of the opaqueness of that supremely difficult work has to do with how it mimes the way repressed material is approached in a nightmare. See Margot Norris, *The Decentered Universe of Finnegans Wake* (Baltimore: The Johns Hopkins University Press, 1974).

32. See, for example, Donald Davie, "Mr. Eliot," in *The Poet in the Imaginary Museum* (Manchester: Carcanet, 1977), pp. 117–21; Denis Donoghue, " 'The Word within a Word,' " in A. D. Moody, ed., *The Waste Land in Different Voices* (London: Edward Arnold, 1974), pp. 185–202; M. L. Rosenthal, "*The Waste Land* as an Open Structure," in Linda Wagner, ed., *T. S. Eliot: A Collection of Criticism* (New York: McGraw-Hill, 1974), pp. 37–48; C. K. Stead, *The New Poetic: Yeats to Eliot* (New York: Harper and Row, 1966), esp. pp. 148–67; and even, in a quirky way, chapter four ("A Dialectical Reading of *The Waste Land*") of Anne C. Bolgan, *What the Thunder Really Said: A Retrospective Essay on the Making of "The Waste Land"* (Montreal: McGill–Queen's University Press, 1973).

33. See above, chapter one, note 33.

34. See above, chapter one, note 10.

35. But see Cleanth Brooks, *Modern Poetry and the Tradition* (Chapel Hill: North Carolina University Press, 1939; rpt. New York: Oxford University Press, 1965), p. 154, and A. D. Moody, *Thomas Stearns Eliot: Poet* (Cambridge: Cambridge University Press, 1979), p. 292.

36. See above, note 10.

37. Trosman, "T. S. Eliot and *The Waste Land*," 716. I have corrected the accuracy of Trosman's first and restored the full text of Trosman's abbreviated second citation. The first comes from Eliot's essay on Pascal (see SE, 358) and is reproduced in *Facs.*, p. 129. The second comes from UPUC, 144–45.

38. Trosman, "T. S. Eliot and *The Waste Land*," 717.

39. See the Litz and Kenner essays in Litz, *Eliot in His Time*.

40. "Introduction" to *Ezra Pound: Selected Poems* (London: Faber and Gwyer, 1928; rpt. 1973), pp. 15–16.

41. Ibid., p. 19.

42. From D. W. Harding, "What the Thunder Said," in Moody, *The Waste Land in Different Voices*, p. 27.

43. "Ezra Pound" (1946). I cite from a reprint in Walter Sutton, ed., *Ezra Pound: A Collection of Critical Essays* (Englewood Cliffs: Prentice-Hall, 1963), p. 19. In another place Eliot refers to the unfinished *Waste Land* as a "mess": see "From T. S. Eliot," in *The Cantos of Ezra Pound: Some Testimonies* (New York: Farrar and Rinehart, 1933), pp. 16–17.

44. It may also be true, as Trosman suggests, that Pound served as both father-confessor and "narcissistic extension" for Eliot, continuing the role that Eliot's therapist Vittoz had so recently played in Lausanne. See Trosman, "T. S. Eliot and *The Waste Land*," 715.

45. "London Letter," *Dial* LXXIII.3 (September 1922), 331.

46. From *Belphegor* (1918). I cite from the English translation by J. I. Lawson introduced by Irving Babbitt (New York, 1929), p. 129. For Eliot's praise of the book, see "The Idea of a Literary Review," *New Criterion* IV.1 (January 1926), 5.

47. "Ulysses, Order, and Myth," *Dial* LXX.5 (November 1923), 483 (emphasis mine).

48. "The Urban Apocalypse," p. 43.

49. *"The Waste Land:* Fifty Years After," p. 6.

50. See below, chapter six, pp. 94–95.

51. See below, chapter six, note 31.

52. See above, note 10.

53. *Facs.*, 129.

54. Eliot's pedantic note to *The Waste Land* is in part humorous, but it is not fundamentally misleading. As John Soldo has pointed out ("The Tempering of T. S. Eliot: 1888–1915," Ph.D. diss., Harvard, 1972), Eliot used a copy of Chapman's *Handbook of Birds of Eastern North America* he received on his fourteenth birthday to identify the hermit-thrush in the neighborhood of the Eliot family summer home on Cape Ann. See Soldo, pp. 182–84.

55. OPP, 26. From "The Music of Poetry" (1942).

56. *Selected Letters*, p. 185. Aiken wrote: "But the skill in the use of time and sound increasingly impresses me, in the later things—Ash Wednesday, for example—there was never a more beautiful gibberish of language, surely? the whole, or detailed, meaning almost nil, but the *effect* lovely."

6. New Life: *The Hollow Men*

1. In their early and influential studies of Eliot, F. R. Leavis and F. O. Matthiessen considered *The Hollow Men* as a pendant to *The Waste Land,* and their conclusions are still accepted by many critics. In 1956, for example, Grover Smith wrote that *The Hollow Men* is an "extension of [*The Waste Land's*] design of quest and failure"; and as recently as 1976 Stephen Spender called the poem a "coda" to its more famous predecessor. See F. R. Leavis, *New Bearings in English Poetry* (1932; rpt. Ann Arbor: University of Michigan Press, 1964); F. O. Matthiessen, *The Achievement of T. S. Eliot: An Essay on the Nature of Poetry* (1935; rev. and enl. ed. Oxford: Oxford University Press, 1972); Grover Smith, *T. S. Eliot's Poetry and Plays: A Study in Sources and Meaning* (1950; rpt. Chicago: University of Chicago Press, 1965), p. 104; and Stephen Spender, *T. S. Eliot* (1975; rpt. New York: Viking, 1976), p. 123.

   But at least since Helen Gardner's *The Art of T. S. Eliot* (1950; rpt. New York: E. P. Dutton, 1959), other readers have interpreted the poem as an expression of Eliot's "new theme of rebirth" and have pointed to the cluster of images it borrows from Dante's *Purgatorio*. The present essay agrees with Gardner and her successors, but would extend the discourse beyond the question of how *The Hollow Men* is to be placed in Eliot's turn toward religion. Like Hugh Kenner in *The Invisible Poet: T. S. Eliot* (1959; rpt. New York: Citadel, 1964), I wish to relate Eliot's changing themes to the development of his style. And like Elisabeth Schneider in *T. S. Eliot: The Pattern in the Carpet* (Berkeley and Los Angeles: University of California Press, 1975), I entertain the possibility that *The Hollow Men* "never quite crystallized" into a unified work of art (p. 106).
2. *The Journals of Arnold Bennett 1921–1928,* ed. Newman Flower (London: Cassell and Company, 1933), p. 52 (entry for 10 September 1924).
3. For Eliot's reading of Aristophanes, see D. D. Paige, ed., *The Letters of Ezra Pound 1907–1941* (New York: Harvest, 1950), p. 171. Eliot's essays are discussed by Kenner in *The Invisible Poet: T. S. Eliot,* pp. 197–221, and by Carol H. Smith in *T. S. Eliot's Dramatic Theory and Practice* (Princeton: Princeton University Press, 1963), *passim.* One of the essays was called "The Beating of a Drum"; it appeared in *Nation and Athenaeum* XXXIV.1 (6 October 1923), 11–12.
4. The sketches were first published in 1926–27 but written much earlier. See Smith, *Eliot's Dramatic Theory,* p. 51.
5. For example, Eliot's 1952 statement to a French audience that "j'ai toujours trouvé que . . . ce qui me plaisait . . . était quelque chose de différent de ce que j'avais pensé devoir écrire" ("I have always found that the work that pleased me . . . was not what I had originally planned to write"); "Charybde et Scylla: lourdeur et frivolité," *Annales du Centre Universitaire Méditerranéen* V (1951/52), 71.) See also OPP, 22.
6. See Paul Valéry, *Le Serpent,* trans. Mark Wardle, Introduction by T. S. Eliot (London: published for the *Criterion* by R. Cobden-Sanderson, 1924), pp. 7–15. Eliot's essay is briefly alluded to by James Torrens in "T. S. Eliot and the Austere Poetics of Valéry," *Comparative Literature* XXIII.1 (Winter 1971), pp. 1–17.

7. Introduction to *Le Serpent,* p. 8.

8. Only the third lecture was ever published, in a shortened form and in French translation. See "Deux attitudes mystiques: Dante et Donne," *Chroniques* 3 (1927), 149–73. Two copies of the Clark Lectures exist—a typescript at King's College, Cambridge, and a carbon at Houghton Library, Harvard University. At the time of this writing, Mrs. Eliot is preparing the entire series for publication.

9. Eliot said in his introduction to the lectures that he was planning to write a book on "The School of Donne" that would be one part of a trilogy to be called "The Disintegration of the Intellect." (The other volumes were to be entitled "Elizabethan Drama" and "The Sons of Ben.")

10. From the third lecture. In the second, Eliot was explicit about the influence of T. E. Hulme on his thinking. It was Hulme, Eliot said, "the most fertile mind of my generation, and one of the glories of [Cambridge] University," who first alerted "us" to the differences between the minds of the thirteenth and nineteenth centuries.

11. From the third lecture. In the fourth, Eliot added: "The interest of Dante lies in the idea or the feeling to be conveyed; the image always makes this idea or feeling more intelligible. In Donne, the interest is dispersed, it may be the ingenuity of conveying the idea by that particular image; or the image itself may be more difficult than the idea; or it may be in the *compulsion,* rather than in the *discovery* of resemblances."

12. Eliot's fascination with the *Vita Nuova* may well have been provoked and guided by Charles Maurras, whose 1912 essay on Dante had been reissued in 1920 as *Le Conseil de Dante.* See James Torrens, "Charles Maurras and Eliot's 'New Life,' " *PMLA* 89.2 (March 1974), pp. 312–32.

13. Eliot on Cavalcanti in the third Clark lecture. Interestingly, Eliot approximates Pound in his description of Trecento poetry and in his illustrations from Cavalcanti and Richard of St. Victor.

14. Rossetti's translation, which was on the recommended reading list Eliot gave out at the end of his first Clark Lecture. I cite from Dante Gabriel Rossetti, ed. and trans., *Dante and His Circle with the Italian Poets Preceding Him* (Boston: Roberts Brothers, 1887), p. 77.

15. See ibid., pp. 43–44.

16. The title of chapter three in Singleton's *An Essay on the Vita Nuova* (Cambridge: Harvard University Press, 1949).

17. Eliot published "Song to the Opherian" in the first (April 1921) number of Wyndham Lewis's *Tyro* under the pseudonym of Gus Krutzsch. The version that was part of the working draft of *The Waste Land* appears in *Facs.,* 98–99.

A nearly complete account of the permutations of material Eliot tried out before settling on the final version of *The Hollow Men* can be found in C. K. Stead, *The New Poetic: Yeats to Eliot* (1964; rpt. New York: Harper and Row, 1966), pp. 168 ff. (One element is omitted: the solo appearance of what became *The Hollow Men* I in *Commerce* III [Winter 1924/25], 9–11.) Stead's discussion supersedes the seriously confused treatment in D.E.S. Maxwell, *The Poetry of T. S. Eliot* (1952; rpt. New York: Humanities Press, 1966), pp. 137–41, 213–17. As Stead is primarily interested in Eliot's general habits of composition, he does not attempt to apply the evidence of

Eliot's revisions to a reading of *The Hollow Men.* For still another look at the poem's growth, see A. D. Moody, *Thomas Stearns Eliot: Poet* (Cambridge: Cambridge University Press, 1979), pp. 118–27.

18. See Rossetti, *Dante,* p. 65.
19. Ibid., p. 63.
20. Eliot may have remembered a similar effect in Browning's "Childe Roland to the Dark Tower Came," with which he associated *The Hollow Men.* See below, note 31.
21. "When we imitated Shelley, it was not so much from a desire to write as he did, as from an invasion of the adolescent self by Shelley, which made Shelley's way, for the time, the only way in which to write" (OPP, 19). Cf. also the Introduction to UPUC, where Eliot said that Shelley was part of the "usual adolescent course" (33).
22. Eliot used the Clark Lectures as the basis for his comparison of Shelley and Crashaw in the review of *The Poems English Latin and Greek of Richard Crashaw* which he published in the *Dial* for March 1928. The review was reprinted as "A Note on Richard Crashaw" in FLA.
23. Cf. also Shelley's lyric "The keen stars were twinkling," which Sencourt says Eliot ridiculed. See Robert Sencourt, *T. S. Eliot: A Memoir* (1971; rpt. New York: Delta, 1973), p. 148.
24. This Dantesque presentation of mature reflection on youthful emotions becomes one of the constants of Eliot's middle and later periods. It is to this attitude that Helen Gardner refers when she remarks on the tonality of "middle age" that pervades *The Hollow Men.* See *The Art of T. S. Eliot,* p. 111.
25. Eliot's habits of composition here repeated the pattern of *The Waste Land,* where the ending of one of the earliest completed parts anticipated the ending of the suite itself: "The Fire Sermon," perhaps the first full movement of *The Waste Land* to be finished, concluded by disintegrating into fragments, just as *The Waste Land* itself would do.
26. Mary, of course, is called both rose and "living star" in *Paradiso* XXIII, and she appears in the center of the multifoliate rose in *Paradiso* XXXII. Eliot may also have been thinking of *Purgatorio* XXXI, where the virtues describe themselves as nymphs on earth but stars in heaven. They are Beatrice's handmaids (as she is Mary's), and they bring Dante "to her eyes."
27. Gardner, *The Art of T. S. Eliot,* p. 113.
28. The letter, dated 30 November 1924, is now in the Ottoline Morrell Collection of the Humanities Research Center of the University of Texas at Austin. With it, Eliot enclosed typescripts of "We are the hollow men" and "Eyes that last I saw in tears."
29. As Philip Headings observed, Eliot alluded to Dostoevsky at the end of "The wind sprang up at four o'clock," where the "Tartar horsemen across death's other river" re-enact the vision of Raskolnikov at the end of *Crime and Punishment.* See Philip R. Headings, *T. S. Eliot* (New Haven: Twayne's, 1964), p. 94. For the enormous impression that Dostoevsky made on Eliot in the Paris of 1910–11, see Eliot as quoted in John C. Pope, "Prufrock and Raskolnikov Again: A Letter from T. S. Eliot," *American Literature* XVIII.4 (January 1947), 319–20.
30. "Wanley and Chapman," *TLS,* 31 December 1925, 907.

31. Where in the fifth lecture he adds Browning's "Childe Roland to the Dark Tower Came" to the list of works in which this phenomenon of doubleness occurs.

32. "John Marston," which first appeared in the *Times Literary Supplement* for 26 July 1934. Grover Smith quotes the Chapman and Dostoevsky passages from this essay in relation to *Sweeney Agonistes* in *T. S. Eliot's Poetry and Plays*, pp. 111–12.

33. Although sometimes—usually at the end of a lyric—Eliot uses "we" instead of "I" to suggest the universality of a moment. Cf. "Eyes that last I saw in tears," which concludes with the line "And hold us in derision."

34. *Commerce* III (Winter 1924/25), 9–11. The poem was dated "Nov. 1924" and was printed alongside a French translation by St.-John Perse.

35. The quotation is from Litz's essay "The Waste Land: Fifty Years After." See *Eliot in His Time*, ed. A. Walton Litz (Princeton: Princeton University Press, 1973), p. 6. (See also Hugh Kenner's essay in the same collection, especially pp. 43–49.)

36. When he wrote to thank John Quinn for Quinn's patronage in 1923, Eliot told Quinn that his aid was "the greatest stimulus to me to commence the work I have in mind, [*Sweeney Agonistes*,] which is more ambitious than anything I have ever done yet" (*Facs.*, xxix).

37. See "The Beating of a Drum," p. 12.

38. "Marianne Moore," *Dial* LXXV. 6 (December 1923), 597. The full statement is worth quoting: "Of course, *all* art emulates the condition of ritual. That is what it comes from and to that it must always return for nourishment. And nothing belongs more properly to the people than ritual. . . ."

39. "Notes on Current Letters," *Tyro* I (Spring 1921), 4.

40. Smith, *Eliot's Dramatic Theory*, p. 71. Smith provides the fullest discussion to date of *Sweeney Agonistes* and of Eliot's theory of primitive drama.

41. Schneider, *T. S. Eliot: The Pattern in the Carpet*, p. 99. Cf. also Pound's Canto 74:

> yet say this to the Possum: a bang, not a whimper
> with a bang not with a whimper. . . .

42. Introduction to *Le Serpent*, p. 9.

43. See Richard Aldington's autobiography, *Life for Life's Sake* (New York: Viking, 1941), p. 261, where Aldington describes a 1920 visit to a rural church with Eliot and recounts the admiration Eliot expressed for Gray's "Elegy" on that occasion. According to Aldington, Eliot commented that "if a contemporary poet, conscious of his limitations as Gray evidently was, would concentrate all his gifts on one such poem he might achieve a similar success." Aldington goes on to connect Eliot's comments with the composition of *The Waste Land*. Without agreeing with him, we ought certainly to note the central place the poem had in Eliot's pantheon of long poems.

44. "Charybde et Scylla: lourdeur et frivolité," p. 81. ("Valéry's poem has what might be called a philosophical structure, an organization composed not only of successive responses to a given situation, but of responses to previous responses. . . . [in his poems] the method of abstraction and the method of poetry are better united than in the work of any other poet.")

45. The conjunction of "Le Cimetière marin" and Gray's "Elegy" in Eliot's re-

marks anticipates Hugh Kenner's observation that the originality of the *Four Quartets* consisted of uniting "a *Symboliste* heritage with an Augustan. . . ." See *The Pound Era* (Berkeley and Los Angeles: University of California Press, 1971), p. 439, and below, chapter nine.

46. See Eliot's remarks on free verse and Jacobean drama in "Reflections on Vers Libre," TCC, 186–87.

47. In "Swinburne as Poet" (1920), SW, 149–50.

48. Symons's translation of Mallarmé. I quote from Richard Ellmann's edition of *The Symbolist Movement in Literature* (1889, rev. 1908; rpt. New York: Dutton, 1958), p. 73.

49. See the discussion of how Pound's revisions particularized Eliot's Johnsonian generalities in Ronald Bush, *The Genesis of Ezra Pound's Cantos* (Princeton: Princeton University Press, 1976), pp. 235–37.

50. See Davie's essay "Pound and Eliot: A Distinction" in Graham Martin, ed., *Eliot in Perspective: A Symposium* (New York: Humanities Press, 1970), pp. 62–82. Davie also speculates on the importance of Valéry.

51. See John Lehmann, "The Other T. S. Eliot," *Listener* LI.1300 (28 January 1953), 178–79, 182.

52. From stanza viii.

53. See Eliot's "Leçon de Valéry" in *Paul Valéry vivant* (Marseilles: Cahiers du Sud, 1946), p. 76.

54. Ibid.

55. I quote from an unpublished 1932 lecture, "The Bible as Scripture and Liturature," in the Houghton Library, Harvard University.

7. "Desire and control"

1. Preface to Charles-Louis Philippe, *Bubu of Montparnasse* (Paris: Crosby Continental Editions, 1932; rpt. New York: Shakespeare House, 1951), p. 7.

2. What he might have done had the reaction been warmer still, we can only guess. As Virginia Woolf wrote in her diary, "There's something hole & cornerish, biting in the back, suspicious, elaborate, uneasy, about him: much would be liberated by a douche of pure praise." (Anne Olivier Bell, ed., *The Diary of Virginia Woolf: Volume Two, 1920–1924* [New York: Harcourt Brace Jovanovich, 1978], p. 302.)

3. Ibid., p. 170.

4. Murry, as Stephen Spender has pointed out, was to be Eliot's favorite whipping boy during the twenties and thirties. See Spender's *T. S. Eliot* (New York: Viking, 1975), p. 80.

5. On the connection between Eliot's Preface and the French right-wing leader Charles Maurras, see Herbert Howarth, *Notes on Some Figures Behind T. S. Eliot* (Boston: Houghton Mifflin, 1964), pp. 175–77, and Bernard Bergonzi, *T. S. Eliot* (New York: Collier, 1972), p. 115. Eliot mentioned Maurras as an element of his "articles of faith" in the letter to Herbert Read quoted just below. As Bergonzi points out, in *Criterion* I.4 (July 1923), 421, Eliot's "Notes" column argued Maurras's thesis that Europe was a Latin culture and could not afford to lose its traditions of classical education.

For Eliot's memories of his first acquaintance with Maurras—in the Paris of his 1910–11 year abroad—see "Hommage à Charles Maurras," in *Aspects de la France et du Monde* for 25 April 1948. The best introduction to Maurras is Albert Thibaudet's "L'Esthétique des trois traditions," which Eliot read in *La Nouvelle Revue Française* for January and March of 1913.

6. See Herbert Read, "T.S.E.—A Memoir," in Allen Tate, ed., *T. S. Eliot: The Man and His Work* (New York: Delta, 1966), p. 21. It should be mentioned that, though Eliot's new stance grew out of his personal crisis, it was hardly unique. Many conservative Englishmen discovered their opinions becoming more rigid in response to post-war unemployment and especially to the 1923 rise of the Labour Party. On 22 January 1923, the day that Ramsay MacDonald became Prime Minister, George V wrote in his diary, "To-day 23 years ago dear Grandmama died. I wonder what she would have thought of a Labour Government?" (Quoted by A.J.P. Taylor in *English History 1914–1945* [New York: Oxford University Press, 1970], p. 209.)

7. See Frank Morley, "A Few Recollections of Eliot," in Tate, *T. S. Eliot,* p. 99.

8. Writing about these incidents in Eliot's life is difficult because Eliot gave different accounts of his feelings to different people. Consider an exasperated letter Virginia Woolf wrote to Richard Aldington: "I will only say now that your account of [Eliot's] conditions at the Bank is quite new to me. It is entirely different from what we had gathered from Tom or Vivien. She definitely told me, that if it were not for her she thought Tom would be happier in the Bank than as literary editor of the *Nation*. In talking to us, Tom has always laid great stress upon the extraordinary kindness which the Bank has shown him. This was one of his stock arguments against leaving. And in our last talk on the subject—about a year ago—he said not a word of complaint about his work or his treatment and led us to think that he had been given promotion, and had every reason to be grateful to them. He certainly said that he was thankful he had stayed on at the Bank. The truth is I expect that he takes different views at different times and to different people." (Nigel Nicolson and Joanne Trautmann, eds., *The Letters of Virginia Woolf: Volume Three, 1923–1928* [New York: Harcourt Brace Jovanovich, 1977], p. 169. The editors provisionally date the letter 16 February 1925, but as note 9 makes clear, it is almost certainly 1924.)

9. For the whole story, see Morley, "A Few Recollections," pp. 99–101. As early as 29 April 1924, Eliot told Virginia Woolf of his "heavensent" release from the Bank. See Anne Olivier Bell, ed., *The Diary of Virginia Woolf: Volume Three: 1925–1930* (New York: Harcourt Brace Jovanovich, 1980), p. 14.

10. Robert Sencourt, *T. S. Eliot: A Memoir* (New York: Delta, 1973), p. 125.

11. *Letters: III*, p. 508 (letter of 7 June 1928). See also Woolf's entry for 8 November 1930 in *Diary: III*, p. 331: "Poor Tom is all suspicion, hesitation & reserve. His face has grown heavier fatter & whiter. There is a leaden sinister look about him. But oh—Vivienne! Was there ever such a torture since life began! —to bear her on one's shoulders, biting, wriggling, raving, scratching, unwholesome, powdered, insane, yet sane to the point of insanity, reading his letters, thrusting herself on us. . . . Yes we have moved again. Tell me, Mrs. Woolf, why do we move so often? . . . And so on,

until worn out with half an hour of it, we gladly see them go. . . . This bag of ferrets is what Tom wears round his neck."

12. *Letters: III*, p. 38 (letter of 18 May 1923).
13. *Diary: III*, p. 14 (entry for 29 April 1925).
14. Sencourt, *T. S. Eliot: A Memoir*, p. 149.
15. Letter of 15 March 1928, in the William Force Stead Collection of the Beinecke Library, Yale University. For Eliot's relations with Stead, see George Mills Harper, "William Force Stead's Friendship with Yeats and Eliot," *Massachusetts Review* 21 (1980), 9–38.
16. Morley, "A Few Recollections," p. 110.
17. Lyndall Gordon, *Eliot's Early Years* (Oxford: Oxford University Press, 1977), p. 130.
18. See Read, "T.S.E.—A Memoir," p. 22.
19. Letter of 10 April 1928, in the Stead Collection.
20. *Letters: III*, p. 38.
21. The autograph manuscript of Eliot's first draft of "Simeon" is now in the Eliot Collection of King's College, Cambridge.
22. See "The Three Voices of Poetry" (OPP, 103).
23. "The Preacher as Artist," *Athenaeum* 4674 (28 November 1919), 1252–53 (emphasis mine).
24. Sencourt, *T. S. Eliot: A Memoir*, p. 127.
25. Cf. Eliot's 1927 remark that it was impossible "to come to the conclusion that Donne believed anything. It seemed as if, at that time, the world was filled with broken fragments of systems, and that a man like Donne merely picked up, like a magpie, various shining fragments of ideas as they struck his eye, and stuck them about here and there in his verse" (SE, 118).
26. "The Beating of a Drum," *Nation and Athenaeum* XXXIV.1 (6 October 1923), 12.
27. See Eliot's "London Letter" in the October 1921 *Dial*, "The Beating of a Drum," "Four Elizabethan Dramatists, A Preface," in the February 1924 *Criterion*, his "Commentary" in the October 1924 *Criterion* and "The Ballet" in the April 1925 *Criterion*.
28. See Audrey T. Rodgers, *The Universal Drum* (University Park: Pennsylvania State University Press, 1979), and David Bernstein, "The Story of Vaslav Nijinsky as a Source for T. S. Eliot's 'The Death of Saint Narcissus,'" *Hebrew University Studies in Literature* IV.1 (Spring 1976), 71–104.
29. See above, chapter one, note 33.
30. In this movement, Eliot's career parallels Wordsworth's, for whom sincerity was also a fundamental concept. See David Perkins, *Wordsworth and the Poetry of Sincerity* (Cambridge: Harvard University Press, 1964).
31. "Donne in Our Time," in Theodore Spencer, ed., *A Garland for John Donne* (Cambridge: Harvard University Press, 1931), p. 8.
32. See, for example, "A Note on Poetry and Belief," *Enemy* I (January 1927); "Shakespeare and the Stoicism of Seneca" (1927) and "Dante" (1929), both in SE; "Poetry and Propaganda," *Bookman* LXX.6 (February 1930); and UPUC.
33. Most notably in Kristian Smidt, *Poetry and Belief in the Work of T. S. Eliot*, rev. ed. (New York: Humanities Press, 1961), pp. 60–79.

34. See John Soldo, "The Tempering of T. S. Eliot, 1888–1915" (Ph.D. diss., Harvard, 1972), p. 230.

35. See SE, 115–18.

36. "The Social Function of Poetry," *Adelphi* XXI.4 (July/September 1945), 154. (This passage was excised in the revised version of the essay Eliot prepared for OPP.)

37. "The Minor Metaphysicals: From Cowley to Dryden," *Listener* III.65 (9 April 1930), 642.

38. "John Dryden III. Dryden the Critic, Defender of Sanity," *Listener* V.120 (29 April 1931), 725.

39. "John Dryden I. The Poet Who Gave the English Speech," *Listener* V.118 (15 April 1931), 621–22.

40. Letter of 3 April 1921, in the Marianne Moore Collection of the Rosenbach Museum, Philadelphia.

41. Letter of 30 May 1925, in the Moore Collection.

42. "Observations," *Egoist* V.5 (May 1918), 70.

43. Introduction to *Marianne Moore: Selected Poems* (New York: Macmillan, 1935), pp. ix–xi (emphasis mine).

44. From "The Metaphysical Poets" (1921). See SE, 248.

45. See F. O. Matthiessen, *The Achievement of T. S. Eliot* (1935; rpt. Oxford: Oxford University Press, 1972), p. 76, and Elisabeth Schneider, *T. S. Eliot: The Pattern in the Carpet* (Berkeley and Los Angeles: University of California Press, 1975), p. 130.

46. "John Dryden I," 621.

47. Ibid., 622.

48. From "Milton I" (1936). See OPP, 161.

49. Wallace Stevens, *Opus Posthumous* (New York: Knopf, 1957), p. 256.

50. Ranjee Shahani, "T. S. Eliot Answers Questions," *John O'London's Weekly* LVIII.1369 (19 August 1949), 497–98. I cite from the reprinted piece in P. Lal, ed., *T. S. Eliot: Homage from India* (Bombay, 1965), p. 132.

51. See SE, 309; *Literary Essays of Ezra Pound* (New York: New Directions, 1968), p. 9; and W. B. Yeats, *Essays and Introductions* (London: Macmillan, 1969), pp. 156–57.

52. Preface to *Transit of Venus: Poems by Harry Crosby* (Paris: Black Sun Press, 1931), pp. viii–ix.

53. From an unpublished 1939 essay, "The Last Twenty Five Years of English Poetry," in the Eliot Collection, King's College, Cambridge.

54. Preface to *Transit of Venus*, pp. vii, iv, v.

55. For details, see Richard Abel, "The Influence of St.-John Perse on T. S. Eliot," *Contemporary Literature* 14.2 (Spring 1973), 213–39.

56. I cite from the 1949 reprint, *Anabasis: A Poem by St.-John Perse* (New York: Harcourt Brace), p. 10.

57. Preface to *Transit of Venus*, p. ii.

58. "Une Lettre de St.-John Perse," *Berkeley Review* I (Winter 1956), 40. Cited by Arthur J. Knodel in "Towards an Understanding of *Anabase*," *PMLA* 79.3 (June 1964), 331. In his book *Saint-John Perse: A Study of His Poetry* (Edinburgh: Edinburgh University Press, 1966), Knodel translates Perse's phrase as: "a very allusive and mysterious play . . . at the extreme verge of what consciousness can grasp" (p. 58).

59. Introduction to *Anabasis*, p. 9.
60. From *Le Figaro Littéraire* for 5 November 1960. See Knodel, "Towards an Understanding of *Anabase*," 329. In Knodel's translation (*Saint-John Perse: A Study of His Poetry,* p. 40): "*Anabase* has as its object the poem of the loneliness of action. Action among men quite as much as the action of the human spirit upon itself. I sought to bring together the synthesis—not the passive, but the active synthesis—of human resourcefulness."
61. "Une feuillet unique," a letter to Jean Paulhan in *Honneur à St.-John Perse: Hommage et témoignages littéraires* (Paris: Gallimard, 1965), p. 19 ("his influence can be seen in some of the poems which I wrote after I finished the translation: he influenced my images and also perhaps my rhythm. Whoever examines my late work will find that this influence perhaps never disappeared"). The volume also contains the letter to Perse that Eliot enclosed along with his first-draft translation in January 1927. In the letter, Eliot says that the poem "me semble un des plus grands et plus singuliers des temps modernes . . . [un] chef-d'oeuvre" ("seems to me one of the greatest and most singular poems of modern times . . . a masterpiece"; p. 419).
62. I cite from the original edition (London: Faber and Faber, 1930).
63. I refer to Eliot's unpublished lecture "Hopkins and Others," given in the undergraduate course (English 26: English Literature from 1890 to the Present Day) he taught at Harvard in the spring of 1933. His notes can be consulted in the Archives Division of the Harvard University Library.
64. This kind of thing is emphasized even more in Eliot's drafts, copies of which are available in the Houghton Library, Harvard University.
65. In a letter attached to Eliot's drafts, Perse complained to Eliot about "bright" and suggested the more precise "flashing," or "lively" or "living." Eliot, however, insisted.
66. After a number of critics guessed as much, Eliot confirmed the fact to Edward Greene. See Edward J. H. Greene, *T. S. Eliot et la France* (Paris: Boivin, 1951), p. 136 n. 2.
67. See the work of Greene and Abel, cited above, notes 55 and 66.
68. Perse's comments are on the title page of Eliot's draft. See note 64.
69. UPUC, 148. For a discussion of this passage, see chapter four.
70. See, for example, R. D. Brown, "Revelation in T. S. Eliot's 'Journey of the Magi,'" *Renascence* 24 (1972), 137, and Elisabeth Schneider, "Prufrock and After: The Theme of Change," *PMLA* 87 (1972), 1114.
71. See Daniel Harris, "Language, History and Text in Eliot's 'Journey of the Magi,'" *PMLA* 95.5 (October 1980), 838–56. Harris points out much the same thing, but applies his observations to a very different reading of the poem.
72. Letter of 5 March 1933, in the Berg Collection of the New York Public Library.
73. See above, note 58.
74. "Note sur Mallarmé et Poe," *La Nouvelle Revue Française* XIV.158 (1 November 1926), 525. Eliot's French can be roughly translated as: worlds which expand sensibility "beyond the frontier of the quotidian, discoveries of new objects fit to call up new emotions."
75. Preface to *Transit of Venus*, p. ix.

8. "Explaining to himself": *Ash Wednesday*

1. Quoted in Helen Gardner, *The Composition of "Four Quartets"* (London: Faber and Faber, 1978), p. 29.
2. Elisabeth Schneider, "Prufrock and After: The Theme of Change," *PMLA* 87 (1972), 1113.
3. An autograph manuscript (marked "earliest" draft) of "Because I do not hope to turn" and a typescript draft of the first five parts of *Ash Wednesday* can be found in the Eliot Collection, Kings College, Cambridge. In addition, a typescript version of "Because I do not hope to turn again," which Eliot prepared after the Kings autograph and before the Kings typescript, exists in the Ottoline Morrell Collection at the Humanities Research Center, University of Texas, Austin. The latter is now attached to an envelope Eliot addressed to Morrell that is postmarked 3(1?) May 1928, but appears to have been taken from a letter of 2 October 1928, also in the collection.
4. The title comes from a popular song recorded by "The Two Black Crows." See I. A. Richards, "On T.S.E.," in Allen Tate, ed., *T. S. Eliot: The Man and His Work* (New York: Delta, 1966), p. 6.
5. From "Address," *From Mary to You*, Centennial Issue (December 1959), 133–36.
6. The phrase is altered from Shakespeare's twenty-ninth sonnet. Eliot had considered the sonnets in his 1927 review of J. M. Robertson's *The Problems of the Shakespeare Sonnets* (*Nation and Athenaeum* XL.19 [12 February 1927], 664, 666) and had devoted much of his review to the question of how poetry is related to an author's life. It is also worth noting that in "Shakespeare and the Stoicism of Seneca" (1927) and in "Dante" (1929) he frequently compared Shakespeare to Dante, almost always with the suggestion that Dante was able to transfer his experience into a poetry more universal than Shakespeare's, the latter being tainted with the mannerisms of Elizabethan (that is to say, Senecan) rhetoric.
7. Cf. SE, 375: "There is in [Baudelaire's] statements a good deal of romantic detritus; *ses ailes de géant l'empêchent de marcher*, he says of the Poet and of the Albatross, but not convincingly."
8. "A Sceptical Patrician," *Athenaeum* 4647 (23 May 1919), 362.
9. It was added between the King's College holograph and the typescript he sent to Ottoline Morrell. See note 3.
10. Eliot writes in the tradition of St. Augustine, who in *Confessions* VIII.5 dissociated two wills: "the old one, the other new, the first carnal, the other spiritual." In "Francis Herbert Bradley" (1927), Eliot had written that we must not distinguish "between a 'private self' and a 'public self' or a 'higher self,' [but] between the individual as himself and no more, a mere numbered atom, and the individual in communion with God. The distinction is clearly drawn between man's 'mere will' and 'the will of the Divine' " (SE, 402). Of course, however, one cannot gloss *Ash Wednesday* simply with those words. The poem gives us not doctrine, but the complicated honesty of personal experience, and what is a simple distinction between the human and the Divine in Eliot's prose becomes in his poetry a tentative organization of the confusions of the self.

11. Dante Gabriel Rossetti, ed. and trans., *Dante and His Circle with the Italian Poets Preceding Him* (Boston: Roberts Brothers, 1887), pp. 27–28.
12. "Wanley and Chapman," *TLS*, 31 December 1925, p. 907.
13. Cf. Auden's observation that each of us must "carry round with him through life,/ A judge, a landscape, and a wife" (*New Year Letter*).
14. See Philip R. Headings, *T. S. Eliot* (New Haven: Twayne's, 1964), p. 77.
15. Elisabeth Schneider, *T. S. Eliot: The Pattern in the Carpet* (Berkeley and Los Angeles: University of California Press, 1975), pp. 114–15.
16. See Paul J. Dolan, "*Ash Wednesday:* A Catechumenical Poem," *Renascence* XIX.4 (Summer 1967), 203.
17. See Karl-D. Uitti, *La Passion littéraire de Rémy de Gourmont* (Paris: Presses Universitaires de France, 1962), pp. 235–36.
18. On Eliot's knowledge of Verlaine's *Sagesse,* see the manuscript of his unpublished lecture "Types of English Religious Verse" (1939), in the Eliot Collection, Kings College, Cambridge.
19. Three of these excised lines were quoted by E. E. Duncan Jones in her essay "*Ash Wednesday.*" See B. Rajan, ed., *T. S. Eliot: A Study of His Writings by Several Hands* (London: Dennis Dobson, 1947), p. 47.
20. See A. D. Moody, *Thomas Stearns Eliot: Poet* (Cambridge: Cambridge University Press, 1979), p. 141: "The seed of the sequence seems to be these two [excised] lines in the 1921 [actually 1924] typescript of 'We are the hollow men'—

> Waters of tenderness
> Sealed Springs of devotion. . . ."

Moody refers to the typescript Eliot sent to Ottoline Morrell in November 1924. See above, chapter six, note 28.
21. See below, p. 149.
22. I cite from Yeats's reprinting in *The Oxford Book of Modern Verse 1892–1935,* which lineated the passage as if it were poetry.
23. "To the Rose upon the Rood of Time," W. B. Yeats, *The Collected Poems* (New York: Macmillan, 1956), p. 31.
24. See above, chapter seven, note 74.
25. See Robert Sencourt, *T. S. Eliot: A Memoir* (New York: Delta, 1973), p. 143.
26. See above, chapter seven, notes 58, 74.
27. See Duncan Jones, p. 48, and Grover Smith, *T. S. Eliot's Poetry and Plays: A Study in Sources and Meaning* (1950; rpt. Chicago: University of Chicago Press, 1965), p. 146.
28. On the King's College manuscript; see note 3.
29. On the functional ambiguities of Eliot's syntax, see William E. Baker, *Syntax in English Poetry* (Berkeley and Los Angeles: University of California Press, 1967).
30. Elisabeth Schneider's interesting reading of the section's last line (she suggests it has the secondary implication of "I only speak it, I do not [or not yet] truly believe it") would seem to be unlikely since, according to Eric Partridge, Eliot had at one time concluded with the line "And my soul shall be healed." See Schneider, *The Pattern in the Carpet,* p. 198, and Eric Partridge, *The Language of Modern Poetry: Yeats, Eliot, Auden* (London: André

Deutsch, 1976), p. 199. (The Kings College typescript contains neither the published version's last line nor the one Partridge cites.)

31. Leonard Woolf supplies Eliot's working titles in *Downhill All the Way: An Autobiography of the Years 1919 to 1939* (New York: Harcourt Brace Jovanovich, 1967), p. 111. The translation is Eliot's own. See SE, 224.

32. Rossetti, *Dante and His Circle*, p. 25.

33. That is, Dante had suggested motherly associations, but for purposes other than Eliot's.

34. "The Eliot Family and St. Louis," appendix to T. S. Eliot, *American Literature and the American Language* (St. Louis: Department of English, Washington University, 1953), p. 29 (emphasis mine).

35. Eliot typed "she" on the Kings College typescript and then excised it.

36. From the King's College typescript, previously cited by Moody, *Thomas Stearns Eliot: Poet*, p. 148. Note that in revision Eliot removed the poem's explicit religious references ("penance," "grace") and added elements of his own private phantasmagoria, especially the bird. Even the jewelled unicorns and the dream have as much to do with the dreams of Eliot's other poetry as with Christian allegory. (The unicorns, apparently, come not from Dante but from a poem of Conrad Aiken's. See Schneider, *The Pattern in the Carpet*, pp. 121–22.)

37. The experience Eliot associates with his nursemaid and with "flood time" and flowers is the miracle that occurs in the consciousness of the devout. The passage of Baudelaire's *Mon coeur mis à nu* with which Eliot ends his *For Lancelot Andrewes* essay on Baudelaire is helpful here, with its acknowledgment of how strength may be drawn from the devotions of a mother:

> Faire tous les matins ma prière à Dieu, réservoir de toute force et de toute justice, à mon père, à Mariette et à Poë, comme intercesseurs; les prier de me communiquer la force nécessaire pour accomplir tous mes devoirs, et d'octroyer à ma mère une vie assez longue pour jouir de ma transformation . . . (FLA, 105).
> ("Every morning to pray to God, the source of all power and justice, and to my father, Mariette and Poe, as intercessors; to supplicate them to grant me the power to accomplish my duty, and to grant my mother a life long enough to celebrate my transformation. . . .")

38. SE, 236. Quoted by Elizabeth Sewell, "Lewis Carroll and T. S. Eliot as Nonsense Poets," in Hugh Kenner, ed., *T. S. Eliot: A Collection of Critical Essays* (Englewood Cliffs: Prentice-Hall, 1962), p. 67.

39. Cf. Eliot on Lawrence in John Baillie and Hugh Martin, eds., *Revelation* (London: Faber and Faber, 1937): "The human mind is perpetually driven between two desires, between two dreams, each of which may be either a vision or a nightmare: the vision and the nightmare of the material world, and the vision and nightmare of the immaterial."

40. I refer to the King's College typescript, which Eliot read aloud to the Woolfs and Mary Hutchinson for criticism. See Leonard Woolf, *Downhill All the Way*, pp. 109–11.

41. See above, chapter five, note 57.

42. I cite from a volume Eliot recommended in a letter to the *New English Weekly* for 12 April 1934: *The Mystical Doctrine of St. John of the Cross: An*

Abridgement Made by C. H. with an Introduction by R.H.J. Steuart, S. J. (1934; rpt. London: Sheed and Ward, 1948), p. 9.

43. As Eliot said about Tourneur's exaggerated revulsion from desire, "Its motive is truly the death-motive, for it is the loathing and horror of life itself." (Yet, he added, "to have realized this motive so well is a triumph; for the hatred of life is an important phase—even, if you like, a mystical experience—in life itself.") See SE, 166.

44. Moody, *Thomas Stearns Eliot*, p. 154.

45. See G. Wilson Knight, "T. S. Eliot: Some Literary Impressions," in Tate, *T. S. Eliot: The Man and His Work*, p. 247.

46. See Eliot's translation, *Anabasis* (New York: Harcourt Brace Jovanovich, 1949), p. 40.

47. See above, chapter two, note 3.

48. "The Literature of Fascism," *Criterion* VIII.31 (December 1928), 282.

49. Quoted in Smith, *T. S. Eliot's Poetry and Plays*, p. 162.

50. Schneider, *The Pattern in the Carpet*, p. 142.

51. See F. O. Matthiessen, *The Achievement of T. S. Eliot* (1935; rpt. Oxford: Oxford University Press, 1972), pp. 82–83.

52. "Ode on Independence Day, July 4th, 1918," published in John Rodker's limited edition collection of Eliot's poems, *Ara Vos Prec*, in 1920 and never reprinted by Eliot. It can be found, however, in James E. Miller, Jr., *T. S. Eliot's Personal Waste Land: Exorcism of the Demons* (University Park: Pennsylvania State University Press, 1977), pp. 48–49.

53. See his review of *The Lion and the Fox* in *Twentieth Century Verse* 6/7 (November/December 1937), 6–9.

54. Quoted in Donald F. Theall, "Traditional Satire in Eliot's 'Coriolan,' " *Accent* XI.4 (1951), 196.

9. "Beyond music"

1. Letter of 31 January 1934, in the Marianne Moore Collection of the Rosenbach Museum, Philadelphia, Pennsylvania.

2. Hugh Kenner, *The Pound Era* (Berkeley and Los Angeles: University of California Press, 1971), p. 439; Donald Davie, "Anglican Eliot," in A. Walton Litz, ed., *Eliot in His Time* (Princeton: Princeton University Press, 1973), p. 194.

3. For a Heideggerian reading of the poem, see William V. Spanos, "Hermeneutics and Memory: Destroying T. S. Eliot's *Four Quartets*," *Genre* XI (Winter 1978), 523–73.

4. See "Note sur Mallarmé et Poe," *La Nouvelle Revue Française* XIV.158 (1 November 1926), 524–26.

5. Letter to Eugenè Lefébure, 17 May 1867, quoted in Walter A. Strauss, *Descent and Return: The Orphic Theme in Modern Literature* (Cambridge: Harvard University Press, 1971), pp. 86, 90. I give Strauss's translation:

   I have created my work by mere elimination, and any truth I have acquired was born only of the loss of an impression that, after flashing, had been consumed and allowed me—thanks to the darkness supplanting it—to penetrate more

> deeply into the sensation of Absolute Darkness. Destruction was my Beatrice. . . .
> . . . Every birth is a destruction, and the life of a moment is the agony in which something lost is resuscitated so that it can be seen, being unknown beforehand . . . I think that in order to be really a man, nature as thinking, one must think with his entire body, the result being thought full and in unison, like those violin strings vibrating immediately with its hollow sound box . . . I am truly decomposed; imagine all this being necessary in order to have a very *single* view of the Universe! Otherwise, one can't feel any other unity than that of one's life.

6. Introduction to Paul Valéry, *The Art of Poetry* (1958; rpt. New York: Vintage, 1961), pp. xvi–xvii. Eliot's counter-statement should be contrasted with Valéry's assertions in "The Poet's Rights Over Language" and "Remarks on Poetry," both reprinted in the same volume.

7. Eliot made similar remarks about the poet's responsibilities, starting in 1922. In Wyndham Lewis's *Tyro* for that year, he wrote that "the traditions of the language, not the traditions of the nation or of the race, are what first concern the writer" and that "whatever words a writer employs, he benefits by knowing as much as possible of the history of these words, of the uses to which they have already been applied. Such knowledge facilitates his task of giving to the word a new life and to the language a new idiom." ("The Three Provincialities," *Tyro* 2 [Spring 1922], 11–13.) For a sampling of Eliot's later comments on the subject, see "Charles Whibley: A Memoir" (1931) and "Byron" (1937).

8. For a moving account of Eliot's struggle with the burden of tradition, see Lawrence Lipking, *The Life of the Poet: Beginning and Ending Poetic Careers* (Chicago: University of Chicago Press, 1981), esp. p. 74.

9. In conversation with Kathleen Raine. See Raine, "St.-John Perse's *Birds*," *Southern Review* III.1 (January 1967), 257 (emphasis mine).

10. I quote from the manuscript of an unpublished address on the "Poetical and Prosaic Use of Words," in the Eliot Collection, Kings College, Cambridge.

11. Letter of 31 October 1934, in the Marianne Moore Collection.

12. Kay Dick, ed., *Writers at Work: The Paris Review Interviews* (London: Penguin Books, 1972), p. 126.

13. "Charybde et Scylla: lourdeur et frivolité," *Annales du Centre Universitaire Méditerranéen* V (1951/52), 81 ("the force of a commonplace but in words no one had ever used before; as with certain lines of Gray, I am struck with astonishment and admiration, as if confronting a miraculous resurrection of the dead").

14. "T. S. Eliot: Some Literary Impressions," in Allen Tate, ed., *T. S. Eliot: The Man and His Work* (New York: Delta, 1966), pp. 246–47.

15. Introduction to G. Wilson Knight, *The Wheel of Fire* (1930; rpt. London: Methuen, 1964), pp. xviii–xix. (Emphasis mine.)

16. G. Wilson Knight, "Myth and Miracle" (1929), in *The Crown of Life* (1947; rpt. London: Methuen, 1966), p. 29.

17. Ibid., p. 31.

18. Introduction to *The Wheel of Fire*, p. xviii.

19. Elisabeth Schneider, *T. S. Eliot: The Pattern in the Carpet* (Berkeley and Los

Angeles: University of California Press, 1975), p. 151. (Schneider quotes from Eliot's 1932 essay "John Ford.")

20. Ibid., p. 153.
21. "Mr. Lucas's Webster," *Criterion* VII.4 (June 1928), 156.
22. "Myth and Miracle," pp. 10, 30.
23. Ibid., 12.
24. Ibid., 24.
25. This and subsequent citations are from "Shakespeare as Poet and Dramatist," an address in two parts Eliot delivered at Edinburgh University in 1937 and at Bristol University in 1941. Never published, the lecture manuscript was presented to the Houghton Library of Harvard University by Emily Hale.

    In the Preface to OPP, Eliot comments that he wished he "could have found [the Shakespeare lectures] worthy of inclusion [in OPP] . . . for what I was trying to say still seems to me worth saying. But the lectures struck me as badly written, and in need of thorough revision" (p. xii). What needs adding is that Eliot's prose was likely to slide in just those circumstances when a subject was close to his heart (the Clark Lectures are another example). Thus it is essays that Eliot remembered without warmth and never published that sometimes tell us most about his career.
26. From the Edinburgh lectures.
27. J. Hillis Miller, *Poets of Reality: Six Twentieth Century Writers* (1965; rpt. New York: Atheneum, 1969), pp. 166, 185.
28. Bernard Bergonzi, *T. S. Eliot* (New York: Collier, 1972), p. 142.
29. From the postscript of a letter to Sir Michael Sadler, dated 9 May 1930, enclosing the manuscripts and typescripts of "Marina," quoted in Richard Abel, "The Influence of St.-John Perse on T. S. Eliot," *Contemporary Literature* XIV.2 (Spring 1973), 235.
30. Introduction to *The Wheel of Fire*, xx.
31. Knight, *The Crown of Life*, p. 100.
32. See "The Noh and the Image," *Egoist* IV.7 (August 1917), 102–3.
33. Introduction to *Selected Poems* by Marianne Moore (New York: Macmillan, 1935), p. xiv.
34. Nancy Hargrove, *Landscape as Symbol in the Poetry of T. S. Eliot* (Jackson: University Press of Mississippi, 1978), p. 113.
35. See especially Erik Arne Hansen, "T. S. Eliot's Landscapes," *English Studies* L.4 (August 1969), 363–79, to which my reading of Eliot's voices is indebted.
36. See Eliot's letter of 9 August 1930 to William Force Stead in the William Force Stead Collection of the Beinecke Library, Yale University.
37. "Sir John Denham," *TLS*, 5 July 1928, p. 501.
38. From "Song" in Seamus Heaney, *Field Work* (New York: Farrar, Straus, and Giroux, 1979), p. 56.
39. See above, chapter six, note 31.
40. "The Borderline of Prose," *New Statesman*, 19 May 1917, p. 158.
41. "Artists and Men of Genius," *Athenaeum* 4704 (25 June 1920), 842.
42. From "Prose and Verse," *Chapbook* 22 (April 1921), 3–10.
43. Edward J. H. Greene, *T. S. Eliot et la France* (Boivin: Paris, 1951), p. 137.
44. For an account of this argument, see above, chapter six.

45. See above, note 4. The fragments of Eliot's "Note" on this and succeeding pages may be translated as follows: "suite . . . métaphysique": "a sequence of studies in progress on metaphysical poetry"; "pour raffiner . . . d'émotion": "to refine and develop the power of his sensibility"; "était . . . émotions": "was an expansion of their sensibility beyond the limits of the quotidian, a discovery of new objects capable of calling up new emotions"; "empêche . . . vers": "prevents the reader from swallowing his lineation or phrasing in one gulp"; "de l'accidentel en réel": "from the accidental to the real" (or better: "from the fanciful to the imaginative"); "ne *croient* . . . intéressent": "does not believe the theories he entertains"; "*incantation* . . . Mot": "incantation which brings out the primitive power of the Word"; "[le] monde tangible": "the sensible world"; "[le] monde des fantômes": "the spectral world."

46. This remark may be compared to one made by the poet whose work so resembled Mallarmé's: in his *Marginalia,* Poe writes that

> there is . . . a class of fancies, of exquisite delicacy, which are *not* thoughts, and to which, *as yet,* I have found it absolutely impossible to adapt language. I use the word *fancies* at random, and merely because I must use *some* word; but the idea commonly attached to the term is not even remotely applicable to the shadows of shadows in question. They seem to me rather psychal than intellectual. They arise in the soul (alas, how rarely!) only at its epochs of most intense tranquility—when the bodily and mental health are in perfection—and at those mere points of time where the confines of the waking world blend with those of the world of dreams. . . . I regard the visions, even as they arise, with an awe which, in some measure, moderates or tranquillizes the ecstasy—I so regard them, through a conviction (which seems a portion of the ecstasy itself) that this ecstasy, in itself . . . is a glimpse of the spirit's outer world; and I arrive at this conclusion . . . by a perception that the delight experienced has, as its element, but *the absoluteness of novelty.* I say the absoluteness—for in these fancies— let me now term them psychal impressions—there is really nothing even approximate in character to impressions ordinarily received. It is as if the five senses were supplanted by five myriad others alien to mortality.

(W. H. Auden, ed., *Edgar Allan Poe: Selected Prose, Poetry and Eureka* [New York: Holt, Rinehart and Winston, 1950], pp. 435–36.)

47. The manuscript of the Turnbull Lectures is now in the Houghton Library, Harvard University. For the circumstances of their delivery (which included Eliot's only meeting with F. Scott Fitzgerald), see T. S. Matthews, *Great Tom* (New York: Harper and Row, 1974), pp. 114–15.

48. I.e., the beginning of "Burnt Norton" II:

> Garlic and sapphires in the mud
> Clot the bedded axle-tree.

On the evidence of a typescript at the Houghton Library, Eliot used these lines earlier in a draft of "Lines for an Old Man" which he dedicated "To Mallarmé." (In its final version, "Lines for an Old Man" retains remnants of Mallarmé's poem, both in the phrase "tell me . . ." and in its syntax.

Eliot's friend Roger Fry translated Mallarmé's tercets this way:

> Say if I am not joyous
> Thunder and rubies at the axles
> To see in this fire-pierced air

> Amid scattered realms
> As though dying purple the wheel
> Of my sole chariot of evening

See *Stéphane Mallarmé: Poems,* trans. Roger Fry (1936; rpt. New York: New Directions, 1951), p. 123.

49. Introduction to Valéry, *The Art of Poetry,* p. xiv.
50. See Bradford Cook, ed. and trans., *Mallarmé: Selected Prose Poems, Essays, and Letters* (Baltimore: Johns Hopkins Press, 1956), p. 41:

> The inner structures of a book of verse must be inborn; in this way, chance will be totally eliminated and the poet will be absent. From each theme, itself pre-destined, a given harmony will be born somewhere in the parts of the total poem and take its proper place within the volume; because, for every sound, there is an echo. Motifs of like pattern will move in balance from point to point. There will be none of the sublime incoherence found in the page-settings of the Romantics, none of the artificial unity that used to be based on the square measurements of the book. Everything will be hesitation, disposition of parts, their alternations and relationships—all this contributing to the rhythmic total-ity, which will be the very silence of the poem, in its blank spaces, as that silence is translated by each stuctural element in its own way.

The same essay also glosses the overtones of "vagueness" and "nuance" as Eliot used those words in the Turnbull Lectures.
51. Joseph Chiari, *Symbolisme from Poe to Mallarmé: The Growth of a Myth* (1956; rpt. New York: Gordian Press, 1970), pp. 142–44. Eliot's praise appears in his Foreword, p. xx.
52. From Eliot's unpublished 1933 lecture on the English poets as letter writ-ers, the remaining notes for which are in the Houghton Library, Harvard University. The passage is quoted in F. O. Matthiessen, *The Achievement of T. S. Eliot* (1935; rpt. New York: Oxford University Press, 1972), p. 90.
53. See Marjorie Perloff, *The Poetics of Indeterminacy: Rimbaud to Cage* (Prince-ton: Princeton University Press, 1981).
54. James Breslin, *William Carlos Williams: An American Artist* (New York: Ox-ford University Press, 1970), pp. 85–86.

10. "Our first world": "Burnt Norton"

1. Letter in Eliot Collection, King's College, Cambridge, quoted in Helen Gardner, *The Composition of "Four Quartets"* (London: Faber and Faber, 1978), p. 67.
2. Henry Ware Eliot's statement was made in a letter of 6 June 1936 to Mar-ianne Moore, now in the Moore collection, Rosenbach Museum, Philadel-phia. Eliot's lecture notes for English 26, "Contemporary English Litera-ture (1890 to the Present Time)" can be found in the Harvard University Archives.
3. Frank Morley, "A Few Recollections of Eliot," in Allen Tate, ed., *T. S. Eliot: The Man and His Work* (New York: Delta, 1966), pp. 104, 108.
4. See, for example, Eliot's "Commentary" in the *Criterion* XIII.52 (April 1934), where he called the roll of the intellectual giants of his youth and retrieved "the memory of a friend [Jean Verdenal] coming across the Luxembourg Gardens in the late afternoon, waving a branch of lilac, a friend who was

later (so far as I could find out) to be mixed with the mud of Gallipoli" (p. 452).

5. See Robert Sencourt, *T. S. Eliot: A Memoir* (1971; rpt. New York: Delta, 1973), p. 153.

6. Morley, "A Few Recollections," p. 106.

7. See Martin Browne, *The Making of T. S. Eliot's Plays* (Cambridge: Cambridge University Press, 1969), p. 6.

8. See Morley, "A Few Recollections," p. 107, and Sencourt, *Memoir*, p. 162.

9. Sencourt, *Memoir*, p. 163. Sencourt claims credit for choosing Eliot's lodgings at Courtfield Road and explains (p. 161) that "next door lived a prominent Anglo-Catholic, Miss Muriel Forwood; among those who lived in houses opening onto the inner lawn were Axel Munthe, author of *The Story of San Michele,* and the leading Anglo-Catholic layman, Athelstan Riley."

10. On Eliot and Emily Hale, see T. S. Matthews, *Great Tom: Notes Towards the Definition of T. S. Eliot* (New York: Harper and Row, 1973), esp. pp. 139–51; Lyndall Gordon, *Eliot's Early Years* (Oxford: Oxford University Press, 1977), pp. 55–57; and Gardner, *Composition,* pp. 35–36.

11. For the restrictions on the Hale-Eliot letters at Princeton University Library (they may not be opened until 1 January 2020), see Matthews, *Great Tom,* p. 151.

12. See Gardner, *Composition,* p. 35.

13. Ibid.

14. Anne Olivier Bell, ed., *The Diaries of Virginia Woolf: Volume Four, 1931–1935* (New York: Harcourt Brace Jovanovich, 1982), p. 178.

15. See his letter to John Hayward of 5 August 1941, quoted in Gardner, *Composition,* p. 29.

16. CPP, 93. Gardner suggests (*Composition,* p. 36) that the link between "Burnt Norton" and "New Hampshire" is due to Emily Hale, who may have been with Eliot in New Hampshire in the spring of 1933.

17. See Gardner, *Composition,* pp. 16, 39.

18. Quoted in ibid., p. 82, from a draft of *Murder in the Cathedral* now in the McKeldrin Library at the University of Maryland.

19. See above, note 15.

20. Lawrence Lipking, *The Life of the Poet: Beginning and Ending Poetic Careers* (Chicago: Chicago University Press, 1981), p. 72.

21. Eliot's phrase in "The Post-Georgians," *Athenaeum* 4641 (11 April 1919), 171. See above, chapter one, note 10.

22. F. R. Leavis, *The Living Principle: "English" as a Discipline of Thought* (New York: Oxford University Press, 1975), p. 158.

23. Cf. also the speech in which Harry asserts that "the past [is] unredeemable" (CPP, 256).

24. See above, chapter eight, note 5.

25. "Mystic and Politician as Poet: Vaughan, Traherne, Marvell, Milton," *Listener* III.64 (2 April 1930), 590.

26. An exception is Barbara Everett, "A Visit to Burnt Norton," *The Critical Quarterly* 16.3 (Autumn 1974), 199–226.

27. Eliot called attention to the influence of *Alice in Wonderland* in an interview with John Lehmann in the *New York Times Book Review* for 29 November 1953. His hint was elaborated with reference to Mallarmé in Elizabeth Sew-

ell, "Lewis Carroll and T. S. Eliot as Nonsense Poets," reprinted in Hugh
Kenner, ed., *T. S. Eliot: A Collection of Critical Essays* (Englewood Cliffs:
Prentice-Hall, 1962), pp. 65–72.

28. In *The Family Reunion,* written afterward, the connection to "Burnt Norton" (and behind it, "New Hampshire") is explicit: looking back from *The
Family Reunion* to "Burnt Norton," we understand that for Eliot, consciously reducing himself to "feet walking" is a way of leaving ordinary
experience behind. So Agatha, who feels a frisson of spookiness along with
her exaltation, declares:

> I only looked through the little door
> When the sun was shining on the rose-garden:
> And heard in the distance tiny voices
> And then a black raven flew over.
> And then I was only my own feet walking
> Away, down a concrete corridor
> In a dead air. Only feet walking
> And sharp heels scraping. Over and under
> Echo and noise of feet.
> I was only the feet, and the eye
> Seeing the feet: the unwinking eye
> Fixing the movement.
>
> (CPP, 276–77)

In *Murder in the Cathedral* also, footfalls represent a transition to a reality
out of time, a reality which may be divine but which is nevertheless fearsome. The passage I am thinking of occurs immediately after Thomas instructs the chorus that the moment of their acceptance of contamination is
distinct from a future moment in memory, when

> the figure of God's purpose is made complete.
> You shall forget these things, toiling in the household,
> You shall remember them, droning by the fire,
> When age and forgetfulness sweeten memory
> Only like a dream that has often been told
> And often changed in the telling. They will seem unreal.
> Human kind cannot bear very much reality.
>
> (CPP, 208–9)

His speech finished, Thomas goes to his death. It is at that point that the
chorus, penetrating the higher reality Thomas describes, reports a horror
that is

> More than *footfall in the passage,*
> More than shadow in the doorway,
> More than fury in the hall.
>
> (CPP, 210; emphasis mine)

29. "Note sur Mallarmé et Poe," *Nouvelle Revue Française* XIV.158 (November
1926), 526 ("There is also the firmness of their steps when they pass from
the sensible world to the spectral one.") See above, chapter nine.

30. See Leavis, *Living Principle,* pp. 158–63, and D. W. Harding, "T. S. Eliot,
1925–1935," in *Scrutiny* 5.2 (September 1936), 171–76.

31. See above, chapter nine, p. 176.

32. See *The Art of T. S. Eliot* (1950; rpt. New York: E. P. Dutton, 1959), p. 46:

"Mr. Eliot has not given us a poem of philosophic argument, though his poem includes philosophic argument."

33. Leavis, *Living Principle*, p. 156.

34. See Donald Davie, *Articulate Energy: An Enquiry into the Syntax of English Poetry* (London: Routledge & Kegan Paul, 1955); Harvey Gross, *Sound and Form in Modern Poetry: A Study of Prosody from Thomas Hardy to Robert Lowell* (Ann Arbor: University of Michigan Press, 1964); and Charles O. Hartman, *Free Verse: An Essay on English Prosody* (Princeton: Princeton University Press, 1980).

35. See "Some Post-Symbolist Structures," in Frank Brady, John Palmer and Martin Price, eds., *Literary Theory and Structure: Essays in Honor of William K. Wimsatt* (New Haven: Yale University Press, 1973), p. 387. Kenner ends his essay by describing "Burnt Norton" ("by intention a counter-poem to *The Waste Land*") as "a sustained homage to Mallarmé."

36. See Hartman, *Free Verse*, pp. 72–73.

37. See *Articulate Energy*, p. 94.

38. In "Pound and Eliot: A Distinction," in Graham Martin, ed., *Eliot in Perspective: A Symposium* (New York: Humanities Press, 1970), pp. 62–82.

39. The exception is line 7, which, read by itself, starts a mood of expectant hope.

40. Introduction to *Selected Poems* by Marianne Moore (New York: Macmillan, 1935), pp. xii–xiii.

41. Eliot's fascination with the OED comes into focus here. See above, chapter nine.

42. "A Commentary," *Criterion* XII.47 (January 1933), 248 (emphasis mine).

43. See Ranjee Shahani, "T. S. Eliot Answers Questions," *John O'London's Weekly*, 19 August 1949, pp. 497–98. I cite from a reprinting in P. Lal, ed., *T. S. Eliot: Homage from India* (Bombay, 1965), p. 132.

44. "Poet as Executant" (1947), in F. R. Leavis, ed., *A Selection from "Scrutiny": Volume One* (Cambridge: Cambridge University Press, 1968), p. 88.

45. See above, chapter seven, note 58.

46. See above, chapter nine, note 52.

47. See *Ferocious Alphabets* (Boston: Little, Brown, 1981). These assertions were anticipated by Hugh Kenner, who wrote in *T. S. Eliot: The Invisible Poet* (1959; rpt. New York: Citadel, 1954) that of the voice of "Burnt Norton," "we may remark first of all its selflessness; it is Old Possum's last disappearing-trick. No *persona* . . . is any longer needed. The words appear to be writing themselves" (p. 293).

48. Leavis, *Living Principle*, p. 177.

49. "Lewis Carroll and T. S. Eliot as Nonsense Poets," p. 69.

50. *The Field of Nonsense* (London: Chatto and Windus, 1952), pp. 37–38.

51. See, for example, Hartman, *Free Verse*, p. 127.

52. Review of *The Mystical Doctrine of St. John of the Cross*, abridged, trans. David Lewis, rev. Dom Benedict Zimmerman, O.D.C., introduction by R.H.J. Steuart, S. J., *Criterion*, XIII.53 (July 1934), 710. Donald Gallup's *T. S. Eliot: A Bibliography* (New York: Harcourt, Brace and World, 1969) attributes the review to Eliot. However, in a letter of 15 August 1952 (now at Milton Academy) Eliot assured Sister Anne C. Delaney that it had been written by McGreevy after all.

53. *The Mystical Doctrine* (1934; rpt. London: Sheed and Ward, 1948), pp. 91, 93–94.
54. Hartman, *Free Verse*, p. 124.

11. "A new and shocking valuation": *Four Quartets*

1. The letters are quoted in Helen Gardner, *The Composition of "Four Quartets"* (London: Faber and Faber, 1978), pp. 16–17 and 24–25.
2. "T. S. Eliot Talks about Himself and the Drive to Create," interview by John Lehmann, *New York Times Book Review*, 29 November 1953, p. 5.
3. On the tone of Eliot's regular evenings at Hayward's flat at 22 Bina Gardens, see Eliot's privately printed *Noctes Binanianae: Certain Voluntary and Satyrical Verses and Compliments as were lately Exchang'd between some of the Choicest Wits of the Age. Collected with the greatest care and now printed without castration after the most correct copies* (London, 1939). (For the purposes of the volume and the evenings that inspired it, Eliot was nicknamed Possum or Elephant; Hayward, Spider or Tarantula; Faber, Coot; and Morley, Whale.)

   Hayward, a promising student, met Eliot at Cambridge in the mid-twenties and went on to edit Donne and Swift. Before the war he became Eliot's closest companion and then, during the period of the *Quartets,* his respected confidant. From 1948 to 1957 the two were flatmates (Eliot called Hayward "landlord") at 19 Carlyle Mansions, Cheyne Walk. See T. S. Matthews, *Great Tom: Notes Towards the Definition of T. S. Eliot* (New York: Harper and Row, 1973), pp. 124–126 and 155–161, and Gardner, *Composition,* pp. 7–8.
4. See E. Martin Browne, *The Making of T. S. Eliot's Plays* (Cambridge: Cambridge University Press, 1969), p. 90.
5. Bonamy Dobrée, "T. S. Eliot: A Personal Reminiscence," in Allen Tate, ed., *T. S. Eliot: The Man and His Work* (New York: Delta, 1966), p. 83.
6. Letter dated "Holy Innocents Day [i.e. Childermas—December 28] 1939," in the Berg Collection of the New York Public Library.
7. See Robert Sencourt, *T. S. Eliot: A Memoir* (1971; rpt. New York: Delta, 1973), p. 152.
8. Ibid., p. 173.
9. For a fuller account of Eliot's intellectual activities during the later thirties, see John Margolis, *T. S. Eliot's Intellectual Development, 1922–1939* (Chicago: Chicago University Press, 1972), pp. 177–218.
10. "Last Words," *Criterion* XVIII.71 (January 1939), 269, 273–74.
11. It did not help that the first English edition of *Four Quartets,* published October 1944, incorrectly announced that the author had "always intended them to be published as one volume, and to be judged as a single work."
12. Eliot later hinted at the frequency of these episodes of self-revaluation when he told a correspondent that he was always discovering that the pictures he made of himself were incomplete, if not actually false. See his letter to Marian V[an] Dorn, 7 November 1954, included in the Marianne Moore Collection, Rosenbach Museum, Philadelphia, Pennsylvania.
13. Kristian Smidt, *The Importance of Recognition: Six Chapters on T. S. Eliot* (Tromso, 1973), p. 39.

14. Letter of "Shrove Tuesday, 1928" to Paul Elmer More, quoted in Margolis, *Eliot's Intellectual Development*, p. 142.

15. Many of Eliot's readers regard the Renaissance spelling as an unproblematic endorsement of the authority of inherited traditions. For examples, see Gardner, *Composition*, p. 42; Hugh Kenner, *The Pound Era* (Berkeley and Los Angeles: University of California Press, 1971), p. 438; George T. Wright, "Eliot Written in a Country Churchyard: The Elegy and *Four Quartets*," *ELH* 43 (1976), 227–43; and Donald Davie, "Anglican Eliot," in A. Walton Litz, ed., *Eliot in His Time* (Princeton: Princeton University Press, 1973), pp. 191 ff.

16. See A. D. Moody, *Thomas Stearns Eliot: Poet* (Cambridge: Cambridge University Press, 1979), pp. 209–10.

17. Letter to Professor H. S. Häusermann, quoted by Häusermann in *English Studies* for August 1941 and cited by Gardner in *Composition*, p. 43.

18. Häusermann's redaction, as given by Gardner in *Composition*, p. 43.

19. Ibid.

20. "Charybde et Scylla: lourdeur et frivolité," *Annales du Centre Universitaire Méditerranéen*, V (1951/52), 81. See above, chapter six, notes 45 and 46.

21. According to Gardner, *Composition*, p. 111, the "ice-cap" was important enough for Eliot to reintroduce it at a late stage of composition. Preparing notes for weaving the not-yet-written fifth section of "East Coker" into what he had already drafted, he connected the image with the theme of desolation and with the counter-theme of "Communion":

> Alone—the ice cap
> Separated from
>   the surfaces of
>   human beings
> To be reunited and
>   the Communion

22. From a letter of 1941 quoted in Gardner, *Composition*, p. 109.

23. See Gardner, *Composition*, pp. 18–19.

24. Ibid., p. 53.

25. From his 1928 preface to Edgar Ansel Mowrer, *This American World* (London: Faber & Gwyer, 1928), quoted in Gardner, *Composition*, p. 48.

26. Reproduced in Gardner, *Composition*, p. 118.

27. From Eliot's Introduction to *The Adventures of Huckleberry Finn*, by Samuel Clemens, 1950; rpt. in the Norton Critical Edition of the Novel, ed. Bradley, Beatty and Long (New York: 1962), pp. 324, 325, 327.

28. Ibid., pp. 324–25, 326.

29. See *Purgatorio* V. 101–29.

30. The first phrase is taken from Thomas Hooker's 1631 sermon "The Danger of Desertion." The second comes from Richard Sibbes's 1630 collection *The Bruised Reed and Smoking Flax*. I am indebted to Andrew Delbanco of Harvard University for drawing my attention to both.

31. In UPUC, Eliot said that such a memory "might lie dormant in [the poet's] mind for twenty years, and re-appear transformed in some verse-context charged with great imaginative pressure" (p. 79).

32. *Composition*, pp. 49–50.

33. Exactly when remains a vexed question. Although Eliot later told John Lehmann and Kristian Smidt he decided on four poems during the writing of "East Coker," Hayward's contemporary remarks suggest otherwise (see note 34). For Eliot and John Lehmann, see above, note 2. For Eliot's comment to Kristian Smidt, see Gardner's *Composition*, p. 18.

34. Hayward's paraphrase of Eliot in a letter to Frank Morley, January 1941, quoted in Gardner, *Composition*, p. 18.

35. As Hayward relayed to Morley in June 1941, Eliot "wants if possible to complete the cycle with a fourth poem—Earth, Air, Water, *Fire*—and has got as far as making a rough, preliminary draft." See Gardner, *Composition*, p. 21.

36. Quoted in Gardner, *Composition*, p. 18.

37. See above, chapter seven, p. 109.

38. Letter of 3 September 1942, quoted in Gardner, *Composition*, p. 26.

39. Quoted in Gardner, *Composition*, p. 109.

40. From Eliot's *Paris Review* interview. See Kay Dick, ed., *Writers at Work* (London: Penguin, 1972), pp. 123, 124. On another occasion, Eliot said that after *The Family Reunion*, "I wanted to sit down and write immediately another play free from [its] faults. Well, the war came and I had other duties and things to do, and I was here and there, so I turned to writing the other three *Quartets,* and they occupied the war years very well. I was able in the conditions in which I was living to write poems of that type and length." ("A Conversation, Recorded in 1958, Between T. S. Eliot and Leslie Paul," *Listener,* September 1969, p. 335.)

41. Helen Gardner, *The Art of T. S. Eliot* (1950; rpt. New York: Dutton, 1959), pp. 38, 37.

42. Donald Davie, "T. S. Eliot: The End of an Era," in Hugh Kenner, ed., *T. S. Eliot: A Collection of Critical Essays* (Englewood Cliffs: Prentice-Hall, 1962), p. 195.

43. Denis Donoghue, "T. S. Eliot's *Quartets:* A New Reading" (1965), in Bernard Bergonzi, ed., *T. S. Eliot, Four Quartets: A Casebook* (London: Macmillan, 1969), p. 231. Donoghue is here speaking primarily of "The Dry Salvages."

44. The remark comes from a draft of "The Three Voices of Poetry." See Moody, *Thomas Stearns Eliot,* p. 203.

45. See ibid., p. 238.

46. "A Commentary," *Criterion* XVI.63 (January 1937), 289–90.

47. "Mr. T. S. Eliot on 'George Herbert,' " *Salisbury and Winchester Journal,* 27 May 1938, p. 12. For more on Eliot's reappraisal of Herbert, see "George Herbert," *Spectator* CXLVIII.5411 (12 March 1932), 360–61 and *George Herbert* (London: Longmans, 1962).

48. From "Types of English Religious Verse," in the Eliot Collection, King's College, Cambridge. It should be noted that "Types of English Religious Verse" does more than point toward "Little Gidding"; it begins to assemble materials. Alluding, for example, to Herbert Grierson's *Cross Currents in the XVII Century* and Basil Willey's *Seventeenth Century Background,* it points to what the fourth *Quartet* would call the "common genius" of seventeenth-century life in "a new religious self-consciousness generated by the religious warfare both physical and intellectual." In the lecture, Eliot locates

the beginning of this self-consciousness in Robert Southwell's "The Burning Babe":

> My faultless breast the furnace is, the fuel wounding thorns;
> Love is the fire, and sighs the smoke. . . .

Then, as he would do in "Little Gidding," Eliot combines these images of fire with a remembrance of the English Civil War and a glance back at the fourteenth century: it was "that great scholar" R. W. Chambers, he said, who had called attention to the popularity in the seventeenth century of works like *The Cloud of Unknowing* and the writings of Richard Rolle and the Lady Juliana of Norwich—"the body of religious prose composed during the great period of English mysticism, the fourteenth century."

49. C. A. Bodelsen, *T. S. Eliot's Four Quartets: A Commentary* (Odense: Copenhagen University, 1958), p. 111.

50. For what will probably remain the fullest articulation of Eliot's symbolic orchestrations, see James Olney, *Metaphors of Self: The Meaning of Autobiography* (Princeton: Princeton University Press, 1972), pp. 275–99.

51. From Eliot's *George Herbert*, p. 13.

52. "Mr. T. S. Eliot on 'George Herbert,' " 12.

53. F. R. Leavis in *The Living Principle: "English" as a Discipline of Thought* (New York: Oxford University Press, 1975), p. 253.

54. P. N. Furbank, *E. M. Forster: A Life* (New York: Harcourt Brace Jovanovich, 1978), II.332.

55. *Criterion* XV.61 (July 1936), 759–60. Had *The Yellow Spot* been as sensationalistic as the *Criterion* review implies, or had the review been in tune with the prevailing attitudes of 1936, the piece would still make unpleasant reading. In fact, although printed with a number of provocative photographs by the leftist Gollancz Press and lacking the reassuring apparatus of scholarly reference (witnesses in Germany then being not eager to be identified), the book struck other reviewers as both fair and important. On the left, Michael Foot wrote in *The New Statesman & Nation* for 21 March 1936 that it was "detailed and well documented" and "must make even the most insensitive reader gasp with horror" (p. 46). In the center, the anonymous *TLS* reviewer called it "timely and valuable." (See the *TLS* for 11 April 1936, p. 307.)

56. *Writers at Work,* p. 127. Helen Gardner, who cites these remarks in *Composition,* notes that in the letter he sent with a proof copy of the *Quartets* to John Hayward, Eliot, although "less satisfied [with the *Quartets* then than afterwards] . . . took the same view that the poems 'got better' as they went on" (p. 4).

57. "Views and Reviews," *New English Weekly* VII.18 (12 September 1935), 351.

58. See above, note 1.

59. Letter of 12 February 1941, in the Eliot Collection, King's College, Cambridge. The raillery ends with four stanzas of a rude ballad as unlike "The Dry Salvages" as they could be.

60. Letter of 14 July 1941, quoted in Gardner, *Composition,* pp. 22–23.

61. Letter of 5 August 1941, quoted in Gardner, *Composition,* p. 24.

62. See above, note 1.

63. Dobrée, "T. S. Eliot: A Personal Reminiscence," p. 86.

64. For the citations in this paragraph, see Gardner, *Composition*, pp. 22–27.
65. William V. Spanos, "Hermenuetics and Memory: Destroying T. S. Eliot's *Four Quartets*," *Genre* XI (Winter 1978), 559. Spanos goes too far, however, in arguing that the "decreative" aspects of the suite are definitive.
66. Gardner, *Composition*, p. 157.
67. Ibid.
68. See ibid., p. 174.
69. Ibid., p. 183.
70. Letter of 27 August 1942, quoted in ibid., pp. 64–65.
71. Harding published his essay in 1943. I quote from a reprint in Kenner, *T. S. Eliot: A Collection of Critical Essays*, pp. 125–28. According to Harding, Eliot's point is to describe

    the dreary bitterness in which a life of literary culture can end if it has brought no sense of spiritual values. The life presented is one, such as Mr. Eliot's own, of effort after clear speech and exact thought, and the passage amounts to a shuddering "There but for the grace of God go I." It reveals more clearly than ever the articles in *The Criterion* did, years ago, what it was in "humanism" that Mr. Eliot recoiled from so violently. What the humanist's ghost sees in his life are futility, isolation, and guilt on account of his self-assertive prowess—"Which once you took for exercise of virtue"—and the measure of aggression against others which that must bring (p. 126).

72. OPP, 295, 307. Around the first World War, according to Richard Ellmann, Eliot's personal reaction to Yeats was chiefly boredom. The Irishman's two subjects of conversation, he then lamented, "[were] George Moore and spooks." See Ellmann, *Eminent Domain* (New York: Oxford University Press, 1967), p. 90.
73. According to his notes in the Harvard Archives Division, Eliot gave two lectures on Yeats and a third on the Irish theatre.
74. "A Commentary," *Criterion* XIV.57 (July 1935), 612–13.
75. Unpublished lecture in the Eliot Collection, King's College, Cambridge.
76. SE, 167; from "Cyril Tourneur" (1930). For earlier expressions of the same view, see Eliot's seventh and eighth Clark Lectures (1926).
77. "The Oxford Jonson," *Dial* LXXXV.1 (July 1928), 68.
78. Ibid.
79. "Donne in Our Time," in Theodore Spencer, ed., *A Garland for John Donne* (Cambridge: Harvard University Press, 1931), p. 10.
80. From Yeats's "The Spur," quoted by Eliot in OPP, 302.
81. Hayward to Frank Morley, February 1940, quoted in Gardner, *Composition*, p. 17.
82. From Yeats's "Vacillation." The echo has been pointed out before, most recently in Gardner, *Composition*, p. 68.
83. See above, chapter one, note 28.
84. "The Oxford Jonson," 68.

Index

Abel, Richard, 258n, 259n, 265n
Accidental objects: in poetry, 20, 41–42, 51–52
Adams, Henry: TSE on, 8, 22, 25, 32, 137, 244n–245n
Adams, J. Donald, 243n
Adolescence, evocations of in TSE's poetry, 90–91; as a state to be transcended, TSE on, 84–85, 143
Aeneid, 11
Aeschylus, 48, 49
Aiken, Conrad, 17, 55, 56, 240n, 262n; praise of TSE's *Poems*, and TSE's reply, 8; on TSE's "beautiful gibberish," 77, 150, 250n; on TSE, 248n; on TSE's marriage, 102; "For T.S. Eliot," 238n
Aldington, Richard, 20, 81, 240n, 254n, 256n
Allan, Mowbray, 246n, 247n
Andrewes, Lancelot, 109–110, 124, 127, 234; TSE on, 113–114
Apollinaire, Guillaume, *Calligrammes*, 179
Aquinas, St. Thomas, 83
Aristophanes, 81, 251n
Aristotle, 48
Arnold, Matthew, 114; TSE on, 24, 77
Ash Wednesday, 5, 39, 86, 95, 98, 107, 109–110, 129–130, 154, 164–165, 174, 188–189, 195, 199, 203; quoted, 34, 75, 77; TSE on, 131; and TSE's life, 132–133, 146–147; organization of, 134; section I, 134–137; section II, 137–143; section II, compared with *The Waste Land*, 139–142; section III, 143–145; section IV, 145–149; section IV, compared with "Burnt Norton," 189; section IV, compared with "Marina," 168; section V, 149–151; section VI, 151–153

Ashbery, John, 179
Auden, W.H., 98, 261n, 266n
Auditory imagination, TSE on the dangers of, 76–77
Augustine, St., *Confessions*, 15, 260n
Awoi No Uye, 49

Babbitt, Irving, 7, 71, 250n
Baudelaire, Charles, 14, 19, 147, 175, 260n, 262n
Beethoven, Ludwig van, 153, 178
Beckett, Samuel, 40
Belief attitudes, 112, 129
Benda, Julien, 71; *Belphegor*, 250n
Bennett, Arnold, 81
Bergonzi, Bernard, 255n, 265n
Bergson, Henri, 10, 18, 243n
Bernstein, David, 257n
Blake, William, 5–6, 43, 73, 111, 234
Bodelsen, C.A., 224, 274n
Bolgan, Anne C., 249n
Bornstein, George, 239n
"Boston doubt," TSE on, 8, 10, 14, 18
Bradley, F.H., 10, 18, 20, 43, 243n, 245n
Breslin, James, 179, 267n
Brooks, Cleanth, 249n
Brown, R.D., 259n
Browne, Martin, 184, 186, 187, 268n, 271n
Browning, Robert, 19, 20, 108; "Childe Roland," 74, 253n, 254n
Burne, Glenn S., 246n, 247n
"Burnt Norton," 39, 94, 116, 118, 123, 130, 148, 158, 169–170, 172–173, 176–178, 183, 186, 219–222, 224–225, 227, 234, 266n, 268n, 270n; quoted, 34, 39, 118, 178; sources of, in TSE's life, 185–189; links to "New Hampshire," 186, 268n; links to *The*

"Burnt Norton," *(Continued)*
  Family Reunion, 188–192; links to
  Murder in the Cathedral, 186–187; section I, 188–192; section I, questions
  raised by, 198–200; language of, 192–
  198; and question of poetic voice,
  199; sections II–V, 201–207; compared with *The Waste Land*, 189, 200;
  compared with *Ash Wednesday*, 202–
  203; compared with "East Coker,"
  211–214
Byron, George Gordon, Lord, 27

Camelots du roi, 17, 153, 242n
Carroll, Lewis, 147–148, 192, 200,
  268n–269n
Cavalcanti, Guido, TSE on, 83, 111–
  112, 252n
Chambers, R.W., 274n
Chapman, George, 26, 94, 244n
Cheetham, Eric, 185
Chiari, Joseph, 177, 267n
Childhood: memories, as recurring im-
  ages, TSE on, 42–43, 184, 217, 272n;
  memories, recurrence in TSE's poetry,
  128, 132–133, 186, 215, 217, 272n; in
  "Animula," 119, 121; in *Ash Wednes-
  day*, 146–147; music of, in TSE's
  verse, 158, 169; in "Landscapes," 170
Childs, Marquis, 146
Chorus, TSE's use of, 95, 97–98, 169
Coffey, P., 241n
Coleridge, S. T., 45, 183–184, 244n
Conrad, Joseph, 47, 160, 215; *Heart of
  Darkness*, 96
Copeland, Charles Townsend, 243n
Coriolan, 17, 153–156; "Triumphal
  March," 153–155; "Difficulties of a
  Statesman," 155–156
Corbière, Tristan, 173; TSE on, 175
Crashaw, Richard, 90, 175–176, 253n
Criterion (journal), 103, 106, 209, 210
Cronin, Anthony, 248n
Crosby, Harry, 124–125, 130

Dance, TSE on, 111, 202, 205
Dante: 14–15, 50, 56, 83–88, 90, 98,
  111–112, 118–119, 236, 252n; *Convivio*, 15; and Mallarmé, 159; *Vita
  Nuova*, 83–88, 90, 98, 133–134, 138,
  164, 252n; *Purgatorio*, 89, 112, 116,
  118–119, 143, 146–148, 158–159,

217, 231–232, 253n; *Purgatorio* and
  Vita Nuova, TSE on correspondence
  between, 133, 146; *Inferno*, 33; and
  "Gerontion," 33–34, 37; and "Little
  Gidding," 229–230; *Paradiso*, 253n
Davie, Donald, 157, 195, 222, 249n,
  255n, 263n, 270n, 272n, 273n
Davies, Sir John, TSE on, 116–118
Delbanco, Andrew, 272n
Denham, John, 171
Dickinson, Emily, 217
Dobrée, Bonamy, 209, 227, 271n, 274n
Donne, John: *Devotions*, 64; TSE on, 51,
  83–86, 109–112, 124, 171, 174, 252n,
  257; "The Blossome," 84
Donoghue, Denis, 222, 249n, 273n; *Ferocious Alphabets*, 199, 270n
Dostoevsky, Feodor: *Crime and Punishment*, 17, 57, 72, 165, 253n; TSE on,
  51–52, 71–72, 94, 172, 242n; *The Idiot*, 57; and "The wind sprang up at
  four o'clock," 253n
Dream(s): in "Gerontion," 40; TSE's interest in, 49; in TSE's early poetry,
  49; and drama, TSE on, 49–50; as
  mode of self-discovery, for TSE, 50–
  51; in *The Waste Land*, 63–66; in Poe's
  work, TSE on, 77–78; of TSE's later
  poetry, 129, 130; in *Ash Wednesday*,
  139. *See also* Nightmare
Dryden, John, TSE on, 114–115, 120,
  173
Duncan Jones, E.E., 143, 261n
Dunne, Annie, 7, 146, 240n

"East Coker," 211–215, 219–222, 227–
  228, 234, 272n; quoted, 178
The Egoist, TSE's writing for, 20–21
Eliot, Ada, 105
Eliot, Charlotte, 5, 7, 54, 155, 242n; vis-
  its TSE in England, 55; on TSE's poetry, 160
Eliot, Henry Ware, 9, 242n, 267n;
  death, 55
Eliot, T.S.: marriage to Vivien, 53; separation from Vivien, 4, 157, 209–210;
  self-conscious disposition toward rhetoric, 20, 25, 243n; expatriation, 5, 9,
  18, 240n; self-doubts, 7–9, 67, 99,
  155–156, 185, 209, 227–228, 240n;
  breakdown, 9, 55, 68; aims of early
  poetry, 5–6, 10–11; emotional charac-

teristics of early poetry, 67, 85–86; conversion, 14, 105, 106, 127, 131; strives to transform himself in his twenties, 17, in his thirties and early forties, 82, 103–106, in his mid-forties, 184–186; writing in French, 17–18; seeks new voice, 18–19; on psychoanalysis and literature, 53; quarrel with parents over his marriage, 53–54; unhappy married life, 55, 104–106, 209–210; reaction to his father's death, 55; on literary borrowing, 58, 101; change in poetic aims after *The Waste Land*, 72–73, 81–83, 86, 98–99, 102–103, 108–109, 112–114, 117–119, 122–123, 129, 142, 157, 176, 192–193, 199, 227; on difference between his intentions and his actual work produced, 81, 251n; reenvisions his life in a double pattern, 77, 94–95, 103, 105, 165, 172–173; sees in Shakespearean romance his own experience of spiritual rebirth, 164–166, 178; interest in what lies "beyond character" and "beyond poetry," 166, 168, 169, 174, 178–179, 199, 201; attempts new start in his marriage, 105–106; striving for linguistic precision, 116–118; style of reciting his poetry, 123, 198–199; renews friendship with Emily Hale, 185; feeling for the history of words, 160, 174, 176–177, 198; spends 1932–33 in America and returns to England, 183–185; agrees to write church pageant, 184–185; Churchwarden at St. Stephen's, 185; on trials of writing, 209; depression, in 1939, 209–211; involvement in public affairs in the thirties, 210; self-accusations, provoked by "Burnt Norton," 211, 214–215, 225, 271n; conditions of his writing, during war years, 221, 273n; conflicts about set poetic form, 6, 108–109, 220, 227

POETRY AND PLAYS:

Anabasis (translation), 125–126, 128, 142, 153, 176, 259n, 263n

"Animula," 103, 119–122, 127, 132, 167, 203

Ariel poems. *See* "Animula," "Journey of the Magi," "Marina," "A Song for Simeon"

Ash Wednesday. See main entry under title

"Burbank with a Baedeker: Bleistein with a Cigar," 23–29, 32, 35–36, 58

"Burnt Norton." *See* main entry under title

"Cape Ann," 169–171

The Cocktail Party, 43, 60, 65–66, 187, 188, 241n

The Confidential Clerk, 7, 36

"A Cooking Egg," 155

Coriolan. See main entry under title

"Cousin Nancy," 23–24

"A Debate Between Body and Soul," 19

"Doris's Dream Songs," 86–92, 94–96

"The Dry Salvages," 4, 7, 153, 215–219, 221–224, 228

"East Coker," 178, 211–215, 219–222, 227–228, 234, 235, 272n; quoted, 178

The Elder Statesman, 8

The Family Reunion, 15–17, 49, 58, 60, 155, 161, 188–193, 209, 239n–240n, 269n

Four Quartets. See main entry under title

"Gerontion," 32–40, 51–52, 54, 108, 151, 155–156, 193, 244n–245n; ms. ending of, 39

The Hollow Men. See main entry under title

"Journey of the Magi," 95, 116, 126–129, 147, 149, 164, 167, 176, 199

"La Figlia Che Piange," 11–14, 17, 18, 58, 67, 134, 148, 189, 242n

"Lines for an Old Man," 266n

"Lines to a Persian Cat," 158

"Little Gidding." *See* main entry under title

"The Love Song of J. Alfred Prufrock." *See* main entry under title

"The Love Song of St. Sebastian," 19, 58

"Marina," 75, 95, 149, 163, 166–169, 172, 218, 265n

Murder in the Cathedral, 97, 115, 161, 169, 170, 185–187, 268n, 269n

"New Hampshire," 158, 169–171, 186, 268n, 269n

"Ode on Independence Day, July 4th, 1918," 155, 263n

"Portrait of a Lady," 42

"Preludes," 42, 49

"Rannoch, by Glencoe," 170–172

"Rhapsody on a Windy Night," 10

Eliot, T.S. *(Continued)*
  The Rock, 123, 169, 205, 212
  "Salutation," 138
  "Som de L'Escalina," 143
  "A Song for Simeon," 95, 107–110,
    127, 164, 167
  "Song to the Opherian," 87, 89, 252n
  Sweeney Agonistes, 17, 41, 58, 73, 81,
    95–98, 153, 162, 254n
  "Three Poems," 91–94
  "Usk," 170–171
  "Virginia," 170–171
  The Waste Land. See main entry under
    title
  The Waste Land drafts, 9, 18, 55, 57,
    82, 240n, 241n, 247n, 249n
  "Whispers of Immortality," 51, 171
  "The wind sprang up at four o'clock,"
    87, 89, 98, 253n
  PROSE:
  "Address," *From Mary to You,* 260n
  After Strange Gods, 235
  "American Literature and the Ameri-
    can Language," 7, 86, 240n
  "Artists and Men of Genius," 265n
  "The Ballet," 257n
  "The Beating of a Drum," 251n,
    254n, 257n
  "Ben Jonson," 47, 244n
  "Beyle and Balzac," 16, 242n, 247n
  "The Bible as Scripture and Litera-
    ture" (unpublished), 247n, 255n
  "The Borderline of Prose," 265n
  "Byron," 264n
  "Charles Whibley: A Memoir," 264n
  "Charybde et Scylla: lourdeur et frivo-
    lité," 251n, 254n, 264n, 272n
  Clark lectures ("Lectures on the Meta-
    physical Poetry of the Seventeenth
    Century," unpublished), 82–86, 90,
    94, 103, 104, 107, 110–111, 165,
    172, 175, 241n, 252n, 253n, 265n,
    275n
  Commentaries (in the *Criterion*), 183,
    210, 240n, 257n, 267n, 270n, 271n,
    273n, 275n
  "A Contemporary Thomist," 9, 241n
  "Cyril Tourneur," 275n
  "Dante" (1920), 56, 112
  "Dante," 85, 88, 116, 133, 246n, 257n,
    260n
  "Donne in Our Time," 111, 257n,
    275n
  Edinburgh lectures ("Shakespeare as

  Poet and Dramatist," unpublished),
    165, 168–169, 265n
  "Eeldrop and Appleplex, I," 45–46,
    246n, 249n
  "The Eliot Family and St. Louis," 7,
    240n, 262n
  "English Literature from 1890 to the
    Present Day" (unpublished lecture
    notes), 27, 183, 232, 244n, 259n,
    267n, 275n
  "English Poets as Letter Writers" (un-
    published), 267n
  "Euripides and Professor Murray,"
    47
  "Ezra Pound," 20, 243n, 250n
  For Lancelot Andrewes, 104, 147, 241n,
    255n, 262n
  "Four Elizabethan Dramatists, A Pref-
    ace," 257n
  "Francis Herbert Bradley," 260n
  "From Poe to Valéry," 77
  "From T.S. Eliot," 250
  "The Function of Criticism," 103
  "George Herbert," 273n
  George Herbert, 273n, 274n
  "Hamlet and His Problems," 47
  "Harold Monro," 244n
  "Hommage à Charles Maurras," 256n
  "The Idea of a Literary Review," 250n
  an interview, in *Grantite Review,* 242n
  an interview, in *Paris Review,* 17,
    242n, 264n, 273n
  introduction to *The Adventures of
    Huckleberry Finn,* 272n
  introduction to *Anabasis,* 259n
  introduction to *Ezra Pound: Literary Es-
    says,* 245n
  introduction to *Ezra Pound: Selected
    Poems,* 239n, 244n, 250n
  introduction to G.W. Knight, *The
    Wheel of Fire,* 163, 243n, 264n, 265n
  introduction to Marianne Moore, *Se-
    lected Poems,* 42, 115, 245n, 258n,
    265n, 270n
  introduction to Josef Pieper, *Leisure,*
    240n
  introduction to Paul Valéry, *Art of Po-
    etry,* 159, 176, 264n, 267n
  introduction to Paul Valéry, "Le Ser-
    pent," 5, 82, 98, 100, 251n, 252n,
    254n
  "Isolated Superiority," 239n
  *John Dryden: The Poet, the Dramatist, the
    Critic,* 114

"John Dryden I. The Poet Who Gave the English Speech," 258n

"John Dryden II. Dryden the Dramatist," 247n

"John Dryden III. Dryden the Critic, Defender of Sanity," 258n

"John Ford," 163, 165

"John Marston," 94, 165, 172, 254n

Knowledge and Experience in the Philosophy of F.H. Bradley, 10, 18, 43, 49, 241n, 245n, 247n

"Lancelot Andrewes," 110, 113–114, 118

"The Last Twenty Five Years of English Poetry" (unpublished), 233, 258n

"Leçon de Valéry," 255n

"Lectures on the Metaphysical Poetry of the Seventeenth Century." *See* Clark Lectures

"Lettre d'Angleterre," 245n

"The Literature of Fascism," 263n

"London Letters," for the *Dial*, 53, 242n, 247n, 248n, 250n, 257n

"Marianne Moore," 254n

"Marivaux," 244n

"The Metaphysical Poets," 20, 258n

"Milton I," 258n

Milton Academy Address, 3–4, 6, 183–184, 192

"The Minor Metaphysicals: From Cowley to Dryden," 258n

"Mr. Lee Masters," 239n, 241n

"Mr. Lucas's Webster," 265n

"Mr. T.S. Eliot on 'George Herbert,'" 273n, 274n

"The Music of Poetry," 77, 177, 250n

"Mystic and Politician as Poet: Vaughan, Traherne, Marvell, Milton," 268n

"The New Elizabethans and the Old," 244n, 247n

"The Noh and the Image," 247n, 265n

"A Note on Poetry and Belief," 257n

"A Note on Richard Crashaw," 253n

"Note sur Mallarmé et Poe," 129, 158, 173–176, 193, 259n, 263n, 266n, 269n

"Notes on the Blank Verse of Christopher Marlowe," 47, 244n

"Notes on Current Letters," 254n

"Notes on the Way," 247n

"Observations," 258n

Oxford Extension Lectures on Modern French Literature, 243n

"The Oxford Jonson," 275n

"The Pensées of Pascal," 105–106

"The Perfect Critic," 245n

"Philip Massinger," 46–47, 108

"Poetical and Prosaic Use of Words" (unpublished), 264n

"Poetry and Propaganda," 257n

"The Possibility of a Poetic Drama," 47

"The Post-Georgians," 6, 240n, 268n

"The Preacher as Artist," 109–110, 257n

preface to Edgar Ansel Mowrer, *This American World*, 272n

preface to *Transit of Venus: Poems by Harry Crosby*, 124–125, 130, 258n, 259n

"Prefatory Note" to Aiken's "An Anatomy of Melancholy," 248n

"Prose and Verse," 265n

"Reflections on Contemporary Poetry I," 20, 41, 51, 244n, 245n

"Reflections on Contemporary Poetry III," 21, 244n

"Reflections on Contemporary Poetry IV," 10, 241n

"Reflections on Vers Libre," 255n

"The Relative Sublime," 246n

review of *The Education of Henry Adams* ("A Sceptical Patrician"), 8, 25, 32, 137, 245n, 260n

review of A.E. Housman, *The Name and Nature of Poetry*, 248n

review of Wyndham Lewis, *The Lion and the Fox*, 263n

review of J.M. Robertson, *The Problems of the Shakespeare Sonnets*, 260n

"Rhetoric and Poetic Drama," 29, 47, 244n

"A Romantic Aristocrat" (revision of "A Romantic Patrician"), 22, 244n

The Sacred Wood, 5–6, 29, 44, 73, 82, 110–111, 115, 245n

"Seneca in Elizabethan Translation," 34

A Sermon (Magdalene College Chapel, 3/7/48), 240n, 243n

"Shakespeare and the Stoicism of Seneca," 112, 257n, 260n

"Sir John Davies," 116–118, 122, 134

"Sir John Denham," 265n

Eliot, T.S. *(Continued)*
  "The Social Function of Poetry," 112,
    258n
  "Style and Thought," 241n
  "Swinburne as Poet," 49, 90, 255n
  "The Three Provincialities," 264n
  "The Three Voices of Poetry," 6,
    108–109, 113, 257n, 273n
  "Tradition and the Individual Tal-
    ent," 27, 43, 45
  "Tradition in the Practice of Poetry,"
    242n
  Turnbull Lectures ("Varieties of Meta-
    physical Poetry," unpublished), 175,
    241n, 266n
  "Types of English Religious Verse"
    (unpublished), 261n, 273n–274n
  "Ulysses, Order, and Myth," 71, 250n
  "Une feuillet unique," 259n
  *The Use of Poetry and the Use of Criti-
    cism*, 30, 43, 44, 77, 162, 172, 183–
    184, 217, 241n, 244n, 245n–246n,
    250n, 253n, 257n, 259n, 272n
  "Views and Reviews," 274n
  "Wanley and Chapman," 253n, 262n
  "What Dante Means to Me," 229, 236
  in "What France Means to You," 242n
  "Whether Rostand Had Something
    About Him" (revised as "Rhetoric
    and Poetic Drama"), 29, 244n
  "Yeats," 233–235
Eliot, Vivien, 4, 53–55, 58, 103, 104–
    105, 182, 185, 209–210, 219, 256n–
    257n
Eliot, William Greenleaf, 7, 242n
Elizabethan drama: TSE's interest in,
    21–22, 29, 38, 172–173, 244n
Ellmann, Richard, 243n, 247n, 275n
Elyot, Sir Thomas, in "East Coker,"
    212–213
Emerson, Ralph Waldo, 6, 7, 9, 24, 102,
    216, 227, 240n, 246n
Emotion(s): TSE's conflicts about, 6–7,
    8–14, 21, 85–86, 117–118, 122, 133,
    212; expressing, TSE on, 41–42;
    Shakespeare's treatment of, TSE on,
    165–166
Euripides, TSE on, 48
Everett, Barbara, 268n

Faber, Geoffrey, 104, 271n
Fitzgerald, F. Scott, 266n
Flaubert, Gustave, 20, 46–48, 178, 244n,

247n; TSE on, 16; *Bouvard et Pécuchet*,
    47
Fletcher, John, 183
Flower, Newman, 251n
Foot, Michael, 274n
Ford, Ford Madox, 74
Forster, E.M., 45, 246n; on "Little Gid-
    ding," 226
Forwood, Muriel, 268n
Four Quartets, 77, 95, 99, 101–102, 115,
    118, 123, 157–159, 174, 177, 179,
    188, 271n; TSE on language of, 161;
    development, 208, 211, 215; develop-
    ment, TSE's account of, 208; four-
    part symmetry, development, 219–
    221, 273n; form, TSE on, 220–221;
    relaxed use of language in, 221–224;
    public voice in, 222–224; TSE's patri-
    otism reflected in, 222–224; as reli-
    gious meditation, 224; theodicy in,
    224–226, 229; composition, as imita-
    tion of himself, TSE on, 227–228;
    TSE on, 227, 274n
Freud, Sigmund, 66, 224
Fry, Roger, 106, 266n–267n
Furbank, P.N., 274n

Gallup, Donald, 270n
Garden(s): of *Ash Wednesday*, 140–142,
    148; of "Burnt Norton," 148, 189–
    192; of TSE's work, varied meanings,
    189
Gardner, Helen, 251n, 260n, 267n,
    268n, 271n, 272n, 273n, 274n, 275n;
    on *The Hollow Men*, 94, 253n; on
    "Burnt Norton," 186, 193; on "East
    Coker," 213; on "The Dry Salvages,"
    218; on composition of "Litttle Gid-
    ding," 228–229
Gerstärker, Friedrich, "Germelshausen,"
    213
Goheen, Robert F., 244n
The Golden Bough, 71, 72
Gordon, Lyndall, 54, 106, 240n, 241n,
    242n, 243n, 247n, 248n, 249n, 257n,
    268n
Gourmont, Rémy de, 45–47, 56, 71,
    140, 245n–246n
Graves, Robert, 25
Gray, Thomas, "Elegy," TSE's admira-
    tion of, 99, 162, 254n, 264n
Greene, Edward, 173, 241n, 242n, 246n,
    259n, 265n

Grierson, Herbert, 273n
Gross, Harvey, 270n

Haigh-Wood, Vivien. *See* Eliot, Vivien
Hale, Emily, 185–186, 268n
Hansen, Erik Arne, 265n
Harding, D.W., 70, 193, 232, 250n, 269n, 275n
Hargrove, Nancy, 265n
Harmon, William, 244n
Harper, George Mills, 257n
Harris, Daniel, 259n
Hartman, Charles O., 270n, 271n
Harvard: TSE at, 3, 7, 9, 18, 174, 183–184
Häusermann, H.S., 272n
Hayward, John, 187, 209, 215, 220, 227–228, 268n, 271n, 273n, 275n
Headings, Philip R., 253n, 261n
Heaney, Seamus, 172, 265n
Heidegger, Martin, 158
Hemingway, Ernest, TSE's respect for, 5, 240n
Herbert, George, TSE on, 224, 225, 273n
Holland, Norman N., 239n
The Hollow Men, 4, 33, 55, 81, 83, 86, 90, 92, 122–123, 165, 171, 230n, 251n, 254n; evolution of, 86–95, 252n–253n; compared with "Prufrock," 89; landscapes of, 90; stylistic technique, 93; voices of, 95–98; TSE's final reworking of, compared with *The Waste Land*, 96–97; use of chorus, 95, 97–98; stylistic developments in, 100–101; compared to "Simeon," 107–108; and Dante, 87–91, 93–94, 98, 133, 251n; and *Ash Wednesday*, 131; TSE on, 157
Honesty: poetic, TSE on, 5–6, 21, 69, 234. *See also* Sincerity
Hooker, Thomas, 272n
Howarth, Herbert, 239n, 255n
Hulme, T.E., 71; influence on TSE's generation, TSE on, 252n
Husserl, Edmund, *Ideas*, 153
Hutchinson, Mary, 262n

Images trouvailles, 42, 57, 69, 248n
Imagism: 52, 76, 112; TSE on, 41, 124; TSE leaves behind, 98, 122, 124, 147
Impersonality: 5, 44–47; TSE's revised

view of, 110–111, 160, 234, 246n. *See also* Personality
Indeterminacy, in TSE's poetry after *The Waste Land*, 128–130, 142, 178–179, 199, 201
Incantation: TSE on, 123; in *The Waste Land*, 75–76, 122; in "Animula," 122; in *The Rock*, 123; in *Ash Wednesday*, 137, 140–142, 150; and Poe, 122; and Mallarmé, TSE on, 174, 176; in "Burnt Norton," 197

James, Henry, 25, 66–67; "The Jolly Corner," 3; novels, TSE's praise of, 8; "The Aspern Papers," 27–28; "Daisy Miller," 27; *The Portrait of a Lady*, 27; "The Beast in the Jungle," 38; TSE on, 47, 76, 183; *The Golden Bowl*, quoted, 53
John of the Cross, St., 95, 158, 203–204; in *Ash Wednesday*, 152
Jonson, Ben, TSE on, 48, 57
Joyce, James: TSE on, 47; *Ulysses*, TSE's review of, 71–72; *Ulysses*, 76–77, 98; *Finnegans Wake*, 125, 200, 249n
Juliana of Norwich, 225, 274n

Keats, John, 20, 81; "Ode to a Nightingale," 62
Kellond, Ellen, 249n
Kenner, Hugh, 34, 41, 58, 72, 157, 194, 245n, 248n, 249n, 250n, 251n, 254n, 255n, 262n, 263n, 269n, 270n, 272n, 273n, 275n
Killorin, Joseph, 248n
Kinsolving, Sally Bruce, 160
Kipling, Rudyard, "They," 187; quoted, 183
Knight, G. Wilson, 153, 163–164, 168, 263n, 265n; *The Wheel of Fire*, TSE's introduction to, 163, 243n
Knodel, Arthur J., 258n, 259n
Kyd, Thomas, 29

Laforgue, Jules, 10, 13, 17, 19, 21, 82, 84, 86, 157, 173–174, 175, 241n, 242n
Lal, P., 258n, 270n
Language: "natural sin of" (TSE), 6, 188, 240n; poet's responsibility to, TSE on, 159–160, 264n; remade, in

Language *(Continued)*
   Mallarmé's verse, 158–159; use of, in "Burnt Norton," 193–198. *See also* Speech
Latini, Brunetto, 230, 232
Lawall, Sarah, 239n
Lawrence, D.H., 76, 246n; TSE on, 3; *Women in Love*, 77; *The Plumed Serpent*, 200
Leavis, F.R., 188, 193, 199, 200, 225, 251n, 268n, 269n, 270n, 274n
Lehmann, John, 99, 255n, 268n, 271n, 273n
Lewis, Wyndham, 47, 264n; *The Lion and the Fox*, 155
Lipking, Lawrence, 188, 264n, 268n
"Little Gidding," 159, 222, 224–237; TSE on, 183, 227; as religious meditation, 224–225; composition, TSE's delay over, 227–228; evolution of, 228–232; and Dante, 229–232; and Yeats, 231, 236; and Swift, 233–236
Litz, A. Walton, 72, 248n, 250n, 263n
Lloyd's bank, TSE at, 54, 104, 256n
"The Love Song of J. Alfred Prufrock," 10–12, 20, 25, 30, 33, 36, 39, 42, 54–55, 61, 75–76, 89–90, 108, 145, 155, 215; autobiographical elements in, TSE on, 241n–242n

Maeterlinck, Maurice, 30
Mallarmé, Stéphane, 17, 99, 114, 123–124, 129, 147, 157–159, 179, 194, 197, 240n, 255n, 266n, 268n; and the reminting of experience, 159, 174, 263n–264n; and *Four Quartets*, 164; TSE on, 157, 173–179, 193; technique, TSE on, 175–176; "M'introduire dans ton histoire," TSE on, 175–176; "The Crisis of Poetry," 176, 240n, 267n; and Dante, 159; and "Burnt Norton," 193–194, 197
Margolis, John, 271n, 272n
Marlowe, Christopher, 21, 29
Marivaux, TSE on, 31
Marston, John, 26, 94
Martin, Grahame, 255n, 270n
Mary Institute, 132, 189
Massinger, Philip, 46, 47, 108
Masters, Edgar Lee, TSE on, 241n
Matthiessen, F.O., 251n, 258n, 263n, 267n

Maurras, Charles, 71, 105, 153, 155, 252n, 255n–256n
Maxwell, D.E.S., 252n
McGreevy, Thomas, 203, 270n
Melville, Herman, 217
Meredith, George, "Lucifer in Starlight," 24
Merton College, Oxford, TSE at, 18
Middleton, Thomas, *The Changeling*, 38
Miller, James E., Jr., 263n
Miller, J. Hillis, 245n, 265n; on TSE's poetry, 166
Milton, John: *Paradise Lost*, 76; TSE on, 76–77
Milton Academy, TSE at, 3–4, 183
Modernism, TSE and, 76–77, 200
Monroe, Harriet, *The New Poetry*, TSE's review of, 21
Moody, A.D., 38, 152, 212, 245n, 250n, 253n, 261n, 262n, 263n, 272n, 273n
Moore, Marianne, 157, 160, 197–198, 258n, 267n; TSE on, 42, 115–116, 197
More, Paul Elmer, 272n
Morley, Frank, 104, 105, 157, 184, 209, 227–228, 256n, 257n, 267n, 268n, 271n, 273n, 275n
Morrell, Ottoline, 94, 96, 97, 260n, 261n
Morris, William, 50
Mowrer, Edgar Ansel, 272n
Munthe, Axel, 268n
Murry, John Middleton, 103, 255n
Music: of poetry and rhetoric, TSE on, 76–77, 176–177; pattern of, in poetry and drama, 163–169, 172–173, 176–177; pattern of, in "Burnt Norton," 195–197, 206–207. *See also* Incantation

Nightmare(s): TSE on, 51–52; "poet's inner world of," TSE on, 52–53; in *The Waste Land*, 52, 55, 57–58, 60–61, 70. *See also* Dream(s)
Noh drama, 49–51
Norris, Margot, 249n

Olney, James, 274n

Paradox, use of, in *Ash Wednesday*, 140–141; in "Burnt Norton," 193

Paris, TSE's "romantic year" in, 5, 17, 184, 242
Partridge, Eric, 261n
Pater, Walter, 141–142
Patmore, Brigit, 240n; on TSE's self-doubts, 7
Perkins, David, 257n
Perloff, Marjorie, 179
Perse, St.-John, 153, 158, 179, 199; impact on TSE, 124–129, 259n; *Anabase*, 124–127, 258n, 259n, 263n; on TSE's use of words, 160; complaints about TSE's translation, 126, 259n; and "Journey of the Magi," 126–129; and *Ash Wednesday*, 129, 142, 147
Personality: 5, 57, 248n; for Gourmont, 44; for TSE, 44–45; Forster on, 45; and impersonality, paradox of, 45–47; in artist's work, 47–48, 247n; TSE's late observations on, 163, 233. *See also* Impersonality
Phillippe, Charles Louis, 102; *Bubu of Montparnasse*, 102, 255n
Philosophy, TSE and, 9–10, 20, 112
Pieper, Josef, 240n
Pinter, Harold, 40
Poe, Edgar Allan, 122, 129; TSE on, 77–78, 174; *Marginalia*, quoted, 266n
Poetic borrowing, TSE on, 58, 101, 108
Poetry: as exorcism, for TSE, 6, 10, 56, 241n; medieval, TSE on, 83; "psychological" vs. "ontological," TSE on, 83, 88, 110; of adolescence, TSE on, 84–85; composition, TSE on, 108–109; and belief, 111–112; philosophical, TSE's interest in, 112, 116; landscape and descriptive, 116, 170–172; rhythms, function of, for TSE, 122; devotional, TSE on, 131; Augustan strain in TSE's, 99, 157, 159–161, 255n; social function of, TSE on, 159, 161; in theatre, TSE on, 161–162; metaphysical, TSE's expanded definition of, 173–174; dislocation of, TSE on, 117, 176–177, 179, 192–193
Poirier, Richard, 57, 249n
Porter, David, 240n
Post-modernism, anticipation of, in "Burnt Norton," 200, 227
Pound, Ezra, 18–20, 41, 44, 69, 76, 104, 123–124, 239n, 243n, 245n, 246n, 250n, 255n; "Les Millwin," 23–24; on composition of TSE's quatrain poems, 24; criticism of "Gerontion" manu-script, 36; "The River Merchant's Wife," 36; criticism of *The Waste Land* manuscript, 57, 70–72; *Cantos*, 126, 148, 254n
Puritans: TSE on, 23; recalled in "The Dry Salvages," 217

Quinn, John, 55, 67, 74, 82, 240n, 243n, 244n–245n, 254n

Raine, Kathleen, 264n
Read, Herbert, 104, 106, 255n, 257n
Reed, Henry, "Chard Whitlow," 169–170
Rhetoric: problem of, TSE on, 19–30, 41–44, 50, 117–118; TSE's disposition toward, 20, 25, 117, 243n; Victorian, 19–20; and modern poetry, TSE on, 20–21; in Elizabethan drama, TSE on, 21–23, 29, 244n; "pathology of" (TSE), 22–23, 29; of Matthew Arnold, TSE on, 24; Elizabethan, TSE's use of, 38; and music, in poetry, 76, 122–123; poetic, and will, 109; and *The Waste Land*, 58–59, 64, 66; and "The Dry Salvages," 222–223
Richard of St. Victor, 83, 252n
Richards, I.A., 246n, 260n
Richmond, Bruce, 104
Riding, Laura, 25
Riley, Athelstan, 268n
Rimbaud, Arthur, 173; TSE on, 175; *Illuminations*, 179
Ritual, in TSE's poetry, 81, 110–111, 254n
Robertson, J.M., 260n
Rodgers, Audrey T., 257n
Rodker, John, 263n
Rolle, Richard, 274n
Romanticism: TSE on, 14–15, 22–23; and "Burbank," 25; and *The Hollow Men*, 90; and "Burnt Norton," 189; and "East Coker," 213
Rosenthal, M.L., 249n
Rossetti, Dante Gabriel, 252n, 253n, 261n, 262n
Rostand, Edmond, TSE on, 30
Russell, Bertrand, 18, 54, 73, 241n, 247n; nightmare, used by TSE in *The Waste Land*, 57, 249n

St. Louis, TSE's memories of, 7, 146, 215–219, 240n

Schneider, Elisabeth, 98, 131–132, 153, 163–164, 251n, 254n, 258n, 259n, 260n, 261n, 262n, 263n, 264n

Schuchard, Ronald, 243n

Schwartz, Sanford, 243n, 246n

Self-dramatization: TSE on, 29–31; in "Gerontion," 34; in *The Waste Land*, 61

Sencourt, Robert, 104–105, 110, 185, 253n, 256n, 257n, 261n, 268n, 271n; on Vivien Eliot, 210

Sewell, Elizabeth, 147–148, 200, 262n, 268n–269n; on TSE, 147–148

Shahani, Ranjee, 258n, 270n

Shakespeare, William, 21, 26, 48, 50; TSE on, 29–30; *Antony and Cleopatra*, 25, 28, 30; *Measure for Measure*, 32–33; *Romeo and Juliet*, 27–28; *Othello*, 30; *Timon of Athens*, 30; *Macbeth*, 49; *Julius Caesar*, 100–101; *Coriolanus*, 30, 153, 155; TSE's mid-life study of, 162–169; *The Winter's Tale*, 157, 165, 168; *Hamlet*, 158, 166, 168; *Pericles*, 163–169, 172; *The Tempest*, 167, 169; music of, TSE on, 168; sonnets, TSE on, 260n

Shelley, Percy Bysshe: 20, 246n; TSE on, 90, 253n

Sibbes, Richard, 272n

Sieburth, Richard, 246n

Silence: in "Burnt Norton," 176–177, 205–206; in poetry, Mallarmé on, 267n

Sincerity: poetic, TSE on, 6, 21, 43, 116, 120, 173; poetic, TSE's revised understanding of, 111–112, 172, 206, 304; of Swift, TSE on, 234; and "Burnt Norton," 206

Singleton, Charles, 85

Skepticism: TSE's, 9, 29; philosophical, of Valéry, 100–101; TSE's use of, in *The Hollow Men*, 101; and belief, TSE on, 105–106

Smidt, Kristian, 211, 257n, 271n, 273n

Smith, Carol H., 251n, 254n

Smith, Grover, 143, 248n, 251n, 254n, 261n, 263n

Soldo, John, 112, 250n, 258n

Sophocles, 169–170

Sorel, Georges, 71

Southwell, Robert, 274n

Spanos, William, 228, 263n, 275n

Speech: in poetry, Eliot on, 29; in poetry, controversy about importance of,

244n; relation to poetry, TSE on, 159–161, 175

Spencer, Theodore, 102, 275n

Spender, Stephen, 251n, 255n

Spenser, Edmund, 62

Stead, C.K., 249n, 252n

Stead, William Force, 105, 110, 257n, 265n

Stendhal, 16

Stevens, Wallace, 76; "Sunday Morning," 77

Strauss, Walter A., 263n

Swift, Jonathan, 160, 208; TSE on, 233–236; echoed in *Four Quartets*, 235–236

Swinburne, Algernon Charles, 19, 20, 49

Symbolism: and TSE's early work, 18, 19, 175; and TSE's later work, 98–99, 122–130, 149–150, 157, 161–162, 164, 172–173, 173–179, 197

Symons, Arthur: *The Symbolist Movement in Literature*, 19, 243n; on Mallarmé, 99

Tate, Allen, 247n

Taylor, A.J.P., 256n

Tennyson, Alfred: TSE on, 5; *In Memoriam*, 19; "Ulysses," 33–34

Theall, Donald F., 263n

Thibaudet, Albert, 256n

Torrens, James, 251n, 252n

Trecento poetry, TSE on, 83, 85, 252n

Trosman, Harry, 68, 248n, 250n

Tourneur, Cyril, 183; TSE on, 263n; *The Revenger's Tragedy*, 38, 40, 52, 173

Turgenev, Ivan Sergeevich, TSE on, 16

Twain, Mark: recalled in "The Dry Salvages," 216, 218; TSE on, 216–217

Uitti, Karl-D., 261n

Valéry, Paul, 3, 99–102, 112, 123, 158; TSE on, 82, 98–99, 159, 162, 176, 254n; "Le Serpent," 82, 98; "Le Cimetière marin," 99–101, 213–214, 254n

Van Dorn, Marian, 271n

Vaughan, Henry, "The Retreat," quoted, 189

Venice: representation of, in "Burbank,"

25, 27, 29; in "The Aspern Papers," 27

Verdenal, Jean, 267n

Verlaine, Paul, 19–20, 140, 261n; "Parsifal," 59; TSE on, 175; "Sagesse," 261n

Villon, François, 78

Vinograd, Sherna S., 245n

Vittoz, Dr. Roger, 55, 69, 248n, 250n

Wanley, Nathaniel, 138

The Waste Land, 5, 15, 33, 48, 51–52, 55, 86, 90–91, 99, 108, 118, 123, 129, 155, 176, 189, 214; origins of, 18, 57, 248n; nightmares in, 51–52, 57–58; TSE's early efforts at composition of, 55–56; "The Fire Sermon," 56–57, 59–63, 70, 253n; function of literary borrowing in, 58–59; characteristic emotions, 59–60, 67; "The Burial of the Dead," 63–66, 70, 72, 248n; Hyacinth garden episode, 64–66, 129, 148; composition, related to TSE's breakdown, 68–70, 254n; fragmentation, TSE's purpose in, 69–70; "Death by Water," 70; "A Game of Chess," 70, 249n; "What the Thunder Said," 70; TSE's reshaping of, 71–72; Grail legend superimposed on, 72, 96, 219; "What the Thunder Said," TSE on, 73; water-dripping song, 74–76, 122; and *The Hollow Men*, 81, 86, 90; reaction to, 103, 255n; compared with *Ash

Wednesday*, 139–140; compared with "Burnt Norton," 199–200, 270n

Watson, George, 242n

Webster, John, 40

Weston, Jessie, 72, 74

Whibley, Charles, 104

Whitman, Walt, 194; recalled, in "The Dry Salvages," 216

Willey, Basil, 273n

Williams, William Carlos, 194; *Spring and All*, 179

Woolf, Leonard, 243n, 262n

Woolf, Virginia, 18, 76, 103–106, 128, 209; *To the Lighthouse*, 77; *Between the Acts*, 200; on TSE, 103, 255n; on Eliots' marriage, 104–105, 256n–257n; on TSE after his return to England, 186

Wordsworth, William, 17, 257n; "Intimations" ode, 189

Wright, George T., 272n

Wyndham, George, 22–23, 25, 36

Yeats, W.B., 19, 20, 124, 258n, 275n; on Victorian rhetoric, 19, 243n; "The Secret Rose," 141–142; "To the Rose upon the Rood of Time," quoted, 142; "Swift's Epitaph," 208; TSE on, 232–235, 275n; and "Little Gidding," 231–236; "The Spur," 275n, quoted, 234–235; "Vacillation," 275n

The Yellow Spot, *Criterion*'s review of, 226, 274n